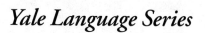

Yale Language Series

Modern
Portuguese
A Reference Grammar

Mário A. Perini

Yale University Press/New Haven and London

Publisher: Mary Jane Peluso

Production Controller: Joyce Ippolito

Editorial Assistant: Emily Saglimbeni

Set in Adobe Garamond type by The Composing Room of Michigan, Inc., Grand Rapids, Michigan.

Printed in the United States of America by R. R. Donnelley and Sons, Harrisonburg, Virginia.

Library of Congress Cataloging-in-Publication Data

Perini, Mário A.

   Modern Portuguese : a reference grammar / Mário A. Perini.

      p.   cm. — (Yale language series)

   Includes bibliographical references and index.

   ISBN 0-300-09155-9 (alk. paper)

   1. Portuguese language—Dialects—Brazil. 2. Portuguese language—Grammar.

  I. Title. II. Series.

PC5444 .P47   2002

469.7′98—dc21   2001046556

A catalogue record for this book is available from the British Library.

The paper in this book meets the guidelines for permanence and durability of the Committee on Production Guidelines for Book Longevity of the Council on Library Resources.

10 9 8 7 6 5 4 3 2 1

To Lúcia, with love

Contents

IV Meaning and Use of Verb Forms

V The Noun Phrase

VI The Sentence

VII The Discourse

VIII Word Formation

IX Final Notes

Appendixes

Foreword

This grammar presents a detailed description of the modern Portuguese language as spoken and written in Brazil. It is intended for the use of English-speaking students at all levels, in particular intermediate and advanced ones, and for the use of their teachers. In writing it I have avoided theoretical discussions, keeping technical terminology to a minimum. On the other hand, every attempt was made to present an up-to-date description reflecting a number of results of recent linguistic research, so that the organization of the work as well as the nomenclature used sometimes departs from what is found in traditional grammars. All indispensable notions are explained in the text, which means that the study of this grammar does not require previous training in linguistics.

I have kept to the usual terminology as far as possible, departing from it only when dealing with notions not contemplated by traditional grammars or when some reanalysis is unavoidable. In such cases, new terms are carefully introduced and fully explained. For instance, I use the terms **simple modals** and **two-word modals** (chapter 22) to refer to two grammatical categories that have no consistent designation in the tradition. And I introduce the notion of *nominal* (chapter 7) to name a general class including so-called adjectives and nouns (which, tradition notwithstanding, are not to be distinguished as separate word classes in Portuguese). I do not apologize for these innovations but merely remark that linguistic science has progressed somewhat during recent decades, whereas traditional terminology is frozen in its state as of 1910 or thereabout.

In this book I have tried to be as complete and comprehensive as possible, and the text reflects some of the immense complexity that is a natural language. In order to make reading and reference as easy as possible, I have, whenever possible, marked less important details as such. What I have not attempted is to present complex facts as if they were simple: my aim throughout the book is to provide a truthful portrait of the language.

Which brings me to my next point: most grammars of Portuguese conceal many features of the language because they are not considered correct, that is, they are not present in the formal standard used in written texts. As a result, the foreign student gets a distorted view of the language and ends up speaking "like a book." Here I parallel the description of the standard (written) language with a description of important points in which the spoken language differs from the standard. In the case of Brazilian Portuguese, these differences are numerous and sometimes rather deep; they have been carefully noted at the appropriate places in the text.

When referring to the spoken language I do not mean the substandard speech of uncultured persons or rural dialects, but the variety of Portuguese used by all educated Brazilians of all professions and regions. Practically no Brazilian actually says things like *dei-lhe um presente* 'I gave him a present,' although this construction is taught in schools and appears usually in writing. Speakers will say instead *eu dei um presente pra ele* 'id.,' keeping the subject pronoun *eu* and substituting the phrase *pra ele* 'to him' in order to avoid the clitic form of the pronoun, *-lhe.* Consequently, really learning Portuguese (as it is used in Brazil) entails acquiring two varieties of the same language. This phenomenon happens in many countries, of course; and in some the difference between the two varieties is even greater than in Brazil (for instance, in countries where Classical Arabic is the official language, but most of the people speak a local variety). While this certainly makes the task of learning Portuguese more complex, nothing is gained in keeping the realities of the language from the student.

The description, therefore, covers a comparatively wide range of usages, from the most conservative found, say, in scholarly works and official documents to the most innovative varieties of the spoken language. Throughout, however, I limit myself to describing what is usually called (somewhat inadequately) the cultured language (*língua culta*), that is, those varieties used by people of some education. Social and regional varieties are, of course, fascinating in their own right, but there is no way to include them here without lengthening the book to an unacceptable degree; this description does not consider archaic language or poetic usages either. What is offered here is a general basis upon which can be built, if desired, a knowledge of all those varieties.

This is not a handbook to be used in day-to-day classroom work; rather, it is a reference work for the student of the language. Accordingly, it does not contain drills or exercises, and the order of presentation follows the logic of grammatical exposition, rather than the step-by-step approach that is necessary in handbooks. Nevertheless, I have not been dogmatic to the point of segregating the different components of the grammar (phonology, morphology, syntax, semantics, and so on) in separate parts of the book. I have not hesitated to "mix" them whenever that seemed more convenient. For example, I have placed the description of tenses and moods (their syntactic use and their semantics) immediately after the chapters on verb inflection because for a student it is more natural to learn forms relating them to their meanings than studying them separately. Also, I have not avoided a certain amount of redundancy, referring to important points again and again whenever necessary.

I do not include in this grammar exhaustive lists of idiosyncratic feminines (*barão / baronesa, genro / nora*), prefixes and suffixes (*ante-por, pro-por, dis-por*), so-called irregular diminutives and augmentatives (*casa / casinhola / casulo*), and so on. Important as they often are, these lists belong in a dictionary, not in a grammar—not least because the semantic relationship between their members is sometimes unpredictable and therefore not amenable to generalization: *casulo* is not a small house (it means 'cocoon'), and the prefix *re-* conveys the meaning "repetition" in *refazer* 'to remake,' but not in *referir* 'to refer' or in *repuxar* 'to stretch energetically.' The preceding observation applies to cases of derivation; as for inflection, of course, all irregularities (irregular verbs, irregular plurals, and so on) are included here because they are systematic in one important respect, that is, in the way the members of each paradigm relate to each other semantically.

I have sometimes indulged in brief theoretical notes and digressions, never without warning the reader about their peripheral nature (such sections are marked with a double asterisk, **). I have done so because I would like this grammar to be equally useful to students of Portuguese, Romance, or general linguistics; and because many points respecting the structure of Portuguese are poorly understood. It is thus important to call the attention of prospective researchers to such problems. The researcher has also been kept in mind in the elaboration of the comments added to some of the items in the bibliography.

Our knowledge of the structure of natural languages is still very far from attaining the stage at which a complete description of any particular language can be written. In spite of the advances of linguistic research, there remain too many practically unexplored areas, and there are serious doubts about most of the points that *have* been investigated. Therefore, the best of grammars cannot help being incomplete. In this work I attempt to give the most complete description allowed by the current state of the science, but I do not sacrifice accuracy for completeness' sake; and I point out doubtful points whenever necessary. This may be occasionally frustrating to the reader who is trying to learn as much as possible of the language, but it is inevitable: the alternative is to present as fact what is no more than speculation.

The text is planned with the English-speaking reader in mind; correspondingly, there are frequent parallel references to the facts of English and Portuguese. The same principle applies to the selection of topics: special emphasis is given to features that differ the most in the two languages, and some others have not been treated at all because they are identical in Portuguese and in English and therefore present no difficulty to the learner—for instance, why go to great lengths to describe the position of the article with respect to its noun if in both languages the facts are identical? Such information might be useful were this book directed to speakers of Russian (which has no articles) or Rumanian (which places the definite article after the noun). Occasionally I also add some reference to parallel phenomena in other Romance languages, particularly Spanish, since so many students of Portuguese have a previous knowledge of Spanish.

I would like to express my gratitude to those who helped me during the long gestation of this book. In particular, I thank my wife, Lúcia Fulgêncio, who read the text and contributed many useful suggestions (which I may still regret not always following); and my dear friend and colleague Curt Blaylock of the University of Illinois, who functioned as a guardian angel watching over both the correctness of my English and the readability of the text in general.

I am also grateful to the Department of Spanish, Italian, and Portuguese of the University of Illinois and to its chairman, Ronald W. Sousa, for making it possible for me to work in Champaign-Urbana during the school years 1997–98 and 1999–2000; and to Mary Jane Peluso and Yale University Press, who believed in my work and supported it. I would like to thank and acknowledge Jordano Quaglia, Yale University, who reviewed the manuscript.

Finally, I will mention two books that formed the foundation for the elaboration of this grammar, books without which my work would have been even more difficult and certainly lower in quality: these are Houaiss and Avery's Portuguese-English dictionary and Earl Thomas's *The Syntax of Spoken Brazilian Portuguese.*

Abbreviations

Arch Archaic form or construction.

NP Noun phrase.

SpBr **(spoken Brazilian)**—Form or construction typically used in the spoken language of Brazil.

Wr **(written language)**—Form or construction used (in Brazil) only in writing.

* Forms marked with a single asterisk are unacceptable or incorrect.

** Forms marked with a double asterisk are theoretical notes and digressions of a peripheral nature.

I Preliminaries

1

The Portuguese Language

Portuguese is the language spoken in Portugal and in Brazil; it has many speakers in several African nations as well, including Angola, Mozambique, Guiné-Bissau, Cabo Verde, and São Tomé, and is also spoken by immigrant minorities in the United States, Canada, and some countries of Western Europe. A conservative estimate puts the number of its monolingual speakers at about 190 million, which makes it one of the great languages of the world—not so widely spoken as English, Mandarin, and Spanish, but more so than French, German, and Italian.

In all that vast area the standard written language is very uniform, differences in spelling and grammatical structure being small; educated Portuguese and Brazilians usually have no difficulty understanding each other's books and newspapers (except when regional vocabulary is used).

As for the spoken language, differences are more salient. The speech of educated Africans usually follows very closely the European model. But in Brazil, where Portuguese is the only language used by the whole population and where it has been evolving independently for almost five centuries, the spoken language differs markedly from European Portuguese. Yet, the European and the Brazilian dialects are mutually intelligible, and free conversation presents no great problems. The linguistic distance between Portugal and Brazil, in what concerns the spoken language, can be roughly compared to that between British and African American English. And within Brazil, dialectal disparities are small, being comparable in importance to the variation of English across the United States.

The linguistic situation in Brazil has given rise to periodic debates about whether or not Portuguese and Brazilian are separate languages. Yet this controversy has never gone beyond academic circles, and most authorities as well as practically all laypersons feel that the two languages are one and the same. I do not go into the issue here, even assuming that it is a substantive question—which it most probably is not. For my purposes it is enough to recognize that many differences exist, mainly in the spoken language. These will be mentioned at the appropriate places; and in the book as a whole, Brazilian Portuguese will be taken as the basic standard of reference.

The distance between the spoken and the written language in Brazil makes it somewhat difficult to describe Brazilian Portuguese. These differences are rather pronounced in regard to certain points, for example, the use of the subjunctive mood (chapter 15); the use of *se* with nonreflexive verbs (chapter 20); nominal and verbal agreement (chapters 34 and 35); the structure of the relative clause (chapter 36); topicalized constructions (chapter 39); and many other important grammatical facts. These divergences are included in the text whenever possible, but it must be borne in mind that description of colloquial Brazilian is still fragmentary. No extensive studies have been made (for a very interesting initial attempt, see Castilho 1990–99)—that is, scholars are still far from being able to write a grammar of the colloquial variety of the language.

On the other hand, the colloquial language is very uniform over the whole territory, and Brazilians of all classes have no trouble whatsoever understanding one another. The standard language as found in books, newspapers, radio, and television is, of course, even more uniform, and it is not possible to tell from grammatical evidence the region from which a text or a broadcast originates.

The standard variety taught in schools has a certain degree of influence on the speech of educated persons, but no one ever comes to the point of using consistently the forms of the written language. That is, the influence of the standard language is never so strong that one can say someone is *speaking* standard Portuguese (except in such hyperformal situations as delivering a prepared speech, for instance). On the other hand, as with most languages, one can evaluate a person's degree of schooling from his or her way of speaking.

The situation may be summarized thus: there is a highly uniform popular language and an even more uniform written standard. In between, one finds several varieties of semistandardized speech, used by more or less schooled people in varying degrees according to the formality of the situation. For instance, a person who says *eles corre* 'they run' in unguarded speech may use the standard form *eles correm* 'id.,' with the required plural ending -*m,* in a formal situation, such as when giving a lecture or speaking on television (one may compare the parallel situation in American English between *he don't* and *he doesn't*).

This constitutes a complex sociolinguistic situation, and there is no way to include all this information in a survey like the one attempted in this book. Every effort will be made to call attention to such variation whenever it seems particularly important. But the phenomenon on the whole has not been satisfactorily described, and its very complexity precludes its inclusion in full in a reference grammar.

Inevitably, thus, the language described in this book is a sort of compromise based on the modern written standard and liberally spiked with comments on features of the spoken language that find their way into the speech of even the most educated people. Any reference to grammatical facts that are confined to very formal written texts will be duly marked, so that the forms in question can be avoided in speaking and, if possible, in writing. To give one example, the simple pluperfect tense (as in *eu fora* 'I had gone') is never used in speaking and is never necessary even in writing, being replaceable by the compound form *eu tinha ido* 'id.'

The first texts in a recognizable form of Portuguese (as distinct from Castilian, Leonese, and other languages of the Iberian peninsula) date from the late twelfth century, and by about 1300 a considerable body of literature had been produced, both in Portugal and in present-day Spain. Apparently, Portuguese, at the time not yet clearly distinguishable from Galician, was felt in those times to be an especially appropriate medium for lyric poetry and was used even by poets whose native language was Castilian. A famous example is the *Cantigas de Santa Maria* (Songs in praise of the Virgin Mary), written in Portuguese by King Alfonso X of Castile.

Portuguese became the official language of the kingdom of Portugal, and in the sixteenth century it followed the fortunes of the Portuguese people in their spectacular expansion through South America, Africa, and Asia. With the publication of the first grammars (Fernão de Oliveira 1536; João de Barros 1540) and dictionaries (Jerônimo Cardoso 1562), the written language was standardized and has maintained a remarkable unity ever since—although there has never existed a controlling academy comparable to the French and Spanish ones. In Brazil the Portuguese language took root and is today the only language spoken by its inhabitants (more than 169 million, according to the 2000 census). In Africa, Portuguese competes with local languages, English, and creoles; nevertheless, it is the official language in the republics of Angola, Mozambique, Guiné-Bissau, Cabo Verde, and São Tomé and is known by educated people in those countries. Finally, I may mention modern Galician, the popular language of Galicia in northwestern Spain, which is so close to Portuguese as to be usually called a co-dialect.

Throughout its eight-century history, the Portuguese language has been the vehicle of an abundant literature, ranging from the medieval *cantigas* to fifteenth-century historians to the great sixteenth-century classical poets (among whom foremost is Luís de Camões), and so on down to modern times. Starting from the mid–seventeenth century, Brazil has been making an ever-increasing contribution, and in recent times African authors have joined the team.

Nowadays the literary output of Portuguese is phenomenal, and authors like the Brazilians Jorge Amado and Paulo Coelho and the Portuguese José Saramago (Nobel

Prize, 1998) are becoming known all over the world. Furthermore, technical material produced abroad is usually translated and published in Brazil and in Portugal, so that Portuguese is also the medium of education at all levels. While many educated people in Portuguese-speaking areas have some reading command of English (often also of French or Spanish), few Brazilians can speak a foreign language fluently, and living or doing business in Portuguese-speaking areas requires some knowledge of the national language.

Portuguese in its written form is close to Spanish (and to Catalan), and a knowledge of those languages is a good first step in understanding Portuguese texts. Yet neither of them is mutually intelligible with Portuguese, especially in their spoken varieties. In Brazil, furthermore, except in the border areas, spoken command of Spanish is a rare phenomenon.

II Pronunciation and Spelling

2

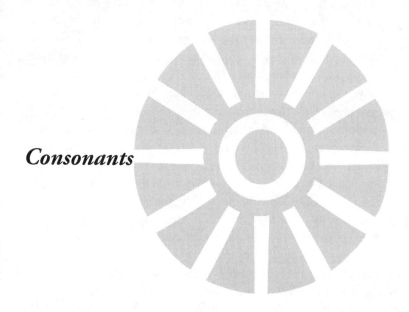

Consonants

Both spelling and pronunciation differ from Portugal to Brazil. Spelling differences are almost insignificant and never hinder word identification; examples are *Antônio* (Br.) vs. *António* (P.); *fato* (Br.) vs. *facto* (P.) 'fact'; *conosco* (Br.) vs. *connosco* (P.) 'with us.'

Pronunciation differences are more important, and a beginner will find it difficult to master both varieties at the same time. My advice is to work consistently on one variety and then study the differences between them, which are pretty systematic. In this book the Brazilian use is described in detail; once that is well known, the jump to understanding European Portuguese is not difficult. Brazilian Portuguese, being spoken in such a large area, also shows some regional variation. The variety described here is a sort of neutral pronunciation, the one used on radio and television, and it is based on the speech of Rio de Janeiro, São Paulo, and Minas Gerais. It is accepted throughout Brazil as a spoken standard.

Although Portuguese spelling is not as regular as it might be, it presents one great advantage: the pronunciation is mostly predictable from the spelling. The problem the learner must face is how to write a spoken form, rarely how to pronounce a written one. There are ambiguous letters, but they are not numerous and fall into few categories. In this and the next three chapters I give as complete an account as possible of how to pronounce words, starting with their written forms. The pronunciation described here is that found in formal educated speech; in normal conversation, as usually happens with most languages, Brazilians tend to slur their utterances to a certain degree.

Before proceeding to describe the pronunciation of Brazilian Portuguese, I should emphasize that I take the written form as the starting point for the description. That is, the rules are stated in terms of the pronunciation of each letter (grapheme) in each relevant environment. For instance, I say things like "the letter **a** is pronounced [ə] when having no accent and appearing at the end of a word." This rule is directed at persons having immediate access to the written word, and it enables the learner to deduce from the written word the correct pronunciation; from the written form *cara* 'face,' one can proceed to the knowledge that the last **a** is to be pronounced [ə].

I have selected this approach for two main reasons. First, as I said, because the pronunciation of Portuguese is predictable to a high degree from the spelling (in the description of English pronunciation, starting from the spelling might not be a very good strategy—at least as the sole resource). Second, because this book is primarily directed to persons learning or teaching Portuguese abroad, that is, people who lack the constant daily contact with the language enjoyed by learners and teachers in Portuguese-speaking areas. For them, the existence of a set of rules allowing one to infer the pronunciation from the spelling (from letters to sounds) is particularly useful. In short, I have selected this approach keeping in mind not the conveniences of linguistic description, but the interests of teaching and learning.

Pronunciation is noted by means of the symbols recommended by the International Phonetic Association; a rough description of each sound is also given, but for an accurate idea of how they sound some contact with live informants or with recordings is indispensable. Transcriptions may be described as broad phonetic, that is, they often represent sound differences even when not linguistically significant (as, for example, the difference in pronunciation of **t** as [tʃ] before [i] and as [t] elsewhere). Transcriptions are enclosed in brackets, [ ].

2.1 The Portuguese writing system

Portuguese is written with the Latin alphabet, plus six diacritics: three accents (acute: **á;** circumflex: **â;** grave: **à**); the tilde: **ã;** the cedilla: **ç;** and the dieresis: **ü.** These are the Portuguese letters, with their names:

Letters

a	*a*	**d**	*dê*	**g**	*gê*
b	*bê*	**e**	*é* or *ê*	**h**	*agá*
c	*cê*	**f**	*efe*	**i**	*i*

(continued)					
j	*jota*	**p**	*pê*	**v**	*vê*
k	*ká*	**q**	*quê*	**x**	*xis*
l	*ele*	**r**	*erre*	**w**	*dáblio*
m	*eme*	**s**	*esse*	**y**	*ípsilon*
n	*ene*	**t**	*tê*	**z**	*zê*
o	*ó* or *ô*	**u**	*u*		

'Ç' is called *cê cedilha;* it is considered a variety of **c** and thus is not included in the alphabet; it is ordered as if it were a regular **c.**

K, w, and **y,** although part of the official Portuguese alphabet, are rare and occur only in unassimilated foreign words (*walkman, kiwi*), in international abbreviations (*km* for *quilômetro*), and in some personal names (*Wanda, Darcy, Kátia, Wanderley, Yara*).

Accents

´	the acute is called	*acento agudo*
^	the circumflex is called	*acento circunflexo*
`	the grave is called	*acento grave*
~	the tilde is called	*til*
¨	the dieresis is called	*trema*

2.2 Pronunciation of consonants

The following letters and digraphs present little difficulty, each being pronounced in only one way:

b is pronounced	[b]	as in English *boy*		ex.: *boi* 'ox'
f	[f]		*fee*	*fé* 'faith'
j	[ʒ]		*usual, vision*	*já* 'already'
k	[k]		*key*[1]	*Kátia* (woman's name)
p	[p]		*pie*[1]	*pai* 'father'
q	[k]		*key*[1]	*quem* 'who'
v	[v]		*veal*	*vaca* 'cow'
ç	[s]		*see*	*aço* 'steel'
ss	[s]		*see*	*osso* 'bone'
sç	[s]		*see*	*desço* '(I) go down'
h	(silent)		[2]	*hoje* 'today'
ch	[ʃ]		*she*	*chá* 'tea'
lh	[λ]		[3]	*alho* 'garlic'
nh	[ɲ]		[4]	*unha* 'fingernail'

Notes

[1]Portuguese [p], [t], [k] lack the aspiration found in English *pie, key, too*. In the English words there is a perceptible puff of air between the consonant and the following vowel; in the Portuguese words *pai* 'father,' *que* 'which,' *tu* 'you' the vowel immediately follows the consonant, without aspiration. Portuguese is, in this respect, similar to French, Spanish, and Italian.

[2]**H** is silent when word-initial, so that *hora* 'hour' and *ora* 'now' are pronounced alike, ['ɔɾə]. But the letter **h** is also found in connection with **c, l,** and **n,** in which case it makes a difference, as shown in the table.

³**Lh** has no exact correlate in English. It is pronounced like **gli** in Italian *paglia,* that is, palatalized **l,** [ʎ]. As in other languages, this sound tends to become [j] (as in English *yes*), but the process is much less advanced in Portuguese than in Spanish, so that pronunciations like *paia* ['pajə] for *palha* 'straw' are frowned upon as uncultured.

⁴The pronunciation of Portuguese **nh** is peculiar to the language. It is like the **y** in English *yes,* but nasalized. It is not identical to Spanish **ñ** or French and Italian **gn,** although these may serve as approximations. The difference is that to pronounce Spanish **ñ** or French / Italian **gn** the tongue comes into contact with the palate, whereas for Portuguese **nh** it only approaches it, so that the result is a nasalized glide [j̃], that is, a semivowel, not a true consonant.

In the word *companhia* 'company' (and only here) **nh** is very often pronounced as **n** [n], even by educated speakers: [kõpɐ̃'nijə].

The following letters have more than one pronunciation:

C			
[s] as in English *force*	—before **e** and **i**	ex:	*céu* 'sky'
[k] as in English *case*	—in all other cases		*cor* 'color'
			cru 'raw'

C behaves identically in Portuguese and in English (except, of course, for the aspiration, which is absent in Portuguese words like *cor, cru*).

Digraphs ending with **c** follow the rules for that letter:

sc [s] as in English *scene*	—before **e** and **i**	ex: *desci* '(I) went down'
sc [sk] as in English *escape*	—in all other cases	*isca* 'bait'
xc [s] as in English *scene*	—before **e** and **i**	*excitar* 'to excite'
xc [sk] as in English *escape*	—in all other cases	*excluir* 'to exclude'

G

[ʒ]	as in English *usual, vision*	—before **e** and **i**	ex:	*gente*	'people'
[g]	as in English *goat*	—in all other cases		*gato*	'cat'
				grão	'grain'

S

[z]	as in English *these*	—between two vowels[1]	ex:	*asa*	'wing'
[z]	as in English *wisdom*	—before a voiced consonant (that is, **b, d, g, v, j, z, m, n, l, r**)[1]		*rasgar*	'to tear'
[z]	as in English *transit* or			*trânsito*	'traffic'
[s]	as in English *dense*	—after **n** and before a vowel[2]		*pensar*	'to think'
[s]	as in English *see, must*	—in all other cases		*só*	'alone'
				isso	'this'
				custar	'to cost'
				ônibus	'bus'

Notes

[1]This rule applies even if the two letters belong to different words; for instance, when uttering *duas vacas* 'two cows' the final *-s* of *duas* is pronounced [z]. Now, if there is a pause, as when one is dictating something on the telephone: *duas . . . vacas* the **s** reverts to its basic pronunciation and does not become [z]. The same for **s** between vowels: in *dois irmãos* 'two brothers' the final **s** of *dois* is pronounced [z].

[2]In this context pronunciation of **s** is unpredictable; it sounds [z] in *trânsito* 'traffic,' but [s] in *pensar* 'to think.'

In Rio de Janeiro and in some areas of the northeast (Salvador, for instance) **s** at the end of a syllable—that is, before a consonant or at the end of a word—is pronounced [ʃ], as in English *she;* or [ʒ], as in English *vision,* when before a voiced consonant. Thus, it is [ʃ] in *três* 'three' and in *três peras* 'three pears,' and [ʒ] in *três bananas* 'three bananas' (this rule applies also to **z,** see below).

Z		
[s] as in English *books* —at the end of a phrase[1]	ex: *paz*	'peace'
[z] as in English *zero* —in all other cases	*zebra*	'zebra'
	azar	'bad luck'

Note

[1]Actually the behavior of **z** at the end of phrases is the same as that of **s:** it is devoiced (becomes [s]) except when followed without pause by a vowel or a voiced consonant. *Paz* 'peace' when alone or at the end of an utterance is pronounced as if it ended with an **s.** But in the phrase *paz na terra* 'peace on Earth' the final **z** is pronounced [z] because of the following voiced consonant **n.**

The rule for **s**, which in certain regions is pronounced [ʃ] or [ʒ] when occurring before a consonant or when utterance-final, applies to **z** as well, e.g., in Rio *paz* 'peace' is pronounced [ˈpaʃ].

T				
[tʃ] as in English	*cheer*	—before the sound [i][1]	ex:	*tia* 'aunt'
[t] as in English	*tea*[2]	—in all other cases		*tu* 'you'
				trem 'train'
				tempo 'time'

Notes

[1] The sound [i] is usually represented in writing by the letter **i**; but the letter **e**, when unstressed, is often pronounced [i] (see chapter 3), and in this case it has the same effect on **t**; for example *elefante* 'elephant' is pronounced [eleˈfɐ̃ tʃi].

[2] But without the aspiration; see above.

D				
[dʒ] as in English *jeans*	—before the sound [i]	ex:	*dia*	'day'
[d] as in English *day*	—in all other cases		*dar*	'to give'
			dragão	'dragon'

As can be seen, the behavior of **t** and **d** with respect to the sound [i] is the same. It should be kept in mind that the conditioning factor is the sound [i], not the letter **i;** see note 1 on **t,** above.

Two observations:

—This alteration of **t, d** before [i] is typical of the speech of south central Brazil. Since it includes the speech of Rio, it is usually taken to be prestigious. But in large areas of Brazil (most of the south, northeast, and the Amazon) many speakers ignore it and pronounce **t, d** alike in all positions: [t], [d].

—**T** and **d** are pronounced with the tongue tip in a slightly more forward position in Portuguese than in English. When saying the English word *day,* the tongue tip touches the upper gums just above the teeth; but for Portuguese *dei* '(I) gave' the tongue should come into contact with the teeth, lying in a more flat position against the gums.

R

[h] as in English *ahead*[1]	—when word-initial	ex:	*rei*	'king'
	—word-final[2]		*cor*	'color'
	—at the end of a syllable		*porta*	'door'
	—double (**rr**)		*erro*	'mistake'
	—when it comes after **l, n,** or **s**		*Israel*	'Israel'
			tenro	'tender'
			melro	'oriole'
[ɾ] as **t** in English *data*[3]	—between two vowels		*cara*	'face'
	—after a consonant other than **l, n, s**		*trem*	'train'
			Brasil	'Brazil'

Notes

[1]This is the most usual pronunciation of **r** in south central Brazil. It varies considerably, though, across the country: in the south it is frequently a rolled sound like Spanish *rr* in *cerro*. In certain areas (western São Paulo, south and west Minas Gerais, part of Goiás) it appears as the English **r** when syllable-final (the latter pronunciation is found to be inelegant).

[2]When a word ends with **r** and is followed without pause by a word beginning with a vowel, the **r** is pronounced as if it were between vowels in a word: *amor eterno* 'eternal love' is pronounced as one word, *amoreterno* [amorɛˈtɛhnu].

[3]This sound is identical to Spanish **r** in *cara*.

Word-final **r** calls for a special remark. Its pronunciation is close to English **h,** as stated above. Yet, *when it is part of a verb form,* it is most often not pronounced at all. Thus, the infinitive form *partir* 'to leave' becomes identical in sound to the past tense form *parti* '(I) have left,' and *quer* '(he/she) wants' becomes [ˈkɛ]. This is not a feature of substandard, uncultured language; it is nearly universal and is found in the fluent speech of practically every Brazilian. The final **r** in verb forms is consistently pronounced only in very formal situations, such as public addresses and such, or when directly mentioning the word, as in *o verbo* **amar** 'the verb *amar.*'

When part of a nonverbal form, final **r** is usually pronounced in southern Brazil but is often omitted in the northeast: instances are *mar* 'sea,' *Itamar* (a man's name), *prazer* 'pleasure,' *amor* 'love.'

The sound here transcribed [h] is a voiceless laryngeal glide (identical to **h in English *hat*) when word-final or before a voiceless consonant. Before a vowel or a voiced consonant, however, it is usually murmured, that is, semivoiced and should be noted as [ɦ] in a more narrow transcription; this sound is found in English *ahead, behind.*

Before consonants one also finds the pronunciation [x] (a voiceless velar fricative) or [ɣ] (its voiced counterpart).

L

[w] as in English *cow*[1]   —at the end of a syllable   ex: *sal*   'salt'

salto 'jump'

(continued)

[l] as in English *lock*	—in all other cases	*lá*	'there'
		flor	'flower'
		ele	'he'

Note

[1]Here too there is some variation. In southern Brazil one finds syllable-final **l** pronounced like **ll** in English *well.* This variant is used by a minority of speakers, though, and tends to disappear in favor of [w]. **L**, pronounced [w], is usually distinctly heard even after [u], so that *sulco* 'groove' is pronounced ['suwku] and is always distinct from *suco* 'juice,' pronounced ['suku].

M and N

M and **n** present some special complexities because they are used to represent not only the sounds [m] (English *my*) and [n] (English *no*), but also the nasalization of the preceding vowel (we will see the effects of nasalizing **m** and **n** above, when we study the pronunciation of the vowels).

As noted, **m** and **n** are marks of nasalization whenever they occur after a vowel and before a consonant; for example, *cinto, tampa, cansar, sempre:* here **m, n** nasalize the preceding vowel and are not themselves pronounced (at the end of a word and in the ending **-ns,** the effect of **m, n** is slightly different and results in nasal diphthongs, see below). Thus, the difference between *fuga* 'flight' and *funga* '(he/she) sniffs' is that the former has an oral **u** and the latter a nasal **u.**

In word-final position, the combination **vowel + m** or **n** is pronounced in several ways, according to the following table:

M, N				
[j̃][1]	—after **e, i**	ex:	*bem*	'well'

(*continued*)

		sim 'yes'
		hífen 'hyphen'
[w̃]¹	— after **a**	*falam* '(they) speak'
silent	— after **o, u**	*bom* 'good'
		um 'one'²
m: [m] as in English *my*		
n: [n] as in English *no* — before a vowel		*mau* 'bad'
		nós 'we'
		cama 'bed'
		cano 'water pipe'

Notes

¹[ɟ] as in English **y** in *day*, and [w̃] as in English **w** in *cow*, but both nasalized.

²In all of the preceding contexts the vowel immediately preceding **n** or **m** is nasalized (see 3.3 below).

Note that final **m** and **n** are silent even when the following word begins with a vowel. Foreigners tend to pronounce *um anjo* 'an angel' as if it were *umanjo,* but this must be avoided, as the correct pronunciation has a nasal vowel followed immediately by the initial *a-* of *anjo,* [ũˈʌ̃ʒu]. As a result, *com um acordo* 'with an agreement' and *comum acordo* 'mutual consent' do not sound alike: the former sounds [kõũaˈkohdu], the latter sounds [komũaˈkohdu].

X

X is pronounced in four ways, and in some cases the pronunciation is unpredictable from the context.

X		
[ʃ] as in English *she*	—when word-initial	ex: *xícara* 'cup'
[ks] as in English *ax*	—when word-final[1]	*tórax* 'thorax'
[s] as in English *East*	—before a consonant	*expor* 'to exhibit'

Note

[1] In only one form final **x** is pronounced [s]: the prefix *ex-*, when taken alone as an independent word: *minha ex* 'my ex (-wife, -girlfriend . . .).'

When it occurs between vowels, **x** can be pronounced in any of the above three ways and also as [z], as in English *zeal*. In this position prediction is impossible, and the student will have to learn the correct pronunciation for every word. For example,

X between vowels			
[ʃ] as in English *she*	ex:	*taxa*	'fee'
[s] as in English *see*		*próximo*	'near'
[ks] as in English *ax*		*fixo*	'fixed'
[z] as in English *zeal*		*exame*	'examination'

W

W occurs rarely in Portuguese. It is found in a few foreign words not yet adapted to Portuguese spelling, as for example in *windsurfe, walkie-talkie,* and, more frequently, personal names: *Wagner, William, Wanderléia.* Pronunciation is unpredictable from context. In words of English origin it is usually pronounced [w]: *William, Wilson, watt;* and in words of German origin it is pronounced [v] (as **v** in English *veal*): *Wagner, Weber.*

3

Vowels

The Portuguese vowel system is more complex than the Spanish but perhaps less so than the English. Portuguese has twelve distinctive vowel sounds, and these include both oral and nasal vowels. Furthermore, the relation between spelling and pronunciation is not as simple as in the case of Spanish or Italian, and this is especially critical in the case of vowels. On the other hand, pronunciation is almost always predictable from the spelling, and on the whole an English speaker learning the pronunciation of Portuguese vowels has a much easier time than a Portuguese speaker learning the English ones. In what follows I give as complete an account as possible of the pronunciation of vowels in Brazilian Portuguese.

3.1 Stress

3.1.1 Stress placement

Since the pronunciation of a vowel sometimes depends on its being stressed or not, I shall start this study of the vowels by looking at stress placement rules. Words in Portuguese are stressed on the last, the penultimate, or the antepenultimate syllable (that is, respectively, the first, second, or third syllable from the end). The spelling gives adequate cues to the placement of the stress, as shown by the following rules:

1. If a vowel bears an acute (′) or a circumflex (^), it is stressed.[1]

2. If no vowel in a word bears an acute or a circumflex, then:

> **2a.** If the word ends in **a, e, o, as, es, os, am, em, ens**, stress the penultimate vowel.[2]

> **2b.** If the word ends in a diphthong,[3] stress the diphthong regardless of whether or not it is followed by **s**.

> **2c.** Otherwise, stress the last vowel.

Notes

[1]As far as the application of the stress rules is concerned, the term "vowel" refers to the letters **a, e, i, o, u,** and **y.** This is phonetically inaccurate, of course, since some of these letters may represent a semivowel (*pai, mau*) or no sound at all (*quero*); here I am using "vowel" merely as a convenient way to refer to those six letters.

[2]The only exception to this rule is the word *porque* 'because,' which is pronounced [puh'ke], with stress on the last syllable, although it has no accent.

[3]Except final **em, am,** which represent nasal diphthongs, that is, [ẽj̃] and [ãw̃], respectively, and which are mentioned in rule 2a above. A diphthong for our purposes is a sequence of any vowel plus **i** or **u,** or any of the following sequences: **ão, ãe, õe.**

The above rules are to be applied in order, so that if it happens that two of them may be applied, the first one is given precedence. For example, the word *órgão* 'organ' might fall under rule 1 (because of the accent) or under rule 2b (because of the diphthong). Rule 1 takes precedence, and the word is stressed on the initial **ó.** Observe that the grave accent (`) and the dieresis (¨) are irrelevant for purposes of stress placement.

Following are some examples of the application of the rules:

Rule 1.

—*Café* 'coffee,' *você* 'you,' *aliás* 'by the way,' *avô* 'grandfather' are all stressed on the last syllable because the vowel in that syllable bears an accent;

—*pêssego* 'peach,' *máscara* 'mask,' *vômito* 'vomit,' *órgão* 'organ,' *imã* 'magnet,' *Hélcio* (man's name) are stressed on the first syllable, for the same reason;

—*Antônio* (man's name), *espécie* 'species' are stressed on the syllable containing the accented vowel.

Rule 2a.

All of the following words are stressed on the penultimate vowel because they have no accent and they have one of the endings listed in rule 2a:

—*casa* 'house,' *bule* 'coffeepot,' *carro* 'car,' as well as their plurals *casas, bules, carros;*

—*amam* '(they) love,' *nuvem* 'cloud' and its plural *nuvens;*

—*Maria* (woman's name), *navio* 'ship.'

Rule 2b.

The following words are stressed on the last syllable, which contains a diphthong:

—*limão* 'lemon,' *alemães* 'Germans,' *papai* 'dad,' *mingau* 'porridge.'

Rule 2c.

Finally, the following words are all stressed on the last vowel because they fall under none of the preceding cases:

—*cantar* 'to sing,' *nacional* 'national,'[1] *rapaz* 'young man,' *xerox* 'xerox,' *irmã* 'sister.'

Note

[1] Words like *nacional* may also be considered as falling under rule 2b because the final **l** is pronounced [w] and the word, therefore, ends in a diphthong. This makes no difference in the outcome, though: in any case *nacional* must be stressed on the final syllable.

Stressed vowels in Portuguese are not merely stronger, but also longer; there is nothing in Portuguese to match the short stressed vowels of English, as in *pit* or *pretty*. A word like *cabana* 'hut' is pronounced [ka'bã:nə]; the ':' indicates a lengthening of the vowel [ã], which is perceptively longer than the other two vowels in the word. It is important to learn this detail, since it is in part responsible for the peculiar rhythm of the spoken language.

3.1.2 Secondary stress

On longer words one hears also a secondary stress, weaker than the main one but important because it contributes to the peculiar rhythm of Brazilian speech. Here lies one of the important differences between Brazilian and English accents: in a word like *literature*, English speakers put an accent on the first syllable, *lit-*, and another on *-tu-*, whereas the Brazilian speaker, when uttering the cognate *literatura*, stresses (primarily) the penultimate, *-tu-*, and (secondarily) the second syllable, *-te-*. This causes the two words to have different rhythm patterns, in spite of their similarity in sound.

In a word like *internacional* 'international' the main stress falls on the last syllable: *in ter na cio **nal;*** and there is a secondary stress on *-na-* and another on *in-*, so that these syllables sound a little stronger than both *-ter-* and *-cio-*. The rule here is that secondary stress falls on alternate syllables, counting backward from the stressed one:

    in *ter **na** cio **nal***

This is the general rule. There are exceptions, and the main one is that when a word is formed with the suffixes *-zinho* (which forms diminutives) or *-mente* (which forms adverbs, like English *-ly* in *rapidly*) the secondary stress must be on the syllable that bears the main stress in the original word. For example, from *pílula* 'pill' one forms *pilulazinha* 'small pill.' The general rule would place secondary stress on the second syllable, *-lu-*, but since *pi-* is stressed on the original word *pílula*, it keeps its stress (now downgraded to secondary status):

    pi *lu la **zi** nha*

The same for *rapidamente* 'rapidly,' from *rápido:*

    ra *pi da **men** te*

In these cases secondary stress used to be marked, the acute accent becoming a grave (`) and the circumflex being kept, so that one wrote *pìlulazinha* and *ràpidamente* and also *pêssegozinho*, from *pêssego* 'peach.' These accents were abandoned in 1971 as a result of one of the spelling reforms Portuguese is periodically subjected to; the reader may find them, along with some others, in books printed before that date.

    Secondary stress appears in a word only before the stressed syllable. Syllables coming after the main stress are uniformly unstressed: in ***máscara*** 'mask,' or in ***casa*** 'house' no secondary stress is perceptible.

3.2 Nasal vowels

Portuguese, like several other languages, but unlike Spanish and English, makes use of the distinction between nasal and oral vowels. Learning this distinction is essential because in many cases nasality is the only sound feature setting words apart. For example, the following pairs of words are distinguished in pronunciation merely because the first word in each pair has an oral vowel whereas the second has a nasal one:

mata	'forest'	*manta*	'blanket'
Leda	(woman's name)	*lenda*	'legend'
ficar	'to stay'	*fincar*	'to ram in'
o	'the'	*um*	'one'
cotar	'to estimate'	*contar*	'to count; to tell'
fuga	'flight'	*funga*	'(he/she) sniffs'

Nasal vowels are always marked in spelling, according to the following rules:

A vowel is nasalized when

A. it bears a tilde: **ã, õ** (the tilde is used only with these two vowels, never with **i, u, e**): *irmã* 'sister,' *mão* 'hand,' *põe* '(he/she) puts'; **or**

B. it comes before **nh:** *banheiro* 'bathroom,' *penhasco* 'cliff,' *tinha* '(he/she) had,' *sonhar* 'to dream,' *unha* 'fingernail' ; **or**

C. it comes before the letters **m, n** followed by another consonant or at the end of a word: *santo* 'saint,' *tempo* 'time,' *cinto* 'belt,' *onda* 'wave,' *tumba* 'grave,' *bunda* 'buttocks,' *marrom* 'brown,' *iam* 'they went,' *hífen* 'hyphen'; **or**

(*continued*)

D. it comes before **m, n** followed by a vowel and is stressed (for the rules governing stress, see 3.1.1 above): *cama* 'bed,' *remo* 'oar,' *fino* 'thin,' *cone* 'cone,' *uma* 'one (fem.).'

The above rules are general and have few exceptions. The exceptions can be summarized as follows:

The first concerns only the word *muito* 'very, many,' which has a nasal **u** even though it does not come under any of the situations described in the rules.

The second exception is some derived words in which the nasal present in the primitive form is kept. For instance, in *comum* 'common' the **u** is nasal according to rule **C** above. In *comumente* 'commonly,' the **u** should be oral because it does not fall under any of the nasalization rules. Nevertheless, the usual pronunciation is with a nasal **u.** The same happens with *caminha* 'little bed,' which has a nasal **a** in the first syllable because it is the diminutive form of *cama* 'bed,' where the **a** is regularly nasal. Now, in the graphically identical *caminha* '(he/she) walks,' the first **a** is oral. This phenomenon is an instance of the tendency of derived words to keep a "reminder" of the primitive form in their pronunciation.

3.2.1 What does a nasal vowel sound like?

Although nasal vowels are frequent in American English, they are never distinctive, that is, their difference from oral vowels is never used for distinguishing one word from another. Consequently, speakers are unaware of their existence. For example, the normal American pronunciation of *hunt* has a nasal vowel, very similar to Portuguese nasal **a** in *canto* '(I) sing.' But the nasal vowel in *hunt* is felt by speakers as being identical to the **u** of *hut,* followed by an **n;** this is not strictly true, as spectrographic analysis shows, but it is psychologically real, and that is the important thing as far as perceiving sounds of the language is concerned. English, then, has oral and nasal vowels but no phonological distinction between them.

English does distinguish between oral and nasal consonants. Pronounce the pair *bee–me* several times and try to detect the difference in sound. You will find that for [m] the air comes out through the nose, whereas for [b] no air comes out through the nose (in fact, during the emission of the consonant no air comes out at all). This effect is achieved by lowering, for the nasals, the velum (the fleshy part of the palate), so that air can escape through the nose. A nasal vowel is produced by the same mechanism; but the velum is only half-lowered, so that air can escape simultaneously through nose and mouth. The student should listen to fluent speakers and try to imitate their enunciation of nasal vowels, that being the only really effective way to learn their pronunciation. It is less difficult than it sounds.

Not all vowel sounds of Portuguese can be nasalized. Of those that can, four correspond very closely to their oral counterparts, the difference being only nasalization: these are "closed" **e** ([e] as in *vê* 'he/she) sees'); "closed" **o** ([o] as in *avô* 'grandfather'); **i**; and **u**. "Open" **e** ([ɛ] as in *pé* 'foot'), and "open" **o** ([ɔ] as in *avó* 'grandmother') are never nasalized.

On the other hand, the vowel **a** changes its sound when nasalized. Stressed oral **a** sounds very low in the mouth, like Spanish or French **a**. But when it becomes nasalized the body of the tongue is raised in the middle of the mouth, so that the resulting sound is very close to the vowel in English *hunt*. Therefore, the difference between *tapa* 'slap' and *tampa* 'lid' is twofold: first, the **a** in *tampa* is nasalized; then, it is perceptibly more closed, resembling English **u** in *hunt*.

3.3 Pronunciation rules for vowels

Following are the rules for the pronunciation of each vowel. They allow the reader to find the right pronunciation for all vowels in all relevant environments, starting from the spelling.

U			
[w] as in English *cow, quick*	—after a vowel at the end of a word, not marked with an accent (whether or not followed by **s**)	ex: *mau*	'bad'
		maus	'bad (pl.)'

(*continued*)

	—between vowels	*Mauá*	(proper name)
	—in the sequences		
	qua, gua	*quatro*	'four'
		água	'water'
	—when marked with		
	a dieresis, **ü**[1]	*tranqüilo*	'quiet'
		agüentar	'to bear'
silent	—in the sequences		
	que, qui, gue, gui[2]	*que*	'which'
		guerra	'war'
	—after **o**	*vou*	'(I) go'
[ū] (nasal)	—before **nh**	*unha*	'fingernail'
	—before **n, m** + consonant	*nunca*	'never'
		tumba	'grave'
	—before **n, m** + word		
	boundary	*atum*	'tuna'
	—before **n, m** when		
	stressed		
		espuma	'foam'
		único	'unique'

(*continued*)

[u] as in English *too*³	—in all other cases	*tu*	'you'
		baú	'trunk'
		árdua	'arduous' ⁴
		Raul	(man's name)

Notes

[1]The dieresis is used in one case only: when **u** must be pronounced in the sequences **gu** and **qu** followed by **e, i.** Normally, **u** is silent in these combinations; when it is pronounced, the dieresis is used to mark the fact.

[2]In the very occasional words containing **quo, u** is most often silent: *quotidiano* 'daily' is pronounced, and sometimes written, *cotidiano.* No word contains **quu.**

[3]English **oo** and Portuguese **u** are not precisely alike. Portuguese **u** is pronounced like Spanish or German **u,** that is, with a more energetic rounding of the lips and retraction of the tongue toward the back of the mouth.

[4]In words like *árdua,* that is, before unstressed final **a** (with or without a following **s**), **u** may also be pronounced [w], so that *árdua* may have two or three syllables. In the masculine form, *árduo,* **u** is usually silent, since the sequence [wu] normally reduces to [u].

I

[j] as in English *day*	—after a vowel at the end of a word,		
	not marked with an accent		
	(whether or not followed by **s**)		
	ex:	*pai*	'father'
		pais	'parents'

(continued)

	—between vowels		
		paiol	'barn'
	—before final **a, o**		
	(whether or not		
	followed by **s**)	*Ásia*	'Asia'
		vários	'several'
	—before a vowel in an unstressed,		
	noninitial syllable	*nacional*	'national'
[ī] (nasal)	—before **nh**	*minha*	'my (fem.)'
	—before **n, m** + consonant	*lindo*	'beautiful'
		limpar	'to clean'
	—before **n, m** + word boundary	*sim*	'yes'
	—before **n, m** when stressed	*fino*	'thin'
[j̃] (nasal)	—after **ã**	*cãibra*	'cramp'
	—after a vowel and before **m, n**	*reina*	'(he/she) reigns'
		boina	'beret'
[i] as in English *see*	—in all other cases	*vi*	'(I) have seen'
		caí	'(I) have fallen'
		viver	'to live'
		raiz	'root'
		Diana	(woman's name)

—**I** is silent in *quieto* 'still,' pronounced as if it were *queto,* ['kɛtu].

—In the ending **-lio / -lia,** when unstressed, the sequence **-li-** is most often pronounced [λ] as if it were written **-lh-,** so that for most speakers *família* 'family' rhymes with *ilha* 'island.'

—In sequences of a vowel + **i,** occurring before the stressed syllable, the pronunciation varies between a semivowel [j] and a vowel [i]. Thus, in *coitado* 'poor thing!' we have [oj], and in *proibido* 'forbidden' we have most often [oi] (two syllables). There is no general rule; but the pronunciation with a diphthong is always acceptable, that is, pronouncing *proibido* with [oj] is not wrong, whereas *coitado* with [oi] is wrong.

E			
[e][1]	—with a circumflex (**ê**)	*pêssego*	'peach'
[ɛ] as in English *pet*	—with an acute (**é**)	*pé*	'foot'
[i] as in English *see*	—before a stressed vowel	*passear*	'to go for a walk'
	—when at the end of a word, (whether or not followed by **s**)[2]	*ave*	'bird'
		aves	'birds'
	—when at the end of an unstressed monosyllable, (whether or not followed by **s**)[3]	*de*	'of'
		lhes	'to them'
		e	'and'

(*continued*)

[j] as in English *day*	—before final unstressed **a, o** (whether or not followed by **s**)		
		área	'area'
		óleo	'oil'
[j̃] (nasal)	—after **ã, õ**	*mãe*	'mother'
		põe	'(he/she) puts'
[ē] (nasal)	—before **nh**	*lenha*	'firewood'
	—before **n, m** + consonant	*lento*	'slow'
		tempo	'time'
	—before **n, m** + word boundary	*hífen*	'hyphen'
		bem	'well'
	—before **n, m** when stressed	*cena*	'scene'
		remo	'paddle'
[e] or [ɛ][4]	—in all other cases	*pelo*	'(body) hair'
		vela	'candle'

Notes

[1]In English, the sound of Portuguese [e] occurs as part of a diphthong, never alone. Take the word *day:* after the [d] sound we have [e], and it is immediately followed by a y-glide, [j]. In order to produce Portuguese [e] you must pronounce the vowel in *day,* but "stop short" of pronouncing the glide. The result is identical to French **é** in *chanté.*

[2]Sometimes this results in a sequence of two [i]'s, which are reduced to only one: *série* 'series' is not pronounced ['serii], but ['seri].

[3]An unstressed monosyllable is a word of one syllable that is an article, a preposition, a conjunction, or a nonsubject pronoun.

[4]Here the pronunciation is unpredictable and must be learned for each word individually: *pelo* '(body) hair' has [e], *vela* 'candle' has [ε]. In the ending **-el,** the **e** is always open, [ε]: *papel* 'paper,' *coronel* 'colonel.'

The conditions for the pronunciation of **o** are similar to those for **e:**

O

[o][1]	—with a circumflex (**ô**)	*avô*	'grandfather'
[ɔ] as in English *flaw*[2]	—with an acute (**ó**)	*avó*	'grandmother'
[u] as in English *you*	—before a stressed vowel	*voar*	'to fly'
	—when at the end of a word, (whether or not followed by **s**)[3]	*gato*	'cat'
		gatos	'cats'
	—when at the end of an unstressed monosyllable, (whether or not followed by **s**)[4]	*o*	'the'
		do	'of the'
		dos	'of the (pl.)'

(*continued*)

[w] as in English *cow*	—before final unstressed a (whether or not followed by s)	*mágoa*	'sorrow'
	—after a stressed vowel	*caos*	'chaos'
[w̄] (nasal)	—after ã	*mão*	'hand'
[ō] (nasal)	—before **nh**	*sonhar*	'to dream'
	—before **n, m** + consonant	*conta*	'account'
		comprar	'to buy'
	—before **n, m** + word boundary	*bom*	'good'
	—before **n, m** when stressed	*soma*	'sum'
		lona	'canvas'
	—when marked with a tilde (**ō**)	*põe*	'(he/she) puts'[5]
[o] or [ɔ][6]	—in all other cases	*soco*	'punch'
		solo	'soil'

Notes

[1]In English, the sound of Portuguese [o], like [e], occurs only as the first part of a diphthong: for example, in *no*. Portuguese [o] is similar to the first part of the English diphthong and is identical to French **eau** in *beau*.

[2]The New England pronunciation, with rounding of the lips: [ˈflɔː]. Many people in the Midwest pronounce [ˈflɒː] without rounding. Portuguese [ɔ] is always rounded.

[3]When a sequence of two [u]'s would result, it is simplified into only one: *contínuo* 'continuous' is pronounced [kõˈtʃĩnu].

[4]As seen above, an unstressed monosyllable is a word of one syllable that is an article, a preposition, a conjunction, or a nonsubject pronoun.

[5]Graphic ** õ** occurs only in the diphthong **õe.**

[6]The situation here is the same as for **e;** the pronunciation is unpredictable and must be learned for every word: *soco* 'punch' has [o], *solo* 'soil' has [ɔ]. The ending **-ol** always has an open **o,** [ɔ]: *farol* 'headlight,' *sol* 'sun,' except in *gol* 'goal,' which has a closed [o].

Two notes on e and o

A. Opening of pre-stress *e* and *o*

When **e** and **o** occur in a syllable previous to the stressed one, they are normally closed, that is, [e] and [o], respectively. Thus, from *mel* [ˈmɛw] 'honey' one gets the derivative *melado* [meˈladu], 'molasses,' where the original [ɛ] becomes [e] in unstressed position; and the same phenomenon is seen in the pair *sol* [ˈsɔw] 'sun,' *solão* [soˈlãw] 'hot sun.'

But there are exceptions. The first exception appears in words in which the stressed vowel is open, that is, [ɛ] or [ɔ]; in these words, an **e** or an **o** in the preceding syllable should also be opened. For instance, *Pelé,* the name of the famous soccer player, is pronounced with two open **e**'s, [pɛˈlɛ], and *bolota* 'acorn' has two open **o**'s, [bɔˈlɔtə]. This happens only when the two vowels have the same articulation point, that is, an open **o** does not cause a preceding **e** to become open, and an open **e** does not cause a preceding **o** to become open; this is seen in *coleta* 'collection,' pronounced [koˈlɛtə].

This rule is valid for the variety of Brazilian Portuguese presented in this book; but in part of São Paulo and most of the south it is often ignored, and many southerners pronounce the first vowel of *Pelé* as a closed [e].

Another exception concerns derived words whose primitives have stressed open vowels: these keep the open vowel even though it is no longer stressed. This happens regularly in derived words with the diminutive suffix *-zinho* and with the adverb-forming suffix *-mente*, e.g., *cafezinho* [kafɛˈzĩju], derived from *café* [kaˈfɛ] 'coffee,' *somente* [sɔˈmẽtʃi], derived from *só* [ˈsɔ] 'only.' This is another instance of the tendency (mentioned in 3.2 above) of derived words to keep a reminder of the primitive form in their pronunciation.

B. Raising of pre-stress *e* and *o*

When **e** and **o** occur in a syllable previous to the stressed one, their pronunciation, according to the above rules, would be [e] or [o], respectively. This can be accepted as an approximation, but it simplifies things a little. Pronouncing, say, *perigo* 'danger' with an [e] in the first syllable is correct; but it sounds slightly too correct, somewhat stilted, more like someone reading aloud than like normal, spontaneous speech. Fluent speakers use [i] in that position, so that the word sounds [pi'ɾigu]. A similar process reduces **o** to [u] as in *to-mate* 'tomato,' pronounced [tu'matʃi]. This is known among linguists as **vowel raising.**

Vowel raising is a general phenomenon, in no way connected with uncultured or popular speech. Unfortunately, it does not seem to be regular, and the beginner will have to pay attention to the speech of native speakers and learn the cases of raising one by one. A few rules of thumb can be of help:

—**e** is always raised when word-initial before **s, n, m** plus a consonant: *estar* 'to be,' *esperar* 'to wait,' *entrada* 'entrance,' *embora* 'away,' etc. are always pronounced with an initial [i];

—raising never occurs before **r** followed by a consonant: the first vowel of *permitir* 'to permit,' *verdade* 'truth' is [e], and the first vowel of *cordeiro* 'lamb' is [o]. Furthermore, word-initial **e, o** before **r** are never raised: *errado* 'wrong,' *oração* 'prayer' begin with [e] and [o], respectively.

Here, the danger for the beginner is raising too many vowels: *perigo* with an [e] and *tomate* with an [o] sound too correct, but *verdade* with an [i] is just plain wrong. Therefore, when in doubt, opt for [e] or [o], as the case may be.

A

[ə] as in English *Cuba*	—whenever it occurs in a word after the stressed syllable (and not before final **n, m**)	*bêbado*	'drunk'
		tia	'aunt'
		tias	'aunts'
		açúcar	'sugar'
[ʌ̃] (nasal)	—before **nh**	*banho*	'bath'
	—before **n, m** + consonant	*campo*	'field'
		cantar	'to sing'

(*continued*)

	—before **n, m** + word boundary	*Ivan*	(man's name)
		lavam	'(they) wash'
	—before **n, m** when stressed	*ramo*	'branch'
		ano	'year'
	—when marked with a tilde (ã)	*lã*	'wool'
[a][1]	—in all other cases	*pá*	'shovel'
		caro	'dear'
		atento	'attentive'
		carrapato	'tick'

Note

[1] The sound of Portuguese [a] is close to the **o** in *pot* (American pronunciation) but noticeably longer, particularly when stressed. It is identical to Spanish **á** in *más*, French **a** in *las*.

Y

Y is a rare letter in Portuguese, occurring in unassimilated foreign words and in some personal names like *Nancy* and *Yara*. It usually follows the same rules as **i**; but in a few cases of borrowed words it keeps the original pronunciation, as in *nylon*, where it sounds [aj] as in English.

3.4 Final devoicing

One last remark on the pronunciation of vowels: Portuguese, as I said, is very close to Spanish in vocabulary and structure, yet it sounds very different to foreign ears. One reason is the abundance of nasal vowels, which do not exist in Spanish. Another is the phenomenon usually called final devoicing. This means that final unstressed vowels, when at the end of a sentence, before a pause, or in some other contexts, are pronounced without vocal cord vibration, that is, they are "whispered." The word *tempo* 'time,' as seen, ends with an [u] sound. But if it comes at the end of a sentence the [u], although articulated in the normal way, is only whispered, without vibrating the vocal cords. In rapid speech, devoicing is sometimes so radical as to totally omit the vowel, so that *tempo* sounds almost like *temp*.

Final devoicing is difficult for a foreigner to grasp; in this case some contact with fluent speakers is essential. On the other hand, devoicing is not strictly compulsory, and you can dispense with it and still speak correct, if a little careful-sounding, Portuguese.

The precise contexts in which final devoicing occurs are as follows:

—at the end of an utterance or before a pause (that is, before silence); for example, the vowels in boldface are devoiced in

*tenho temp**o***	'(I) have time'
*cerveja em lat**a***	'canned beer'

—very often between two voiceless consonants (**p, t, c, f, s, x, q**); for example,

*lat**a** pequena*	'small can'

When a word is stressed on the antepenultimate syllable and the last vowel is devoiced, devoicing often extends to all sounds (including consonants) occurring in the word after the stressed syllable, as in *lingüística* 'linguistics,' *rápido* 'rapid,' where boldface letters represent devoiced sounds.

3.5 I-insertion

A characteristic feature of Brazilian (as against European) pronunciation is insertion of an [i]-sound to break certain consonant clusters, to avoid a consonant cluster at the beginning of a word, or to avoid a final consonant. The [i] thus inserted behaves like any other vowel: it can have secondary stress (see 3.1.2) and a **t** or a **d** before it becomes [tʃ] and [dʒ], respectively, as they do before any other [i].

I-insertion happens in three contexts:

—In word-initial position, before a cluster of **s** plus a consonant. These clusters never appear in native Portuguese words, but they are frequent in borrowings like the English loanwords *stress* and *spray,* pronounced [isˈtɾɛsi] and [isˈpɾej], respectively.

—In word-final position, whenever a word would end in a consonant other than **s** or **r.** This also happens in loanwords, in acronyms, and in only one native word, the preposition *sob* 'under,' pronounced ['sobi]. Thus *USP*, which stands for *Universidade de São Paulo* 'São Paulo University,' is pronounced ['uspi]. Examples of English origin are *bug, kart, staff,* all of which add a final [i] when pronounced. In the case of *kart,* the **t** becomes [tʃ], as expected.

—Whenever there is a cluster starting with a consonant other than **r, s, m, l,** or **n.** This occurs often in Portuguese words: *advogado* 'lawyer,' pronounced *adivogado* (five syllables); *optar* 'to choose,' pronounced *opitar; pneu* 'tire,' pronounced *pineu* or *peneu; objeto* 'object,' pronounced *obijeto,* and so on.

This results in the only cases of words stressed on the fourth syllable from the end; for instance, the word *rítmico* 'rhythmic' would seem to be stressed on the antepenultimate syllable. But since the cluster -**tm**- is broken by the insertion of an [i], the word actually has four syllables and is stressed on the first: ['hitʃimiku].

3.6 Glide insertion

3.6.1 Before final *s, z*

In words ending in a stressed vowel plus the [s] sound (written **s** or **z**), a [j]-glide is often added before the final [s] sound, as in

três	'three'	['tɾejs]	or	['tɾes]
francês	'French'	[fɾɐ̃'sejs]	or	[fɾɐ̃'ses]
rapaz	'young man'	[ha'pajs]	or	[ha'pas]
arroz	'rice'	[a'hojs]	or	[a'hos]

Glide insertion before final [s] is very common in Rio and in Minas, less so in the south. The precise conditions under which insertion occurs are not known. It seems to be more general after **e, a** than after other vowels, so that for many speakers *mais* 'more' and *mas* 'but' are pronounced alike, but in *avôs* 'grandfathers,' *avós* 'grandparents, grandmothers' insertion never takes place.

3.6.2 Between vowels

In sequences of stressed **o** or **e** plus a vowel in another syllable, a glide is inserted between the two vowels, so that a diphthong results. When the first vowel is **o,** the glide [w] is inserted: the word *boa* 'good (fem.)' is pronounced ['bowa], that is, with a glide, [w], between the two vowels. When the first vowel is **e,** the glide [j] is inserted, and in this case it is generally written: *feio* 'ugly (masc.),' pronounced ['feju]. But even in the rare cases in which no **i** appears between the vowels the glide is present, e.g., the family name *Corrêa,* which is pronounced as if were *Correia* (it is sometimes also spelled this way).

When the first stressed vowel is **i,** the glide [j] is inserted in the variety we are studying, but many speakers in other regions join the two vowels directly, e.g., *fio* 'thread, cable,' pronounced ['fiju] in Minas and Rio, but ['fiu], or even ['fiw] in Bahia.

4

Diphthongs, Triphthongs, Hiatuses

4.1 Diphthongs: Regular cases

Portuguese has several diphthongs. Most require no special explanation, being simply sequences of a vowel plus a semivowel, i.e., a vowel sound that does not form a syllable—so that the sounds of a diphthong always belong to one and the same syllable. Examples are **au,** as in *aula* 'class,' pronounced as a sequence of [a] plus [w] and very similar to English **ow** in *how;* and **ai** as in *pai* 'father,' similar to English **y** in *my.* These diphthongs are pronounced according to the general rules given above for the vowels and need no special treatment. In any case, the complete list follows (with English correlates whenever possible):

Oral diphthongs						
ai	[aj]	as in English	*my*	ex:	*pai*	'father'
au	[aw]	as in English	*how*		*mau*	'bad'

(continued)

éi	[ɛj]			*papéis*	'papers'
ei	[ej]	as in English	*say*	*lei*	'law'
eu	[ew]			*eu*	'I'
éu	[ɛw]			*véu*	'veil'
oi	[oj]			*boi*	'ox'
ói	[ɔj]	as in English	*boy*	*rói*	'(he/she) gnaws'
iu	[iw]			*riu*	'(he/she) laughed'
ui	[uj]			*cuidado*	'care'

—**Accent on** *éi, éu, ói:* These three diphthongs (with open **e, o** + semivowel) are always accented, in order to keep them distinct from **ei**, **eu, oi** (closed vowel + semivowel).

—**Reduction of** *ai, ei:* The sequence **ei,** normally a diphthong, is pronounced [e], that is, a closed **e,** when it occurs before **r, j, ch,** or **x.** For instance, *feira* 'open-air market,' *beijo* 'kiss,' and *peixe* 'fish' are pronounced as if they were written *fera, bejo, pexe,* respectively. A few people pronounce the diphthong in these cases, probably under the influence of the spelling. The same process is also common before **m:** *queimar* 'to burn' is often pronounced *quemar,* and *teima* 'stubbornness' sounds *tema.* But in these cases the diphthong *can* be pronounced without loss of naturalness.

The sequence **ai** undergoes an analogous reduction, but only before the sound [ʃ]: *caixa* 'box,' *baixo* 'low' are pronounced [ˈkaʃə], [ˈbaʃu], respectively.

—**Pseudo-diphthong** *ou:* The sequence **ou** is pronounced [o], that is, as a simple vowel, not as a diphthong. Thus, *couro* 'leather' and *coro* 'choir' are pronounced alike.

—**Nasal** *ui:* The sequence **ui** is pronounced as a nasal diphthong in the word *muito* 'very; many'; see the following section.

—Rising versus falling diphthongs:** this distinction is not made here because so-called rising diphthongs are normally produced by the general rules and therefore require no special discussion. Thus, in the word *rádio* 'radio' the final **-io** is pronounced in only one syllable, [ju], by virtue of the application of the general rules given above. The fact that [ju] is, technically, a (rising) diphthong does not need to be emphasized here, since this information is not necessary for pronunciation purposes.

—**"New" diphthongs:** the fact that **l** at the end of a syllable is pronounced [w] by most speakers gives rise to diphthongs in many words which originally did not have them. Thus, *sal* 'salt' is pronounced ['saw], *futebol* 'soccer' is pronounced [futʃi'bɔw], and *voltar* 'to come back' is pronounced [vow'tah].

As noted above, this pronunciation [w] for syllable-final **l** is not universal. In Portugal and in some areas of southern Brazil, final **l** is pronounced [ɫ], like English **ll** in *well*.

4.2 Nasal diphthongs

Nasal vowels also combine with semivowels to form diphthongs. In these cases **the whole diphthong** is nasal, that is, both segments, the vowel and the semivowel, are nasalized. Thus, the diphthong written **-em** sounds like English **ay** in *day*, but nasalized throughout (although the phonetic transcription usually puts the tilde on the vowel only: [ẽj], where more rigorously one should have [ẽj̃]).

Nasal diphthongs are not spelled in a straightforward way; for instance, the diphthong [ẽj̃] may be spelled **em**: the **e** becomes nasal by effect of the following **m**, according to a general rule; and the **m** itself is pronounced as a nasal semivowel, [j̃]. A better way to describe the phenomenon is to consider nasal diphthongs as units and to say simply that the sequence **em** (in word-final position) is pronounced [ẽj̃]. Therefore, I give below the list of all nasal diphthongs, with their respective pronunciations. There are five nasal diphthongs:

Nasal diphthongs

[ɐ̃j̃]	written **ãe, ãi,** or **ai**	*mãe* 'mother,' *cãibra* 'cramps'[1]
[ɐ̃w̃]	written **ão, am**	*irmão* 'brother,' *falam* '(they) speak'[2,3]
[ẽj̃]	written **em, ém, en, én**	*correm* '(they) run,' *porém* 'however,' *reféns* 'hostages'[4]
[õj̃]	written **õe** or **õem** or written **oi** when stressed preceding **n, m**	*nações* 'nations,' *põem* '(they) put'[5] *boina* 'beret'
[ũj̃]	written **ui**	*muito*[6] 'very, many'

Notes

[1]The spelling **ai** for this nasal diphthong occurs only in a few words where it is stressed and precedes a nasal consonant: *Jaime* (a man's name). Some speakers pronounce these words with an oral diphthong.

[2]The spelling **am** is used for the diphthong when it is unstressed (and word-final) in verb forms: *andam* 'they walk.' In nouns **ão** is always used, even when unstressed: *órfão* 'orphan.'

[3]The word **não** 'no; do not' is regularly pronounced [nᾶw̃], as expected. But when it comes immediately before a verb (that is, when it functions as the negative particle) it very frequently sounds [nũ], as if it were written *num: não gostei* '(I) did not like,' then, sounds like *num gostei*. If **não** does not immediately precede a verb it must be pronounced in the regular way: for instance, when used as an independent negation: *não!* 'no!' or when negating a nominal: *não-especialista* 'nonspecialist,' or when part of a double negation: *não faz isso não* 'don't do that'—here the first *não* is usually reduced to [nũ], but the second one must be pronounced [nᾶw̃] (see 31.3.4 for more details).

[4]The spelling **ém,** with accent, is used when the diphthong is word-final and stressed. The sequences **en, én** are pronounced as diphthongs when final or when preceding a final **s:** *bens* 'possessions' is pronounced ['bẽjs].

[5]**Õem** is found only in the form *põem* 'they put,' a form of the verb *pôr* 'to put,' and in corresponding forms of verbs derived from *pôr: compõem, impõem,* etc.

[6]This diphthong occurs only in the word *muito,* 'very, many,' pronounced always with a nasal, and in the popular pronunciation of *ruim* 'bad,' ['hũj]. As for the latter word, purists defend a pronunciation in two syllables, that is, oral **u** followed by nasal **i:** [hu'ĩ], but the pronunciation with a diphthong is the most usual.

4.3 Triphthongs

Triphthongs are sequences of a semivowel plus a vowel plus a semivowel. English has triphthongs in the exclamation *wow!* and in the word *way.* Triphthongs, like diphthongs, always belong to one and the same syllable.

Potentially, then, we might have a triphthong whenever a letter like **i, u,** which are often pronounced as semivowels, precedes a diphthong. The triphthongs actually occurring in Portuguese are as follows:

Triphthongs

[waj]	written **uai**	—in the sequences **guai, quai** *Paraguai* 'Paraguay'

(*continued*)

			quais	'which (pl.)'
[wej]	written **üei**	—in the sequence **güei**	*agüei*	'(I have) watered'
[waw]	written **ual**	—in the sequences **gual, qual**	*igual*	'equal'
[wʌ̃w̃]	written **uão** or **uam**	—in the sequences **guão,**	*saguão*	'lobby'
		quão, guam	*quão*	'how much'
			águam	'(they) water'
[wẽj̃]	written **üem**	—in the sequence **güem**	*águem*	'(they) water [subj.]'
[wõj̃]	written **uõe**	—in the sequence **guõe**	*saguões*	'lobby (pl.)'

Triphthongs have a very limited distribution in the language, occurring in but a few words and always after **q** or **g.**

**4.4 Hiatuses

A **hiatus** is simply the separation of two vowels between different syllables. One example is *saí* [sa'i] '(I) went out': we say that there is a hiatus between **a** and **í.** Hiatuses do not require special study, as they are all derived automatically from the application of the pronunciation rules given above. But it may be useful to summarize separately the conditions under which hiatuses do and do not appear.

The general conditions are very simple and may be stated in terms of contact of the letters that are normally pronounced as semivowels—that is, **u** (and **o** when pronounced [u] or [w]) and **i** (and **e** when pronounced [i] or [j])—with any other vowels. When these vowels are pronounced [w] or [j], respectively, we have diphthongs; when they are pronounced [u] or [i], we have hiatuses.

The rules are as follows:

1. Whenever **i, u** precede a stressed vowel, the sequence is to be pronounced as a hiatus—that is, each vowel belongs to a syllable.

Ex.: *iodo* [i'odu] 'iodine'; *atuar* [atu'a] 'to act.'

Exceptions
a) When **i, u** are between vowels, they are pronounced as semivowels, [j] and [w], respectively, which gives rise to a diphthong: *caiar* [ka'jah] 'to whitewash'; *Mauá* [ma'wa] (proper name).
b) **U** is pronounced as a semivowel in the sequences **gua, qua,** and when it bears a dieresis: *aguar* [a'gwa] 'to water,' *quatro* ['kwatru] 'four,' *sagüi* [sa'gwi] 'little monkey.'
2. Whenever **i, u** follow a vowel, they are pronounced as semivowels, and the sequence is a diphthong and belongs to the same syllable.
Ex.: *pai* ['paj] 'father'; *mau* ['maw] 'bad.'
Exceptions
a) When **i, u** bear an accent (**í, ú**) the sequence has a hiatus: *saída* [sa'idə] 'exit,' *saúde* [sa'udʒi] 'health.'
b) When **i, u** are followed by **z, l** at the end of a word, the sequence has a hiatus: *raiz* [ha'is] 'root'; *Raul* [ha'uw] (man's name).
c) In certain words the sequence **i, u** + vowel may be pronounced with a hiatus or as a diphthong. Such words are derived from words having a hiatus, or are formed with prefixes + a word beginning with a vowel: *raizeira* [hai'zerə] 'healer, medicine woman,' derived from *raiz* [ha'is] 'root'; *reunir* [heu'nih] 'to bring together,' derives from *re-* + *unir* 'to unite.' Yet these words can also be pronounced [haj'zerə] and [hew'nih], respectively.
3. The sequences **ui** and **iu** (without accent) are pronounced as diphthongs, [uj] and [iw], respectively: *ruivo* ['hujvu] 'red-haired,' *saiu* [sa'iw] '(he/she) went out.'

5

Joining Words

When people speak, word boundaries do not appear; words are run together, so that the sequence *shut up* sounds (and is sometimes written) *shuddup,* as if it were one word. This also happens in Portuguese; we have already seen one case, that of final **r** before a word beginning with a vowel: in *amor eterno* 'eternal love' the final **r** of *amor* [aˈmoh] is pronounced [ɾ] as in *amoroso* 'loving,' that is, the word boundary is disregarded, and the sequence is pronounced as if it were *amoreterno* [aˌmoɾeˈtɛhnu]. We have also seen that word-final **s** is pronounced [z] when the following word begins with a vowel or a voiced consonant: *os olhos* 'the eyes,' *duas vacas* 'two cows' are pronounced with final [z] in the first word: [uzˈɔʎus], [ˈduəzˈvakəs].

In this section I shall present a few more cases of special phenomena occurring at word boundaries (the technical designation for these phenomena is **sandhi**). For the student who wants to acquire a fluent, natural-sounding pronunciation of the language they are indispensable.

5.1 Vowel + vowel

5.1.1 Final vowel deletion

In many cases in which a word-final vowel comes immediately before a word-initial vowel, and there is no pause or intonation break between them—that is, when they are pronounced in the same breath—one of the vowels disappears in normal pronunciation. Thus, in *casa enorme* 'huge house' the final *-a* of *casa* is not heard, and the sequence sounds as if it were *casinorme* ['kazi'nɔhmi]. The final *-a* can be pronounced, but this gives the impression of somewhat slow, careful speech, as if the speaker were trying to be understood over a poor telephone connection.

In other cases both vowels are pronounced, although the first one is reduced, becoming a glide, a sound like English **y** in *yes*. In *bule amassado* 'dented coffeepot' both the final [i] of *bule* and the initial [a] of *amassado* must sound, but they do so in only one syllable: ['buljama'sadu].

The following rules govern this type of vowel reduction:

When both vowels are **unstressed**:

1. If the first vowel is [i] or [u], and the second is not identical to the first,

the first vowel becomes a glide: [i] becomes [j], [u] becomes [w].

2. In all other cases the first vowel is omitted.

When either vowel is stressed, reduction does not occur, and the vowels are usually pronounced separately, even if they are identical: in *fruta ácida* 'sour fruit' both **a**'s are pronounced.

These rules do not apply in slow speech. Yet certain sequences of identical vowels are always reduced: one cannot pronounce both **a**'s in *pia azul* 'blue sink,' for instance.

5.1.2 Preposition contraction

In one case the vowel deletion process described above may be obligatory even in slow, careful speech and is furthermore represented in writing: in sequences of the prepositions *a, de, em,* and *por* plus an article, a demonstrative, or the pronoun *ele / ela* 'he / she.'

Prepositions occur typically preceding a noun phrase, and noun phrases very often begin with an article or a demonstrative; therefore, the sequence **preposition** + **article / demonstrative / pronoun** is very frequent. For instance, we may have *de* 'of' before *o carro* 'the car' in

A porta do carro
'The door of the car'
One might expect *a porta de o carro,* but when *de* occurs before *o* the two contract

into *do.* This contraction is obligatory, and the sequence *de o* does not occur.[1] When the preposition is *por,* it changes its form, becoming *pel-,* so that *por* + a is realized as *pela:*

> *Entramos pela porta da frente.*
> 'We entered through the front door.'

Note

[1]In formal written language *de o* (*de a,* etc.) are kept separate if *o* is the first word of a following clause. Thus, one writes *a hora <u>de o</u> presidente falar* 'the moment the president speaks' [literally, 'the time <u>of the</u> president to speak']. This rule, however, is falling into disuse, so that one finds most often *a hora <u>do</u> presidente falar.*

There are also cases of optional contraction. In such cases contraction is more usual in Portugal, while Brazilians prefer to use the two words separately, as in *as asas dum anjo* 'the wings of an angel' (Port.) versus *as asas <u>de um</u> anjo* 'id.' (Braz.).

The elements that can contract with preceding prepositions are the articles (both definite and indefinite) and the demonstratives *esse* 'this,' *este* 'this,' and *aquele* 'that,' as well as their neuter forms *isso, isto, aquilo,* and the personal pronoun *ele:*

> *A casa daquela bruxa*
> 'That witch's house'

> *Tenho medo disso.*
> 'I am afraid of this.'

> *Você só pensa naquilo.*
> 'That's all you think about.'

A complete table of contractions is found in appendix 3. The following rules account for all of them (optional cases of contractions are within brackets, [ ]):

Rule 1. The preposition *a* contracts only with *o, a,* and the demonstratives beginning with *a-;* and the sequence *a* (prep.) + *a-* (first letter of the following word) becomes *à.*

Contractions

$a + o(s) \rightarrow ao(s)$

$a +$ **any form beginning with** $a\text{-} \rightarrow à\text{-}$ e.g.

$a + a$ (article) $\rightarrow à$

$a +$ aquele $\rightarrow àquele$

Examples

Dei um presente <u>à</u> vizinha.
'I gave a present <u>to the</u> neighbor.'

Cheguei atrasado <u>ao</u> concerto.
'(I) arrived <u>at the</u> concert late.'

Vou <u>àquela</u> festa vestido de Ali Babá.
'I am going <u>to that</u> party costumed as Ali Baba.'

Note

The resulting **à** is pronounced as a regular **a**; thus, the contraction *àquele* is pronounced in the same way as the noncontracted demonstrative *aquele*. *Ao* is pronounced [aw].

Rule 2. The preposition *de* becomes *d-*, and the preposition *em* becomes *n-*. They contract with all articles, demonstratives, and with *ele;* but contraction with *um(a)* is avoided in writing,[1] although it is frequent in the spoken language.

Note

[1] By Brazilians, mentioned above; the Portuguese often write *dum, numa,* etc.

Contractions

de + o	→	*do*
de + um	→	[*dum*]
de + esse	→	*desse*
em + a	→	*na*
em + ela	→	*nela*
em + uma	→	[*numa*]

Examples

A janela <u>da</u> sala
'The window <u>of the</u> living room'

Vivo pensando <u>nela</u>.
'I spend my life thinking <u>of her</u>.'

Rule 3. The preposition *por* becomes *pel-*. It contracts only with the

definite article.

Contractions

por + *o*   →   *pelo*

por + *a*   →   *pela*

Examples

O ladrão fugiu <u>pela</u> janela.
'The burglar escaped <u>through the</u> window.'

5.2 Syllable deletion

Another word-boundary phenomenon is syllable deletion. It is the Portuguese version of something found in many languages, including English. For instance, when someone says *next stop* one might expect to hear the sequence [st] twice, because *next* ends with it and *stop* begins with it. But what is heard is *nekstop:* the sequence [st st] is simplified to [st]. In this case deletion is virtually obligatory, and pronouncing both occurrences of [st] yields a somewhat strange result.

In Portuguese there is a similar phenomenon: syllable sequences are simplified at the boundary of words. One example is *Faculdade de Medicina* 'medical school': *Faculdade* ends in *-de,* pronounced [dʒi]; and the following preposition, *de,* is also pronounced [dʒi]. The result should be the sequence [dʒi dʒi], but only one of these two syllables is pronounced, so that the sequence sounds as if it were written *Faculda'de Medicina.*

The two syllables do not have to be identical in order to follow the rule; simplification occurs, for instance, in *limite de palavra* 'word boundary,' where the final *-te* of *limite* is deleted, although it is not identical with the following *de;* another example is *gente direita* 'honest people,' pronounced *gen' direita.* The disappearance of the first syllable is so complete that some assimilation rules apply to the remainder of the word, as in *imposto de renda* 'income tax': the **s** in *imposto* is voiceless, [s], because it comes before a **t;** but in *imposto de renda* the final *-to* vanishes, and the **s** is voiced into [z] because it then comes into contact with a **d:** [ĩ'poz dʒi 'hẽdə].

The contexts in which syllable simplification occurs are not precisely known, but some indications can be made. First, both syllables must be unstressed. Thus, in *gente digna* 'honorable people' no simplification takes place because the initial *di-* of *digna* is stressed. Second, the vowel in the first syllable must be [i] or [u]. Therefore, simplification occurs in *caldo de cana* 'sugar-cane juice,' where the two syllables in contact are [du] and [dʒi], but in *fralda de bebê* 'baby's diaper' both the final *-da* of *fralda* and the preposition *de* are pronounced. And the consonants must be [t] or [d]: no simplification occurs to delete *-co* in *coco da Bahia* 'Bahia coconut' or *-po* in *campo de futebol* 'soccer field.'

Finally, the results of not applying the simplification rule vary; in *Faculdade de Medicina* there is always deletion; but in *caldo de cana* deletion appears to be optional, and the phrase may sound natural even if both *-do* and *de* are pronounced. Simplification is also optional when the two words in question do not form a phrase but are separated by a major syntactic boundary, as in *a gente dizia que* . . . 'people said that . . . ,' where the final *-te* of *gente* may or may not be pronounced without harm to fluency, because *a gente* is the subject of the sentence and *dizia* is part of the predicate.

6

Notes on Spelling

As we have seen, Portuguese pronunciation rules are fairly systematic; with comparatively few exceptions, pronunciation of every word can be predicted from its spelling.

Things are different when one takes the opposite road: predicting spelling from pronunciation. Here the degree of unpredictability is high, and in some cases the only solution is to learn the spelling as something independent from pronunciation. For instance, the reader may have remarked that the sound [s] between vowels can be written in several ways: **c, ç, s, sç, ss, sc, x, xc.** This means that very often a word can be written in more than one way, yet only one is considered correct. For instance, *passa* 'raisin' might also be written *paça* or *pasça,* without any change in the way it is pronounced. Why is *passa* the only correct spelling?

The answer is that you must spell *passa* because that is the way it has always been spelled. And if you think this is irrational (which it is), remember that English spelling is even more difficult for Brazilians to learn! Of course, etymological reasons are generally mentioned to explain these idiosyncrasies; yet they fail to satisfy many people because, first, there are many words whose etymology is unknown; then, because in some cases etymology, although known, is not followed; and, finally, because we question why we should write *passa* with *-ss-* only because the Romans, two thousand years ago, did so. There is no good answer to these objections; but things being the way they are, not the way they should be, Portuguese spelling will for the moment remain full of unnecessary difficulties.

In this section I give a few rules that concern accent placement and syllabification, which are quite systematic. And I add a list of sounds that may present spelling problems; the list does not solve the problems but at least delimits them, so that a student will not waste time wondering how to write ['bifi] 'steak,' which has only one possible spelling, *bife;* but will be alert to the real dangers, like the aforementioned [s] between vowels.

6.1 Accents

As mentioned, there are three accents, the acute (á), the circumflex (â), and the grave (à). The tilde (ã) and the dieresis (ü) are not considered accents, but the distinction is not really important, so they will be treated here as accents.

6.1.1 The acute and the circumflex

The acute and the circumflex have the basic function of marking the stressed vowel in a word. The **circumflex,** ˆ , is used whenever the vowel to be accented is a closed **e** [e], a closed **o** [o], or a nasal **a, e,** or **o** (the circumflex is never used on **u, i**). One exception: the endings -**ém,** -**éns,** which take an acute even though the vowel is nasal. For example, *pêssego* 'peach,' *fôlego* 'breath,' *lâmpada* 'light bulb,' *apêndice* 'appendix,' *ônibus* 'bus.'

The **acute,** ´ , is used in all other cases: *Ásia* 'Asia,' *América* 'America,' *lírio* 'lily,' *óleo* 'oil,' *também* 'also,' *parabéns* 'congratulations,' *íntimo* 'intimate,' *único* 'only.'

In order to state the accent rules, one must first divide words into three categories, according to the place of stress relative to the end of the word. Portuguese stress, as we saw in 3.1, can fall on the last syllable (*café* 'coffee'), on the penultimate (*casa* 'house'), or on the antepenultimate (*pílula* 'pill'). Thus there are three types of words, each of which will be taken into account when stating the accent rules.

Let's start with words stressed on the antepenultimate syllable. The rule is very simple:

Accent rule 1. When a word is stressed on the antepenultimate syllable, it has an accent on the stressed vowel.

Examples: *lâmpada* 'light bulb,' *tímido* 'shy,' *pálido* 'pale,' *pêssego* 'peach,' *século* 'century,' *ônibus* 'bus,' *cólera* 'wrath.'

For words stressed on the penultimate syllable, the rule is as follows:

Accent rule 2. When a word is stressed on the penultimate syllable, it has an accent on the stressed vowel if it ends in:

—a diphthong (whether or not followed by **-s**), except those written **am, em, ens;**[1]

—**i, is, u, us;**

— **r, l, n.**

Otherwise, it has no accent.

Note

[1]For purposes of accentuation, the endings **-io, ia, uo, ua** may be considered diphthongs; therefore, a word having these endings takes an accent if the stressed syllable is the penultimate, e.g., *história* 'history,' *contínuo* 'continuous,' *água* 'water.' If the stress falls on the **i** or **u,** no accent is necessary: *navio* 'ship.'

Examples: *órgão* 'organ,' *pônei* 'pony,' *júri* 'jury,' *ônus* 'burden,' *açúcar* 'sugar,' *fácil* 'easy,' *hífen* 'hyphen,' *Antônio* (man's name);
casa 'house,' *bule* 'coffeepot,' *carro* 'car,' *homem* 'man,' *homens* 'men,' *falam* '(they) speak.'

For words stressed on the last syllable, the rule is as follows:

Accent rule 3. When a word is stressed on the last syllable, it has an accent on the stressed vowel if it ends in:

-em, -ens;

-a, -e, -o, -as, -es, -os.

Otherwise, it has no accent.

Examples: *também* 'also,' *parabéns* 'congratulations,' *está* '(he/she) is,' *café* 'coffee,' *paletó* 'jacket,' *cafés, paletós;*

portão 'gate,' *falei* '(I) have spoken,' *falou* '(he/she) has spoken,' *aqui* 'here,' *tatu* 'armadillo,' *mulher* 'woman,' *papel* 'paper.'

A supplementary rule is needed for some vowel sequences, viz.:

Accent rule 4. In the sequences

ai, au, ei, oi, ou, iu, ui

the second vowel has an accent if

—it does not belong to the same syllable as the first one; and

—it is not followed in the same syllable by **nh,**

—or by **l, z** in the same syllable.

Examples
—*Aí* [a'i] 'there': the word contains the sequence **ai**, not followed by **nh** or by **l, z** in the same syllable; **a** and **i** do not belong to the same syllable. Then, we accent the second vowel. Analogous cases: *país* 'country,' *baú* 'trunk,' *viúvo* 'widow,' *roído* 'gnawed.'

—*Raiz* [ha'is] 'root': the word contains the sequence **ai,** not in the same syllable. But the second vowel in the sequence is followed by **z** in the same syllable. Therefore, no accent. Analogous cases: *rainha* 'queen,' *Raul* (man's name).

Furthermore, accents are used in some special cases:

—To mark stressed monosyllables ending in *a, e, o, as, es, os.* A stressed monosyllable, in short, is a word of one syllable which is not an **article,** a **preposition,** a **conjunction,** or a **nonsubject clitic pronoun.** In this case the monosyllable will take the acute or the circumflex, according to the way the vowel is pronounced: *dá* '(he/she) gives,' *pé* 'foot,' *lê* '(he/she) reads,' *dó* 'pity,' *Jô* (nickname).

As for unstressed monosyllables, they are never accented: *de* 'of,' *por* 'by,' *que* 'that (conj.),' *os* 'the (pl.),' *lhe* 'to him/her.'

—In the sequences **ee** and **oo** when word-final (with or without a subsequent **s** or **m**): *vêem* 'they see,' *enjôo* 'nausea, motion sickness,' *vôos* 'flights.'

—On the diphthongs **éu, éi, ói,** in order to mark their pronunciation with open vowels, that is, respectively, [ɛw], [ɛj], and [ɔj]: *chapéu* 'hat,' *papéis* 'papers,' *herói* 'hero.' When without the accent, **eu, ei, oi** are pronounced with closed vowels: [ew], [ej], [oj].

—In some cases graphically identical words are distinguished by putting an accent on one of them:

Têm, '(they) have,' *vêm* '(they) come,' forms of the verbs *ter* and *vir,* respectively, in order to distinguish them from their respective singulars *tem* '(he/she) has,' *vem* '(he/she) comes.' This extends to corresponding forms of the derived verbs like *conter* 'to contain,' *reter* 'to hold,' *provir* 'to arise from,' and a few others.

Pôr 'to put,' in order to distinguish it from the preposition *por* 'by.'

Pôde '(he/she) could,' in order to distinguish it from *pode* '(he/she) can.'

Pára 'stop' (indicative or imperative), in order to distinguish it from the preposition *para* 'for.'

Porquê 'reason' (*não entendi o porquê da sua demissão* '(I) didn't understand the reason for your dismissal') in order to distinguish it from *porque* 'because.'

6.1.2 The tilde

The **tilde** is used to mark nasal **ã** and **õ** when there is no other nasalization sign. Thus, in *cama* 'bed' the **a** is nasal but bears no tilde because the following **m,** plus the fact that the vowel is stressed, leaves no doubt about the nasality of the vowel. Now, in *irmã* 'sister' the final vowel is nasal, but it is not followed by an **n** or **m.** Therefore, it bears a tilde to show that it is nasal. The most typical use of the tilde is on final nasal diphthongs: **-ão, -õe, -ãe.**

In one case the tilde is used even though the diphthong is followed by a nasal consonant: in the verb form *põem* '(they) put,' from *pôr* 'to put.' The singular is *põe* '(he/she) puts,' and the *-m* is preserved in order to show that *põem* is plural. This is a purely graphic resource: *põe* and *põem* are pronounced alike, ['põj]. The same rule works for the compounds of *pôr: compõem* '(they) compose,' *dispõem* '(they) arrange,' *impõem* '(they) impose,' and a few others.

6.1.3 The grave, the dieresis, and the apostrophe

The **grave** is used only on the letter **a;** and, in fact, only in three words: *à, àquele / àquela, àquilo.* Its use is grammatically determined, and it follows the rules given in section 32.5.

The **dieresis** is used in the sequences **gu** and **qu** before **i** or **e** whenever the **u** is pronounced: in *aquilo* 'that,' *guerra* 'war' the **u** is silent (as it always is in the sequences **qui, que, gui, gue**): [aˈkilu], [ˈgɛhə]; in *tranqüilo* 'quiet,' *agüentar* 'to bear' the **u** sounds, and therefore it bears a dieresis: [tɾɐ̃ˈkwiluɭ, [agwẽˈta].

The **apostrophe, '** , is little used in Portuguese. It appears where part of a word has been deleted for metrical purposes, as in

> . . . *de crenças, de esp'rança e fé*
> '. . . of beliefs, hope, and faith'

The apostrophe is a reminder that the word *esperança* 'hope,' which normally has four syllables, is to be pronounced with three syllables. The apostrophe also occurs in certain contractions: *d'água* as in *copo d'água* 'glass of water,' *minh'alma* for *minha alma* 'my soul,' and some other cases. In these cases it is also acceptable to omit the apostrophe: *dágua, minhalma.*

6.2 Syllabification

Syllabification in Portuguese never follows etymologic criteria as it does in English. It is strictly phonological, that is, it depends entirely on pronunciation, which makes it amenable to general rules and therefore easier to learn. The following rules govern syllable separation in Portuguese:

---

1. Two adjacent consonants belong to different syllables, except in the case of **p, b, t, d, c, g, v, f** followed by **r** or **l;** the latter sequences belong to the same syllable with the following vowel.

Examples: *par-te* 'part,' *cam-po* 'field,' *lap-so* 'oversight,' *cal-do* 'broth'; but *co-bra* 'snake,' *in-fla-mar* 'to inflame,' *a-trás* 'behind.'

The only exception is words beginning with two consonants, when obviously both must belong to the same syllable regardless of their nature: *psi-co-lo-gi-a* 'psychology,' *mne-mô-ni-co* 'mnemonic,' *Pto-lo-meu* 'Ptolemy.'

In these cases the first syllable (*psi-, mne-, Pto-* in the above examples) is normally broken in pronunciation whenever it does not begin with the groups specified in the rule. Thus, *prato* 'dish' is pronounced as two syllables because it begins with **pr-**; but in *Ptolomeu* an [i] is inserted between the two initial consonants, so that the pronunciation is [pitolo'mew] (see 3.5 for the rule of **i**-insertion).

The rule applies equally to sequences of identical consonants, which are divided into two syllables: *as-sar* 'to bake,' *cor-rer* 'to run.'

In the very rare cases of sequences of three consonants, only the last one is separated, e.g., *subs-tantivo* 'noun.'

---

2. For two adjacent vowels,

  2a. they belong to the same syllable if they form a diphthong,

  diphthongs in Portuguese being the following:[1]

  ai ei éi oi ói ui

  au eu éu iu (ou)[2]

  ãe ãi ão õe

  (final unstressed) **ia ea eo ie io oa ua ue uo**

 2b. otherwise, they belong to different syllables.

Notes

[1] I am not listing final **-em, -am,** which are pronounced as diphthongs; they are never separated either.

[2] **Ou** is a false diphthong, since it is pronounced [o].

Examples (stressed vowels in **boldface**): *au-la* 'class,' *he-rói* 'hero,' *pai* 'father,' *mãe* 'mother,' *viu* '(he/she) saw,' *á-rea* 'area,' *sé-rio* 'serious,' *má-goa* 'sorrow';
ba-ú 'trunk,' *sa-ir* 'to go out,' *pa-ís* 'country,' *Ra-ul* (man's name), *pi-a* 'sink,' *fi-o* 'cable,' *la-go-a* 'lake.'

---

3. When a diphthong is followed by a vowel, as in *saia* 'skirt,' usage

varies, and both *sa-ia* and *sai-a* are found.

The latter practice is preferable since it follows a general rule.

6.3 Spelling problems: A summary

As mentioned earlier, Portuguese spelling is not very systematic—much less so, for instance, than Spanish or Italian, although more so than English and French. In this section I list the main difficulties learners will encounter when trying to figure out how to spell a word they already know how to pronounce.

One word of caution, however: it is not advisable to try to learn rules as a way to surmount some of the problems of Portuguese orthography, since a great part of it is simply not reducible to rules at all. To mention the worst problem, the sound [s] can be written in no fewer than nine ways, and the choice of this or that spelling depends on factors such as the etymology of the word, the history of the word (what language it was borrowed from and when), and, last but not least, the fantasy of grammarians. I suggest that the student attack these problems by learning the spelling of words individually.

That said, it is possible to enumerate the main difficulties; the following list is to be taken as cautionary. It outlines the broad areas in which rules are of little help:

Sound	Possible spellings	Examples	
[s]	ç	*caçar*	'to hunt'
	c (before **i, e**)	*cem*	'100,' *cinco* '5'
	s	*sem*	'without,' *bastante* 'enough'
	z (in sentence-final position)	*paz*	'peace'
	x	*próximo*	'next'
	xc (before **i, e**)	*exceto*	'excepted'
	sc (before **i, e**)	*descida*	'descent'
	ss	*passa*	'raisin'
	sç	*desça*	'climb down (imperat.)'
[ʃ]	x	*xarope*	'syrup'
	ch	*chá*	'tea'
[k]	c	*casa*	'house'
	q (before nonsyllabic **u**)	*quase*	'almost'
	qu (before **i, e**)	*querer*	'to want,' *quilo* 'kilo'
	k (rarely)	*Kátia*	(woman's name)
[ʒ]	j	*já*	'already'
	g	*gente*	'people'

(continued)

[z]	**z**	*zebra*	'zebra'
	s (between vowels)	*casa*	'house'
[v]	**v**	*vaca*	'cow'
	w (rarely)	*Wagner*	(man's name)
[w]	**u**	*mau*	'bad'
	l (syllable-final)	*mal*	'evil'
	w (rarely)	*Wilson*	(man's name)

There is still the problem of word-initial **h,** which, as noted above, is not pronounced; its presence in a word must be learned case by case: *homem* 'man,' *habilidade* 'ability.'

Finally, there is the nasal diphthong [Ãj], which may be written **ãe, ãi,** or **ai** (the latter when stressed and before a nasal consonant). It is not common and occurs in a few words only; it is probably sufficient to learn the following four cases: *mãe* 'mother,' *cãibra* 'cramp,' *Jaime* (man's name), and the plural ending *-ães* as in *pães* 'loaves,' *capitães* 'captains.'

6.4 Punctuation and capitalization

6.4.1 Punctuation

Punctuation is used in much the same way in Portuguese and in English, the differences being relatively insignificant. Three points may be mentioned as being the most relevant:

—In enumerations of the type *A, B, and C* English often puts a comma before the last member, whereas in Portuguese the last member has the conjunction only, with no comma:

Convidei Selma, Saulo e Simone.
'(I) have invited Selma, Saulo, and Simone.'

—Turn-taking in dialogue is indicated in English by a paragraph and quotation marks; in Portuguese one uses the paragraph and the dash, —:

Portuguese

—Por que vocês se esconderam?—perguntei.
—Estávamos com medo do vampiro.

English

"Why did you hide?" I asked.
"We were afraid of the vampire."

—In English, quotation marks always follow a comma or a period, regardless of whether it belongs to the quoted passage or not:

English

He said: "My sister is ill."
He said that "his sister," even though he has no sister, was ill.

In the second sentence, the comma does not belong to the quoted speech, yet it appears before the unquote.

In Portuguese, the quotation marks are supposed to enclose exactly the portion of the text which is intended as a direct quotation:

Portuguese

Ele disse: "Minha irmã está doente."
Ele disse que "sua irmã", embora ele não tenha irmã, estava doente.

6.4.2 Capitalization

Here again the differences are few. The two languages differ in some details, though:
—In Portuguese, modifiers relative to countries and peoples are not capitalized; neither are names of languages or national designations:

Raquel fala japonês.
'Raquel speaks Japanese.'

Takao é japonês.
'Takao is Japanese.'

Aqui do lado mora um japonês.
'A Japanese lives next door.'

But the names of academic subjects (including languages) are normally capitalized:

Ela tem um mestrado em Francês.
'She has an M.A. in French.'

Tirei nota baixa em Biologia.
'(I) got a low grade in biology.'

—In poetry, each line is usually capitalized:

E assim, quando mais tarde me procure
Quem sabe a morte, angústia de quem vive,
Quem sabe a solidão, fim de quem ama,
                    [Vinícius de Moraes]

This is not a universal rule, and some authors prefer not to capitalize every line.

—It is not usual in Portuguese to capitalize titles when used to refer to persons:

O presidente declarou que a inflação é insignificante.
'The president stated that inflation is insignificant.'

—Portuguese does not capitalize names of months and days of the week:

A reunião é no primeiro domingo de janeiro.
'The meeting is on the first Sunday in January.'

—Finally, Portuguese has the curious habit of *not* capitalizing some words that refer to relatives, such as *papai* 'Daddy,' *mamãe* 'Mom,' *vovô* 'Grandfather,' *vovó* 'Grandmother,' *titia* 'Auntie,' and *titio* 'Uncle.'

6.5 Use of the hyphen

The hyphen is used with oblique pronouns, when unstressed and postposed to the verb (see chapter 29 for their grammatical use): *ajudei-a* '(I) helped her,' *pode-se acrescentar açúcar* 'one can add sugar,' etc. It is also used in the increasingly rare "mesoclitic" forms, such as *ajudar-me-ia* '(he/she) would help me.' No hyphen is used when the oblique pronoun occurs before the verb: *ela me ajudou* 'she helped me.'

Apart from this use, the hyphen occurs in compound words, such as *auto-retrato* 'self-portrait,' *mal-humorado* 'ill-humored,' and many others. There are rules purporting to describe more or less precisely when such sequences are to be written with a hyphen and when as a single word, resulting in *super-homem* 'superman' besides *supernovo* 'extra-new.' These rules are the object of periodic changes, which are more or less ignored by the press; and in any case they are not sufficient to define the problem with any rigor. For instance, the *Manual Geral da Redação da Folha de São Paulo,* published by one of the foremost Brazilian newspapers, gives twelve rules on when to employ the hyphen, plus a list of 618 items that are written with a hyphen. That being the situation, my advice is not to worry too much about the matter and to consult a dictionary when in doubt (but be sure to consult only one dictionary, as they usually do not agree with each other).

III Inflection

7

Number and Gender in NP-Words

7.1 Inflection

As is the case with all Romance languages, Portuguese inflection is relatively complex, particularly in regard to the verb system. Most of the complexity comes from the fact that the verb varies for all persons in all tenses—as against English, in which, for instance, the form corresponding to the subject *you* is never distinct from the form that occurs with *they* (*you are* / *they are*) and in which there is no person inflection in the past tense. The subjunctive, very little used in present-day English, is still alive in Portuguese, and the future and pluperfect can be formed with endings as well as with auxiliaries as in English. Furthermore, Portuguese distinguishes, in the past tense, between perfect and imperfect forms.[1] On the other hand, some verb forms are seldom used in the modern language, and these are duly marked as such in the tables given below.

Note

[1]The complete designations are **preterit perfect** and **preterit imperfect.** In this grammar, for short, they will be called simply **preterit** and **imperfect,** respectively. I follow here Thomas's (1969) and Butt and Benjamin's (1995) terminology.

In this grammar **inflection** is treated separately from **derivation.** Inflection means, in practice, variation of verbs for tense, person, number, and mood; and variation of nominals for number and gender. These are highly systematic paradigms and can be described in tables of the usual kind. Some other phenomena are often called inflection, but they are much more idiosyncratic and belong in a chapter on derivation, that is, word formation. Among these are the formation of superlatives like *chatíssimo* 'extremely boring'; diminutives like *carrinho* 'little car'; and augmentatives like *mãozona* 'big hand.' They will be treated in chapter 41.

The study of inflection has, so to speak, two faces: first, one must learn how a word is inflected: for instance, whether or not it has a plural and how the plural (if any) is formed. Second, there is the question of how to use the different forms: when to employ the plural, how to impose agreement between different words and phrases, what the meaning of each verb tense is, and so on. In this chapter only the first of these questions will be treated; I list below, in as systematic a way as possible, all forms each nominal and verb can have in the language. The way to use these forms and their precise meaning will be the subject of later chapters.

7.2 NP-words and nominals

Let's start with inflection in pronouns, articles, numerals, and nominals. **Nominals** correspond to what are generally termed nouns and adjectives. This classification is, I believe, more adequate for Portuguese than the traditional one, which distinguishes nouns from adjectives as two separate word classes.

The class comprising nominals, pronouns, articles, and numerals will be called **NP-words,** from their property of appearing as constituents of the noun phrase. It is useful to bring all these items together in one, so to speak, superclass because their grammatical behavior is similar in many important points: these are the only items that make their plural in *-s;* and that either belong to a gender (masculine or feminine) or agree in gender. Besides, they are the only items that can refer to entities, that is, name things of the world.

The alternative (found in traditional grammars) is to treat their inflection, their agreement rules, etc., separately, which causes a great deal of repetition in grammatical statements. It makes little sense to learn that nouns make their plural in *-s* and then, later, to learn that adjectives (and pronouns, and articles) make their plural in *-s.* I decided, then, to introduce the novel term **NP-word,** which allows us to capture these grammatical facts in a unified manner.

Moreover, all words traditionally called nouns and adjectives belong to the general class of nominals. Nominals can occur in two main semantic functions: they may be **referential**—when they refer to a thing, a person, or some abstract entity—or they may be **attributive**—when they add to the concept of a thing, person, or entity some quality or determination. For instance, in *aquela nuvem negra* 'that black cloud' the nominal *nuvem* 'cloud' is referential because it introduces the concept of a thing; and the nominals *aquela* 'that' and *negra* 'black' add to this concept a determination (*aquela*) and a quality (*negra*) and are thus attributive.

Nominals are also brought together under one label because there is really no good reason to distinguish nouns from adjectives in Portuguese. (The interested reader will find a brief discussion of this terminological and theoretical innovation in 7.4.1 below; for a full discussion and justification, see Perini *et al.* 1996. For the moment, all the general student must know is what was just explained in the preceding paragraphs: this chapter covers inflection in nominals (nouns + adjectives), pronouns, articles, and numerals all together.)

In the next sections I discuss inflection in NP-words, which is not as complex as it is in verbs. Portuguese NP-words, unlike Russian and German ones, have no cases, and the main points of contrast with English are, first, the existence of grammatical gender: *casa* 'house' is feminine, and *carro* 'car' is masculine; and, second, the requirement that some NP-words agree with others in gender and number. For instance, one must say *a* casa amarel*a* 'the yellow house,' but *o* carro amarel*o* 'the yellow car,' *os* carros amarel*os* 'the yellow cars.'

7.3 Number

7.3.1 General rules

Portuguese, like English, has two numbers, singular and plural. The traditional (and easiest) way to state their respective forms is to start with the singular and form the plural from it. Therefore, the rules given below have the shape of plural-formation rules.

Before stating the rules, it may be useful to comment on the double character of number. A Portuguese word is marked for number in two ways: it may have a number by itself, usually by virtue of its meaning, like *homens* 'men.' Here the word is plural for semantic reasons, that is, it refers to more than one man; we may call this phenomenon **governing number,** and it is typical of nominals used referentially. And there are cases in which a word has number in order to agree with another word in the same phrase or even elsewhere in the sentence; in English this occurs only with the words *this* and *that,* which become *these* and *those* when attached to plural nouns: *this man, these men.* What is exceptional in English is the general rule in Portuguese, and almost all words—including articles, possessives, and determiners in general—agree when used attributively: *homem famoso* 'famous man,' pl. *homens famosos* 'famous men'; *o homem* 'the man,' pl. *os homens* 'the men'; this will be called **governed number.** Agreement sometimes does not show; for example, *simples* 'modest, simple' has the same form in the singular and in the plural, as seen in *homem simples* 'modest man,' pl. *homens simples.* In such cases one says that the singular and plural forms are identical.

There is one word that occurs in a position where it would be expected to agree but does not; this is *que,* 'what; which' (as an interrogative or an exclamative); *que* does not change even when attached to a plural nominal: *que homem?* 'which man?,' *que homens?* 'which men?'

The general plural-forming rule is very simple:

---

1. To form the plural of an NP-word, add *-s* to the singular form

singular		plural	
cidade	'city'	*cidades*	
carro	'car'	*carros*	
mão	'hand'	*mãos*	
orelha	'ear'	*orelhas*	
grande	'large'	*grandes*	
o	'the (sing.)'	*os*	'the (pl.)'
aquele	'that'	*aqueles*	'those'

All Portuguese NP-words end in *-s* when in the plural. But the way this *-s* is added to the singular may vary, according to the way the singular itself ends. The most relevant features of the singular, for purposes of plural formation, are whether or not the last syllable is stressed; and the particular consonant or diphthong found at the end of the word. The following additional rules describe all special cases of plural formation:

---

2. If the singular ends in *-l*

2a. If the last syllable is stressed, drop *-l* and add *-is*. If this results in *-iis*, drop one of the *i*'s:

| *papel* | 'paper' | *papéis* |

(continued)

jornal	'newspaper'	*jornais*
azul	'blue'	*azuis*
lençol	'(bed) sheet'	*lençóis*
infantil	'childish'	*infantis*

2b. If the last syllable is unstressed *-il* or *-el*, drop *-il* / *-el* and add *-eis:*

fóssil	'fossil'	*fósseis*
fácil	'easy'	*fáceis*
possível	'possible'	*possíveis*

This rule has exceptions, only three of which must be mentioned: *mal* 'evil, woe' and *cônsul* 'consul,' which make the plural *males* and *cônsules,* respectively; and *gol* 'goal (in soccer),' which makes the plural *gols,* pronounced ['gows].

On the accent on *papéis* and *lençóis*

Since the **e** in *papel* and the **o** in *lençol* are open, [ɛ], [ɔ], they get an accent in the plural, following the general rule that the diphthongs [ɛj] and [ɔj] are always marked with an acute (section 6.1).

3. If the singular ends in *-s* or *-x* and the last syllable is unstressed, there is no change, and the plural is identical to the singular

simples	'simple'	*simples*

(*continued*)

lápis	'pencil'	*lápis*
tórax	'thorax'	*tórax*

If the stress falls on the last syllable, the word adds -*es* as per rule 5 below: *país* 'country,' pl. *países*.

4. *If the singular ends in* -*m, drop* -*m and add* -*ns*

bom	'good'	*bons*	
marrom	'brown'	*marrons*	
um	'a, one'	*uns*	'some'
armazém	'grocery store'	*armazéns*	
fim	'end'	*fins*	
nuvem	'cloud'	*nuvens*	

The change of -*m* into -*n* is, of course, a mere orthographic resource to avoid the sequence -*ms*, which does not occur in Portuguese. If we look at pronunciation, though, these words are regular, making their plural by adding a final [s] after the final (nasal) vowel or diphthong.

For the accent on *armazém, armazéns,* see chapter 6.

5. In other cases, when the singular ends in a consonant, add -*es*

cor	'color'	*cores*

(*continued*)

rapaz	'boy'	*rapazes*	
português	'Portuguese'	*portugueses*	
ás	'ace'	*ases*	
açúcar	'sugar'	*açúcares*	'sugars (kinds of sugar)'

There are some exceptions, all recent borrowings from English: *pôster, gângster, shopping center,* which just add an *-s: pôsters, gângsters, shopping centers.* This is the universal usage, although grammars and dictionaries give these items as regular.

On the accent on *português* and on *ás*

The accent disappears in the plural *portugueses, ases* because now the word is accented on the penultimate and ends in *-es*.

6. If the singular ends in *-ão*

6a. If the last syllable is unstressed, add *-s*

órfão	'orphan'	*órfãos*

6b. If the last syllable is stressed, add *-s;* or drop *-ão* and add *-ões* <u>or</u> *-ães*[1]

irmão	'brother'	*irmãos*
ladrão	'thief'	*ladrões*
pão	'loaf'	*pães*

Note

[1]The cases described in rule 6b are idiosyncratic, as there is no regular way to form the plural from the singular when the latter ends in stressed *-ão;* therefore, each case must be learned individually. The most common plural ending is *-ões,* and whenever the word is an augmentative, it takes *-ões: casarão* 'big old house,' pl. *casarões.*

---

7. Some NP-words (apart from those ending in *-s* and *-x*) do not have plural forms:

laranja	'orange (color)'	*rosa*	'pink'
grená	'purplish red'	*gelo*	'ice-colored'
baita **SpBr**	'big'		

The above rule applies to these words when used attributively—that is, when they express a quality attributed to an object, as in *vestido <u>laranja</u>* 'orange dress.' Most of them can also be used referentially—that is, to refer to objects, as in *uma <u>laranja</u>* 'an orange.' In these cases they do have plurals. Thus, one says *vestidos <u>laranja</u>* 'orange dresses,' but *essas <u>laranjas</u>* 'these oranges.' The same NP-words, when acting as modifiers, also lack gender inflection.

7.3.2 Special cases

There are some special cases of plural formation:

7.3.2.1 *Opening of* o *in the plural*

Many words with stressed vowel [o] (closed **o**) change this vowel into [ɔ] (open **o**) when adding the *-s* to form the plural. Thus, the plural of *porco* 'pig,' pronounced ['pohku], is *porcos* ['pɔhkus], with [ɔ]. In other cases vowel opening does not occur, e.g., *bolo* ['bolu] 'cake,' plural *bolos* ['bolus], both with [o]. This is not predictable and must be learned individually.

The following is a list of the most common words that have closed **o** [o] in the singular and open **o** [ɔ] in the plural:

corpo	'body'	*ovo*	'egg'
destroço	'wreck'	*poço*	'well'
disposto	'willing'	*porco*	'pig'
esforço	'effort'	*porto*	'harbor'
fogo	'fire'	*posto*	'gas station'
grosso	'thick'	*povo*	'people'
imposto	'tax'	*reforço*	'reinforcement'
jogo	'game'	*socorro*	'help'
miolo	'brains'	*tijolo*	'brick'
olho	'eye'		
osso	'bone'		

To these items one must add all words formed with the very common suffix *-oso*, which occurs in words like *gostoso* 'tasty,' *amoroso* 'loving,' *venenoso* 'poisonous'; all these words open their stressed **o**'s in the plural.

There is a historical tendency to limit the scope of this rule, and some words that are registered in traditional grammars as undergoing it have ceased to open their [o]'s in modern speech: *almoço* 'lunch' and *forno* 'oven' are nowadays regular. But the words in the above list are always pronounced in the plural with open **o**.

7.3.2.2 Words with the suffix -zinho

The suffix *-zinho,* feminine *-zinha,* is used to form diminutives: *pão* 'loaf,' *pãozinho* 'little loaf.' When pluralized, these derived words mark the plural in *both* their elements, as if *-zinho* were a separate word. Therefore, to make the plural of *pãozinho* it is not enough to add an *-s;* one must also change the element *pão* into its plural *pães: pãezinhos.* The final *-s* of *pães* is omitted, thus avoiding the sequence **sz,** which never occurs in Portuguese.

On the other hand, a word like *pá* 'shovel' becomes *pás,* then we add *-zinho* (in the feminine plural form, *-zinhas*) and delete the *-s* of *pás,* so that the result is *pazinhas.* Here the process is not apparent, and the plural is regular. The difference shows in words ending in **r, l,** or in the diphthong **-ão,** that is, those words that not only add *-s,* but also undergo other changes when becoming plural, as can be seen in the following examples:

			Diminutive singular	Diminutive plural
balão	'balloon'	(pl. *balões*)	*balãozinho*	*balõezinhos*
alemão	'German'	(pl. *alemães*)	*alemãozinho*	*alemãezinhos*
pastel	'turnover'	(pl. *pastéis*)	*pastelzinho*	*pasteizinhos*

With words ending in **s** and **z,** however, *-zinhos* is added directly to the singular form, so that from *rapaz* 'young man' (plural *rapazes*), *francês* 'Frenchman' (plural *franceses*) one gets *rapazinhos, francesinhos,* not the expected * *rapazezinhos,* * *francesezinhos.*

There is a tendency to ignore this rule in the spoken language. In particular, words ending in **-r,** like *flor* 'flower,' usually fail to add the *-e* before the suffix, so that one normally hears the plural *florzinhas* **SpBr** (such forms are increasingly common in the written language as well).

7.3.2.3 Compound nominals

The plural of compound nominals is a traditional bugbear in Portuguese grammar. Yet, for once, things are less complex than they are believed to be. The rules given below provide a complete description of how compound nominals are pluralized.

For our purposes, a compound nominal is one composed of more than one word, joined with a hyphen(s). Examples are *beija-flor* 'hummingbird,' *guarda-chuva* 'umbrella,' *pé-de-cabra* 'crowbar.'

Some words are often called compounds because of their etymology, although they are not written with a hyphen: *aguardente* 'sugar brandy,' *fidalgo* 'nobleman,' and some others. In spite of their origins, however, these words behave exactly like any other (non-compound) word, and there is no reason to call them compounds. In particular, their plural follows the general rules: *aguardentes, fidalgos,* and so on.

In real compounds, the plural departs from regular cases only when they are composed of **two nominals without a preposition.** The rule is as follows:

Rule 1. In compounds composed of two nominals without a preposi-

tion, both elements take the -*s* of the plural:

couve-flor	'cauliflower'	**pl.**	*couves-flores*
água-marinha	'aquamarine'		*águas-marinhas*
quinta-feira	'Thursday'		*quintas-feiras*
cirurgião-dentista	'dental surgeon'		*cirurgiões-dentistas*

There are several exceptions, about which it should be noted that (a) they are not clearly delimited in traditional grammars, and (b) their very status as exceptions is questionable. For instance, it is said that *escola-modelo* 'model school' makes the plural *escolas-modelo,* that is, adding the -*s* to the first element only. One current grammar (Cunha and Cintra 1985) explains this by saying that *modelo* here is a "noun functioning as a specific determiner." Another (Kury 1972) states that only *escola* takes -*s* because one can "understand a preposition" between the two elements; *escola-modelo* would be equivalent to *escola para modelo* (a phrase which, if acceptable at all, certainly means something else). None of these criteria is sufficiently clear, and these cases are better described as exceptions. On the other hand, I suspect that if someone says or writes *escolas-modelos,* thereby inserting this compound into the general rule, few people will raise objections.

Rule 2. When the compound nominal is used as a modifier (i.e., at-

tributively) and is written with a hyphen, only the second element

varies, both in gender and in number:

> (*continued*)
>
> *problema econômico-financeiro* 'economic-financial problem' (masculine sing.)
>
> *políticas econômico-financeiras* 'economic-financial policies' (feminine pl.)

In all other cases—that is, whenever the compound is not composed of two nominals—the plural mark is added to the last element if there is no preposition joining them:

> **Rule 3.** Compounds not composed of two nominals and without a preposition follow the general plural rule, and take *-s* at the end of the word:
>
> | | | | |
> |---|---|---|---|
> | *guarda-roupa* | 'wardrobe' | **pl.** | *guarda-roupas* |
> | *grão-duque* | 'grand duke' | | *grão-duques* |
> | *vice-presidente* | 'vice-president' | | *vice-presidentes* |

Guarda-roupa is composed of a verb form (*guarda* 'keeps') plus a nominal and means literally 'clothes keeper'). There are many similar compounds in Portuguese: *pára-lama* 'fender' (literally, 'mud stopper,' from *parar* 'to stop'), *arranha-céu* 'skyscraper,' from *arranhar* 'to scrape,' and so on. As for *grão-duque* 'grand duke,' the first element never occurs as an independent word and may be analyzed as a prefix. In all these cases, then, compounds behave like noncompounds, which also take *-s* at the end.

Of course, it may be difficult for the beginner to identify *guarda-* in *guarda-roupa* as a verb form. At the beginning, many of these compounds will have to be learned as exceptions; on the other hand, mistakes in forming the plural of compounds are not too serious, and many Brazilians (when they try to obey grammatical injunctions) have as hard a time with them as foreigners.

Finally, when there is a preposition between the two main elements, the plural mark is added to the first member:

Rule 4. In compounds joined by a preposition, add *-s* to the first element:

pé-de-moleque	'peanut praline'	*pés-de-moleque*
pão-de-ló	'a kind of cake'	*pães-de-ló*
mula-sem-cabeça	'headless mule (a popular myth)'	*mulas-sem-cabeça*

This is equally regular because it follows the general rule for noun phrases. That is, just as we say *casa de madeira* 'wood house,' pl. *casas de madeira*, we say *pé-de-moleque*, pl. *pés-de-moleque*, as if there were no hyphen.

7.3.2.4 One-number words

There are many NP-words that occur only in the singular, and a few only in the plural. Among those that have only the singular, I list some traditionally termed pronouns, such as

isto	'this'
isso	'this'
aquilo	'that'

These words correspond to the above translations when occurring alone in the phrase, as in *this is absurd,* which translates into Portuguese as *isso é absurdo;* note that in this position English *this, that* also lack plural forms. When *this, that* occur next to a noun, their Portuguese counterparts are *este, esse, aquele,* which do have plural forms: *esse homem* 'this man,' *esses homens* 'these men.'

Other pronouns occurring only in the singular are:

quem	'who'
alguém	'someone'
ninguém	'no one'
tudo	'everything'
nada	'nothing'
algo	'something'
cada	'each'

These pronouns present no special difficulty, since their English counterparts behave in similar ways: *who, someone, each,* etc. also have no plural.

Many nominals, usually corresponding to English mass-nouns, occur only in the singular:

ouro	'gold'
arroz	'rice'
coragem	'courage,' etc.

Words occurring only in the plural are few. One example is *férias* 'vacation,' which is always plural: *suas férias vão ser curtas* 'your vacation will be short (literally, your vacations . . .).' Some others, like *óculos* 'eyeglasses,' have become singular in the spoken language, so that one writes *meus óculos estão quebrados* 'my eyeglasses are cracked,' but one says *meu óculos quebrou* **SpBr,** literally 'my eyeglasses is cracked'; note that the word keeps its final *-s*, which is no longer felt as a plural marker.

Finally, some NP-words occur only in the plural by virtue of their meaning, like *vários* 'several,' *diversos* 'id.'

7.3.2.5 Erudite plurals

In imitation of English usage, one sometimes finds Latinate plurals like *campi* (pl. of *campus*), *corpora* (pl. of *corpus*). These forms are restricted to the speech and writing of academics; most people will just say *campus* in the plural.

7.4 Grammatical gender

Gender (like number) is the designation of two distinct, although related, grammatical phenomena. Take, for example, the word *janela* 'window.' This word is said to be **feminine** because all NP-words directly qualifying or determining it must have a special form, also called feminine. This occurs when the NP-word is used referentially and is called **governing gender** because it determines the gender of agreeing elements in the NP. Thus, we say *uma janela aberta* 'an open window,' where *uma* and *aberta* must be in the feminine because they are governed by the feminine item *janela*. This is called **governed gender** and occurs when the NP-word is used attributively. Now, the word *livro* 'book' is **masculine** because NP-words qualifying it take on another form, the masculine form: *um livro aberto* 'an open book.'

A word used referentially must have a gender, that is, be feminine or masculine. Correspondingly, all agreeing elements in an NP must be in the same gender as their governing element (I come back to this point in 7.4.2 below).

**7.4.1 Heads and modifiers: A first view

In order to properly understand what is going on when an NP-word agrees in gender with another, a short semantic excursus is in order. The first thing to observe is which of the several NP-words in a phrase is the one that determines the gender (and the number) of the whole structure, and with which other NP-words in the phrase will have to agree.[1]

Note

[1]Not all items agree with the head, however. Some do not agree for morphological reasons, being invariable, like *laranja* 'orange (color)' and *baita* 'big.' Qualifiers introduced by a preposition also do not agree; for instance, in the noun phrase *o velho tapete português de vovó* 'Granny's old Portuguese rug,' the head is *tapete* 'rug'; *o* 'the,' *velho* 'old,' and *português* 'Portuguese' agree with the head. But *de vovó* 'Granny's' does not and cannot agree because it is a prepositional phrase.

In noun phrases like

Aqueles rapazes gordos
'Those fat boys'

Uma janela aberta
'An open window'

Algumas observações importantes
'Some important remarks'

there is one word that defines what it is that we are speaking about. In *aqueles rapazes gordos* we are speaking about boys; in *uma janela aberta,* about a window; and in *algumas observações importantes,* about remarks. This word is the **head;** in the phrases above the heads are, respectively, *rapazes* 'boys,' *janela* 'window,' and *observações* 'remarks.'

The other members of the phrase are included in order to delimit the scope of the head, so that in, say, *aqueles rapazes gordos* the receptor learns that the speaker wants to refer to boys; not to any boys, but to fat boys; and not to any fat boys, but to those fat boys. But the fact remains that the speaker is always referring to boys. The delimiting elements (*aqueles, gordos, uma, aberta, algumas, importantes*) will be called **modifiers.** The head is said to have governing gender; modifiers agree with the head and have governed gender.

A head can also be defined as the element of the noun phrase that carries referential meaning; and the modifiers are the elements that carry attributive meaning. A noun phrase may have several modifiers, but it has at most one head (which may be compound, as in *João e Maria* 'João and Maria').

Of course, this is precisely what happens in English: a noun phrase always has a central reference, which is expressed by the head; and it may include one or more modifiers, one of whose functions it is to help the receptor identify properly what entity the speaker is trying to evoke. The system has a few complexities that do not concern us here. Neither does the way a listener or a reader identifies which item in the NP is the head (the curious reader will find a discussion of the problem, with a proposed solution, in Perini *et al.* 1996, 57–106).

Some nominals may function only as heads (e.g., *janela* 'window'); some function only as modifiers (e.g., *aberto* 'open'); some, finally, function either as heads or as modifiers. An example of the latter class is *gordo,* which can occur either as a modifier, meaning 'fat,' as in *rapaz gordo* 'fat boy,' or as a head, meaning 'fat person,' as in *os gordos comem muito* 'fat people eat a lot.' This correlates with the meaning of each item, and therefore it is not necessary to distinguish three morphological classes among nominals. Learning the exact range of meanings a nominal has leads automatically to learning its functional possibilities: head, modifier, or both. To be more specific, learning the word *janela* 'window' means learning that it refers to an object and that it does not denote a quality; *gordo* 'fat,' by contrast, refers to an object and denotes a quality. From this information one can derive automatically the syntactic properties of each word: *janela* is always a head, *gordo* can be a head or a modifier.

This is why there is no reason to distinguish adjectives from nouns in Portuguese: Every nominal which can name an object can be a head (and would traditionally be called a noun); some of these can also occur as modifiers, that is, not naming but qualifying or determining the head. And all nominals (and NP-words in general) that cannot name objects occur, in a noun phrase, obligatorily as modifiers.

7.4.2 Heads and governing gender

The main principle underlying gender agreement is that **whenever a word is a head it has governing gender,** that is, heads are always feminine or masculine, and this shows in the agreement. There are no exceptions; having governing gender is an obligatory accompaniment of being the head of a noun phrase. Even foreign words must be marked for gender. For instance, suppose we want to speak of root beer, a drink that is unknown in Brazil and lacks a Portuguese name. We must give it a gender and say something like

Ponha o "root beer" na geladeira.
'Put the root beer in the refrigerator.'

Root beer is marked as masculine, as shown by the form of the article *o.* Alternatively, it might be feminine, *a "root beer"* (since in this particular case no one use has been established); but it cannot be used in Portuguese without a gender.

The student therefore needs to learn the gender for every nominal capable of functioning as the head of a noun phrase; and, unfortunately, in most cases this is not predictable from its meaning or pronunciation. A few useful hints are given below (7.4.5), but there are many nominals that are feminine or masculine for no known reason: *tribo* 'tribe' is feminine, *cabo* 'handle' is masculine; *mão* 'hand' is feminine, *pão* 'loaf, bread' is masculine; *maquete* 'scale model' is feminine, *disquete* '(computer) disc' is masculine, and so on.

7.4.3 Modifiers and governed gender

When a word has **governed gender** it usually shows agreement. For example, the word *vermelho* 'red' agrees in number and gender and therefore has a feminine form, *vermelha*, and each form has a plural: *vermelhos, vermelhas.* Thus one must say *livro vermelho* 'red book,' *casa vermelha* 'red house,' *livros vermelhos* 'red books,' and *casas vermelhas* 'red houses.'

But the word *laranja* 'orange,' which designates both the fruit and the color, does not agree, even when it occurs as a modifier: *livro laranja,* 'orange book,' *casa laranja* 'orange house,' *livros laranja, casas laranja.*

The conditions governing gender agreement will be discussed in chapter 34. In this section we are concerned with the way feminine and masculine forms of nominals are formally related. In the case of NP-words working as modifiers and therefore usually coming in pairs of masculine and feminine forms, the rules are tolerably simple, although a little more complex than for plural formation. We will study these rules first, then have a look at governing gender in nominals, which is far less systematic.

Summarizing, the main task facing the student in regard to NP-words with governed gender is to learn how the feminine differs from the masculine; for NP-words with governing gender, it is to learn whether the word is masculine or feminine.

7.4.4 Gender of modifiers

I follow tradition in taking the masculine form as basic and deriving the feminine from it. The first group are NP-words that differ for masculine and feminine; then, there is a group of NP-words that do not vary for gender (although they do for number).

Group 1. NP-words with different forms for the masculine and the feminine

---

1. If the masculine ends in -*o*, drop the -*o* and add -*a;*

if it ends in -*u* or in -*ês*, add -*a*.

masc.		fem.
vermelho	'red'	*vermelha*
nu	'naked'	*nua*
português	'Portuguese'	*portuguesa*

Português has an accent because stress falls on the last vowel and the word ends with *-s;* the feminine form, *portuguesa,* does not need an accent because stress falls on the penultimate vowel (see 6.1 above).

Exceptions: The following words have identical forms for both genders:

hindu	'Indian (from India)'
zulu	'Zulu'
cortês	'polite'
descortês	'impolite'

Several words used in colloquial style or in slang do not vary in gender: *bocó* 'stupid,' *gagá* 'senile,' *borocochô* 'depressive,' *biruta* 'crazy,' *bacana* 'cute.' Recent loanwords, not yet assimilated (and usually keeping their original spelling), do not vary either: *light,* as in *uma dieta light* 'a light diet,' *soft* as in *estilo soft* 'soft style.'

---

2. If the masculine ends in *-ão,* change the ending into *-ona* or into *-ã*

comilão	'gluttonous'	*comilona*
alemão	'German'	*alemã*
são	'healthy'	*sã*

As always, the *-ão* ending is a problem; there is no general way to predict the feminine from the masculine, and each word must be learned individually.

---

3. If the masculine ends in *-eu,* change the *-eu* into *-éia*

hebreu	'Hebrew'	*hebréia*
plebeu	'plebeian'	*plebéia*
ateu	'atheist'	*atéia*

The only important exception is *judeu* 'Jewish,' which makes *judia*.

Group 2. NP-words with only one form for the masculine and the feminine

If the masculine ends in *-a, -e, -i, -l, -z, -r, -m;* or if it ends in *-s* preceded by an unstressed vowel, the feminine and the masculine are identical

hipócrita	'hypocritical'
indígena	'(American) Indian'
forte	'strong'
nacional	'national'
azul	'blue'
capaz	'able'
feliz	'happy'
simples	'modest; simple'
familiar	'familiar'
exemplar	'exemplary'
virgem	'virgin'
ruim	'bad'
marrom	'brown'
comum	'common'

Exceptions are

bom	'good'	*boa*
um	'a; one'	*uma*
algum	'some'	*alguma*
espanhol	'Spanish'	*espanhola*
andaluz	'Andalusian'	*andaluza*

and words formed with the suffix *-or,* which means 'agent' and corresponds approximately to English *-ing* or *-er:*

trabalhador	'worker; hard-working'	*trabalhadora*
invasor	'invader; invading'	*invasora*

7.4.4.1 *Opening of* **o** *in the feminine*

We saw above that some NP-words having a stressed closed **o,** [o], change this [o] into an open **o,** [ɔ], in the plural. The very same words (when they have a feminine form) open their [o] in the feminine. In the following examples, the masculine is pronounced with a [o], and the feminine with a [ɔ]:

grosso	['gɾosu]	'thick'	*grossa*	['gɾɔsə]
disposto	[dʒis'postu]	'willing'	*disposta*	[dʒis'pɔstə]

(See list in 7.3.2.1)

The rule also applies to all NP-words formed with the suffix *-oso: carinhoso* 'tender,' *gostoso* 'delicious,' *feioso* 'ugly,' *formoso* 'beautiful,' etc.

7.4.5 Inherent gender

The rules noted in the preceding section apply to NP-words when they function as modifiers and generally agree with their heads. When a nominal is a head, as we saw, it does not *agree,* but must *belong* to a gender. The main problem here is to learn, for each item, whether it is masculine or feminine. In general, the gender must be learned for each item individually; but there are some partial rules that can lighten the task, and these are given in what follows.

7.4.5.1 *Grammatical and natural gender*

The relationship between grammatical gender and the expression of natural gender (that is, sex) is somewhat complex in Portuguese. It is sometimes held that there is no relationship at all, and many examples seem to support this idea. Thus, *livro* 'book' is masculine, *casa* 'house' is feminine, and there is no semantic reason for that; and the same applies to many thousands of words that designate inanimate objects. Furthermore, it is possible to refer to a male with a feminine word (e.g., *vítima* 'victim,' *testemunha* 'witness,' *criança* 'child,' all feminine, but referring to males or females indifferently), and it is also possible, if less frequent, to refer to females with a masculine word: *cônjuge* 'spouse,' masculine, but correct when referring to either spouse; also *bebê* 'baby (of either sex).'

On the other hand, when it comes to words referring to persons or some animals, there is an undeniable tendency to use masculine words for males and feminine for females. It is no accident that *homem* 'man' and *cavalo* '(male) horse' are masculine, and *mulher* 'woman' and *égua* 'mare' are feminine. In many cases the two words are akin, and then they often show the typical endings *-a* for feminine, *-o* for masculine, as in *porco* '(male) pig' vs. *porca* 'sow,' *gato* '(male) cat' vs. *gata* '(female) cat,' and so on. And sometimes the words are identical, but even then they must appear as feminine when referring to females, masculine when referring to males; this shows in the agreement, as in *uma pianista romântica* 'a romantic (female) pianist' vs. *um pianista romântico* 'a romantic (male) pianist.'

It is thus possible to formulate rules, albeit partial, to deduce the gender of a word from certain features of its meaning. Following is a list of such partial rules. Gender is indicated in the examples by the definite article *o* 'the (masc.),' *a* 'the (fem.).'

---

1. For nominals that name human beings, those referring to women are feminine, those referring to men are masculine

a mãe	'the mother'
o pai	'the father'
o professor	'the (male) teacher'
o pianista	'the (male) pianist'
a médica	'the (female) doctor'
o médico	'the (male) doctor'

The same rule applies to many names of animals, mostly those that refer to domestic ones or to large mammals

o leão	'the lion'
a leoa	'the lioness'
o cavalo	'the horse'
a égua	'the mare'

These are often the same animals for which English distinguishes males and females with different words. For other animals, there is only one name, sometimes feminine, sometimes masculine, which designates either sex:

a raposa	'the fox (male or female)'
o pernilongo	'the mosquito (m. or f.)'
a águia	'the eagle (m. or f.)'
o jacaré	'the alligator (m. or f.)'
a baleia	'the whale (m. or f.)'

Exceptions: The following words refer to human beings, yet have only one gender, valid for either sex

a pessoa	'the person (m. or f.)'
a criança	'the child (m. or f.)'
a vítima	'the victim (m. or f.)'
a testemunha	'the witness (m. or f.)'
o bebê	'the baby (m. or f.)'
o cônjuge	'the spouse (m. or f.)'

To these we may add a few more colloquial words, usually of a derisive character: *a peça* 'the creature (m. or f.)'; *a besta* 'the idiot (m. or f.).'

7.4.5.2 Other rules

---

2. Names of oceans, rivers, and mountains as well as the names of months and points of the compass are masculine

o Atlântico	'the Atlantic'
o São Francisco	'the São Francisco (river)'
o Himalaia	'the Himalayas'
setembro passado	'last September'
o oeste	'the West'

---

3. Names of cities are feminine

a Paris de Toulouse-Lautrec	'Toulouse-Lautrec's Paris'
a linda Ouro Preto	'the beautiful Ouro Preto'

There are few exceptions:

o Rio de Janeiro
o Cairo
o Porto 'Oporto'
o Recife

Natives of Recife usually refer to their city in the masculine, with the article: *o Recife é lindo* 'Recife is beautiful.' But in the rest of Brazil it is more usual to apply the general rule, making *Recife* feminine, without the article: *Recife é linda.*

The gender of proper names like the above tends to follow the gender of the generic word that describes it, e.g., names of oceans are masculine and the word *oceano* 'ocean' is also masculine. Although this tendency is not absolute, it is too regular to be just a coincidence; and, besides, the language seems to tend to make it more and more regular.

Thus, names of neighborhoods in my hometown, Belo Horizonte, are sometimes masculine (*o Barro Preto*), sometimes feminine (*a Pampulha*). But all neighborhoods built in the past thirty or forty years have masculine names, even when the name itself is feminine in the language: *o Guarani, o Santa Lúcia*. This may be related to the masculine gender of the word for 'neighborhood,' *bairro*. Another example is names for commercial and industrial companies, which have feminine general designations, (*companhia* 'company,' *loja* 'shop,' *fábrica* 'factory') and are always feminine: *a Ford, a Marcelo* (a carpet shop), as opposed to *o Marcelo,* which refers to a man called Marcelo. One more example: names of streets, squares, and avenues are always feminine, and so are the words *rua* 'street,' *praça* 'square,' *avenida* 'avenue': *eu moro na Maranhão* 'I live on Maranhão (street),' as opposed to *eu moro no Maranhão* 'I live in (the state of) Maranhão.'

---

4. Words ending in unstressed *-o* [excluding words ending in *-ão*] are masculine, and words ending in unstressed *-a* are feminine.

This is no more than a tendency, albeit a strong one, and it is worth learning. A survey of the 1,000 most frequent words in Portuguese shows that 268 of them are NP-words ending in *-a* or in *-o,* and of these only 5 do not follow the rule. These are all words ending in *-a* that are masculine:

dia	'day'
problema	'problem'
poeta	'poet'
sistema	'system'
artista	'artist'

and two of them, *poeta* and *artista,* can also be feminine.

Among the exceptions, many fall under the following subrules:

a. almost all words ending in *-ma* are masculine: *problema* 'problem,' *sistema* 'system,' *tema* 'theme,' *drama* 'drama';[1] and

b. all words formed with the suffix *-ista* can be masculine or feminine, when referring to men or women respectively: *o artista* 'the (male) artist,' *a artista* 'the (female) artist,' and equally for *pianista* 'pianist,' *socialista* 'socialist,' etc.

Note

[1]Common feminine words in *-ma* are *soma* 'sum,' *fama* 'renown,' *lima* 'file (tool), sweet lime.' *Grama* 'gram' is given as masculine in the grammars, but most people use it as feminine: *duzentas gramas* 'two hundred grams'; but the compounds of *grama*, like *quilograma* 'kilogram,' are always masculine.

Apart from specifying the above rules and observations, little can be done to help the student learn the gender of nominals. In most cases inherent gender is unpredictable and will have to be learned individually.

8

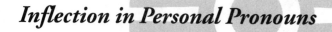

Inflection in Personal Pronouns

8.1 The modern Brazilian system

8.1.1 Personal pronouns

In Portuguese, as in English, personal pronouns are peculiar words in that they change according to the syntactic function they perform. Thus, one says *eu cheguei* 'I have arrived,' but *Marcos **me** viu* 'Marcos saw me,' where *eu* 'I' and *me* 'me' are considered different forms (cases) of the same pronoun.

Portuguese personal pronouns may have as many as five cases, corresponding to the following contexts: as a subject; as a direct object; as an indirect object, without a preposition; after the preposition *com* 'with'; and after other prepositions. Taking *eu* 'I' as an example, we have the following:

eu trabalho aqui	'I work here'
*Marcos **me** viu*	'Marcos saw me'
*Marcos **me** deu uma ajuda*	'Marcos gave me some help'
*Marcos trabalha **comigo***	'Marcos works with me'
*Marcos trabalha para **mim***	'Marcos works for me'

Notice that the form occurring after *com* is written together with the preposition; if this results in a double consonant (*com* + *migo*), it is simplified: *comigo* (in Portugal the two consonants are kept: *commigo, connosco*). Observe that the forms corresponding to direct object (*Marcos **me** viu*) and to indirect object (*Marcos **me** deu uma ajuda*) are identical for *eu*; for third person pronouns they differ, being, respectively, *o / a* and *lhe* (the use and meaning of pronoun forms are detailed in chapter 29).

The pronoun system as used in the spoken language is not the same as that found in written texts. It also varies from region to region, both from Portugal to Brazil and within Brazil itself. Furthermore, there is a set of special honorific forms, used in special circumstances, so that the whole system is more complicated than its English correlate. In the table below, I describe general Brazilian usage; any deviations are included in the appended notes.

Table 8.1
Personal pronouns (current Brazilian usage)

	Subject	Direct object	Indirect object	After *com*	After other prepositions
'I'	*eu*	*me*	*me*	*comigo*	*mim*
'you (sing.)'	*você*	*te* *você* *[o/a]*	*te* *[lhe]*	*com você*	*você*
'he / she'	*ele/ela*	*ele/ela* *[o/a]*	*[lhe]*	*com ele/ela*	*ele/ela*
'we'	*nós*	*nos*	*nos*	*conosco*	*nós*
'you (pl.)'	*vocês*	*vocês* *[os/as]*	*[lhes]*	*com vocês*	*vocês*

Table 8.1
Personal pronouns (current Brazilian usage) (*continued*)

	Subject	Direct object	Indirect object	After *com*	After other prepositions
'they'	*eles/elas*	*eles/elas* [*os/as*]	[*lhes*]	*com eles/elas*	*eles/elas*

The table shows only special forms to be used with *com* and with the other preposi-tions when these are irregular, e.g., *comigo* 'with me,' *para mim* 'for me'; in the remaining cases the pronoun does not change in this context, e.g., *com você, para ele*. Forms within brackets [ ] are largely confined to the written language.

—Some case forms corresponding to *você* 'you' and its plural, *vocês*, are identical to the forms corresponding to *ele / ela* 'he / she' and their plurals. Traditional grammars con-sider *você(s)* a third person pronoun, which is correct as long as form is concerned: it has many case forms in common with *ele / ela*, and verbs agree with it in the same way—*você vai* 'you go,' *ela vai* 'she goes'—and in the plural, *vocês vão* 'you (pl.) go,' parallel to *elas vão* 'they go.' Therefore, pronouns like *você* (and some others, see below), as well as their ac-companying verb forms, will be referred to in this book as "third person," in spite of the fact that they refer to the listener. "Person" is to be understood as a formal, morphosyntac-tic category, not a semantic one.

The older second person pronouns, *tu* 'you (sing.)' and *vós* 'you (pl.)' are obsolete in southeastern Brazil. *Tu* is still heard in some regions of Brazil (extreme south, some areas of the northeast, sometimes in Rio)[1] and is in normal use in Portugal, whereas *vós* seems to have entirely disappeared from current usage (*vocês* being used as the plural of *tu*).

Note

[1] Usually with third person verb forms: *tu vai com a gente?* **SpBr** 'are you going with us?'

—As shown in the table, so-called third person pronouns (*ele / ela, você,* and their plurals) tend to become regular NP-words, abandoning special case forms. For these pronouns, the only case form intensively used nowadays in the spoken language is *te,* objective form of *você;* but even this competes with the regular form, so that one hears both *eu te amo* and *eu amo você* for 'I love you.' *Lhe* is replaced by *a* or *para* followed by the general form: *Marília lhe deu uma ajuda* **Wr** 'Marília gave him / her some help' becomes *Marília deu uma ajuda a ele / ela,* and *eu lhe entreguei o embrulho* **Wr** 'I handed him /her the packet' is now *eu entreguei o embrulho para ele / ela.*

—*Mim* is the first-singular form used with prepositions other than *com;* one always says *para mim* 'for me,' *sem mim* 'without me' etc. But with *entre* 'between,' which is usually followed by two noun phrases, the normal form is *eu: entre ela e eu* 'between her and me'; *entre ela e mim* sounds stilted, ultracorrect.[1]

Note

[1] *Para* (and more rarely other prepositions) may be immediately followed by a pronoun in its subject form, but only when the latter is the subject of a clause—that is, when *para* introduces not the pronoun, but the whole clause, as in *isso tudo é <u>para eu</u> limpar?* 'is all this for me to clean?' There is a tendency to use the oblique even in these cases: *isso tudo é <u>para mim</u> limpar?* **SpBr,** but such constructions are usually regarded as substandard.

—*Nós* 'we' and corresponding case forms are still in wide use, but there is a strong tendency to substitute *a gente,* which patterns as a third person nominal. Thus, one can say *nós saímos às oito* 'we went out at eight,' but also *a gente saiu às oito* 'id.' *A gente* is also used as an object and after prepositions: *eles insultaram a gente* 'they insulted us,' *traz aí uma cerveja para a gente* **SpBr** 'bring us a beer.'

—The indirect object can always be expressed by a preposition (usually *a* or *para*) plus the pronoun in its regular form for use with prepositions. Thus, *lhe* is the indirect object form of *ele / ela,* but it is used almost exclusively in writing. In common speech one finds *para ele:*

Eu lhe dei um cachorrinho.	**Wr**
Eu dei um cachorrinho para ela.	**SpBr**
'I gave her a little dog.'	

For the use of *ele,* etc. as objects in the spoken language, see chapter 29.

—The subject form is used in certain constructions in which current English uses the object form. First, after *como* 'like' and *quanto* 'as much as': *ela é gorda como eu* 'she is fat like *me*.' Second, as a complement of *ser* 'to be': *sou eu* 'it is *me*.'

8.1.2 Proclitic *você* becomes *cê*

The pronoun *você* when preceding a verb form is usually reduced in pronunciation, becoming *cê* (in certain regions also *ocê*). Thus, *você tem medo disso?* 'are you afraid of that?' sounds *cê tem medo disso?* When *você* does not immediately precede a verb form (e.g., when it is an object) it generally does not reduce: *eu amo você* 'I love you.' The reduced form *cê* is avoided in postverbal position, where *ocê* can be used: *Vou ajudar ocê / *cê.* 'I'm going to help you.'

Reduction to *ocê* also occurs after certain prepositions, and in such cases the preposition and the pronoun agglutinate in the way described in section 5.1.2: *de você* becomes *docê; para você* becomes *procê.* Reduction of *você* is typical of the spoken language and appears only in writing when the author wishes to impart a colloquial flavor to the text.

8.1.3 Reflexive pronoun *se*

There is no Portuguese form exactly corresponding to English *-self* as in *myself.* In the first person (and in the second, when used), Portuguese expresses reflexivity with the normal case forms of pronouns: *eu me machuquei* 'I have hurt myself,' where the object form *me* is used as it is in *o cachorro me machucou* 'the dog hurt me'; *nós só podemos contar conosco* 'we can count only on ourselves,' with the same form used in nonreflexive contexts like *ela vai jantar conosco* 'she is going to have dinner with us.'

For all other pronouns (*você, vocês, ele / ela, eles / elas*)—that is, for third person pronouns—there is a special reflexive pronoun, *se*. Thus, 'he hurt himself' is translated as *ele se machucou*, with the reflexive pronoun *se* in its direct object form. The forms of the reflexive pronoun are as follows:

Table 8.2
Reflexive pronoun *se*

Direct object	Indirect object	After *com*	After other prepositions
se	*se*	*[consigo]*	*[si]*

As indicated, *consigo* and *si* are mainly used in the written language. They are replaced in speech by the prepositions followed by the general forms *você, ele, ela,* as the case may be, reinforced with *mesmo* (sometimes *próprio*), which in this case may be translated as '-self': *ele fala com ele mesmo* **SpBr** (instead of . . . *consigo mesmo*) 'he talks to himself'; *ela só traz almoço para ela mesma* **SpBr** (instead of . . . *para si mesma*) 'she brings lunch only for herself.'

For the use of reflexives with so-called **reflexive verbs** (*casar-se* 'to get married,' *arrepender-se* 'to repent'), see chapter 20.

8.1.4 Honorific forms of address

Portuguese has several alternative forms of address, comparable to English *Your Excellency, Your Highness,* but used daily in a much wider variety of situations. Their use is governed by such sociological categories as the relative age of speakers; their degree of intimacy; their respective social class and power relations, as evaluated by the speaker; and the degree of formality of the situation.

By far the most common of these forms is *o senhor,* feminine *a senhora* 'you,' used when addressing someone who is older or a comparative stranger to whom one wishes to show some degree of respect. Other forms are:

Vossa Excelência —used to address judges in court and high government officials such as members of Congress, state governors, and the president;

Vossa Majestade —used to address the king or the emperor;

Vossa Excelência Reverendíssima (usually shortened to *Vossa Reverendíssima*)
      —used to address high officials of the Catholic Church;

Vossa Santidade —used only to address the pope;

Vossa Alteza —used to address princes of the royal and imperial houses;

Vossa Senhoria —generally used in written communication, in order to give it a formal character.

Colloquially, one also hears *o doutor,* as in *o doutor vai querer um cafezinho?* 'are you going to have a coffee?'; *o doutor* is used in order to show appreciation by the speaker of a presumed higher social status of the addressee—independently of the real existence of a doctoral degree (use of *o doutor* in this sense gives some impression of subservience).

All these forms pattern exactly like *você,* both with respect to their case forms and with respect to verbal agreement—that is, they are always used with third person verb forms.

O senhor / a senhora is still in very general use. All other forms are more or less obsolete, either for historical reasons (there is no one left in Brazil or in Portugal to call *Vossa Majestade*) or because they all tend to be replaced by *o senhor.* In a recent television broadcast showing preparations for the installation of a new president, I observed that the television commentators as well as other persons charged with organizing the ceremony used *o senhor* to address both the incumbent and the president-elect.

On the other hand, *você*, the familiar form of address, is making inroads into former *o senhor* territory. Fifty years ago it was mandatory to call one's parents *o senhor / a senhora;* nowadays this is exceptional, and *você* is substituted instead.[1]

Note

[1] *A senhora* is used to address all women, regardless of marital status; nowadays the use of *a se-nhorita* for unmarried women sounds almost ridiculous. Correspondingly, the formal way to refer to women is by prefixing *dona* (abbreviated *D.*) to the first name: *dona Clara;* the use of *senhora* (or *se-nhorita*) with the last name sounds too formal and is found only in writing.

Forms such as *Vossa Excelência* and the like change the initial possessive to *Sua* when referring to someone (as opposed to addressing him or her). The same happens in English, so that one says *Sua Excelência ainda não chegou* 'His Excellency has not yet arrived.' When used as vocatives, though, unlike their English counterparts, they lose their possessive: *Ex-celência, por favor vire-se para a câmera* '(Your) Excellency, please turn toward the camera.'

8.1.5 Cliticization

Case forms that (a) are used to express direct and indirect objects, (b) are not used after prepositions, and (c) are not identical with their respective subject forms, are called clitics. This means that they are but weakly stressed in speech, and this fact has some syntactic and orthographic consequences. Syntactically, clitics may appear either after or before the verb, as can be seen in the two alternative forms of saying 'I have killed him': *matei-o* and *eu o matei.* The orthographic consequence is that clitics are joined to the verb by a hyphen when they are postposed.

The conditions under which clitics may appear before or after the verb are fully stated in chapter 29. For the moment, it is enough to mention the fact, which affects the following forms:

me

te

o/a, os/as

lhe, lhes

(continued)

nos

se   [3rd person reflexive]

The forms *o / a* and their plurals *os / as* become *-lo / -la, -los / -las* when immediately following an infinitive verb form, which in its turn loses the final *-r* and is accented (if ending in *-a or -e*) to show that stress still falls on the last syllable. Thus, *matar* means 'to kill'; but if we want to say (or, rather, write, since these forms are seldom heard in speech) 'I want to kill him,' we must apply the above rule, saying *eu quero matá-lo* **Wr** (colloquial *eu quero matar ele* **SpBr**).

After verb forms ending in a nasal sound, the same pronouns become *-no / -na, -nos / -nas: amam-nas* **Wr** '(they) love them,' *põe-no* **Wr** '(he/she) puts it.'

8.2 European, archaic, and literary forms

Besides the forms given above, there are some other pronoun forms that should be known (at least passively), although they do not occur in general Brazilian usage. They are common in the speech of Europeans and in that of some Brazilians, and they occur in texts of a special or conservative character. These are the so-called second person pronouns, namely, *tu* 'you (sing.)' and *vós* 'you (pl.).' Their case forms are as shown in the following table:

Table 8.3
Tu **and** *vós*

	Subject	Direct object	Indirect object	After *com*	After other prepositions
'you (sing.)'	*tu*	*te*	*te*	*contigo*	*ti*
'you (pl.)'	*vós*	*vos*	*vos*	*convosco*	*vós*

Tu is usual in Portugal as the most intimate form of address (*você* being felt by European speakers as being slightly more formal) and is also used in certain regions of Brazil, particularly in the south (Paraná, Santa Catarina, and Rio Grande do Sul) and in certain areas of the northeast. *Vós* has dropped from normal use, being heard only in certain varieties of religious speech as a form of addressing God.

These pronouns, like first person ones, do not have special reflexive forms; the normal objective forms do service as reflexives: *tu* <u>te</u> barbeias 'you shave yourself,' *vós* <u>vos</u> enganais **Wr** 'you (pl.) are mistaken.'

9

Numerals

Numerals are traditionally divided into two types: **ordinals** and **cardinals.** Ordinals denote order: *primeiro* 'first,' *décimo-terceiro* 'thirteenth,' whereas cardinals denote quantity: *oito* 'eight,' *vinte e cinco* 'twenty-five.'

Ordinals pattern like other NP-words having governed gender. They therefore vary in gender, changing their final *-o* into *-a* to form the feminine from the masculine: *terceiro andar* 'third floor (masc.),' *terceira casa* 'third house (fem.),' and in number, adding *-s* to form the plural: *os terceiros lugares* 'the third places (in a competition).' The only problem peculiar to ordinals, then, is the way they are formed from corresponding cardinals, and this will be discussed below.

9.1 Numeral formation

Although numeral formation is not, strictly speaking, a case of inflection, I include it in this section for the sake of compactness.

9.1.1 Cardinals

Cardinals are simple from *zero* 'zero' to *vinte* 'twenty.' Some are historically derived from sequences of separate words, but their ancient parts have become so intimately agglutinated that they are better treated as simple forms. No one, except linguists, knows that *dezesseis* 'sixteen' was originally *dez e seis* 'ten and six.' These simple forms are as follows:

0 : *zero*	
1 : *um* (masc.), *uma* (fem.)	11 : *onze*
2 : *dois* (masc.), *duas* (fem.)	12 : *doze*
3 : *três*	13 : *treze*
4 : *quatro*	14 : *quatorze*
5 : *cinco*	15 : *quinze*
6 : *seis*	16 : *dezesseis*
7 : *sete*	17 : *dezessete*
8 : *oito*	18 : *dezoito*
9 : *nove*	19 : *dezenove*
10 : *dez*	20 : *vinte*

Dezesseis (16), *dezessete* (17), *dezoito* (18), and *dezenove* (19), being treated as single words, are pronounced [dʒize'sejs], [dʒizɛ'setʃi], [dʒi'zojtu] and [dʒize'nɔvi], respectively.

In certain special contexts, in particular when saying telephone numbers, the numeral '6' is pronounced *meia* (from *meia dúzia* 'half a dozen'). Thus, when giving the phone number 386 6461, one usually says *três oito meia, meia quatro, meia um* (also *três oito meia, sessenta e quatro, sessenta e um*).

9.1.1.1 Round numbers

The words for multiples of 10 and 100 are also simple:

30 : *trinta*	200 : *duzentos*
40 : *quarenta*	300 : *trezentos*
50 : *cinqüenta*	400 : *quatrocentos*
60 : *sessenta*	500 : *quinhentos*
70 : *setenta*	600 : *seiscentos*
80 : *oitenta*	700 : *setecentos*
90 : *noventa*	800 : *oitocentos*
100 : *cem* (*cento* when in composition)	900 : *novecentos*

As noted earlier, multiples of 100 from 200 up vary for gender: *quatrocentos carros* '400 cars,' *quatrocentas casas* '400 houses.'

'One thousand' is *mil,* and it does not vary for plural. With *mil* the numeral *um* is not usually preposed, except sometimes in writing a check (when all ambiguity must apparently be eschewed); thus, we have *mil* '1,000,' *dois mil* '2,000' (attention: feminine *duas mil*), *cinco mil* '5,000,' etc.

Millions are expressed by *milhão / milhões (de),* that is, always with a preposition before the designation of the quantified items, and so on for *bilhão* and *trilhão: um milhão de habitantes* 'one million inhabitants.'

9.1.1.2 Twenty-one, and so on

The other numbers are formed from the preceding ones following the models below:

From 21 to 99: multiple of ten + *e* + unit

21 :   *vinte e um*
48 :   *quarenta e oito*
99 :   *noventa e nove*

Hundreds are also connected by *e*

---

106 :   *cento e seis*
147 :   *cento e quarenta e sete*
380 :   *trezentos e oitenta* (masc.)
918 :   *novecentas e dezoito* (fem.)

Thousands, millions and up are connected by a comma when co-occurring with more than one order, but with *e* when co-occurring with only one additional order **or** when the first order down (hundreds for *mil*, thousands for *milhão*) is empty

---

1.641 :	*mil, seiscentas e quarenta e uma*	'1,641 (fem.)'
4.860 :	*quatro mil, oitocentos e sessenta*	'4,860 (masc.)'
3.460.030 :	*três milhões, quatrocentos e sessenta mil e trinta*	'3,460,030'
70.004 :	*setenta mil e quatro*	'70,004'
25.010 :	*vinte e cinco mil e dez*	'25,010'
1.001 :	*mil e um*	'1,001 (masc.)'
1.026 :	*mil e vinte e seis*	'1,026'
1.100 :	*mil e cem*	'1,100'
6.400 :	*seis mil e quatrocentas*	'6,400 (fem.)'
10.040 :	*dez mil e quarenta*	'10,040'

| 1.000.400 : | *um milhão e quatrocentos* | '1,000,400 (masc.)' |
| 11.900.000: | *onze milhões e novecentos mil* | '11,900,000' |

9.1.2 Ordinals

The ordinal system in Portuguese is complex—excessively so, as even native speakers usually acknowledge. This comes from the fact that ordinals for numbers above twenty are formed on a model borrowed from Latin, which (a) uses many designations taken directly from Classical Latin, such as *quadringentésimo* for '400th,' *nonagésimo* for '90th,' and (b) insists on marking *every number* as ordinal, instead of just adding an ordinal mark at the end of the whole number (as more sensible languages like Italian, French, and English do). This results in long sequences such as *milésimo quingentésimo sexagésimo sexto* '1,566th,' as if we said in English *thousandth five-hundredth sixtieth-sixth*.

As expected, this clumsy system is in very limited use, and speakers generally find a way to express ordinals otherwise. The main alternative is to use a different turn of the sentence, as in *o candidato número sessenta e seis* 'candidate number 66,' instead of *o sexagésimo sexto candidato* 'the 66th candidate.'

Ordinals from one to ten as well as those for multiples of ten and for *cem* '100' and *mil* '1,000,' when used alone, are in normal use. Those from eleven to nineteen are an intermediate case: they are used more often than, say, those for the hundreds and are known to all speakers but still are avoided whenever possible. Finally, the more exotic forms such as *trecentésimo* '300th,' *septuagésimo* '70th' are unknown to most speakers. Following is the list of ordinals; those used in everyday speech are in boldface.

1º	**primeiro**	*11º*	*décimo primeiro*	*21º*	*vigésimo primeiro*
2º	**segundo**	*12º*	*décimo segundo*	*22º*	*vigésimo segundo*
3º	**terceiro**	*13º*	*décimo terceiro*		*etc.*
4º	**quarto**	*14º*	*décimo quarto*	*30º*	*trigésimo*
5º	**quinto**	*15º*	*décimo quinto*	*40º*	*quadragésimo*
6º	**sexto**	*16º*	*décimo sexto*	*50º*	*qüinquagésimo*
7º	**sétimo**	*17º*	*décimo sétimo*	*60º*	*sexagésimo*

(*continued*)

8º	**oitavo**	*18º*	*décimo oitavo*	*70º*	*septuagésimo*
9º	**nono**	*19º*	*décimo nono*	*80º*	*octogésimo*
10º	**décimo**	*20º*	*vigésimo*	*90º*	*nonagésimo*
100º	**centésimo**	*600º*	*seiscentésimo*	*1,000,000º*	*milionésimo*
200º	*ducentésimo*	*700º*	*septingentésimo*	*1,000,000,000º*	*bilionésimo*
300º	*trecentésimo*	*800º*	*octingentésimo*	*etc.*	
400º	*quadringentésimo*	*900º*	*nongentésimo*		
500º	*qüingentésimo*	*1,000º*	**milésimo**		

To these we may add *último* 'last,' *penúltimo* 'penultimate,' and *antepenúltimo* 'third from the end.'

How does one write the ordinal for *dois mil* '2,000' and the like? The general rule calls for *segundo milésimo,* but in fact I have never seen such forms in actual use, and no grammar mentions them. This shows clearly how artificial these forms are.[1]

Note

**[1]Thomas (1969) states that "the ordinals are avoided a great deal in [spoken Brazilian]." That this is a fact is shown in Duncan's (1971) frequency dictionary, where the only ordinals that occur with appreciable frequency are *primeiro* 'first,' *segundo* 'second,' *terceiro* 'third,' and *quarto* 'fourth.' In Duncan's corpus of about 500,000 running words, even such presumably common ordinals as *sétimo* 'seventh,' *décimo* 'tenth' did not occur at all.

9.1.3 Fractions

As in English, ordinals are used also to express fractions: *um quinto* 'one fifth,' *um milésimo* 'one thousandth.' There are some exceptions, though:

$\frac{1}{2}$ is *meio* or *um meio;*[1]

$\frac{1}{3}$ is *um terço.*

Note

[1] *Meio* is used before a head nominal: *meio melão* 'half a melon,' *um meio* is used to refer to the abstract fraction: *quatro vezes um meio* 'four times ½.'

For fractions beyond *um décimo* 'one tenth' the element *avos* is added to the cardinal:

$\frac{1}{12}$ is *um doze avos;*

$\frac{1}{32}$ is *um trinta e dois avos*

and so on. For larger round numbers, the cardinal is used again:

$\frac{1}{100}$ or 0,01 is *um centésimo;*

0,001 is *um milésimo;*

but

1/99 is *um noventa e nove avos.*

9.2 Notes on the use of numerals

Some observations on the use of numerals:

—First of all, it must be noted that ordinals usually come before the nominals they modify: *a primeira namorada* 'the first girlfriend,' except when used to number monarchs and centuries: *Dom Pedro Segundo* 'Dom Pedro the Second,' *o século sexto* 'the sixth century.' Nevertheless, sometimes one finds postposed *primeiro* (not other ordinals) in poetic language: *nunca se esquece o amor primeiro* 'one never forgets his first love.'

—With the numbering of kings, popes, and centuries, ordinals are used up to ten; from then on, cardinals are used: *Dom João Quarto* 'Dom João the Fourth,' but *Luís Quatorze* 'Louis XIV.' Likewise, *século terceiro,* or *terceiro século* 'third century,' but *século dezoito* 'eighteenth century.'

—With days of the month one uses *primeiro* 'first,' but then one proceeds with cardinals: *primeiro de maio* 'May first,' *dez de novembro* 'November tenth.'

—As in English, postposed cardinals are used for pages and chapters of a book, houses and apartments, etc., as in *página vinte e cinco* 'page 25,' *apartamento seis* 'apartment 6.' For chapters, one also finds postposed ordinals: *capítulo três* or *capítulo terceiro* 'chapter 3.'

—Fractions, except *meio* '½,' are followed by *de* when occurring before a nominal: *meio melão* 'half a melon,' but *um quarto de melão* 'one fourth of a melon' (compare the identical use of English *of* in this context).

9.3 Gender and number in numerals

9.3.1 Gender

The only cardinals that vary in gender are *um* 'one,' *dois* 'two,' and the names for multiples of 100 from 200 to 900. *Um* 'one' becomes *uma* in the feminine, and *dois* becomes *duas*: *um carro* 'one car,' *uma casa* 'one house'; *dois carros, duas casas.*

As for the multiples of 100, they all end in *-os* (being inherently plural), and they make their feminine regularly, changing *-os* into *-as.* Thus, we have *trezentos carros* 'three hundred cars,' but *trezentas casas* 'three hundred houses.' According to all grammars, these numerals keep their forms even when followed by other numerals as complements, as in *trezentos e quarenta carros* 'three hundred and forty cars,' *trezentas e quarenta e cinco casas* 'three hundred and forty-five houses.' In such cases, however, speakers most often use the masculine (that is, the unmarked) form of the multiple of 100; that is, while keeping the agreement in *trezentas casas* 'three hundred houses,' they tend to say *trezentos e quarenta e cinco* casas 'three hundred and forty-five houses.'

All other numerals are invariable in gender: *três carros* 'three cars,' *três casas* 'three houses'; *mil / cem / setenta carros* 'one thousand / one hundred / seventy cars,' *mil / cem / setenta casas.*

9.3.2 Number

Some cardinals in Portuguese vary in number. These are restricted to the names of large numbers, like *milhão* 'million,' plural *milhões, bilhão* 'billion,' plural *bilhões.* They behave in this respect like normal NP-words indicating quantity, and just as one says *dois quilos de laranjas* 'two kilos of oranges,' one says *dois milhões de laranjas* 'two million oranges'—literally, 'two millions of oranges.' But when *milhão, bilhão* are followed by other numerals, the preposition *de* is omitted: *dois milhões e quatrocentas mil laranjas* '2,400,000 oranges.'

Ordinals behave morphologically like normal modifiers, agreeing with their heads: *o primeiro rapaz* 'the first boy,' *a primeira moça* 'the first girl,' *a décima quarta moça* 'the fourteenth girl.'

9.4 Use of commas and dots in writing numbers

Portuguese follows the French and American way of counting, so that *um bilhão* corresponds to 1,000,000,000. The use of commas and dots follows the continental usage, that is, a comma is used to separate decimals, as in 2,75, read *dois vírgula setenta e cinco,* which corresponds to American 2.75; American '.25' is written 0,25, and read *zero vírgula vinte e cinco.* In large numbers, dots (never commas) are used to separate classes by groups of three, as in 1.000.000 (*um milhão*); an alternative way of writing these numbers is with spaces instead of dots: 1 000 000.

10

Articles, Determiners, Possessives, and Relatives

To close our study of NP-word inflection, I list below the articles, determiners (taken here in a very general sense), and possessives. Most of these items behave like modifiers in general, inflecting for gender and for number; any behavioral particularities are duly noted.

10.1 Articles

Portuguese has two articles, definite *o* and indefinite *um:*

	Masculine singular	Masculine plural	Feminine singular	Feminine plural
'the'	*o*	*os*	*a*	*as*
'a, some'	*um*	*uns*	*uma*	*umas*

Um translates English *a* when in the singular: *um cachorro* 'a dog,' *uma casa* 'a house'; but when plural it corresponds to English *some: umas casas* 'some houses.' And, as we've seen, *um* does double duty as a numeral, 'one.'

There are several important differences between Portuguese and English as concerns the use of articles; these are the subject matter of chapter 26.

10.2 Other determiners

Other determiners are:

	Masculine singular	Masculine plural	Feminine singular	Feminine plural
'this'	*este*	*estes*	*esta*	*estas*
'this'	*esse*	*esses*	*essa*	*essas*
'that'	*aquele*	*aqueles*	*aquela*	*aquelas*

10.2.1 *Este* vs. *esse*

According to traditional grammars, the difference in use between *este* and *esse*, both translated as 'this,' is that *este* is considered to be associated to the first person and *esse* to the second person. Thus, *este livro* 'this book' refers to a book that is close to the speaker, and *esse livro* refers to a book close to the listener. *Aquele livro*, 'that book,' refers to a book that is not close to either the speaker or the listener.

Furthermore, *este* is used to refer to something that follows in a text, whereas *esse* refers to something that precedes: *ele respondeu com estas palavras:* 'he answered in these words:' if the words follow; but if the words are given previously, we should say *ele respondeu com essas palavras.*

Actually, though, very few speakers (and writers) make the distinction as described in the previous paragraphs. In the spoken language *este* has practically disappeared, being replaced in all cases by *esse;* in writing, more often than not people use *esse* or *este* indifferently. *Aquele,* however, remains distinct, and no speaker fails to make the distinction between *aquele livro* and *este / esse livro.* The system tends, then, to become analogous to the English one, which distinguishes only *this* and *that.*

In the written language, *este* and *aquele* may be used as English *former* and *latter:*[1]

> *Houve um conflito entre a França e a Inglaterra; <u>aquela</u> pretendia anexar o Sudão, e <u>esta</u> queria manter sua influência no vale do Nilo.*

> 'There was a conflict between France and England; the <u>former</u> intended to annex Sudan, and the <u>latter</u> wanted to keep her influence in the Nile Valley.'

Note

[1]In Portuguese as in English, this construction is clumsy, sometimes hard to decipher, and therefore its use is not to be encouraged.

10.2.2 Neuter forms: *Isto, isso, aquilo*

The determiners *este, esse, aquele* have neuter forms, viz., *isto, isso, aquilo.* These forms do not vary in gender or number. Their use presents some difficulties to an English speaker because their English correspondents are, again, *this* and *that*—and yet the two groups cannot be used interchangeably. The following rules should help distinguish between neuter and nonneuter determiners.

Only nonneuter determiners (*este, esse, aquele*) are used when

—reference is made to a human being; or

—the determiner is followed by an NP head.

Examples:

> *Esse é um preguiçoso.*
> 'This [guy] is lazy.'

> *Aquela janela deve ficar fechada.*
> 'That window must stay closed.'

In these cases *isto, isso, aquilo* cannot be used.

When we refer to inanimate things *and* the determiner comes alone in its noun phrase, we may have either neuter or nonneuter forms, but they are still not equivalent. In such contexts, nonneuter determiners are anaphoric, that is, they refer to some NP-word previously mentioned in discourse, as, for example, in *Comprei dois livros. Este veio com defeito* 'I bought two books; this one came with a defect.' Since Portuguese lacks a word for English *one* (used as a pronoun), the determiner appears alone.

In other cases the neuter form must be used. It is always translatable as 'this / that thing': *isso é um camarão?* 'is this (thing) a shrimp?'; *aquilo precisa ser jogado no lixo* 'that (thing) must be thrown into the garbage can.'

Another way to explain the difference between *este, esse, aquele* and *isto, isso, aquilo* is to say that the latter are used whenever one wishes to refer to an entity that is (a) inanimate, and (b) not identified by its name, be it explicit in the phrase, be it recoverable from the preceding context.

A final rule of thumb that may help in distinguishing these two kinds of determiners is that whenever *this, that* are the singular of *these, those* they correspond to Portuguese *esse, aquele*, not to *isso, aquilo: that book* [**plural** *those books*] translates as *aquele livro.*

10.2.3 *Todos, ambos, todo*

These items vary in gender regularly: *todas as mulheres* 'all the women,' *todos os rapazes* 'all the boys'; *toda mulher* 'every woman,' *todo rapaz* 'every boy.' Now, their number inflection presents some complexities, which correlate with semantic and syntactic differences. We may distinguish three uses:

1. *Todo* in the singular, without a following article, means 'every; any,' as in

> *Todo cidadão tem direitos.*
> 'Every citizen has rights.'

> *Toda criança aprende a ler com facilidade.*
> 'Any child learns to read with ease.'

In this case the noun phrase has a generic meaning, as shown in the examples.

2. *Todo* in the singular, followed by an article or a demonstrative like *este, esse, aquele,* means 'whole,' 'all,' as in

> *Toda a cidade foi inundada.*
> 'The whole town was flooded.'

> *Todo esse barulho por nada.*
> 'All this noise for nothing.'

3. *Todos* in the plural, followed by an article or a demonstrative, means 'every; all,' as in

> *Todos os cidadãos têm direitos.*
> 'All the citizens have rights.'

> *Todas as cidades foram inundadas.*
> 'Every town was flooded.'

In this use *todos os cidadãos* means something very similar to *todo cidadão,* but the noun phrase does not have a generic meaning.[1]

The article or demonstrative does not appear if *todos* is followed by a personal pronoun: *todos vocês* 'all of you.'

Note

[1] That is, the two constructions, *todo cidadão* and *todos os cidadãos,* are not synonyms: *todo cidadão* refers to citizens intensionally, and *todos os cidadãos* extensionally. Thus, *todo cidadão tem direitos* means, strictly speaking, 'for all **x, if **x** is a citizen, **x** has rights,' whereas *todos os cidadãos têm direitos* means 'it is true that all **x** have rights.' One consequence is that *todo cidadão* occurs in generic expressions, but not in specific ones (nailed down to a specific place and time), whereas *todos os cidadãos* is appropriate in both contexts. For instance, *todos os cidadãos votaram antes do almoço* 'all citizens voted before lunch,' is acceptable, but * *todo cidadão votou antes do almoço* is not—compare with *todo cidadão vota antes do almoço,* 'every citizen votes before lunch,' which is acceptable. This difference, however, is irrelevant in most cases and can be disregarded in a general description.

Ambos 'both' functions exactly like *todos,* likewise occurring only in the plural and always followed by the definite article or by a determiner: *ambas as funções* 'both functions,' *ambos aqueles homens* 'both those men.' *Ambos* is rarely used in speech, being more typical of written texts. In speech it is replaced by *os dois* or *todos (os) dois:* instead of

> *Quero ambas as camisas.*   **Wr**
> 'I want both shirts.'

one should say

> *Quero as duas camisas.*

or

> *Quero todas as duas camisas.*

The requirement that an article follow *todos,* as well as *todo* in *toda a cidade* 'the whole town,' is less and less obeyed, so that even in writing one sometimes finds phrases like *todas casas* 'all the houses,' *todo carro* meaning 'the whole car': *ele limpou todo carro* **SpBr** 'he cleaned the whole car.' This construction is frowned upon by some, but it is common in written texts and usual in speech.

10.2.4 *Tudo*

Tudo is a neuter form with a near perfect correlate in English, which is *everything:*

> *Tudo aqui me deprime.*
> 'Everything here depresses me.'

10.2.5 *Qualquer, cada, que*

Qualquer 'any, whatever' does not vary in gender, but it does in number, becoming *quaisquer* in the plural (because it comes from an earlier two-word sequence, *quais quer*). To be sure, this strange form is avoided whenever possible and does not occur in the spoken language; yet, it appears occasionally in written texts.

The singular, though, is very common in all styles; it can be translated as 'any' or 'whatever' and occurs both preposed and postposed to the head:

> *Qualquer idiota sabe disso.*
> 'Any idiot knows that.'

Leia qualquer tese.
'Read any thesis at all.'

Qualquer casaco me serviria.
'Any coat would be of use to me.'

Me procure a qualquer hora.   **SpBr**
'Meet me any time.'

Examples with postposed *qualquer*:

Ele está procurando um livro qualquer.
'He is looking for a (= any) book.'

Me empreste aí um casaco qualquer.   **SpBr**
'Lend me any old coat.'

Qualquer is also used sometimes in the meaning of 'vulgar' or 'nondescript,' as in *uma mulher qualquer* 'a vulgar woman.' In such phrases, which sound slightly old-fashioned, it is always postposed.

Cada 'each, every' does not vary for gender and is always singular: *cada homem e cada mulher* 'each man and each woman.' The sequence *cada um* means 'everyone' or 'each one' (but see below for its anaphoric use):

Cada um deve fazer o que puder.
'Everyone must do whatever he can.'

It also can mean 'every' when followed by a noun, as in

Cada homem é uma ilha.
'Every man is an island.'

but this use is somewhat rare, *todo* being preferred:

Todo homem é uma ilha.
'id.'

This is very clear in the expression *todo dia* 'every day,' which sounds much more natural than *cada dia* 'id.' More often, *cada* followed by a noun corresponds to 'each':

Cada aluno receberá quatro tarefas.
'Each student will be assigned four tasks.'

Qualquer and *cada* co-occur with *um(a)* when used anaphorically:

—Que livro você recomenda?
—Qualquer um.
"Which book do you recommend?"
"Any one."

—Quantas camisetas eu devo dar aos jogadores?
—Duas para cada um.
"How many T-shirts do I have to give to the players?"
"Two each."

Interrogative and exclamative ***que*** 'what, which' is invariable in both gender and number:

Que alunas fantásticas!
'What fantastic students!'

Que livros você tirou na biblioteca?
'Which books did you borrow from the library?'

Que bobagem!
'What nonsense!'

All other determiners are morphologically regular. Their syntactic use as well as their meaning is examined in chapter 27.

10.3 Possessives

Number inflection in possessives is regular and requires no special rules: *meu* 'my' makes the plural *meus,* and likewise for *seu* 'his/her, your,' pl. *seus; nosso* 'our,' pl. *nossos,* etc. Gender, however, is irregular for *meu* 'my,' *seu* 'his/her, your,' as well as for *teu* 'your'; the other two, *nosso* 'our' and *vosso* 'your,' are regular:

	Masculine	Feminine
'my'	*meu*	*minha*
'your'	*[teu]* *seu*	*[tua]* *sua*
'his/her'	*seu* *dele* 'his' *dela* 'her'	*sua* *dele* 'his' *dela* 'her'
'our'	*nosso*	*nossa*
'your'	*[vosso]* *[seu]* *de vocês*	*[vossa]* *[sua]* *de vocês*
'their'	*seu* *deles* 'their [masc.]' *delas* 'their [fem.]'	*sua* *deles* 'their [masc.]' *delas* 'their [fem.]'

Possessive forms

A few comments on the meaning and use of the possessives:

—*teu* **and** *vosso*—The forms *teu* and *vosso*, possessive forms corresponding to *tu* and *vós*, respectively, are not in current use like the others. *Vosso* is used only in connection with *vós*, which means that it is practically extinct, appearing only, and rarely, in religious discourse. As for *teu*, it is not only used by speakers who use *tu* (part of southern and northeastern Brazil), but also appears sometimes as the possessive form in connection with *você.* That is, some speakers who use only *você* as the familiar form of address may say *teu pai* 'your father,' as well as the regular *seu pai* 'id.' For most speakers of the variety we are taking as basic, though, *teu* is never used, and 'your father' is always *seu pai.*

—**use of *dele(s)***—The reader may have noticed that the form for 'his/her' and for 'their' is the same, viz. *seu:* that is, both 'his/her father' and 'their father' translate as *seu pai.* Furthermore, *seu* can also mean 'your' because it is the possessive form corresponding to *você* 'you.' This results, in principle, in a confusing situation that is resolved in practice by the use of the forms *dele, dela,* literally 'of his,' 'of hers' (*de* + *ele*), and their plurals *deles, delas.* Thus, if we want to say 'her father,' the phrase *seu pai* is usually avoided, and we say *o pai dela* instead, and similarly for *o pai delas* 'their (fem.) father,' *o pai dele* 'his father,' etc. As we've seen, the use of *dele,* etc., also provides a distinct form for 'their,' which is missing in the traditional table. *Dele,* etc., unlike the other possessives, are always postposed to the head.

This is the normal state of things in Brazilian Portuguese. And, consequently, the possessive *seu,* while still in general use, tends to specialize in the meaning 'your'; that is, a phrase like *seu pai* is understood, whenever possible, as 'your father,' not as 'his father,' etc. The possessive form for the second person plural (in the old language, *vosso*) should also be *seu: seu pai* should also mean 'your (pl.) father.' This never happens, however, in modern usage. The current form is *o pai de vocês,* that is, one uses the alternative form of the possessive, given in the table above.

Seu meaning 'his / her' is used nowadays only in a few set phrases in which there is no possibility of ambiguity, as in

> *Lá vem o Daniel e <u>suas</u> piadas de mau gosto.*
> 'Here comes Daniel with his tasteless jokes.'

> *Todo homem deve defender <u>seus</u> filhos.*
> 'Every man must defend his children.'

For the construction exemplified by *ele <u>me</u> quebrou o nariz* 'he broke my nose,' in which the possessive meaning is conveyed by an oblique pronoun, see chapter 29.

10.4 Relative and interrogative pronouns

10.4.1 Relatives

The relative pronouns are as follows:

que	'which'
o qual / a qual / os quais / as quais	'which'

quem	'who'
cujo / cuja	'whose'
onde	'where'

The pronoun *o qual* agrees in number and in gender with its antecedent, as shown in

A cidade <u>na qual</u> eu morei **Wr**
'The city [**feminine singular**] in which I have lived'

O bairro <u>no qual</u> eu morei **Wr**
'The neighborhood [**masculine singular**] in which I have lived'

As cidades <u>nas quais</u> eu morei **Wr**
'The cities [**feminine plural**] in which I have lived'

Os bairros <u>nos quais</u> eu morei **Wr**
The neighborhoods [**masculine plural**] in which I have lived'

Cujo agrees with the following nominal:

O rapaz <u>cujo</u> pai me telefonou **Wr**
'The boy whose [**masculine singular**] father called me'

O rapaz <u>cuja</u> mãe me telefonou **Wr**
'The boy whose [**feminine singular**] mother called me'

O rapaz <u>cujos</u> pais me telefonaram **Wr**
'The boy whose [**masculine plural**] parents called me'

O rapaz <u>cujas</u> meias eu lavei **Wr**
'The boy whose [**feminine plural**] socks I washed'

As indicated above, both *o qual* and *cujo* are used almost exclusively in the written language. The use of relative pronouns in both registers is described in chapter 36.

10.4.2 Interrogatives

The interrogative pronouns are as follows:

que?	'what?'
o que?	'what?'
quem?	'who?'
qual?	'which?'
quanto? / quanta? / quantos? / quantas?	'how much / how many?'

The interrogative pronouns *qual* and *quanto* agree with the following nominal:

> *Quais calças você vai vestir?*
> 'Which [**feminine plural**] pants are you going to wear?'

> *Qual camisa você vai vestir?*
> 'Which [**feminine singular**] are you going to wear?'

> *Quantos copos você já bebeu?*
> 'How many [**masculine plural**] glasses have you already had?'

The use of these interrogatives in sentences is described in chapter 31. *Que* and *quanto* are also used in exclamations:

> *Quanta chuva!*
> 'What a lot of rain!'

> *Que casa maravilhosa!*
> 'What a wonderful house!'

11

The Verb

Like Romance languages in general, Portuguese has a verb structure that is much more complex than the English one. Yet many of its forms have dropped from actual use, a process that is particularly advanced in the Brazilian variety of the language. In its most adipose version, found in grammars, a verb includes sixty-eight separate forms (distinguished by tense, mood, person, and number); these reduce to a more manageable thirty-three in current Brazilian spoken usage.

This complex situation precludes a simple presentation of verbal paradigms. Correspondingly, I give them in two stages: first, I present all tenses, including only the four person forms that occur in Brazilian speech. Then, the paradigms are completed with second person forms, useful for understanding the traditional literature (up to about the 1920s), European books and newspapers, and occasional texts written in very formal or archaizing language. The paradigms are given in full in appendix 1.

11.1 Mood, tense, person, number

aspect

Portuguese verbs vary in **mood, tense, person,** and **number.** Of these categories mood is the most elusive. The main mood difference is one opposing the indicative to the subjunctive; for example, take the forms *ronca* and *ronque,* which both may mean '(he/she) snores.' The way most grammars attempt to give the rules governing the use of one or the other leaves much to be desired. Some state that the indicative is used to express a reality, the subjunctive a hypothesis. That this is not true is clearly shown by the following pair of sentences:

> *Ela ronca demais, talvez.*
> 'She snores too much, perhaps.'

> *Talvez ela ronque demais.*
> 'Perhaps she snores too much.'

The two sentences are virtually synonymous; yet we find the indicative in the former, the subjunctive in the latter.

In fact, I believe that mood differences are not exhaustively describable in terms of meaning; rather, mood is a complex phenomenon, having a semantic and a formal face. The question is considered in chapters 14–17, where the use and meaning of moods are discussed at some length. For the moment, suffice it to remark that traditional grammar distinguishes three moods, namely, the **indicative,** the **subjunctive,** and the **imperative.** Besides these, there are three **nominal forms,** that is, the **infinitive,** the **gerund,** and the **participle.** In the present section and in the paradigms, traditional nomenclature will be adopted (in an English translation), but this does not imply uncritical acceptance, as will become clear in due time. The idea is merely not to burden the exposition with a terminological discussion that may obscure matters for some students.

Tense is in certain ways connected with time, but the connection is far from simple (a situation that obtains in English as well). Thus, one can say that the future is almost always used to express an event that has not yet taken place, as in *Sônia comerá todas as pizzas* 'Sônia will eat all the pizzas,' and the past usually expresses something that has already happened, as in *Sônia comeu todas as pizzas* 'Sônia ate all the pizzas.'

But one can say *Sônia vai ao cinema amanhã* 'Sônia goes to the movies tomorrow,' where the present tense *vai* is used to refer to a future event; or *em 1500 os primeiros navios portugueses chegam ao Brasil* 'in 1500 the first Portuguese ships reach Brazil,' where the present tense expresses a past event. One can also refer to a future event by using the past tense, as in *quando vocês chegarem eu já comi tudo* 'when you arrive I will have eaten everything (literally, I have eaten everything).' This is a widespread phenomenon, and while one cannot say there is no connection between tense and time, the connection is complex; it is described in chapters 18 and 19.

In our paradigms three main tenses appear: **present, past** (Port. *pretérito*), and **future.** Furthermore, there is a tense picturesquely termed **future of the past** (Port. *futuro do pretérito*), which is usually considered a variety of the future; in fact, it corresponds to the English **conditional,** and to avoid confusion I will use the English term here. Past tenses are further distinguished into **preterit, imperfect,** and **pluperfect.**

This leaves us with a list of six tenses, namely, present, preterit, imperfect, pluperfect, future, and conditional. These are all represented in the indicative mood, whereas the subjunctive has a reduced list: only present, imperfect, and future—nine tenses, to which must be added the **personal infinitive,** a highly peculiar resource of the Portuguese language, which brings the total to ten tenses.

These are the **simple** tenses, that is, those that are represented by single words, like *come* '(he/she) eats' (present); *comi* '(I) have eaten' (preterit); *comíamos* '(we) ate' (imperfect); *comeriam* '(they) would eat' (conditional), and so on. Besides these, there are several **compound** forms, formed with auxiliaries, e.g., *tínhamos comido* '(we) had eaten,' *estou comendo* '(I) am eating,' etc. Compound forms are best taken up in connection with the auxiliaries (chapter 13).

Person is the property verbal forms have of referring to an entity as being in some kind of semantic relationship with the event denoted by the verb. For example, in *comi* '(I) ate' the verb form (in particular, the ending *-i*) informs us that the agent of the action is the speaker; in *comeu* it informs us that the agent is not the speaker.

Here the semantic relationship is one of agent-action, but this depends on the verb. Many verbs do not express an action at all, like *ser* 'to be,' *amar* 'to love,' and in such cases the semantic relationship shown in the person ending is something different—for example, in *amo* '(I) love' the ending *-o* shows that the **experiencer** of the experience denoted by the verb is the speaker. With the verb *apanhar* 'to take a beating' the personal ending shows who is the **patient** of the action: *apanhamos* '(we) took a beating'; and so on.

When a subject appears, it either indicates the same entity already identified by the verbal ending (thus making the expression redundant), or specifies it further, when the ending is not sufficiently explicit. For instance, we may say *comi* '(I) ate,' without an overt subject, or *eu comi* 'I ate,' with the overt subject *eu*. The two sentences are synonymous, but the second one contains a redundancy in that it refers twice to the speaker: through the ending *-i* and through the presence of the pronoun *eu*. Now, in *ele comeu* '(he) ate' we have a different situation because the third person singular ending *-eu* may refer to many entities: *ela* 'she,' *ele* 'he,' *você* 'you,' not to speak of *Maria, Antônio, meu irmão* 'my brother,' etc. In such cases the presence of the subject is not redundant because third person endings are too vague, and some complementation is called for. And, in fact, third person verb forms, without subject, occur only in specified circumstances (see chapters 20, 21, 38).

All this is not too different from what occurs in English, of course. But Portuguese verbs are richer in personal endings than English ones. In current spoken Brazilian, we can distinguish four persons:

1st singular—as in	*amo*	'(I) love'
3rd singular—as in	*ama*	'(he / she) loves'

(*continued*)

1st plural—as in   *amamos*   '(we) love'

3rd plural—as in   *amam*   '(they) love'

The reader will remark the absence of second person forms. This is because third person forms do duty for reference to the addressee, as in *você ama* 'you love,' with the same ending as in *ele ama* 'he loves.'

Second person forms do exist, but they are not used in the variety here described; the second person singular is alive, though, in Portugal and in some areas of southern and northeastern Brazil, and in poetry as well:

2nd singular—as in   *amas*   'you (sing.) love'

The second plural, as I said earlier, is used only in very restricted contexts, for example, in some types of religious speech. It is usual in literature up to the nineteenth century:

2nd plural   —as in   *amais*   'you (pl.) love'

We have, then, six forms for each tense, but only four are in normal use nowadays in standard Brazilian.

Number is also expressed by so-called personal endings, since they distinguish between singular and plural forms. A Portuguese verb is traditionally conjugated in conjunction with typical pronouns for each person:

eu amo	'I love'
[tu amas]	'you (sing.) love'
ele ama	'he loves'
nós amamos	'we love'
[vós amais]	'you (pl.) love'
eles amam	'they love'

The two forms in brackets are absent from current speech and will be included only in the supplementary paradigms, section 11.3.3.

Finally, I may mention the tendency to substitute *a gente* (+ third person verb forms) for *nós* in the spoken language, so that instead of *nós amamos* 'we love' one often hears *a gente ama* 'id.' *Nós,* nevertheless, along with its corresponding forms in -*mos,* remains in frequent use, so that one cannot speak of a further reduction in the verb system.

11.2 Conjugations

Regular verbs are organized into three **conjugations,** according to the way they inflect for tense and mood, differences of person and number among conjugations being small. For instance, take the three verbs *cantar* 'to sing,' *vender* 'to sell,' *partir* 'to leave'; their infinitive forms differ, and this is the easiest way to ascertain the conjugation a verb belongs to: verbs ending in -*ar* in the infinitive belong to the **first conjugation,** verbs in -*er* belong to the **second conjugation,** and verbs in -*ir* belong to the **third conjugation.** There are some verbs in -*or,* namely *pôr* 'to put' and its compounds, like *impor* 'to impose,' *dispor* 'to organize,' *repor* 'to replace,' and several others. These verbs are best analyzed as belonging to a conjugation of their own—in other words, they are irregular—and all inflect exactly like *pôr*.

This results in three sets of endings for many forms, one for each conjugation, so that, for instance, the preterit, first person plural of *cantar* 'to sing' is *cant*<u>*amos*</u> '(we) sang,' that of *vender* 'to sell' is *vend*<u>*emos*</u> '(we) sold,' and that of *partir* 'to leave' is *part*<u>*imos*</u> '(we) left'. The ending -*a* in the form *canta* means that it belongs to the indicative, whereas in *venda* or *parta* the *-a* marks the form as belonging to the subjunctive. The conjugation a verb belongs to must, therefore, be kept in mind when inflecting it. In the following sections I list all the forms a verb of each conjugation can assume (complete paradigms for the three conjugations are summed up in appendix 1). Regular verbs will be covered first; irregular verbs present their own difficulties, which are best understood when considered in comparison with regular ones.

As I said earlier, in the following sections I shall list only the personal forms present in modern Brazilian usage; therefore, forms for the second person (singular and plural) are listed separately in section 11.3.3.

11.3 The regular verb

11.3.1 Tense (and mood) formation

Two main problems should be considered when conjugating a verb: mood and tense formation and person formation. In this section we consider mood and tense formation. It is in fact only one process (and in modern studies one speaks of **mood-tense** endings) because there are no separate morphological markings for mood and tense. There is, therefore, no need to consider them separately, and we may speak simply of **tense formation.**

In what follows I present all tenses of the Portuguese verb, both those that are still in normal use and those that have become obsolete (the latter being duly marked as such). My concern in this section is how to derive all forms from a few basic ones. For each form only a rough translation is provided, and no attempt is made to describe accurately its meaning and use—this will be done, for all tenses and moods, in chapters 14–19.

I have organized the presentation of tenses in the following way: the rules of the present section are for forming the first person singular of each tense; the remaining persons are formed from the first singular by means of the rules given in section 11.3.2 below.

In order to derive all tenses of a regular verb, we need only one primitive form, that is, the infinitive. For irregular verbs, as we will see, more primitive forms are necessary.

The infinitive gives us the two bits of information we need in order to apply the rules: (a) the **radical** (which is obtained by dropping the final ending, *-ar, -er,* or *-ir* as the case may be), and (b) the conjugation the verb belongs to: to repeat, verbs in *-ar* belong to the first conjugation, verbs in *-er* to the second conjugation, and verbs in *-ir* to the third conjugation.

For example, suppose someone wants to find out the future of the verb *comer* 'to eat.' The radical is *com-,* and the verb belongs to the second conjugation because its infinitive ends in *-er.* Consulting the table, we find that the ending corresponding to the future of the second conjugation is *-erei.* Therefore, the future of *comer* (first person singular) is *com- + -erei* = comerei.

Below is a table of endings for all tenses. Tenses within brackets, [ ], are nowadays largely restricted to the written language.

Table 11.1
Tense endings (first person singular where applicable)

		1st conj. *falar*	2nd conj. *vender*	3rd conj. *partir*
Indicative	Present	*-o*	*-o*	*-o*
	Imperfect	*-ava*	*-ia*	*-ia*
	[Future	*-arei*	*-erei*	*-irei*]+
	Conditional	*-aria*	*-eria*	*-iria* +
	Preterit	*-ei*	*-i*	*-i*
	[Pluperfect	*-ara*	*-era*	*-ira*]+
Imperative	(colloquial)	*-a*	*-e*	*-e*
	(formal)	*-e*	*-a*	*-a*
Subjunctive	Present	*-e*	*-a*	*-a*
	Imperfect	*-asse*	*-esse*	*-isse* +
	Future	*-ar*	*-er*	*-ir* +
Nominal forms	Impersonal infinitive	*-ar*	*-er*	*-ir* +
	[Personal infinitive	*-ar*	*-er*	*-ir*] +
	Gerund	*-ando*	*-endo*	*-indo* +
	Participle	*-ado*	*-ido*	*-ido*

—Tenses marked with + are those in which the difference between the conjugations consists merely of the presence, at the beginning of the suffix, of *a, e,* or *i,* for the first, second and third conjugations, respectively, e.g., *-asse, -esse, -isse.*

—About the two forms of the imperative, see section 11.3.2 below.

—**Nominal forms,** except the personal infinitive, do not inflect for person or number (they correspond to the English gerund *singing,* infinitive *(to) sing,* and past participle *sung*).

—The reader will probably notice that the future subjunctive and the personal infinitive endings are identical. This is so in all regular verbs; but, as will be seen in the next chapter, they differ in many irregular verbs.

11.3.1.1 Deletion of final -r in verbs

The infinitive, as we've seen, ends in *-r.* It has already been remarked that this *-r* is pronounced only in very careful, deliberate speech, as when mentioning 'the verb *cantar*'; more usually, it is not pronounced at all, so that *cantar* is pronounced [kɐ̃'ta], e.g., *ela vai cantar* 'she is going to sing,' pronounced ['ɛlə 'vaj kɐ̃'ta]. In only one case, *vir* 'to come,' the resulting final vowel is nasalized, so that *vir* is pronounced ['vĩ], e.g., *ele queria vir* 'he wanted to come,' usually pronounced ['eli ki'ɾijə 'vĩ].[1]

Note

[1]The pronunciation ['vi], without nasalization, also occurs but more rarely.

Final *-r* is deleted in *all* verb forms, not only in the infinitive: *for,* the future subjunctive of *ser* 'to be' is pronounced ['fo], and *quer* 'he wants' sounds ['kɛ]. In nonverbal forms, final *-r* is pronounced: *lar* 'home' is not homophonous with *lá* 'there.' *Andar* loses its final **r** when it is an infinitive, 'to walk'; but it can also be a noun, meaning 'floor (of a building)': *moro no terceiro andar* 'I live on the third floor,' and then the final **r** is pronounced.[1]

Note

[1]Many speakers in the northeast omit final *-r* in all words, indistinctly.

11.3.2 Person endings: The modern Brazilian system

Person formation is partly regular, so that it is possible to state a few general rules, in order to avoid learning all the forms one by one. The rules given below (as tables) will enable the student to build all forms currently used; the complete paradigms may be found in appendix 1.

Let's begin with the table below, which allows derivation of personal forms from the first singular form:

Table 11.2a
Person endings

When the 1st singular ends in	the 3rd singular ends in	the 1st plural ends in	the 3rd plural ends in	
	-a	-amos	-am	[1st conjugation]
-o	-e	-emos	-em	[2nd conjugation]
	-e	-imos	-em	[3rd conjugation]
-a	-a	-amos	-am	all
-e	-e	-emos	-em	3
-r	-r	-rmos	-rem	conjugations

This table works for all verb forms with the first singular endings shown. Thus, if the first singular is *(eu) cante,* we know that the other forms will be *(ele) cante, (nós) cantemos, (eles) cantem.* If the first singular ends in *-o* (which happens in the present indicative), we must first know the conjugation the verb belongs to—in other words, we must also have the infinitive. Since *cantar* 'to sing' belongs to the first conjugation, *(eu) canto* corresponds to *(ele) canta, (nós) cantamos, (eles) cantam;* for *partir* 'to leave' (third conjugation), we have *(eu) parto, (ele) parte, (nós) partimos, (eles) partem.* The first singular ends in *-r* in the future subjunctive and in the personal infinitive; we then have, for instance *(eu) cantar*, from which we derive *(ele) cantar, (nós) cantarmos, (eles) cantarem.*

The tenses that do not conform to the table are those that have other endings in the first singular or that have no first singular form at all (that is, the imperative). For these there are special rules:

For the future

Endings to be added to the infinitive form			
1st singular	3rd singular	1st plural	3rd plural
-ei	*-á*	*-emos*	*-ão*

For the preterit

Table 11.2b
Person endings (future and preterit)

1st singular	3rd singular	1st plural	3rd plural	
-ei	*-ou*	*-amos*	*-aram*	1st conjugation
-i	*-eu*	*-emos*	*-eram*	2nd conjugation
-i	*-iu*	*-imos*	*-iram*	3rd conjugation

For the imperative

The imperative requires a special note. In the written language and in the speech of some persons, it is formed in the following way:

Table 11.2c
Person endings (imperative, standard form)

3rd singular	3rd plural	
-e	-em	1st conjugation
-a	-am	2nd and 3rd conjugation

Thus, the imperative of *cantar* is *cante* 'sing (when addressing one person),' *cantem* 'sing (when addressing several persons),' and likewise *venda, vendam; parta, partam*. These forms are identical to the corresponding ones of the present subjunctive.

But there is another way to form the imperative, and this is predominant in the spoken language; in written texts it occurs mainly in dialogue, when the author wants to give the text a character of orality. It is formed in the following way:

Table 11.2d
Person endings (imperative, colloquial form)

3rd singular	3rd plural	
-a	-em	1st conjugation
-e	-am	2nd and 3rd conjugation

The two sets differ only in the singular. Both are frequently used by the same persons, and the choice of one or the other is usually governed by the degree of formality of the situation. Thus, a speaker may say *canta, menino* **SpBr** 'sing, child' in one situation, but *cante, menino* in another, more formal situation.

Stress of the first plural form

In first plural forms, stress sometimes falls on the same syllable as in the other persons and sometimes "jumps" one syllable toward the end of the word. For example, we have *can-*

tava '(I) sang,' which is stressed on *-ta-*, and *cantávamos* '(we) sang,' stressed on the same *-ta-* syllable; in contrast, we have *canto* '(I) sing,' stressed on *can-*, but *cantamos* '(we) sing,' stressed on *-ta-*.

The rule that governs the place of stress in first plural forms is the following:

> In first plural forms, stress falls on the syllable preceding the *-mos* ending (that is, the penultimate) whenever the other forms are stressed on the radical; otherwise, stress falls on the third syllable from the end.

Thus, the present indicative is stressed on the radical: *canto;* therefore, in the first plural the stress jumps ahead, *cantamos;* in the imperfect indicative, stress falls on the ending, *cantava,* and it stays on the same syllable in the first plural: *cantávamos.*

Final *-s* deletion in the *-mos* suffix

In casual speech the first person plural suffix *-mos* reduces to *-mo,* without the final *-s.* For instance, a sentence like *nós chegamos do Rio* 'we arrived from Rio' becomes *nós chegamo do Rio* **SpBr.** When a vowel follows, sandhi (see 5.1) takes place normally: *nós chegamos a tempo* 'we arrived on time' becomes *nós chegam' a tempo* **SpBr.**

11.3.3 Second person endings

Although second person forms have dropped from everyday use in most of Brazil, it is necessary to know them in order to read the traditional literature. The second person singular is still heard in Portugal and in some regions of Brazil and is also relatively frequent in poetry. Most Brazilians use *você,* pl. *vocês* as the preferred mode of address; and those who, in Brazil as in Portugal, employ *tu* for the singular, in the plural substitute *vocês* (or equivalent forms; see section 8.1.4) for old *vós,* so that the latter as well as its accompanying verb forms is definitely archaic.

The following table is to be understood in the same way as the one given in section 11.3.2. It makes it possible to derive second person forms from first person ones.

Table 11.3a
Second person endings

When the 1st singular ends in	the 2nd singular ends in	the 2nd plural ends in	
	-as	-ais	[1st conjugation]
-o	-es	-eis	[2nd conjugation]
	-es	-is	[3rd conjugation]
-a [present subjunctive]	-as	-ais	
-a [other tenses]	-as	-ais	all
-e	-es	-eis	3
-r	-res	-rdes	conjugations

The table works for all tenses, except the following two:

Table 11.3b
Second person endings (preterit)

1st singular	2nd singular	2nd plural	
-ei	-aste	-astes	1st conjugation
-i	-este	-estes	2nd conjugation
-i	-iste	-istes	3rd conjugation

For the imperative

Since the imperative has no first person form, the base is the radical (the infinitive, minus the ending *-ar, -er, -ir*), to which the following endings should be added:

Table 11.3c
Second person endings (imperative)

2nd singular	2nd plural	
-a	-ai	1st conjugation
-e	-ei	2nd conjugation
-e	-i	3rd conjugation

Now, these endings are for the imperative when used without a negative word like *não* 'do not,' *nunca* 'never,' and the like. When the imperative is negative, however, second person endings are the same as in the present subjunctive. Thus, the affirmative *canta* 'sing' corresponds to the negative *não cantes* 'do not sing'; likewise, we have *correi* **Arch** 'run (pl),' but *nunca corrais* **Arch** 'never run (pl)'; *parte* 'go away,' but *não partas* 'do not go away.'

It must be stressed that in Brazil all these forms occur only in the written language, mostly in relatively ancient texts. They are not a part of the modern language, and few Brazilians can use these forms correctly. Nowadays, as we saw above, the third person is substituted, which makes the negative in the regular way, merely by adding the negative particle: *corra* 'run,' *não corra* 'do not run'; or, more colloquially, *corre* 'run,' *não corre* **SpBr** 'do not run.'

Stress on the second plural form

The second plural endings *-is* and *-ais* are always stressed. As for *-eis,* the following rule applies:

> In second plural forms in *-eis,* stress falls on the ending itself whenever the other forms are stressed on the radical; otherwise, stress falls on the third syllable from the end.

This is the same rule applying to stress in all first plural endings. For example, in present indicative *ando* '(I) walk,' the stress falls on the radical, and therefore we have *andais* 'you (pl) walk'; but in imperfect *andava* '(I) walked,' the stress is on the ending -*ava,* therefore *andáveis* 'you (pl) walked.'

The rules given above allow the student to conjugate a regular verb in its entirety, provided that he knows the first person singular of the tense he wants and the conjugation the verb belongs to.

11.3.4 Apparent irregularities

11.3.4.1 Orthographic adjustment

Before studying real irregularities, we will have a quick look at some cases in which perfectly regular verbs may look irregular by virtue of the spelling conventions of the language.

For instance, the fact that the letter **c** is pronounced [s] when before **i** and **e** causes a verb like *atacar* 'to attack' to change the final **c** of its radical into **qu** when the following suffix begins with **e,** to avoid its being pronounced [s]. Thus, the infinitive is *atacar,* and the present indicative is *ataco,* etc., but the present subjunctive is *ataque, ataquemos,* in order to preserve the pronunciation [k] in the final consonant of the radical. Observe that, phonologically speaking, *atacar* is regular, the change from **c** to **qu** being purely orthographic. This phenomenon occurs in the following cases:

When the radical ends in	it changes into	Example	
c before **a, o**	**qu** before **e, i**	*atacar, ataque*	'attack'
c before **e, i**	**ç** before **a, o**	*descer, desço*	'climb down'
ç before **a, o**	**c** before **e, i**	*começar, comece*	'begin'
g before **a, o**	**gu** before **e, i**	*pagar, pague*	'pay'
g before **e, i**	**j** before **a, o**	*agir, ajam*	'act'
gu before **e, i**	**g** before **a, o**	*distinguir, distingo*	'distinguish'

Verbs having **j** as the final consonant of the radical in the infinitive do not change **j** into **g** before **e, i:** *viajar, viajemos* 'travel.' As for **qu** before **e, i,** it would regularly become **c** before **a, o;** but as there is no regular verb ending in *-quer* or *-quir,* this change does not happen in practice.

11.3.4.2 Verbs ending in -ear

Verbs ending in **-ear** should make their present indicative in **-eo, -ea,** and so on. But since these endings are always pronounced as two syllables, and since the sequence ['eu] (two syllables) does not occur in the language, a semivowel [j] is inserted between the two vowels and is represented in spelling by **i.** This occurs whenever the **e** is stressed, thus from *passear* 'to take a walk' we have *passeio, passeia, passeie,* etc. When the **e** is unstressed, no insertion occurs: *passear, passeamos, passeando.* All verbs in **-ear** undergo this insertion, e.g., *ratear* 'to misfire,' *rechear* 'to stuff,' *marear* 'to cause to be seasick,' *colear* 'to slither.'

12

Irregular Verbs

Most irregular verbs show changes in the radical—which, in regular ones, is invariable; for instance, *cuspir* 'to spit,' which makes *cuspo* '(I) spit' but *cospe* '(he/she) spits.' There is also a small group of verbs that take some different suffixes from the ones found in regular verbs; for instance, *estar* 'to be' makes its present indicative *estou, está* (besides regular *estamos*). We will start with the first group, which can be divided into several subclasses, as listed and discussed in what follows.

12.1 Vowel shift in the radical

Many verbs having **e** or **o** as the last vowel in the radical (hereafter called the **radical vowel**) are subject to special rules, which differ according to conjugation. In many cases the rules specify whether an **e** or an **o** is to be pronounced open, [ɛ], [ɔ], or closed, [e], [o]. These rules do not apply to cases in which these vowels are followed by nasal consonants (**n, m, nh**), since in such cases **e** and **o** become themselves nasalized [ẽ] and [õ], and nasal **e** and **o** are always closed (see 3.2).

In the third conjugation, similar rules apply to verbs with **i** or **u** as the last vowel in the radical.

First conjugation

In most verbs of the first conjugation, radical **e** is pronounced open, [ɛ], whenever it is stressed; otherwise, it is pronounced closed, [e]: *levar* 'to take away' makes *levo* '(I) take away,' pronounced ['lɛvu], *levam* '(they) take away' ['lɛvãw], but *levamos* '(we) take away' [leˈvãmus].

In a few exceptions, verbs keep the closed [e] throughout their conjugation: *chegar* 'to arrive,' *desejar* 'to desire.' *Fechar* 'to close' belongs traditionally to this group, but nowadays it is more generally inflected like *levar: fecho* '(I) close' is pronounced ['feʃu] by most speakers.

Radical **o** is pronounced open, [ɔ], whenever it is stressed; otherwise, it is closed, [o]: *rolar* 'to roll' makes *rolo* ['hɔlu] '(I) roll.'

The only exceptions are verbs with radical *ending* in **o,** that is, without any consonant between the radical vowel and the suffix, which have a closed [o] in all forms: *voar* 'to fly' makes *vôo* ['vou] '(I) fly,' *voa* ['vowə] '(he/she) flies,' and the same for *soar* 'to sound,' *doar* 'to donate,' and *coar* 'to strain.'

Roubar 'to steal' has **ou** in the radical, which is supposed to be pronounced [o] and often is: *roubo* '(I) steal' may be pronounced ['hobu]. However, many speakers apply the opening rule to **ou,** so that *roubo* very often sounds ['hɔbu] as if the verb were *robar.* The same occurs with *estourar* 'to explode.' Both pronunciations are acceptable, although only the first is sanctioned by grammatical tradition. A similar phenomenon occurs with *endoidar* 'to become mad,' which derives from *doido* ['dojdu] 'mad' but has an open [ɔ] in the same forms as *rolar,* as in *ele endoida* [ĩˈdɔjdə] *quando vê dinheiro* 'he goes mad when he sees money.'

Second conjugation

Radical **e, o** are pronounced [ɛ], [ɔ], respectively, whenever they are stressed (and oral, see above), except in the first person singular of the present indicative and the forms derived from it: present subjunctive and third person forms of the imperative. For instance, *beber* 'to drink' makes its present indicative as follows:

eu bebo	'I drink'	['bebu]
ele bebe	'he drinks'	['bɛbi]
nós bebemos	'we drink'	[beˈbẽmus]
eles bebem	'they drink'	['bɛbẽj]

Likewise, *mover* 'to move' has the following forms:

eu movo	'I move'	['movu]
ele move	'he moves'	['mɔvi]
nós movemos	'we move'	[mo'vĩmus]
eles movem	'they move'	['mɔvẽj̃]

There are no exceptions to this rule.

Third conjugation

The alternations found in the third conjugation are somewhat different. Verbs with radical **e** change this **e** into **i** when it is stressed in the first person singular of the present indicative and in the forms derived from it (present subjunctive and third person of the imperative); in all other cases the **e** is pronounced open, [ɛ], when stressed (and oral). For instance, *servir* 'to serve' has the following forms in the present indicative:

eu sirvo	'I serve'	['sihvu]
ele serve	'he serves'	['sɛhvi]
nós servimos	'we serve'	[seh'vĩmus]
eles servem	'they serve'	['sɛhvẽj̃]

The following verbs follow this model: *conseguir* 'to manage,' *preferir* 'to prefer,' *referir* 'to refer,' *repetir* 'to repeat,' *seguir* 'to follow,' *sentir* 'to feel,' *vestir* 'to dress.'[1]

Note

[1]Here, as below, I give the most frequent among the verbs following this model—that is, those included in the 1,500 most frequent words of the language according to Duncan 1971.

In some exceptions, verbs change the **e** of the radical into **i,** when stressed, in *all* forms: *agredir* 'to attack' makes

eu agrido	'I attack'
ele agride	'he attacks'
nós agredimos	'we attack'
eles agridem	'they attack'

Other verbs that behave like *agredir* are all verbs ending in *-gredir,* like *progredir* 'to progress'; and also *prevenir* 'to warn.'

Verbs with **u** or **o** in the radical have **u** in forms derived from the first person of the present indicative, and open **o,** [ɔ], in all other cases in which the radical vowel is stressed. For instance, *dormir* 'to sleep' and *fugir* 'to run away' have the following forms:

eu durmo	'I sleep'		*eu fujo*	'I run away'	
ele dorme	'he sleeps'	['dɔhmi]	*ele foge*	'he runs away'	['fɔʒi]
nós dormimos	'we sleep'		*nós fugimos*	'we run away'	
eles dormem	'they sleep'	['dɔhmẽj]	*eles fogem*	'they run away'	['fɔʒẽj]

Among the verbs following this rule are *acudir* 'to succor,' *cobrir* 'to cover,' *construir* 'to build,' *descobrir* 'to find out,' *destruir* 'to destroy,' *dormir* 'to sleep,' *fugir* 'to run away,' *subir* 'to go up.'

Some verbs, however, keep the **u** throughout: *instruir* 'to educate' makes *eu instruo, ele instrui, nós instruímos, eles instruem.* The following verbs follow this model: *assumir* 'to take on,' *iludir* 'to deceive,' *influir* 'to influence,' *presumir* 'to presume,' *resumir* 'to summarize,' *curtir* 'to tan; to enjoy,'[1] and a few others that are rarely used.

Note

[1]The original meaning of *curtir* is 'to tan' (said of leather, for instance). Nowadays it is also used in the sense of 'to enjoy.' The connection between the two ideas is anybody's guess.

12.2 Irregular verbs

Most true irregular verbs undergo changes in the radical. For instance, *perder* 'to lose' makes the first person singular of the present indicative *perco* '(I) lose'; and *fazer* 'to make' makes its preterit *fiz* '(I) made.' In some cases, the radical does not change, but the suffixes are idiosyncratic, as in *estar* 'to be,' which has a radical *est-* throughout the conjugation, but makes its present indicative, first person, *estou,* and the present subjunctive *esteja.* Verbs that undergo particularly radical changes in their conjugation are termed **anomalous;** an example is *ser* 'to be,' which has in its present indicative the forms *sou* '(I) am,' *é* '(he/she) is,' and makes the preterit *fui* '(I) was,' and the present subjunctive *seja.*

A useful notion in the study of the irregular verbs is the concept of **primitive forms.** These are the forms of a verb from which others can be derived in a regular manner; that is, all or most irregularity concentrates on the primitive forms, so that it is not advisable to disregard them (and, say, teach each form as if it were totally idiosyncratic). For example, a principle which works for all verbs is that the **preterit indicative,** the **pluperfect,** the **imperfect subjunctive,** and the **future subjunctive** all derive from the same form of the radical. Thus, the verb *caber* 'to fit' makes the preterit irregularly, *coube.* But the other three tenses are derived from this one regularly: *coub-era, coub-esse, coub-er.* Information of this kind is, so to speak, too good to throw away.

There are several such partial regularities obtaining for irregular verbs. It was in order to capture them that primitive forms were devised. For most irregular verbs, the primitive forms are the only ones to be learned separately. This system works for most irregular verbs, and those that depart from it in general have but one extra irregular form. Anomalous verbs, on the other hand, are excessively unruly and therefore not entirely predictable from their primitive forms. Portuguese has thirty-two really frequent irregular verbs. Eight of them are anomalous; the remaining twenty-four—which I will call simply **irregular**—are tolerably systematic, as described below.

The description given in this chapter may be utilized by teachers as a guideline to the regularities that should be eventually mastered by the student—chiefly, of course, through planned exercises and texts, although in some cases, with some students, direct grammatical information may also be useful.

The primitive forms needed to describe an irregular verb are as follows:

Infinitive	e.g., *poder* 'to be able'
Present indicative, 1ˢᵗ person singular	*posso*
Present indicative, 3ʳᵈ person singular	*pode*
Preterit, 1ˢᵗ person singular	*pude*
Preterit, 3ʳᵈ person singular	*pôde*
Past participle	*podido*

Besides, there are three verbs that make the future irregularly, and two verbs that make the present subjunctive irregularly. Some verbs have two forms for the past participle; about the use of these two forms, see 12.5 below.

Finally, some verbs have an open [ɛ] instead of the regular [e] in the endings of all forms derived from the preterit which begin with **e** (unless a nasal consonant follows because in that case the **e** is nasalized). Thus, the imperfect subjunctive of the regular verb *vender* 'to sell' is *vendesse,* pronounced [vẽˈdesi], but for the verb *saber* 'to know' the corresponding form is *soubesse,* pronounced with an open **e**, [soˈbɛsi] (in *soubemos* 'we knew' the **e** is nasal because it is stressed and followed by **m** and therefore cannot be pronounced [ɛ]). The items in question include all anomalous verbs except *ser* and *ir,* plus the irregular verbs

> *caber*   'to fit in'
> *dizer*   'to say'
> *fazer*   'to make'
> *poder*   'to be able'
> *querer*   'to want'
> *saber*   'to know'
> *trazer*   'to bring.'

In appendix 2 this irregularity is marked for each verb.

All forms of an irregular verb are derived from the six primitive forms given above. The following table gives the source of each form:

Primitive form	Derived forms
Infinitive *pod-er* →	**Present indicative, all forms except 1st singular and 3rd singular**
	pod-es, pod-emos, pod-eis, pod-em
	Imperfect indicative
	pod-ia, pod-ias . . .
	Gerund
	pod-endo
	Future[1]
	pod-erei, pod-erás . . .
	Conditional[1]
	pod-eria, pod-erias . . .
	Imperative, 2nd singular and 2nd plural [Wr]
	pod-e, pod-ei
Present indicative, 1st singular *poss-o* →	**Present subjunctive**[2]
	poss-a, poss-as . . .
	Imperative, 3rd person
	poss-a, poss-am

(*continued*)

Primitive form	Derived forms
Present indicative, 3rd singular *pod-e* →	**(only itself)**[3]
Preterit, 1st singular *pud-e* →	**Preterit, except 3rd singular**
	pud-e, pud-este, pud-emos,
	pud-estes, pud-eram
	Pluperfect
	pud-era, pud-eras . . .
	Imperfect subjunctive
	pud-esse, pud-esses . . .
	Future subjunctive
	pud-er, pud-eres . . .
	ꝑest
Preterit, 3rd singular *pôd-e* →	**(only itself)**
Past participle *pod-ido* →	**(only itself)**

✳

Notes

[1]Three verbs have irregular future and conditional: *fazer* 'to make' makes *farei, faria; dizer* 'to say' makes *direi, diria;* and *trazer* 'to bring' makes *trarei, traria.*

[2]Two verbs have irregular present subjunctive: *querer* 'to want' makes *queira,* etc.; and *saber* 'to know' makes *saiba,* etc.

[3]The present indicative, third singular is included because of six verbs that do not derive this form from the infinitive in the regular way:

fazer	'to make,'	3rd sing. present indicative	*faz*
dizer	'to say'		*diz*
trazer	'to bring'		*traz*
rir	'to laugh'		*ri*
ler	'to read'		*lê*
ver	'to see'		*vê*

Observe that this same form does duty as the imperative in the spoken language: *faz um omelete para mim* **SpBr** 'make an omelette for me.' Two verbs (both meaning 'to be') are exceptional: *ser* (third singular, present indicative *é*) makes the imperative *seja;* and *estar* (third singular, present indicative *está*) makes *esteja* (substandard *teje*).

A couple of examples may be useful to illustrate the use of primitive forms and of the above table in the derivation of the other verb forms. Suppose we want to derive the imperfect subjunctive of *caber* 'to fit.' The table tells us that the imperfect subjunctive derives from the preterit, first singular; and in appendix 2 we find that the preterit, first singular of *caber* is *coube*. The radical is *coub-,* and to this radical we add the endings of the imperfect subjunctive, which yields *coub-esse, coub-esses, coub-esse, coub-éssemos, coub-ésseis, coub-essem.* Furthermore, from the appendix we know that *caber* is one of the verbs that have an open [ɛ] in the endings of the imperfect subjunctive (as well as in all endings in preterit-derived tenses that begin with an **e**); this justifies the acute accent in *coubéssemos.* For *perder* 'to lose,' which does not take the open [ɛ] but has the regular closed [e], the accent is a circumflex, as for regular verbs of the second conjugation: *perdêssemos.*

Take some forms of *fazer* 'to make.' Suppose we want the present subjunctive, first person plural. From the table we know that the present subjunctive is derived from the present indicative, first singular, that is, *faço.* We delete the personal ending, and we come to the radical *faç-.* The table gives the ending *-amos* for the present subjunctive, first plural (second conjugation), which, added to the radical, yields *façamos.*

Or suppose we want the complete paradigm of the present indicative. We already have two forms, *faço* and *faz.* The remaining forms are derived from the infinitive, *fazer.* We drop the ending *-er;* to the radical, *faz-,* we add the second conjugation personal endings *-emos, -em.* The complete present indicative, therefore, is as follows:

eu faço	'I make'
ele faz	'he makes'
nós fazemos	'we make'
eles fazem	'they make'

Let's derive the future subjunctive, third person plural. This tense is derived from the preterit, first person singular, which is *fiz;* since there is no final vowel to be dropped, the radical is *fiz-.* The ending of the future subjunctive, third plural, is *-er,* which gives *fizer* (with an open [ε], as determined by the rule, since the primitive form ends in *-e*). We then add the third person plural ending, *-em,* getting *fizerem.* Observe that in this case, as in several others, the future subjunctive (*fizer*) differs from the personal infinitive (*fazer*).

The same process can be applied to all irregular verbs (excluding anomalous ones), yielding most forms. In a few cases, however, there is an additional irregular form, not derivable in the usual way. The list found in appendix 2 gives the primitive forms for the most common irregular verbs as well as any additional irregularities they may have.

12.3 Anomalous verbs

Finally, we come to eight anomalous verbs that are irregular to an extreme. Here derivation rules are of little help, and the best way to describe them is to state their tenses in full (person inflection is more regular and often follows the general models). These verbs are the following:

dar	'to give'
estar	'to be'
haver	'there to be'
ir	'to go'
pôr	'to put'
ser	'to be'
ter	'to have'
vir	'to come'

As they are highly irregular, it is not convenient to attempt any generalization, as was done for irregular verbs in the preceding section. The best solution is simply to give their complete conjugations, which appear in appendix 2.

12.4 Defective verbs

Some verbs, for no discernible reason, lack certain forms and are called **defective.** They all belong to the third conjugation and may be described in two main groups, namely:

First, verbs that lack the **first person singular of the present indicative** and consequently the present subjunctive and the imperative forms that derive from it. For example, *demolir* 'to demolish': one can say *ele demole* 'he demolishes,' *elas demoliram* 'they have demolished,' but not * *eu demolo,* or * *que eu demola.* The verbs that pattern after *demolir,* apart from some very unusual ones, are *abolir* 'to abolish' and *emergir* 'to emerge.'

Second, verbs that lack all forms in which the stress falls on the radical; that is, in the present indicative they only have the first person plural (and the second plural in the old language); and they lack the present subjunctive and the persons of the imperative derived from it. Of the verbs following this model, only two are of any frequence nowadays: *punir* 'to punish,' and *falir* 'to go bankrupt.' Thus, one can say

> *A companhia <u>faliu</u> por causa dos impostos.*
> 'The company went bankrupt because of taxes.'

But if we want to say the same thing in the present, we must use a circumlocution in place of *falir*:

> *Essa companhia <u>abre falência</u> de três em três anos.*
> 'This company goes bankrupt every three years.'

This is so because in *faliu* the stress falls on the ending (*-iu*), whereas in * *fale* the stress would fall on the radical. Likewise, one can use *castigar* 'to punish' to supply the missing forms of its synonym *punir*.

12.5 Double participles

Many verbs have two participles, one regular, the other irregular; for instance, *expulsar* 'to expel' has the regular *expulsado* and the irregular *expulso*. The use of the two participles in most cases is not indifferent: the regular one is used after the auxiliary *ter* (*haver*), and the irregular one with *ser* (that is, in passive sentences), or without any auxiliary, e.g.,

> *O diretor já tinha <u>expulsado</u> três alunos.*   [**regular participle**]
> 'The director had already expelled three students.'

> *Três alunos foram <u>expulsos</u> pelo diretor.*   [**irregular participle**]
> 'Three students have been expelled by the director.'

> *Os alunos <u>expulsos</u> recorreram à justiça.*   [**irregular participle**]
> 'The expelled students went to court.'

The most frequent cases of double participle are the following:

Verb		Regular participle	Irregular participle
aceitar	'to accept'	*aceitado*	*aceito*[1]
acender	'to light'	*acendido*	*aceso*
eleger	'to elect'	*elegido*	*eleito*[1]

entregar	'to deliver'	*entregado*	*entregue*[1]
expressar	'to express'	*expressado*	*expresso*
exprimir	'to express'	*exprimido*	*expresso*
expulsar	'to expel'	*expulsado*	*expulso*[1]
imprimir	'to print'	*imprimido*	*impresso*
matar	'to kill'	*matado*	*morto*
morrer	'to die'	*morrido*	*morto*
pagar	'to pay'	*pagado*	*pago*[1]
pegar	'to catch'	*pegado*	*pego*[1]
prender	'to arrest'	*prendido*	*preso*
salvar	'to rescue'	*salvado*	*salvo*[1]
soltar	'to set free'	*soltado*	*solto*
suspender	'to discontinue'	*suspendido*	*suspenso*

Note

[1]Many speakers use the irregular participle of these verbs in all cases: *eu já tinha* <u>*entregue*</u> *todos os jornais* 'I had already delivered all the papers.' Here one would expect the regular participle, *entregado,* because the auxiliary is *ter;* yet, the irregular participle is probably the preferred form. In particular, the regular participle of *pagar* and *pegar* is practically extinct, in spite of being upheld in traditional grammars. With *salvar,* the regular participle *salvado* is nowadays used in the sense of 'saving (information in a computer),' but the irregular one, *salvo,* is usual in the sense of 'saving (a life)': *eu tinha salvado esse arquivo* 'I had saved this archive,' but *essa cirurgia já tinha salvo muitas vidas* 'that surgery had already saved many lives.'

13

Auxiliaries

Some verbs can be combined with the gerund, the infinitive, and the participle of other verbs, making up sequences semantically similar to simple verb forms. For example, the sequence *vou comer* expresses the future and is the preferred colloquial alternative to *comerei* 'I will eat.' These constructions are similar to English sequences such as *have eaten, going to eat,* and the like. They are usually called **compound tenses,** the first verb form being the **auxiliary.** I describe them in this chapter as sequences of auxiliaries + main verbs.

Portuguese auxiliaries can be used before a participle, an infinitive, or a gerund:

Auxiliaries used with the participle

ter : *eu tenho comido* 'I have been eating'

haver : *eu havia comido* **Wr** 'I had eaten'

Besides these, there is the construction with *ser* + participle, as in *eu fui insultado* 'I was insulted,' that is, the so-called passive voice (see chapter 21).

Auxiliary used with the infinitive

ir: *eu vou comer*   'I will eat'

Auxiliaries used with the gerund

estar: *eu estou comendo*   'I am eating'

andar: *eu ando comendo*   'I have been eating'

vir: *eu venho comendo*   'I have been eating'

ir: *eu vou comendo*   'I keep eating'

These constructions express fine shades of meaning and are sometimes difficult to discriminate; their translation into another language is not always easy. Although they belong, properly speaking, to the chapter on syntax, they will be described here because sequences of auxiliary + main verb are often alternatives to simple forms of the verb, e.g., the sequence *eu havia comido* 'I had eaten,' which replaces the obsolete pluperfect, *eu comera* 'id.'

13.1 Auxiliary + participle

There are two auxiliaries that enter into construction with the participle: *ter* and *haver*. Only *ter* can be used in the present indicative; in all other tenses *ter* and *haver* can occur, the difference being that *haver* occurs exclusively in written texts, while *ter* is both literary and colloquial. The general meaning of the construction is of a completed event (what linguists call **perfective aspect**) when the auxiliary is in a past or in a future tense; and of an event that happened in the past and has continued down to the present when the auxiliary is in the present. For instance,

eu tenho comido		'I have been eating'
eu tinha comido		'I had eaten'
eu terei comido	**Wr**	'I will have eaten'
eu teria comido		'I would have eaten'

All these forms may occur (in writing) with *haver* instead of *ter,* except the first one, i.e., the sequence of *haver* in the present indicative + past participle, which does not occur in present-day Portuguese.

13.2 Auxiliary + infinitive

The only auxiliary used with the infinitive is *ir* (there are many **main verbs,** called **modals,** that come with the infinitive; see chapter 22). When *ir* is in the present indicative, the construction is equivalent to the future: *vou convidar Carla* 'I will invite Carla.' This construction with *ir* has totally replaced the simple future form, *convidarei,* in the spoken language. In spite of what is stated in some grammars, its meaning is not limited to expressing an immediate future: *o mundo vai acabar dentro de três bilhões de anos* 'the world will end in three billion years.'

Ir is not used as an auxiliary in the way just described when the main verb is *ir* itself; in such cases, one must use the present. Thus, *I will go* translates not as * *eu vou ir,* but simply as *eu vou.*

With *ir* in the past, the sequence *ir* + infinitive means a future relative to some time in the past, as in

Eu ia convidar a Carla para a festa de ontem.
'I was going to invite Carla for yesterday's party.'

The use of *ir* in the future + infinitive is rare and means the same as when *ir* is in the present:

O prefeito irá inaugurar o edifício de manhã.
'The mayor will dedicate the building in the morning.'

The form *vamos* is used as a sort of auxiliary of the imperative, corresponding to English *let's:*

Vamos repetir a festa.
'Let's repeat the party.'

In this use, *vamos* is most often pronounced [vãw].

With all other forms, *ir* occurs only in its main verb capacity, that is, as 'to go':

eu fui convidar	'I went (somewhere) in order to invite'
eu tinha ido convidar	'I had gone (somewhere) in order to invite'
vai convidar	'go and invite (imperative)'

With the preterit, this construction also has a peculiar meaning: *eu fui convidar a Carla,* besides having the meaning mentioned above, means something close to 'I was stupid enough to invite Carla.' This meaning arises only when *ir* is in the preterit tense and is generally used in conjunction with a continuation such as . . . *e ela estragou a festa* ' . . . and she ruined the party.'

13.3 Auxiliary + gerund

All constructions of auxiliary + gerund denote an event considered in its development rather than at its end or beginning. For instance, *estamos trabalhando* means 'we are working,' and *ando trabalhando demais* means 'I have been working too much' (and I am still working too much). The auxiliaries found with the gerund are the following:

estar   'to be'
The meaning of *estar* with the gerund is identical to that of *be* plus gerund in English.

Estamos trabalhando.
'We are working.'

Estivemos trabalhando.
'We have been working.'

andar   'recent event, continued in the present (or at the time referred to by the tense of *andar*),' corresponding to English *have been* + gerund:

Eu ando comendo demais.
'I have been eating too much.'

Eu andava comendo demais.
'I had been eating too much.'

vir   (same meaning as *andar*)

> *Eu venho comendo demais.*
> 'I have been eating too much.'

Vir + gerund is comparatively infrequent, as compared with *andar* + gerund.

ir   in most cases may be translated as English *keep* + gerund:

> *Enquanto você descansa, eu vou arrumando os livros na estante.*
> 'While you rest, I'll keep arranging the books on the shelf.'

There is also a curious case of double auxiliary: ***querer*,** when used in the gerund after the auxiliary *estar* and followed by an infinitive, expresses a future event that is both imminent and perceptible in some way:

> *O teto está querendo cair.*
> 'The roof is about to fall (and is showing signs of it).'

As a main verb, *querer* means 'to want.'

A final note on these auxiliaries: *andar, acabar,* and *estar* also occur with qualificative nominals ("adjectives") as well as with some adverbial phrases, and in such constructions they keep their auxiliary meaning:

> *Eles andam furiosos.*
> 'They have been furious (lately).'

> *Eles acabaram furiosos.*
> 'They ended up furious.'

> *Eles estão de férias.*
> 'They are on vacation.'

13.4 Sequences of auxiliaries

In Portuguese, as in English, auxiliaries may occur in sequence, as in *tenho estado trabalhando demais* 'I have been working too much': here we have *ter* + participle and *estar* + gerund in the same construction.

The order of auxiliaries in such complex sequences is fixed (as it is in English): one must place first the auxiliaries used with the participle, second the auxiliaries used with the infinitive, and third the auxiliaries used with the gerund. Each auxiliary or main verb takes the form required by the preceding one, so that if we have, as in the example above, a sequence of **ter** + **participle** plus **estar** + **gerund,** the auxiliary *estar* must come in the participle because it follows *ter.* The main verb must come in the gerund because the preceding auxiliary is *estar* + gerund.

This sounds more complicated than it is in practice; the examples below should make the situation sufficiently clear. Let's first analyze the example:

> *Tenho estado trabalhando.*
> 'I have been working.'

This sequence can be analyzed as follows:

tenho	**esta-**	**_-do_**	**trabalha-**	**_-ndo_**
1	**2**	**3**	**4**	**5**
1:	auxiliary	*ter*		
2:	auxiliary	*estar*		
3:	participle ending	(required by *ter*)		
4:	main verb	*trabalhar*	'to work'	
5:	gerund ending	(required by *estar*)		

This system is perfectly parallel to the English one, exemplified in *I have been working.*

As a rule, speakers use one auxiliary per sentence, sometimes two (but with restrictions, see below), practically never more than two. Therefore, sentences like *tenho estado sendo visto,* presumably 'I have been being seen' are never found in practice, except perhaps as grammatical examples. And even sequences of two auxiliaries are not all possible, the only comparatively frequent combinations being the following:

ter + **participle**   —   **estar / andar** + **gerund**

> *Tenho estado estudando muito.*
> 'I have been studying a lot.'

> *Tenho andado estudando muito.*
> 'id.'

ir + **infinitive**   —   **estar** + **gerund**

> *Vou estar almoçando quando você chegar.*
> 'I will be eating lunch when you come.'

** *13.5 What is an auxiliary?*

Many verbs also occur before infinitives, gerunds, and participles but are not considered auxiliaries. An example is *querer* 'to want,' as in *elas querem entrar* 'they (fem.) want to come in.' Although this is a theoretical question, it may not be out of place to give here the reasons *querer* and the like are not considered auxiliaries. The practical-minded reader can skip this section without detriment to his or her study of the language.

There has been some discussion about exactly what is to be considered an auxiliary. In this book I adopt a compromise solution, keeping our practical goals in mind. For us, the features that distinguish an auxiliary from a main verb are the following:

a. An auxiliary adds to the construction a semantic ingredient that is not predictable from its meaning when taken separately. Thus, *ir* means 'to go,' that is, expresses a motion of some sort; but *eu vou cantar* means a future, 'I will sing,' and has nothing necessarily to do with motion. Analogously, *andar* when taken alone means 'to walk,' but before a gerund it denotes a recent event, still under way: *andar* is a main verb in *eu ando duas horas por dia* 'I walk two hours a day,' but it is an auxiliary in *eu ando comendo demais* 'I have been eating too much.'

b. Auxiliaries do not admit a different subject for the main verb: one can say *estou tentando* 'I am trying,' *tenho tentado* 'I have been trying,' *vou tentar* 'I will try,' but there is no way to give the verb *tentar* 'to try' in any of these constructions an independent subject, different from the subject of *estar, ter,* and *ir,* respectively. In contrast, *quero entrar* 'I want to go in' admits an independent subject for *entrar* 'to go in,' although in this case it must become a subjunctive: *quero que você entre* 'I want you to go in.'

c. The auxiliary is not taken into consideration when selecting complements. All main verbs make certain requirements on complements: some must have an object, as for example *fazer* 'to make,' which never occurs alone; others must have an animate subject, like *desejar* 'to wish,' and so on. But whatever the requirement is for the simple form of a verb, it is also valid for a sequence of auxiliary + main verb: *tenho feito* 'I have made,' *vou fazer* 'I will make,' *estou fazendo* 'I am making' also require an object, just as *vai desejar* '(he/she) will wish,' *tenho desejado* '(I) have wished' require an animate subject. That is, the presence of the auxiliary is irrelevant for purposes of selection of complements. Now, when we have a sequence of, say, *desejar* 'to wish' plus an infinitive, selection of complements must take into account both *desejar* and the verb that follows it. Thus, one cannot say * *eu desejei fazer* 'I wished to make,' without an object, because *fazer* requires an object; and one cannot say * *o queijo desejava cair* 'the cheese wished to fall down' because *desejar* requires an animate subject.

The irrelevance of the auxiliary for selection can be clearly seen in cases of passive sentences. We may passivize a sentence without regard to the presence of the auxiliary, and the passive will be acceptable if the active is (and if the main verb admits of passivization). Thus, we may say

Meu primo vai vender essa fazenda.
'My cousin will sell this farm.'

And also

Essa fazenda vai ser vendida por meu primo.
'This farm will be sold by my cousin.'

But if we have a sequence of verb + infinitive, and the first verb is not an auxiliary, the passive may not be acceptable because the requirements of the first verb have not been met:

Meu primo quer vender essa fazenda.
'My cousin wants to sell this farm.'

But

* *Essa fazenda quer ser vendida por meu primo.*
* 'This farm wants to be sold by my cousin.'

which is just as unacceptable in English, for the same reasons.
d. A fourth feature of auxiliaries is that negation must be attached to the auxiliary, never to the main verb. For instance, we can say *nós não temos comido carne* 'we have not eaten meat,' but never * *nós temos não comido carne.* This restriction is sometimes relaxed in the colloquial language, so that one may hear sentences like *eu vou não me mexer daqui até que você volte,* literally 'I am going not to move from here until you're back.'

Strict application of the above criteria yields a rather short list of auxiliaries in Portuguese: *ter, haver* (+ participle); *ir* (+ infinitive); *estar, andar, vir, ir, acabar* (+ gerund); *ser* (+ participle, in passive constructions); and the sequence *estar querendo* (+ infinitive). Some grammars give a longer list of auxiliaries used with the infinitive, but these are better analyzed as main verbs and are discussed in chapter 22 under the heading **modals.** Examples of modals are

Ele devia calar a boca.
'He should shut up.'

Sônia continuou a trabalhar.
'Sônia kept working.'

A firma deixou de pagar a gratificação.
'The company failed to pay the bonus.'

In all these cases, and several others, one or more of the four features defining auxiliaries is absent. First, they normally have the same meaning when used with the infinitive and when used alone: *Sônia continuou o trabalho* 'Sônia continued (her) work.' Second, they admit of independent negation for both verbs: *Sônia não continuou a trabalhar* 'Sônia didn't keep working' vs. *Sônia continuou a não trabalhar* 'Sônia kept not working.'

IV Meaning and Use of Verb Forms

14

Mood

14.1 Semantic and syntactic factors

The main problem in regard to **mood** is the conditions of use of the **indicative,** the **subjunctive,** and the **infinitive.** As will be seen, these conditions are complex and involve both factors of form (syntax) and of meaning (semantics). The use of the **imperative,** also considered an independent mood, presents no special difficulty, being closely similar to its English equivalent.

Mood is a mixed category having to do with both meaning and form. Mood differences are often used to express certain shades of meaning (so that in certain contexts using the subjunctive or the indicative entails a difference in meaning); but in other cases the occurrence of a specific mood results simply from the presence of a governing item, without any apparent semantic reason for it. In this chapter and the following ones I list all the situations in which one or another mood must (or may) be used; as will be seen, the list of situations is heterogeneous, reflecting the fact that mood itself is a grammatically heterogeneous category. Some generalizations have been reached, though, and they form the basis of the exposition given in this part of the grammar.

The complex nature of mood has caused some fluctuation in the analyses found in traditional grammars; for instance, the conditional (*eu faria* 'I would make') is considered a tense of the indicative in current grammars, but it was formerly analyzed as a mood in itself (called ***condicional*** 'conditional'). As for nominal forms, that is, the infinitive, the gerund, and the participle, no one seems to know for sure whether to consider them moods or not.

These theoretical questions need not concern us here. For our purposes, four moods will be considered, namely, the indicative, the subjunctive, the infinitive, and the imperative; I also examine the gerund and the participle (whether or not they are to be considered independent moods).

How the four moods are used often depends mainly on their meaning and/or role in communicative situations. For instance, the imperative is used almost exclusively to express orders or requests; but, on the other hand, an order or a request can also be expressed by the indicative, as in

> *Vocês <u>vão sair</u> da cama imediatamente!*
> **indicative**
> 'You are going to jump out of bed right now!'

The semantic rules governing the use of moods are not simple. And, besides, there are also formal factors that partly govern the use of moods; for instance, the adverbial *talvez* 'perhaps' requires that a following verb be in the subjunctive, whereas other items that equally denote doubt require the indicative:

> *Talvez ela <u>esteja dormindo</u>.*
> **subjunctive**
> 'Perhaps she is sleeping.'

but

> *Provavelmente ela <u>está dormindo</u>.*
> **indicative**
> 'Probably she is sleeping.'

No complete description of these factors has ever been devised, and mood is certainly one of the difficult points for English speakers learning Romance languages. Yet some rules can be stated, and these will hopefully help the student avoid most of the pitfalls laid by the language.

14.2 Main and subordinate clauses

Mood depends in great measure on whether the verb in question belongs to a main clause or to a subordinate one. **Subordinate clauses** are formally marked, for instance, by preposing the word *that* in *I see that he is drunk* (the subordinate clause is the underlined portion of the sentence). In English, the marks are often dispensed with, so that one can say *I see he is drunk*, without any subordination mark. In Portuguese this does not happen, and subordinate clauses are marked as such in all cases.[1] The mark may be a special word (conjunctions or relative pronouns), placed before the clause; or it may be a special ending on the verb (infinitive or gerund endings). In this section I give some criteria for distinguishing between subordinate clauses and main clauses.

Note

[1] There is, to be sure, a very marginal case in which a subordinate bears no subordination mark. In formal language, such as in official reports, the subordinate following the verbs *esperar* 'to hope,' *desejar* 'to wish,' *solicitar* 'to solicit' may appear without the proper conjunction, which should be *que*, e.g., *esperamos sejam estes esclarecimentos suficientes* 'we hope (that) these explanations be sufficient.' This use is rare and gives an impression of extreme formality, even pedantry.

14.2.1 How to identify subordinate clauses

A subordinate clause may be identified by the following marks:

a. Conjunctions

The main conjunction is *que* 'that,' which can occur either alone or preceded by several prepositions and adverbs:

> *Soubemos **que** <u>mamãe chegou</u>.*
> 'We have learned that Mom has arrived.'

> *O patrão mandou **que** <u>vocês fiquem até as cinco</u>.*
> 'The boss ordered you to stay until five [literally, . . . ordered that you stay . . .].'

> ***Já que** <u>os preços subiram</u>, vamos pedir aumento.*
> 'Since prices have gone up, we will ask for a raise.'

> *Jogo xadrez **sempre que** <u>posso</u>.*
> 'I play chess whenever I can.'

Other frequent conjunctions are *embora* 'although,' *caso* 'in case,' *porque* 'because,' *quando* 'when,' *se* 'if, whether,' *como* 'as,' *conforme* 'as' (a list of all important conjunctions is given in chapter 37):

> ***Embora** <u>seja caro</u>, o restaurante é péssimo.*
> 'Although it is expensive, the restaurant is awful.'

> **Caso** <u>você veja seu pai</u>, dê a ele minhas lembranças.
> 'In case you see your father, give him my greetings.'

> Não sei **se** <u>está chovendo em Brasília</u>.
> 'I do not know if it is raining in Brasília.'

b. Relative pronouns

Relative pronouns are the following: *que* 'which, who,' *quem* 'who,' *cujo* 'whose,' *o qual* 'which,' *onde* 'where.' The precise use of each is described in chapter 36. Here I want to note only that they, too, function as marks of subordinate clauses (and, unlike conjunctions, they are part of the subordinate):

> Quero uma secretária **que** <u>saiba alemão</u>.
> 'I want a secretary who knows German.'

> A velha **cujo** <u>marido morreu</u> mora ali.
> 'The old woman whose husband died lives there.'

> Este é o professor <u>com **quem** eu trabalhava</u>.
> 'This is the teacher I used to work with [literally, . . . with whom I used to work].'

As this sentence shows, a relative pronoun may be preceded by a preposition, here *com* 'with.'

c. Endings

A subordinate clause may also be marked by a special verb ending. Thus, infinitives and gerunds, whenever not used with auxiliaries, constitute (with their dependent elements) subordinate clauses:

> Todos desejam **pegar** <u>o seu autógrafo</u>.
>   **infinitive**
> 'Everyone wishes to get your autograph.'

> Sandrinha trabalha **cantando** <u>alegremente</u>.
>   **gerund**
> 'Sandrinha works (while) singing merrily.'

A **main clause** is characterized (negatively) by the absence of any of the marks listed above. Main clauses may appear alone in a sentence, as in

> Quero uma secretária.
> '(I) want a secretary.'

Or they may appear with one or more subordinates in the same sentence; in this case, one says that the main clause is **the whole sentence,** so that the subordinate clause is part of the main clause:

> *Quero uma secretária que saiba alemão.*
> '(I) want a secretary who knows German.'

> **Main clause:** *Quero uma secretária que saiba alemão.* (= the whole sentence)
> **Subordinate clause:** . . . *que saiba alemão.*

Generally speaking, each clause has one verb form;[1] and the mood of each verb form depends, in large measure, upon its being in a subordinate clause or not. Thus the subjunctive and the infinitive occur almost exclusively in subordinate clauses, the imperative only in main clauses,[2] and the indicative may occur in both main and subordinate clauses.

Notes

[1] The exception is when we have a sequence of an auxiliary plus a main verb, as in *estou comendo* '(I) am eating,' *tínhamos chegado* '(we) had arrived.' In these cases, the notion of mood applies to the auxiliary, which follows the same rules as simple verb forms (see chapter 13 for a study of sequences of auxiliary + main verb).

[2] That is, in a main clause and not in a subordinate one. Since the subordinate clause is part of the main clause, its verb is, rigorously speaking, also in the main clause. The opposition here is between a verb belonging to a subordinate clause and a verb (called **main verb**) that does not belong to any subordinate.

Most of the problem lies in subordinate clauses. A main clause may contain an imperative, an indicative, and exceptionally a subjunctive or an infinitive; but the conditions for the occurrence of each are clearly distinct and very simple to state. Accordingly, we begin our study with mood in main clauses; we then tackle the more delicate problem of mood in subordinate clauses.

14.3 Mood in main clauses

The indicative and the imperative are the characteristic moods found in main clauses:

> *Vocês ainda não lavaram o meu carro.*
> **indicative**
> 'You (pl.) have not yet washed my car.'

Lavem o meu carro, por favor.
imperative
'Please wash my car.'

The conditions under which these two moods are used are identical in Portuguese and in English. We saw above that an order or a request may be expressed by an indicative as well as by an imperative, and this also applies to both languages:

Você *vai lavar* meu carro imediatamente!
indicative
'You will wash my car right now!'

This sentence conveys an order, although its verb is in the indicative.

The subjunctive and the infinitive can also occur in main clauses, but only in restricted contexts. Considering first the subjunctive,

> The subjunctive may occur in a main clause when it expresses a wish
>
> (or a curse):

(DESEJO QUE) *Deus nos proteja desses tecnocratas!*
Ø
subjunctive
'(May) God protect us from those technocrats!'

Diabos o levem!
subjunctive
'(May) devils carry you away!'

[handwritten margin note: actually elliptical subordinations because below, one can see the n.C. marker 'que']

The conjunction *que* is sometimes included:

Que seu projeto tenha sucesso!
subjunctive
'(May) your project meet with success! [literally, that your project meet . . .]'

Furthermore,

the subjunctive appears in main clauses when it is governed by the adverb *talvez* 'perhaps.'

This adverb, when preceding a verb, requires that it be in the subjunctive:

Talvez eu <u>tenha entendido</u> mal.
'Perhaps I have misunderstood (it).'

This happens only when *talvez* precedes the verb. If it is placed after the verb, the latter comes in the indicative:

Eu <u>entendi</u> mal, talvez.
'I have misunderstood (it), perhaps.'

Besides *talvez*, the following items also govern the subjunctive:

quiçá	'perhaps'	**Arch**
oxalá	'let's hope that'	**Wr**
tomara	'let's hope that'	

Tomara always occurs with *que:*

Tomara que você <u>tenha</u> sucesso.
Oxalá você <u>tenha</u> sucesso.   **Wr**
'Let's hope that you be successful.'

Some speakers also use the subjunctive after *possivelmente* 'possibly' and *provavelmente* 'probably'; for these speakers both of the following are acceptable:

Provavelmente ele <u>está</u>   /   <u>esteja</u> com raiva de você.
                indicative   subjunctive
'Probably he is angry with you.'

Finally, there is a curious use of the imperfect subjunctive, meaning something like a "past imperative," in contexts like

—*Maria caiu da escada e quebrou o braço.*
—*Pois <u>tivesse</u> mais cuidado!*
"Maria fell down the stairway and broke her arm."
"Why wasn't she more careful? [literally, Well, be she more careful!]"

This use of the imperfect subjunctive reflects some irritation on the part of the speaker.

The infinitive occurs in main clauses only in sentences expressing an order or an instruction not directed to anyone in particular:

<u>*Diminuir*</u> *a velocidade.*
'Reduce speed.'

<u>*Deixar*</u> *esta porta sempre fechada.*
'Keep this door closed at all times.'

This use is characteristic of written signs and instructions (such as recipes, for instance). It is not correct to use this construction when explicitly addressing someone; in such cases, one must use the imperative:

João, <u>deixe</u> essa porta sempre fechada.
'João, leave this door always closed.'

If the addressee is implicit, the infinitive may be used (always in writing):

Por favor, <u>ligar</u> para Maria Luísa.
'Please call Maria Luísa.'

A variant of this context is the infinitive found in some fixed expressions of command used by the military:

<u>*Virar*</u> *à direita!*
'Turn right!'

15

Subjunctive vs. Indicative in Subordinate Clauses

15.1 The status of mood in subordinates

In subordinate clauses we find three moods: the indicative, the subjunctive, and the infinitive. Of these, only the indicative and the subjunctive are used with a preceding complementizer (the most typical of which is the conjunction *que* 'that'); the infinitive has no introducing word, and its subordinate status is, as we saw in 14.2, marked by the infinitive ending itself. For instance,

Vimos **que** *os meninos* <u>*quebraram*</u> *o jarro.*
indicative
'(We) saw that the children broke the vase.'

Convém **que** *você* <u>*troque*</u> *os pneus.*
subjunctive
'It would be good for you to change the tires.'

Minha mãe quer <u>*ir*</u> *ao cinema.*
infinitive
'My mother wants to go to the movies.'

When a verb occurs in a subordinate clause, its mood is governed by an item present in the main clause, which may be a **verb,** a **preposition,** a **conjunction,** or a **nominal.** For instance, whenever the main clause has the verb *querer* 'to want,' the subordinate verb must be in the subjunctive or in the infinitive, never in the indicative:

> *A professora quer que eu   <u>leia</u>   tudo isto.*
> **subjunctive**
> 'The teacher wants me to read all this.'

> *A professora quer   <u>ler</u>   tudo isto.*
> **infinitive**
> 'The teacher wants to read all this.'

The preposition *sem* 'without' requires a subjunctive or an infinitive, but the preposition *desde* 'since, provided' allows either the indicative or the subjunctive:

> *Ela saiu sem você   <u>visse</u>.*
> **subjunctive**
> 'She left without your seeing it.'

> *Ela saiu sem você   <u>ver</u>.*
> **infinitive**
> 'id.'

> *Ela não parou de chorar desde que você   <u>saiu</u>.*
> **indicative**
> 'She hasn't stopped crying since you left.'

> *Podemos ir a qualquer restaurante, desde que   <u>seja</u>   limpo.*
> **subjunctive**
> 'We can go to any restaurant, provided it is clean.'

Note that with *desde* the meaning of the preposition changes according to the mood of the subordinate verb: when it means 'since,' it requires the indicative, but in the meaning of 'provided' it requires the subjunctive. This happens with several prepositions and may be expressed in a clearer way by stating that the mood of the subordinate verb is governed by some semantic element present in the preposition.

Conjunctions may also make mood requirements. For instance, *já que* 'since, now that' requires the indicative:

> *Já que ninguém se   <u>apresenta</u>,   eu mesmo vou.*
> **indicative**
> 'Since nobody is volunteering, I am going myself.'

The conjunction *embora* 'although' requires the subjunctive:

> *Embora o cachorro* <u>*seja*</u> *barulhento, eu gosto dele.*
> **subjunctive**
> 'Although the dog is noisy, I like him.'

In certain cases a nominal can also govern a subordinate verb; this happens when a subordinate clause is a complement to the nominal, as in

> *A possibilidade de que você* <u>*venha*</u>
> **subjunctive**
> 'The possibility that you come'

> *A notícia de que você* <u>*veio*</u>
> **indicative**
> 'The news that you came'

As can be seen, the nominal (*possibilidade* 'possibility,' *notícia* 'news') is followed by a preposition; but, since the preposition is the same (*de*) in both cases, we must impute the selection of mood to the nominal, not to the preposition. The preposition in such cases may be said to be "transparent" for mood assignment purposes; this is always the case with *de*.

A very common construction is formed by a clause subordinate to a sequence of the verb *ser* + a nominal, as in

> *É importante que ele* <u>*compareça*</u>.
> **subjunctive**
> '(It) is important that he show up.'

> *É evidente que ele* <u>*compareceu*</u>.
> **indicative**
> '(It) is evident that he has shown up.'

Here again the nominal (*importante, evidente*) determines the mood of the subordinate.

In what follows, I consider first cases in which the mood of the subordinate is governed by a verb or a nominal in the main clause. I have limited the description given in the next section to the most important classes of verbs and nominals in their most common uses—ignoring certain constructions found only in formal style. Such details, when needed, are added in supplementary notes.

I start with some useful generalizations having to do with the intended meaning of the subordinate clause in relation to the main one. Three types of meaning are traditionally assigned to the subjunctive: **suasion, uncertainty,** and **emotion.** While these designations are somewhat vague, they provide a useful beginning, and I take them in turn in the sections below. These three meaning categories apply whenever we have a subordinate verb governed by a verb or a nominal in the main clause, with the conjunction *que* 'that.' Cases of mood governed by other conjunctions or by prepositions + *que* will be considered separately in section 15.6.

15.2 Subjunctive of suasion

The clearest statement of this semantic factor governing the use of subjunctives is the one found in Bull (1965) and intended for Spanish; it works for Portuguese as well:

> "Any purpose, intention or wish, on the part of the agent of the governing verb or nominal, to influence the action of the subject of the dependent verb implies the use of the subjunctive" [or the infinitive].[1,2]

Notes

[1]Bull's rule means that the indicative is never used with these verbs; they may appear in Portuguese with a subjunctive or with an infinitive: *mandei que lavassem o carro / mandei lavar o carro.* With many of them, the infinitive appears when the subjects of the two clauses are understood as being identical: *queremos que Maria seja eleita* 'we want Maria to be elected,' *queremos ser eleitos* 'we want to be elected.' See chapter 16 for details.

[2]I am using the term *agent* rather loosely here; in a sentence like *João ama Maria* 'João loves Maria,' no action, and therefore no agent, is involved. We cannot speak simply of a subject because the same semantic relation occurs in *o amor de João por Maria* 'João's love for Mary,' where the word *João* is certainly no subject (since there is no verb), and yet its semantic relation with *amor* and *Maria* is the same as in the preceding sentence. Since we can hardly go into the vexed question of how to analyze this element, I will speak of an agent and hope that the reader will know what I am talking about.

In the cases described by the above rule we speak of **subjunctive of suasion.** This rule is responsible for contrasts like the following:

> *Marina **sabe** que Mônica   <u>almoça</u>   às 12 horas.*
> **indicative**
> 'Marina knows that Mônica eats lunch at 12.'

> *Marina **quer** que Mônica   <u>almoce</u>   às 12 horas.*
> **subjunctive**
> 'Marina wants Mônica to eat lunch at 12.'

The first sentence denotes something Marina (the subject of the main clause) knows for a fact, and that fact is expressed in the subordinate *Mônica almoça às 12 horas;* therefore, the indicative is used. The second sentence denotes Marina's wish to influence Mônica's behavior, and therefore the subjunctive is used (in English, in this case, the same difference is shown by the use of the indicative in the first sentence and the infinitive in the second sentence).

Another example:

> ***Notei*** *que Márcia   <u>estava</u>   pronta.*
> **indicative**
> '(I) noticed that Márcia was ready.'

> ***Mandei*** *que Márcia   <u>estivesse</u>   pronta.*
> **subjunctive**
> '(I) ordered that Márcia be ready.'

The rule applies, then, to verbs in clauses that depend on main verbs like the following:

aconselhar	'to advise'
adorar	'to love'
conseguir	'to manage'
deixar	'to let'
desejar	'to wish'

(continued)

detestar	'to hate'
exigir	'to demand'
gostar	'to like'
insistir	'to insist'
mandar	'to order'
obrigar	'to force'
odiar	'to hate'
pedir	'to ask, to request'
permitir	'to allow'
precisar	'to need'[1]
proibir	'to forbid'
querer	'to want'

etc.

and many others, all of which express a "purpose, intention or wish, on the part of the agent of the main verb or nominal, to influence the action [or whatever it is that the subordinate verb denotes] of the subject of the dependent verb."

Note

[1] *Precisar* 'to need' is not a suasion verb, but it patterns like *querer: preciso que você me ajude* '(I) need you to help me,' *preciso sair mais cedo* '(I) need to leave earlier.'

The rule also applies in cases in which the main clause contains a nominal, which is the governing element:

> A **exigência** *de que vocês* <u>*trabalhem*</u> *no domingo veio da diretoria.*
> **subjunctive**
> 'The requirement that you work on Sundays came from management.'

> *Recebemos* **ordens** *de que se* <u>*preparasse*</u> *um verdadeiro banquete.*
> **subjunctive**
> 'We received orders that quite a banquet should be prepared.'

The facts here are parallel to what we just saw with verbs: the nominals *exigência* 'requirement' and *ordens* 'orders' express the wish of someone to influence someone else's behavior and therefore require the subjunctive. Now with *informação* 'information,' for instance, no such semantic feature is present, and the subordinate verb remains in the indicative:

> A **informação** *de que vocês* <u>*trabalham*</u> *no domingo veio da diretoria.*
> **indicative**
> 'The information that you work on Sundays came from management.'

As far as I can ascertain, this rule has no exceptions. Note that the purpose, intention, or wish referred to in the rule is a property of the **agent of the main verb or nominal,** not of the **speaker.** Thus, when someone, say, Laura, utters the sentence

> *O diretor* **mandou** *que Alex* <u>*consertasse*</u> *o elevador.*
> **subjunctive**
> 'The director ordered Alex to fix the elevator [literally, . . . that Alex fix the elevator].'

one does not understand that Laura herself wants to influence Alex's actions; such an intention is attributed to the director, that is, to the entity referred to by the subject of the main verb *mandou* 'ordered.' Correspondingly, the subordinate verb (*consertasse*) comes in the subjunctive.

15.3 Subjunctive of uncertainty

The second rule governing the occurrence of the subjunctive can be stated as follows:

> Whenever the main verb or nominal denotes **uncertainty, doubt,** or
>
> **denial** on the part of the main agent about the events described in the
>
> subordinate clause, the latter must be in the subjunctive.

I call this **subjunctive of uncertainty.** Examples of the application of the rule are

> *É **possível** que Elvis   esteja   vivo.*   [**uncertainty**]
>   **subjunctive**
> '(It) is possible that Elvis is alive.'

> *Os estudantes **duvidam** que o professor   conheça   a matéria.*   [**doubt**]
>   **subjunctive**
> 'The students doubt that the teacher knows the subject.'

> *O acusado **negou**   que   possuísse   alguma arma.*   [**denial**]
>   **subjunctive**
> 'The defendant denied that he owned any gun.'

> *A **possibilidade** de que Elvis esteja vivo foi mencionada no debate.* [**uncertainty**]
>   **subjunctive**
> 'The possibility that Elvis is alive was mentioned in the discussion.'

Here also the uncertainty, doubt, or denial mentioned in the rule is attributed to the **agent**
of the main clause, not to the **speaker.**
   Nominals expressing **falsehood**—such as *falso* 'false,' or *mentira* 'lie'—function in
the same way, since they denote denial of truth, and also require the subjunctive:

> *É **falso**   que o presidente   pretenda   se reeleger.*
>   **subjunctive**
> '(It) is false that the president intends to seek reelection.'

> *Era **mentira**   que a casa   estivesse   pegando fogo.*
>   **subjunctive**
> '(It) was a lie that the house was on fire.'

The rule that refers to words denoting uncertainty, doubt, or denial is not as reliable as the rule given earlier for verbs of suasion because it has some exceptions: some verbs, like *suspeitar* 'to suspect,' *desconfiar* 'to suppose,' *pensar* 'to think,' which apparently belong in the same semantic category as *duvidar* 'to doubt,' are most often constructed with the indicative:[1]

> *Carla* **suspeita** *que o vizinho* <u>*é*</u> *um espião.* [also: . . . <u>*seja*</u> *um espião.*]
>   **indicative**   **subjunctive**
> 'Carla suspects that the neighbor is a spy.'

With *achar* 'to think' **in the present,** only the indicative is possible:

> *Você* **acha** *que eu* <u>*estou*</u> *mentindo?*
>   **indicative**
> 'Do you think I am lying?'

But when *achar* is in the past, the subjunctive is acceptable:

> *Você* **achou** *que eu* <u>*estava*</u> / <u>*estivesse*</u> *mentindo?*
>   **indicative**   **subjunctive**
> 'Did you think I was lying?'

Note

**[1]To be sure, I tend to believe that these cases are not real exceptions, and that a more careful statement of the rule would leave them out of the cases in which the subjunctive is mandatory. To see why, consider *duvidar* 'to doubt,' which takes the subjunctive, and *suspeitar* 'to suspect,' which takes the indicative. Both verbs denote some sort of uncertainty, but they present this uncertainty in different ways; with *duvidar,* the uncertainty is, so to speak, the main ingredient, whereas in *suspeitar* the main ingredient is a (growing) certainty about whatever it is that the subordinate clauses states. All this is, of course, mere speculation at present; no research has been done on the subject from this point of view; but when the problem is examined closely, we may well find that the subjunctive of uncertainty (when governed by a verb) is governed by semantic factors without exception.

15.4 Subjunctive of emotion

The third rule governing the use of the subjunctive is as follows:

> When the main verb or nominal denotes an **emotion** on the part of the
>
> agent, the subordinate verb must be in the subjunctive.

The rule works for verbs denoting such emotions as fear, sorrow, joy, etc.:

*O povo **teme** que <u>venha</u> aí um novo pacote econômico.*
　　　　　　　subjunctive
'The people fear that a new set of economic measures may be coming.'

***Lamento** muito que a escola <u>tenha</u> que fechar.*
　　　　　　　　　subjunctive
'I am so sorry that the school has to close down.'

*Foi **ótimo** que <u>chovesse</u> ontem.*
　　　　　　subjunctive
'It was great that it rained yesterday.'

*O **medo** de que <u>houvesse</u> uma nova guerra*
　　　　　　subjunctive
'The fear that a new war might happen'

15.5 Mood in factual clauses

It is often said in traditional grammars that the indicative is the mood used in the expression of facts; but this is a simplification because the subjunctive is also used in the same capacity. The two moods complement each other in a quite systematic manner, and in order to describe this phenomenon it will be necessary to go briefly into an important semantic opposition: the opposition between **assertion** and **presupposition.**[1]

Note

[1]In this section we are concerned only with clauses introduced by the conjunction *que* 'that.' Clauses introduced by other connectives—including those composed of a preposition + *que*, such as *logo que* 'as soon as,' *desde que* 'since'—follow special rules; see 15.6 below.

Let's begin with the following examples:

É evidente que ele   está   bêbado.
indicative
'(It) is evident that he is drunk.'

É uma pena que ele   esteja   bêbado.
subjunctive
'(It) is a pity that he is drunk.'

From either sentence we gather that he is, in fact, drunk; yet, in the first one the subordinate verb is in the indicative (*está*), and in the second one it is in the subjunctive (*esteja*).

The reason for this difference in mood is that the factuality of the subordinate clause is presented in different ways in the two sentences. In the first one, the nominal *evidente* 'evident' has as its main semantic function to assert the speaker's belief that whatever follows is true (this comes from the meaning of *evidente,* a word that means something that is 'clearly true'). Now, in the second sentence, *é uma pena que ele esteja bêbado* 'it is a pity that he is drunk,' the nominal *pena* 'pity' is not used to assert the truth of what follows; instead, it asserts that what follows is a sad thing—this is the speaker's opinion. The meaning of the word *pena* 'pity' has nothing to do directly with truth; it is rather used to convey the speaker's feelings on the contents of the subordinate. Now, the receptor deduces that the subordinate must also be true because the speaker is unlikely to comment on the sad character of an event while not believing it to be true. We then say that the contents of the subordinate clause ('that he is drunk') are asserted in the first sentence, presupposed in the second one. This may seem a somewhat subtle distinction, but it is crucial in describing when to use the indicative or the subjunctive in factual sentences. The rule is the following:

Whenever a subordinate clause expresses a fact (in the speaker's opinion) it must be in the indicative if that fact is asserted and in the subjunctive if it is presupposed.

A few more examples are in order. For instance, in

> *Afirmo que o governo* <u>*errou*</u>.
> **subjunctive**
> '(I) state that the government is wrong.'

the speaker uses the verb *afirmo* 'I state' in order to assert his belief that the government is wrong. Consequently, the subordinate verb must be in the indicative. Now, in

> *Lamento que o governo* <u>*tenha errado*</u>.
> **subjunctive**
> '(I) am sorry that the government is wrong.'

the verb *lamento* 'I am sorry' asserts not the speaker's belief that the government is wrong, but rather the speaker's regret about that particular fact—which, in turn, is presupposed, that is, inferred to be true by the receptor. Consequently, the subordinate verb is in the subjunctive.

15.6 Connective-governed mood

When a finite subordinate clause is preceded by a connective, the connective may govern the mood (indicative or subjunctive) of the subordinate. This happens with conjunctions in general; the exception is *que,* when it occurs alone, in which case the preceding verb or nominal is the governing item. But compound conjunctions, which often end in *que,* do govern the mood of the subordinate, e.g., *para que* 'so that,' *já que* 'since,' *assim que* 'as soon as,' and many others, listed and discussed below.

Coordinators (such as *mas* 'but,' *e* 'and,' *ou* 'or' [see chapter 37]) do not govern the mood of the clauses they connect, that is, coordinate clauses have independent mood.

Instances of conjunction-governed mood are

> *Fechamos a porta* **para que** *o cachorro não* <u>*entrasse*</u>.
> **connective** **subjunctive**
> '(We) closed the door so that the dog would not come in.'

> *Fechamos a porta,* **já que** *o cachorro* <u>*tinha entrado*</u>.
> **connective** **indicative**
> '(We) closed the door, since the dog had come in.'

> **Se** *ela* <u>*quisesse,*</u> *eu bem que casaria com ela.*
> **connective subjunctive**
> 'If she wanted (it), I would gladly marry her.'

In these examples the mood of the subordinate is selected according to the connective used: *para que* 'so that' always requires a subjunctive, and *já que* 'now that' requires an indicative. Many of these connectives are, as in the above examples, composed of a preposition + *que;* others (like *quando* 'when,' *se* 'if,' *enquanto* 'while') are simple.

The connective *se* requires a subjunctive when in its conditional reading; but it may also be used in the meaning 'since, now that,' and in this case it takes the indicative:

> **Se** *você está tão cansada, por que* <u>*continua*</u> *a andar?*
> **connective**   **indicative**
> 'If you are so tired, why do you keep walking?'

The conditions governing mood in clauses introduced by connectives are rather complex; and since no really valid generalizations have ever been formulated, I list below all important connectives, along with the requirements for their usage. There are five patterns, described in turn in what follows.

15.6.1 Connectives used with the indicative only

Group 1. Connectives used with the indicative only

assim como	'in the same way that'
dado que	'given that'
já que	'now that'
porque[1]	'because'
visto que	'given that'

Note

[1] Except when negated; see 15.8.

These connectives are always followed by a clause with the verb in the indicative, regardless of tense. In practice, this means that the two verbs are independent of each other, and the selection of tense, for instance, depends exclusively on the intended meaning of each verb, not on any governing relation between them. Examples are:

Vou esconder   *os biscoitos,*   **já que**   *o cachorro entrou* / *está entrando* / *vai entrar.*
future   **past**   **present**   **future**
'(I) will hide the crackers, since the dog came in / is coming in / will come in.'

Visto que   *chove muito em Manaus,*   *levei* / *levo* / *vou levar*   *um guarda-chuva.*
              present   **past** **present** **future**
'Given that it rains a lot in Manaus, (I) took / take / will take an umbrella.'

15.6.2. *Quando, como,* etc.

Group 2. Connectives used with the <u>present</u> indicative, <u>past</u> indicative[1] or <u>imperfect</u> subjunctive, and <u>future</u> subjunctive

como	'as'
depois que	'after'
enquanto	'while'
logo que	'as soon as'
quando	'when'
quanto mais . . . mais[2]	'the more . . . the more'
sempre que	'whenever'

Notes

[1]That is, preterit or imperfect indicative.

[2]And its variants *quanto menos . . . menos, quanto menos . . . mais, quanto mais . . . menos.* The subordinate verb is the one that appears in the place marked '. . .', e.g., *quanto mais ele dormir, mais sono vai ter* 'the more he sleeps [**future subjunctive**] the more sleepy he'll grow.'

As we've seen, mood correlation with these connectives depends on the tense used in the subordinate; thus, although a connective like *quando* 'when' can appear with the imperfect or the future subjunctive, its occurrence with a present subjunctive (**quando eu vá*) is totally unacceptable. Cases in which the latter combination is found in Spanish (*cuando yo vaya*) appear in Portuguese with the future subjunctive (*quando eu for*).[1]

Note

[1]With *logo que* and *sempre que* the present subjunctive is also acceptable, if not very common: *eu te telefono logo que você tenha terminado de almoçar* 'I will call you as soon as you have finished lunch.'

When the subordinate clause contains an auxiliary (plus a verb in a nonfinite form) the mood requirement applies to the auxiliary, which is the only element in the sequence that varies in mood. Thus, we may say

Eu ia limpar a cozinha **quando** *você* <u>tivesse</u> *acabado de comer.*
'I would clean the kitchen when you had finished eating.'

Here we have the sequence *tivesse limpado* in the subordinate; the auxiliary *tivesse* is in the imperfect subjunctive, as required by the conjunction *quando.*

Further examples of the use of mood with these connectives are the following:

Quanto mais *o governador* <u>mente</u>, **menos** *o povo* <u>acredita</u>.
                    present indicative   **present indicative**
'The more the governor lies, the less the people believe (him).'

> ***Quanto mais*** *o governador* <u>*mentisse*</u>, ***menos*** *o povo acreditaria.*
> ### imperfect subjunctive
> 'The more the governor lied, the less the people would believe (him).'

> ***Quanto mais*** *o governador* <u>*mentia*</u>, ***menos*** *o povo acreditava.*
> ### imperfect indicative
> 'The more the governor lied, the less the people believed (him).'

> ***Quanto mais*** *o governador* <u>*mentir*</u>, ***menos*** *o povo acreditará.*   **Wr**
> ### future subjunctive
> 'The more the governor lies, the less the people will believe (him).'

> *Eu telefonaria* ***logo que*** <u>*tivesse*</u> *consertado o carro.*
> ### imperfect subjunctive
> 'I would call as soon as I had fixed the car.'

> *Chiquinha vai chorar* ***quando*** *seu pai* <u>*viajar*</u>.
> ### future subjunctive
> 'Chiquinha will cry when her father leaves on a trip.'

15.6.3 *Caso, antes que, para que,* etc.

Group 3. Connectives used with the present and imperfect subjunctive only

a fim de que	'in order to'
a menos que	'unless'
a não ser que	'unless'
a que	'to [before a subordinate clause]'[1]
ainda que	'although, even if'
antes que	'before'
caso	'in case'

(continued)

contanto que	'provided that'
embora	'although'
mesmo que	'even if'
nem que	'even if'
para que	'so that, in order to'
sem que	'unless, without [as in *without anyone knowing*]'

Note

[1]*A que* is rare; it occurs with some verbs that require *a,* in the few cases when this *a* is followed by a clause, e.g., *A diretoria se opõe a que o edifício seja reformado* 'Management is opposed to having the building restored [literally, . . to that the building be restored].'

These connectives are never used with the future subjunctive;[1] instead, they take the present subjunctive when the subordinate clause refers to a future event, e.g.,

*Vamos entrar em casa **antes que** chova.*

present subjunctive

'Let us go inside before it rains.'

Note

[1] *Mesmo que* and *nem que* occur sometimes in the spoken language with the future subjunctive: *mesmo que ele contar tudo* . . . **SpBr** 'even if he tells it all . . . '

Other examples:

Embora *o tempo <u>estivesse</u> chuvoso, ninguém saiu do campo.*
        imperfect subjunctive
'Although the weather was rainy, no one left the stadium.'

Eles se encontram **sem que** *ninguém*   <u>saiba</u>.
                       present subjunctive
'They meet without anyone knowing.'

Isso tudo é **para que** *as crianças*   <u>possam</u>   *brincar.*
                   present subjunctive
'All this is so that the children can play.'

15.6.4 Connectives used with the indicative or the subjunctive

---

Group 4. Connectives used with the indicative or the subjunctive

até que	'until'
de maneira que	'so that'
de modo que	'so that'
desde que	'since, provided that'
mal	'hardly'

> (*continued*)
>
> These connectives, like those in group 3, cannot be used with the future subjunctive; the present subjunctive is used instead, e.g.,
>
> *Ela vai reclamar* **até que** *alguém* <u>ouça</u>.
>
> **present subjunctive**
>
> 'She will complain until someone listens.'

The choice of mood used with these connectives causes a difference in meaning. This is very clear with *desde que,* which with the subjunctive has the conditional meaning 'provided' and with the indicative has the temporal meaning 'since':

Os policiais não vão te incomodar **desde que** *você se* <u>comporte</u>.
subjunctive
'The policemen won't bother you, provided that you behave.'

Os policiais o procuram **desde que** *ele* <u>fugiu</u>.
indicative
'The policemen look for him since he escaped.'

With the remaining items, the difference is more subtle, e.g.,

Helena se calava **logo que** *Antônio* <u>começava</u> *a falar.*
indicative
'Helena was silent as soon as Antônio started to speak.'

Helena se calava **logo que** *Antônio* <u>começasse</u> *a falar.*
subjunctive
'Helena was silent as soon as [and if] Antônio started to speak.'

The first sentence gives as a fact that Antônio did start to speak at certain times, whereas the second is noncommittal—it states only that if and when Antônio started to speak, Helena became silent.

15.6.5 *Se* 'if'

This conjunction is peculiar in its uses and deserves separate study. We may distinguish four main uses of *se,* examined in turn in what follows.

15.6.5.1 *Conditional* se

Se may express a condition of the event expressed in the main clause, as in

> **Se** *você* <u>*pedir,*</u>   *ele certamente vai te ajudar.*
>   **future subjunctive**
> 'If you ask (him), he will certainly help you.'

> **Se** *ele* <u>*está*</u>   *sonegando, vai acabar levando uma multa.*
> **present indicative**
> 'If he is evading taxes, he will end up being fined.'

The following rule accounts for the mood in the subordinate in these cases:

A conditional clause introduced by *se* may be in the

>> ***present indicative,***

>> ***past indicative,***   **or**

>> ***future subjunctive.***

Further examples are:

> **Se** *alguém* <u>*precisa*</u>   *de ajuda, posso dar uma mãozinha.*
>   **present indicative**
> 'If someone needs help, (I) can give a hand.'

> **Se** *Marcos* <u>*fez*</u>   *isso, errou.*
>   **preterit indicative**
> 'If Marcos did that, he was wrong.'

> **Se** *você* <u>*fizer*</u>   *esse tratamento, vai ficar totalmente curado.*
>   **future subjunctive**
> 'If you follow this treatment, you will be totally cured.'

Se ela <u>estava</u> no Rio, certamente viu os fogos de artifício.
imperfect indicative
'If she was in Rio, (she) certainly saw the fireworks.'

15.6.5.2 Counterfactual *se*

Counterfactual *se* may be considered a variant of conditional *se:*

> When the subordinate verb is in the imperfect subjunctive, there is a
>
> strong intimation that what it denotes is neither true, nor likely to be-
>
> come true:

conditional

Se você <u>fizesse</u> esse tratamento, ficaria totalmente curado.
 imperfect subjunctive
'If you followed this treatment, you would be totally cured.'

Se <u>tivesse</u> chovido ontem, o jogo teria sido adiado.
imperfect subjunctive
'If it had rained yesterday, the game would have been postponed.'

This reading arises only when the subordinate verb is in the imperfect subjunctive.

15.6.5.3 Factive *se*

The clause introduced by *se* may also express a fact, as in

Se você <u>resolveu</u> todos os seus problemas, por que continua reclamando?
'If you have solved all your problems, why do you keep complaining?'

This sentence makes it clear that you *have* solved all your problems, and the speaker just asks why you keep complaining. In this meaning, *se* is often translatable as *since*. Another example is

Se a cidade é tão grande, não vai ser difícil encontrar um apartamento.
'Since the city is so large, it will not be difficult to find an apartment.'

When introducing a factual clause, *se* always takes the indicative.

15.6.5.4 Nominalizing se

Finally, *se* may be used to introduce an indirect question, as in

*Ninguém sabe **se** essa cerveja <u>presta</u>.*
'Nobody knows whether this beer is any good.'

*Camila perguntou **se** Sérgio <u>estava</u> em casa.*
'Camila asked if Sérgio was at home.'

When introducing an indirect question, *se* corresponds to English *if* or

whether; and the subordinate verb is in the indicative.

15.7 Mood in relative clauses

I now turn to the functioning of mood in relative clauses—that is, clauses introduced by the relative words, viz.,

que	'who, which'
quem	'who, whoever'

(continued)	
o que	'what, whatever'
o qual	'who, which'
cujo	'whose'
onde	'where'
quanto	'as much as'

Examples of sentences containing relative clauses (underlined) are:

A pianista <u>que tocou ontem</u> é portuguesa.
'The pianist who played yesterday is Portuguese.'

A pianista <u>cujo estilo te impressionou</u> é portuguesa.
'The pianist whose style impressed you is Portuguese.

A pianista <u>sobre a qual falei</u> é portuguesa.
'The pianist about whom I spoke is Portuguese.'

O teatro <u>onde a portuguesa tocou</u> fica na rua da Bahia.
'The theater where the Portuguese (woman) played is on Bahia street.'

<u>Quem quiser ir ao concerto</u> pode pegar um bilhete na porta.
'Whoever wants to attend the concert may get a ticket at the door.'

Vou te dar <u>quanto você precisar</u>.
'(I) will give you as much as you need.'

The structure of relative clauses is studied in chapter 36. Here it is sufficient, first, to be able to identify them—not a difficult task, since they always begin with a relative word, with or without a preceding preposition. And, second, to notice that a relative clause is typically a **modifier**—that is, it is part of a noun phrase, and the head of this noun phrase immediately precedes the relative pronoun.[1] Thus, in

A pianista <u>que tocou ontem</u> é portuguesa.
'The pianist who played yesterday is Portuguese.'

the sequence *a pianista que tocou* 'the pianist who played' is a noun phrase, and it is the subject of the verb phrase *é portuguesa* 'is Portuguese.' The nominal *pianista* is the head of the noun phrase, and it is called the **antecedent** of the relative pronoun.

Note

[1]In English this is not always true, e.g., *all* **men** *will die* <u>*who make an attempt on our king's life*</u>. But in Portuguese the antecedent must occur immediately before the relative clause: *todos os* **homens** <u>*que atentarem contra a vida de nosso rei*</u> *morrerão*.

Some relative clauses have no overt head, e.g.,

<u>*Quem quiser ir ao concerto*</u> *pode pegar um bilhete na porta.*
'Whoever wants to attend the concert may get a ticket at the door.'

Here *quem quiser ir ao concerto* 'whoever wants to attend the concert' is a relative clause, but there is no preceding head, and therefore the relative pronoun has no antecedent. The entity referred to is implicit, and the referent is indeterminate: *quem* 'who' refers to a nonidentified person, *o que* 'what' to a nonidentified thing, etc. Headless relative clauses are introduced by *quem* 'who(ever),' *o que* 'what(ever),' *quanto* 'as much as,' and *onde* 'where,' e.g.,

<u>*O que você tentar*</u> *você vai conseguir.*
'Whatever you try, you'll get.'

Vou para <u>*onde ninguém vai me achar*</u>.
'(I) am going where nobody will find me.'

The verb in relative clauses may be in the subjunctive or in the indicative, and this difference in mood corresponds to a difference in meaning. The difference may be stated as follows:

> In relative clauses, the indicative is used to express a belief on the part of the speaker that the NP containing the relative clause refers to a specific, existent entity; the subjunctive is used when the enclosing NP refers to a hypothetical, not necessarily existent, entity.

Returning to our examples, we have:

> *A pianista que* ___**tocou**___ *ontem é portuguesa.*
> **indicative**
> 'The pianist who played yesterday is Portuguese.'

Here the verb of the relative clause is in the indicative, and the sentence deals with a real person, presumed to exist. Compare with

> *A pianista que* ___**tocar**___ ___*nesta sala*___ *vai ficar decepcionada.*
> **subjunctive**
> 'The (= any) pianist who plays in this room will be disappointed.'

The noun phrase *a pianista que tocar nesta sala* does not refer to a specific person, but rather to any person found in the situation described; that is, *whoever* plays in this room will be disappointed. It is not even understood that some person will, in fact, play in this room; *if* this happens, disappointment will ensue.

Another example is

> *Estou procurando uma secretária que* ___*tem*___ *cabelo ruivo.*
> **indicative**
> '(I) am looking for a secretary who has red hair.'

> *Estou procurando uma secretária que* ___*tenha*___ *cabelo ruivo.*
> **subjunctive**
> '(I) am looking for a (= any) red-haired secretary.'

In the first sentence (with the indicative), the speaker refers to a specific person, presumed to exist. In the second sentence (with the subjunctive), the speaker merely gives the description of what he is looking for, with no specific person in mind, and it may even turn out that no red-haired secretary exists. This semantic difference cannot be expressed in English by means of the subordinate verb—although, of course, it may be expressed by other means, e.g.,

> 'I am looking for a secretary, and she has red hair.'

as against

> 'I am looking for any red-haired secretary.'

15.8 The future subjunctive

Since the future subjunctive is very different from any existing verb form of English, it may be useful, at the risk of being redundant, to summarize the conditions under which it is used. The future subjunctive is used in two contexts:

a. after certain connectives, namely, those in group 2 (section 15.6.2), e.g., *como* 'as,' *quando* 'when,' and with *se* 'if,' when the main verb has future or imperative meaning. Examples:

> *Por favor, me ligue **logo que** você puder.*
> 'Please call me as soon as you can.'

> ***Sempre que** chover, esta cobertura vai se abrir automaticamente.*
> 'Whenever it rains, this cover will open automatically.'

b. in relative clauses, when the enclosing NP refers to a hypothetical, not necessarily existent, entity, and the situation is understood to have future reference. Examples:

> *Eles vão roubar tudo o que puderem.*
> 'They will steal all they can.'

> *Coloque aqui as peças que apresentarem algum defeito.*
> 'Put the parts that show some defect here.'

15.9 Subjunctive induced by negation

There is still one important factor that induces the appearance of the subjunctive, namely, negation. With verbs, it often happens that the affirmative form requires the indicative, but the negative accepts (but never requires) the subjunctive. The most common example is *achar* 'to think,' e.g.,

> *Eu acho que o cantor está agradando.* [**cf.** * *Eu acho que o cantor esteja agradando.*]
>   **indicative**   **subjunctive**
> 'I think that the singer is making a good impression.'

but

> *Eu não acho que o cantor está / esteja agradando.*
>   **indicative subjunctive**
> 'I don't think that the singer is making a good impression.'

There is no difference in meaning between the two versions of the sentence.

This does not happen with all verbs; with *ver* 'to see' only the indicative is possible, even when the verb is negated:

Eu não vi que o cantor   <u>*estava*</u>   /   **<u>estivesse</u>*   *agradando.*
                         indicative   subjunctive
'I didn't see that the singer was making a good impression.'

Some of the most common verbs that behave like *achar* (indicative when affirmative, indicative or subjunctive when negated) are

alegar	'to allege'
anunciar	'to announce'
comunicar	'to communicate'
confirmar	'to confirm'
contar	'to tell'
informar	'to inform'
mencionar	'to mention'
revelar	'to disclose'
sonhar	'to dream'

As we see, most of these verbs express "ways of saying," that is, they are verbs of communication.

Now, turning to **connectives:** when *porque* 'because' or *que* 'that' are negated (that is, when they are preceded by the negative particle *não*) the following subordinate clause must be in the subjunctive—although, as we saw in 15.6, *porque* requires the indicative when affirmative. Examples are as follows:

Ela sorriu, **não porque**   <u>*tivesse*</u>   *gostado.*
                            subjunctive
'She smiled, but not because she had enjoyed (it).'

*Preciso te castigar—**não que** isso me   dê   prazer.*
subjunctive
'(I) must punish you—not that this gives me [any] pleasure.'

15.10 The subjunctive in the spoken language

The description given in the preceding sections of the uses of the subjunctive applies to the modern written language and to the more formal varieties of the spoken language. But in the spontaneous speech of even educated Brazilian speakers the subjunctive has a more restricted use, and in particular the present subjunctive tends to disappear. The process is not equally advanced in all parts of the country; the subjunctive seems to be better preserved in the northeast than in Minas Gerais or in the south. The following notes should, then, be taken as preliminary indications; the student who wants to keep on the safe side is advised to use the subjunctive in the traditional way.

The difference between the two moods when in a relative clause (described in 15.7) is not equally felt by all Brazilians; for many, there is no semantic difference at all, and these persons normally use the indicative in all cases. For instance, we saw in 15.7 that there is a difference in meaning between the sentences

Estou procurando uma secretária que   tem   cabelo ruivo.
indicative
'(I) am looking for a secretary who has red hair.'

Estou procurando uma secretária que   tenha   cabelo ruivo.
subjunctive
'(I) am looking for a red-haired secretary.'

Here, the indicative marks the referent of the noun phrase (that is, the secretary) as presumed to exist in fact, whereas with the subjunctive the noun phrase is understood as a mere description of what the subject is looking for. Many speakers, however, use only the indicative in relative clauses, which then becomes ambiguous between the two meanings (just as it is in English).

In certain regions (Minas Gerais, for instance) one hears very often the indicative used with verbs that, in the standard language, require the subjunctive. Thus, for standard

Eu quero que você me   ajude.
subjunctive
'I want you to help me [literally, I want that you help me].'

many Mineiros will say

> *Eu quero que você me   ajuda.*   **SpBr**
> **indicative**
>
> 'id.'

This use of the indicative never appears in writing, but it is frequent in the speech of people of all classes. It occurs with all verbs except *ser* and *estar,* which keep their subjunctive form even in this context:

> *Eu quero que você seja feliz.* [**not** * *Eu quero que você é feliz.*]
> 'I want you to be happy.'

It is important to reiterate that this retraction in the use of the subjunctive is much more advanced in the case of the present subjunctive than in the case of the imperfect or the future subjunctive. For the latter two tenses the standard use, as described in this chapter, is normal also in the spoken language.

16

Uses of the Infinitive

16.1 Character of the Portuguese infinitive

The infinitive (*amar, vender, partir,* etc.) is very widely used in Portuguese. In many cases it is used in contexts in which English employs an infinitive or a gerund, and the two languages are similar in most of these cases; but the Portuguese infinitive has certain idiosyncrasies, which will be pointed out at the appropriate points. The infinitive is also used, in restricted contexts, in main clauses (see chapter 14 above); here we will be concerned with its use in subordinate clauses.

The infinitive has been called a **nominal** form of the verb, meaning that it has some characteristics of a verb and some of a nominal.[1] It is "verbal" in that it can have a subject, an object, etc., as normal verb forms do (in Portuguese it can even, as we will see, agree with its subject); and it is "nominal" in that it can occur as the head of a noun phrase.

Note

**[1]In spite of its dual nature, the infinitive is included in grammars together with the forms of the verb because it is morphologically part of the verb paradigm.

16.1.1 The infinitive as head of a noun phrase

If there is a key to the use of the infinitive in Portuguese, it is its nominal character. The construction headed by the infinitive is a noun phrase and occurs in contexts in which regular (noninfinitive) noun phrases can occur. In

There is a subject; it's Big Pro [handwritten]

Tomar café de manhã é uma tradição brasileira.
'Drinking coffee in the morning is a Brazilian tradition.'

Subordinate clause [handwritten]

the infinitive *tomar* (which corresponds here to an English gerund, *drinking*) has an object (*café*), thus behaving like a verb; but it is also the head of the NP *tomar café de manhã* 'drinking coffee in the morning'—which, in its turn, is the subject of *é uma tradição brasileira* 'is a Brazilian tradition.' In the same context we may have a noninfinitive noun phrase, e.g.,

> *O carnaval é uma tradição brasileira.*
> 'Carnival is a Brazilian tradition.'

In *tomar café de manhã é uma tradição brasileira* the infinitive is (the head of) a **subject**—and behaves, therefore, as a nominal. The clause headed by an infinitive can occur in any of the syntactic functions of an NP, e.g.,

as a **subject:**

> *Perdoar é divino.*
> 'To forgive is divine.'

> *Nadar é bom para a saúde.*
> 'Swimming is good for (your) health.'

as an **object:**

> *Todos nós detestamos almoçar muito cedo.*
> 'We all hate eating lunch too early.'

> *O velhinho sabia fazer bonecas.*
> 'The old man knew how to make dolls.'

as the **complement of a preposition:**

> *Ela não conhece a alegria de ter um filho.*
> 'She does not know the joy of having a child.'

Oito hóspedes chegaram sem avisar.
'Eight guests arrived without warning.'

as the **complement of the verb *ser* 'to be':**

Meu maior medo é quebrar uma perna.
'My greatest fear is to break a leg.'

The infinitive in any of these functions may be preceded by a determiner and quali-
fied by a modifier, e.g.,

subordination

Ninguém suporta esse seu reclamar constante.
'Nobody can stand your constant complaining [literally, this your complaining].'

Ela gostava de ouvir o cantar dos passarinhos.
'She liked to listen to (the) singing of the birds.'

A vida dele é um eterno pedir favores.
'His life is a permanent asking (of) favors.'

The infinitive with a determiner and/or a modifier, however, is not very common in the
colloquial language, being largely confined to writing.

As we've seen, the Portuguese infinitive may correspond to the English infinitive or
to the gerund. And it may be observed that in all these cases the infinitive clause may be replaced by a noninfinitive noun phrase, e.g.,

O perdão é divino. [**cf.** *Perdoar é divino.*]
'Forgiveness is divine.'

O exercício físico é bom para a saúde. [**cf.** *Nadar é bom para a saúde.*]
'Physical exertion is good for (your) health.'

and so on.

In some cases, an English *that*-clause may be translated as a Portuguese infinitive:

Meu medo é o preço aumentar.
'My fear is that the price might go up.'

In English, *that*-clauses are preferred whenever the subordinate clause has an overt subject;
but in Portuguese the infinitive is very freely used in this case, as shown in the above ex-

ample. When no overt subject appears in the subordinate, we may have the infinitive in both languages:

> *Meu medo é <u>ficar doente</u>.*
> 'My fear is to fall ill.'

Here the (elliptical) subject of the subordinate is the idea of "I," which is introduced previously by the presence of the possessive *meu* 'my.' Now, in

> *Meu medo é <u>o preço aumentar</u>.*
> 'My fear is that the price might go up.'

the subject of the subordinate is *o preço* 'the price,' a concept not previously introduced; therefore, English prefers to use a *that*-clause, whereas in Portuguese we find an infinitive with the overt subject *o preço* 'the price.'[1]

❋

Note

[1]A noninfinitive clause is also possible: *Meu medo é que <u>o preço aumente</u>.*

In some cases, the infinitive does not correspond to a nominal—for instance, when it is used with an auxiliary (*vou <u>correr</u>* '(I) will <u>run</u>'), or with a modal verb (*devemos <u>ajudar</u>* '(we) must <u>help</u>'), or in the construction exemplified by *um livro difícil de <u>ler</u>* 'a book hard to <u>read</u>.' In all these cases, English and Portuguese are similar, so they present no serious learning problems.

Note that the Portuguese gerund can *never* be used as the head of an NP; that is, sentences like

>
> * <u>Nadando</u> é bom para a saúde.*
> 'Swimming is good for the health.'

> * Eu adoro <u>tocando</u> piano.*
> 'I enjoy playing piano.'

are totally unacceptable. Whenever the English gerund is used as the head of an NP (and is, therefore, a subject, an object, or the complement of a preposition) it must be translated in Portuguese as an infinitive (the uses of the Portuguese gerund are described in chapter 17).

16.1.2 The personal infinitive

Before we examine the conditions of the use of the infinitive, a preliminary note on the "personal infinitive" may be useful. The Portuguese infinitive has two remarkable characteristics: it very often has an overt subject, and it agrees with it. For example,

> *Foi uma alegria <u>meus filhos me **visitarem**</u>.*
> 'It was a joy (for) my children to visit me.'

Here the infinitive (*visitarem* 'to visit') agrees with *meus filhos* 'my children,' which is then called its subject; when the infinitive agrees it is termed **personal infinitive.** The conditions under which infinitive agreement takes place are described in chapter 35 and will not be considered in this section. Apart from the fact that it agrees, the personal infinitive is a normal infinitive, and its occurrence results from the general rules given in this chapter.

16.2 When (and how) to use the infinitive

The verb of the main clause is the element that determines whether and how the infinitive is to occur in the subordinate clause. In what follows I systematically present each group of verbs, with the conditions they impose on the occurrence of the infinitive. This, of course, is one more example of the general fact that the verb in the main clause governs the mood of verbs in the subordinate clause. Each of the following sections considers the occurrence of the infinitive with a class of verbs; and each is titled according to a typical member of each class.

16.2.1 With *querer* 'to want'

> With some verbs, like *querer* 'to want,' the subjunctive is obligatory when the subjects of the main and of the subordinate clauses are different; but if the subjects are to be understood as identical ("coreferential") the infinitive, without an overt subject, is obligatory in the subordinate.

This construction is found in all Romance languages. For instance,

*Tia Carolina quer que <u>você **faça** aquele famoso bolo</u>.*
'Aunt Carolina wants you to make that famous cake   [literally, . . . wants that you make . . .].'

*Tia Carolina quer **fazer** <u>aquele famoso bolo</u>.*
'Aunt Carolina wants to make that famous cake.'

In the first sentence the subject of the main clause is *Tia Carolina* 'Aunt Carolina,' and the subject of the subordinate is *você* 'you'; therefore, both subjects are expressed, and the subordinate must be in the subjunctive. In the second sentence, the two subjects are to be understood as corefential—that is, Aunt Carolina wants to make the cake herself; therefore, the subordinate has no overt subject, and its verb is in the infinitive.

This type of alternation happens with the following verbs:

querer	'to want'
desejar	'to wish'
detestar	'to hate'
esperar	'to hope'

16.2.2 With *tentar* 'to try'

With other verbs, like *tentar* 'to try,' the two subjects are necessarily coreferential:

*Ela tentou **vencer** o concurso.*
'She tried to win the contest.'

Sentences with *tentar* 'to try' and different subjects for the two clauses, like

** Ela tentou que você **vencesse** o concurso.*
* She tried for you to win the contest.

are unacceptable, both in English and in Portuguese. Since the same rule seen above for *querer* applies to these verbs, they end up occurring always with the infinitive:

With verbs like *tentar* 'to try,' the subordinate is always in the infinitive.

Verbs that behave like *tentar* are

ameaçar	'to threaten'
buscar	'to seek, to try'
procurar	'to seek, to try'
dever	'must'
ousar	'dare'
costumar	'usually'[1]
saber	'can'[2]

Notes

[1] *Costumar* is a verb, but it expresses an idea that is normally expressed in English with the aid of adverbs like *usually, normally,* etc.:

> *Meu patrão costuma insultar todo mundo.*
> 'My boss usually insults everybody.'

The English construction is with the adverb + the verb expressing the main idea (*usually insults*); the Portuguese construction is with *costumar* + the infinitive of the main verb (*costuma insultar*).

[2] *Saber* has two meanings: it may denote a skill or ability, as in

> *Ela sabe falar russo.*
> 'She can speak Russian.'

In this reading *saber* is usually translated as *can*, and patterns like *tentar*. *Saber* may also denote information-getting or -possessing, as in

Ela sabe que o marido bebe.
'She knows that (her) husband drinks.'

In this reading *saber* does not function like *tentar,* but requires the indicative in the subordinate.

16.2.3 With *ver* 'to see'

Besides being the head of a noun phrase, as seen in the preceding section, the infinitive appears in other constructions. The most important of these is with a group of verbs that we may call **verbs of perception** because most of them express some kind of sensorial perception: *ver* 'to see,' *ouvir* 'to hear,' *sentir* 'to feel'; and also some **verbs of suasion** (see 15.2), like *mandar* 'to order,' *deixar* 'to let,' and *dizer* when meaning 'to order.' These verbs take a finite *que*-clause (with the indicative if the main clause has a verb of perception, with the subjunctive if it has a verb of suasion) or an infinitive:

> With verbs like *ver* 'to see,' the infinitive or the indicative may appear in the subordinate, but there is a difference in meaning between the two constructions.

Taking *ver* 'to see' as an example, we may say

*O guarda viu que o rapaz **pulou** a cerca.*
'The policeman saw that the boy jumped over the fence.'

Besides this construction, we may have

*O guarda viu o rapaz **pular** a cerca.*
'The policeman saw the boy jump over the fence.'

Here English and Portuguese are similar; as the glosses show, there is a semantic difference between the two constructions. The first sentence (in either language) expresses some kind of perception that does not have to come from direct experience: the policeman may have seen that the boy jumped over the fence because of marks on the top of the posts, for instance. Now, the sentences in the second set express the fact that the policeman saw the boy as he jumped over the fence. In other words, in the first sentences the object of *viu* 'saw' is *que o rapaz pulou a cerca* 'that the boy jumped over the fence,' which denotes a fact. But in the latter sentences the object of *viu* 'saw' is *o rapaz* 'the boy,' which denotes a person; that is why, presumably, we understand *viu o rapaz* 'saw the boy' as a semantic unit in the second group, but not in the first one.

All verbs accepting these two constructions show a clear semantic difference between the two, e.g.,

> *O guarda ouviu que <u>o rapaz **pulou** a cerca</u>.*
> 'The policeman heard that the boy jumped over the fence.'

Here, in both languages, the receptor understands that the policeman heard a report that the boy had jumped over the fence; but in

> *O guarda ouviu o rapaz **pular** <u>a cerca</u>.*
> 'The policeman heard the boy jump over the fence.'

we understand that the policeman heard the noise made by the boy when he jumped over the fence.

With verbs of suasion, English prefers the infinitive, while Portuguese allows both the infinitive and *que* with the subjunctive—again, with a semantic difference:

> *A diretora mandou que <u>Maria **ficasse** no porão</u>.*
> 'The director gave orders (to the effect) that Maria stay in the basement.'

> *A diretora mandou Maria **ficar** <u>no porão</u>.*
> 'The director told Maria to stay in the basement.'

The second Portuguese sentence, but not the first, implies that the order was given personally to Maria. To see this more clearly, we may take the following sentence:

> * *A diretora mandou os barris **ficarem** <u>no porão</u>.*
> * 'The director told the barrels to stay in the basement.'

This sentence is odd because we have to understand that she addressed the barrels directly. The strangeness disappears if we use the *que*-construction:

> *A diretora mandou que <u>os barris **ficassem** no porão</u>.*
> 'The director gave orders (to the effect) that the barrels stay in the basement.'

The infinitive construction, as found with the above verbs of perception and suasion, has some peculiar features, which may be mentioned here—although they are not precisely a learning difficulty, because here again English and Portuguese are very similar. These peculiarities arise from the fact that the NP immediately preceding the infinitive behaves in some respects like the object of the main verb and in other respects like the subject of the infinitive.

Thus, the NP in question may be an objective pronoun:[1]

*A diretora _me_ mandou **ficar** no porão.*
'The director ordered me to stay in the basement.'

*O guarda _o_ viu **pular** a cerca.*   **Wr**
'The policeman saw him jump over the fence.'

Note

[1]In which case it usually appears before the main verb; see chapter 29 for the syntactic behavior of clitic pronouns.

This fact seems to indicate that the NP in question is the object of the main verb. On the other hand, the same NP behaves like the subject of the infinitive because the infinitive may (optionally; see chapter 35) agree with it:

O guarda viu os rapazes _pular / pularem a cerca_.
'The policeman saw the boys jump over the fence.'

Here both versions are equally acceptable.[1]

Note

[1]In these cases, to be sure, there is a lot of variation among speakers; I have found some who reject the impersonal infinitive in *o guarda viu os rapazes pular a cerca,* and some who accept it without restriction.

Also, when the NP is a personal pronoun, it may (especially in the spoken language) appear as a subject form:

Deixa <u>eu ficar mais um pouco</u>.   **SpBr**
'Let me stay a little longer.'

Mandei <u>ela sair daqui imediatamente</u>.   **SpBr**
'(I) ordered her to get out of here immediately.'

In the written language one would find *deixe-<u>me</u> ficar mais um pouco,* with the objective form of the pronoun.[1]

Note

**[1] The double behavior of the NP before the infinitive in this construction is a traditional problem in syntactic theory; it has received several superficially different solutions, which all boil down to the observation that the NP that precedes the infinitive is the object of the main verb or the subject of the subordinate one, depending on the angle you look at it.

The fact that the preinfinitive NP behaves in some ways like an object is also shown by the (limited) possibility of its occurring as the subject of a passive sentence, as in

<u>Este teatro</u> *foi mandado restaurar pelo governo de Minas Gerais.*
'This theater was ordered rebuilt by the government of Minas Gerais.'

This construction is not usual nowadays, being apparently confined to some formulas.
The most important verbs that pattern like *ver* and *mandar* are the following:

ver	'to see'
ouvir	'to hear'
sentir	'to feel'
mandar	'to order'
deixar	'to let'
fazer	'to force'[1]

Note

[1] *Fazer* also means 'to make.' It means 'to force' when it appears in the construction studied in this section, e.g., *A polícia fez o suspeito assinar uma confissão* 'The police forced the suspect to sign a confession.'

16.2.4 Preposition-taking verbs

Some verbs of suasion pattern just like *ver* 'to see' and *mandar* 'to order,' with the difference that they require the presence of a preposition before the preinfinitive NP, or before the infinitive itself, or both.

permitir   'to allow'
Permitir 'to allow' requires the preposition *a* before the NP; compare the following sentences with *ver* and *permitir*, respectively:

> *O cozinheiro viu <u>Manuel</u> entrar na cozinha.*
> 'The cook saw Manuel go into the kitchen.'

> *O cozinheiro permitiu <u>a Manuel</u> entrar na cozinha.*
> 'The cook allowed Manuel to go into the kitchen.'

Apart from the presence of the preposition, the two constructions are identical.
       Verbs that pattern like *permitir* are

receitar	'to prescribe'
recomendar	'to recommend'

proibir   'to forbid'
Proibir patterns like *ver* but requires the preposition *de* before the infinitive (no preposition before the preceding NP); compare

> *O cozinheiro viu Manuel <u>entrar na cozinha</u>.*
> 'The cook saw Manuel go into the kitchen.'

O cozinheiro proibiu Manuel de entrar na cozinha.
'The cook forbade Manuel to go into the kitchen.'

pedir 'to ask for'

Pedir 'to ask for' requires two prepositions: *a* before the NP and *para* before the infinitive; again, comparing the two constructions, we have

O cozinheiro viu Manuel entrar na cozinha.
'The cook saw Manuel go into the kitchen.'

O cozinheiro pediu a Manuel para entrar na cozinha.
'The cook asked Manuel to go into the kitchen.'

This construction is ambiguous, in that we may understand that either the cook or Manuel is to go into the kitchen.

aconselhar 'to advise'

Aconselhar 'to advise' requires the preposition *a,* which may occur *either* before the infinitive or before the preceding NP:

O cozinheiro aconselhou Manuel a entrar na cozinha.
O cozinheiro aconselhou a Manuel entrar na cozinha.
'The cook advised Manuel to go into the kitchen.'

The two constructions are synonymous; the first is probably the most common.

16.2.5 Free alternation

With many verbs and connectives the infinitive can be freely substituted for the indicative or the subjunctive. An instance of the infinitive alternating with the subjunctive is

*Lamento profundamente que sua firma **tenha** falido.*
*Lamento profundamente sua firma **ter** falido.*
'(I) deeply regret that your company went bankrupt.'

These two sentences are synonymous and equally natural. The infinitive can also, less frequently, alternate with the indicative:

*Meu grande problema é que eu **ganho** muito pouco.*
*Meu grande problema é eu **ganhar** muito pouco.*
'My great problem is that I earn very little.'

Here again, the two versions can be considered synonymous.

In the above examples, the verb (*lamentar* 'to regret,' *ser* 'to be,' respectively) is the governing element, which determines whether or not the parallel infinitive construction is possible.

A **connective** can also govern the possibility of free alternation with the infinitive; for instance, we may have both the subjunctive and the infinitive after *antes de* 'before':

> *O cachorro morreu antes que <u>o veterinário</u> **chegasse**.*
> *O cachorro morreu antes de <u>o veterinário</u> **chegar**.*[1,2]
> 'The dog died before the vet arrived.'

Notes

[1]Observe that the particle *de* is omitted before the conjunction *que*. This is valid for other connectives formed with *de* or *a*, such as *depois de* 'after,' *de maneira a* 'so that,' but not for *a fim de* 'in order to,' which always keeps its *de*, even before *que*; on this, see 32.3.

[2]Here *de* + o is not contracted into *do* (as per the rule stated in 5.1.2) because *de* is considered to come before the whole clause *o veterinário chegar*—in other words, there is a clause boundary between *de* and *o*. On the other hand, in the spoken language (and increasingly in writing) the contraction occurs nevertheless, in spite of some opposition from teachers and grammarians, so that one hears, and reads, *antes do veterinário chegar*.

But we cannot have an infinitive after *logo* 'as soon as':

> *O cachorro morreu logo que <u>o veterinário</u> **chegou**.*
> * *O cachorro morreu logo <u>o veterinário</u> **chegar**.*
> 'The dog died as soon as the vet arrived.'

We saw above that the infinitive behaves in many ways like a nominal, and this shows in its selection of connectives. We may state the following general rule:

Whenever a connective that occurs before a *que*-clause can also occur before a nonsentential NP, it can also occur with an infinitive clause; connectives that cannot occur before nonsentential NPs also cannot occur with infinitive clauses.

Thus, returning to our examples above, we saw that *antes* 'before' occurs both with *que*-clauses and with infinitive clauses:

> *O cachorro morreu antes que <u>o veterinário</u> **chegasse**.*
> *O cachorro morreu antes de <u>o veterinário</u> **chegar**.*
> 'The dog died before the vet arrived.'

This derives from the fact that *antes* can also appear before a nonsentential NP:

> *O cachorro morreu antes do gato.*
> 'The dog died before the cat (died).'

The connectives that can occur with infinitives (and, consequently, with nonsentential NPs) are listed below. Some of them end in a particle (usually called a preposition); this particle is omitted before *que,* except with *a fim de,* which keeps it:

> *O veterinário foi chamado a fim de que examinasse o cachorro.*
> 'The vet was called to examine the dog.'

These are the connectives that can occur with an infinitive clause:

a fim de	'in order to'
antes de	'before'
depois de	'after'
para	'in order to'
sem	'without'
até	'until'

The rule has two exceptions: *de maneira a* and *de modo a,* both meaning 'so that,' are connectives that cannot occur with nonsentential NPs, yet admit of the infinitive. These connectives also lose their *a* before *que:*

Coloque a tampa de maneira que cubra a lente.
Coloque a tampa de maneira a cobrir a lente.
'Put the lid so that it covers the lens.'

16.3 Other infinitive constructions

We have just studied the main constructions in which the Portuguese infinitive appears. Apart from these, it is also used in several minor constructions that I review here.

16.3.1 *Difícil de ler* 'difficult to read'

The following construction occurs in English and Portuguese:

Este livro é difícil de ler.
'This book is difficult to read.'

The only difference is that Portuguese requires the preposition *de* before the infinitive. This construction is possible with a group of nominals, all of which express a judgment about the easiness or pleasantness of a task:

difícil	'difficult'
duro	'tough'
fácil	'easy'
bom	'good'
ruim	'bad'
agradável	'pleasant'
desagradável	'unpleasant'

16.3.2 With auxiliaries and modals

As we saw in chapter 13, the infinitive appears after the auxiliary *ir* to form the most usual future form, as in

> *Marília <u>vai sair</u> para São Paulo às quatro.*
> 'Marília will leave for São Paulo at four.'

This sequence of *ir* + infinitive is one of the normal ways to express the future in modern Portuguese.

Another use of the infinitive with an auxiliary is an alternative form of the *estar* + gerund sequence; thus, one can say

> *Está chovendo.*
> '(It) is raining.'

The gerund in this construction can be replaced by *a* + infinitive:

> *Está <u>a chover</u>.*
> 'id.'

The construction with *a* + infinitive is usual in Portugal; in Brazil, only the gerund is used in speaking, but *a* + infinitive sometimes occurs in writing.

Modals are verbs (or sequences of a verb + a particle, as in *ter que*) that occur only with a subjectless infinitive or gerund, e.g.,

> *O teto <u>pode cair</u> a qualquer momento.*
> 'The roof may fall at any moment.'

> *A chuva <u>começou a incomodar</u> todo mundo.*
> 'The rain started to bother everybody.'

> *Marcelo <u>acabou telefonando</u>.*
> 'Marcelo ended up calling.'

Modals and their use are studied in chapter 22.

16.3.3 Idioms

The infinitive appears in some idioms; the most important are listed below.

ao + infinitive
The sequence *ao* + infinitive is used as a synonym of *quando* 'when' + indicative; thus, the following sentences are equivalent:

> *Ela percebeu tudo <u>ao entrar no quarto</u>.*
> *Ela percebeu tudo <u>quando entrou no quarto</u>.*
> 'She realized everything when she entered the room.'

no + infinitive

In the colloquial language, we find *no* + infinitive, with the same meaning as *ao* + infinitive:

> *No virar de lado, todos os pratos quebraram.*   **SpBr**
> 'When they turned on their side, all the dishes broke.'

por + infinitive

Por + infinitive denotes an activity that was programed but has not yet been performed:

> *Tenho ainda uns quatro capítulos por escrever.*
> '(I) still have four chapters to write.'

Some idioms are composed of a modal with a fixed following verb, e.g.,

> *Ela fez por merecer uns tapas.*
> 'She did something that deserves a few slaps.'

We might consider *fazer por* as a modal like the ones seen in the preceding section; but it occurs only with *merecer* 'to deserve,' not freely with other verbs. For this reason I prefer to list the whole sequence, *fazer por merecer,* as an idiom. Another example is

> *O conferencista deu a entender que estava irritado.*
> 'The lecturer hinted that he was annoyed.'

Dar a in this reading occurs only with *entender*.

article + infinitive

Being a nominal form, the infinitive can also occur preceded by an article. This, to be sure, is a pretty rare construction and occurs preferably in writing:

> *O comprar por prazer é um privilégio.*   **Wr**
> '(The) buying for pleasure is a privilege.'

> *Ouvia-se por toda parte um zumbir de abelhas.*
> 'One heard everywhere a buzzing of bees.'

que + infinitive

We saw above that the conjunction *que* and the infinitive are mutually exclusive: whenever we have *que,* the following verb must be in the subjunctive or in the indicative. Yet there is a curious construction with *que* + infinitive, exemplified by

> *Tenho muito que fazer.*
> '(I) have a lot to do.'

I do not believe this *que* should be analyzed as a conjunction, though. It is most probably a reduced form of the free relative *o que* 'what,' which is confirmed by the possibility of adding *o* to the sentence:

> *Tenho muito o que fazer.*
> 'id.'

This construction occurs normally only in this context, that is, after *ter muito / pouco / bastante* 'to have a lot / little / enough to.'

17

Gerund, Participle, Imperative

17.1 Gerund

As noted previously, the use of the gerund (*amando, vendendo, partindo*) is more restricted in Portuguese than in English. For instance, the sentences below have the gerund in English but other forms in Portuguese:

> *Swimming is good for your health.*
> Port: **infinitive**—*Nadar é bom para a saúde.*

> *My uncle finally stopped smoking.*
> Port: **infinitive (with preposition)**—*Meu tio finalmente parou de fumar.*

> *We have never visited a Spanish-speaking country.*
> Port: **relative clause**—*Nunca visitamos um país que fala espanhol.*
>   or ***de* + NP**—*Nunca visitamos um país de fala espanhola.*

> *He had a face resembling a cabbage.*
> Port: **relative clause**—*Ele tinha uma cara que parecia um repolho.*

In what follows I try to present the cases in which the gerund is used in Portuguese, both when it corresponds to the English gerund and when it corresponds to other English forms.

17.1.1 With auxiliaries and modals

As discussed in chapter 13, the gerund is used with four auxiliaries; I give the list below, with examples showing the meaning of each:

estar

> *Estou trabalhando demais.*
> '(I) am working too much.'

andar

> *Ando trabalhando demais.*
> '(I) have been working too much.'

vir

> *Venho trabalhando demais.*
> '(I) have been working too much.'

ir—As observed in chapter 13, *ir* + gerund expresses an event considered in the context of another event, e.g.,

> *Enquanto você frita as batatas, eu <u>vou comendo</u>.*
> 'While you fry the potatoes, I eat (them).'

The gerund also occurs with some modals, e.g.,

> *Eles <u>acabaram concordando</u> conosco.*
> 'They ended up agreeing with us.'

See chapter 22 for a detailed study of modals.

17.1.2 Adverbial use of the gerund

The gerund is frequently used as an adverbial element, usually denoting something that takes place at the same time as the event described by the main verb. For instance,

> *Ela entrou no salão <u>gritando</u>.*
> 'She entered the room yelling.'

Seu irmão telefonou <u>pedindo ajuda</u>.
'Your brother phoned asking for help.'

Antônio encontrou Bruna <u>passeando na praia</u>.
'Antônio met Bruna (while) walking on the beach.'

In the last example the gerund (*passeando*) is ambiguous because it may mean either that Antônio or that Bruna was walking on the beach. This happens whenever the subordinate has a gerund, and the main sentence has a subject and an object.

The gerund is also used to translate the English construction *by* + gerund:

O ferreiro dobra o ferro <u>esquentando-o</u>.
'The blacksmith folds the iron by heating it.'

The gerund is often used to express a cause, as in

<u>Estando sem emprego</u>, mandei meu currículo para várias escolas.
'Being jobless, I sent my C.V. to several schools.'

Or it may express just a concomitant event:

<u>Gabriela chegando</u>, tudo vai ficar mais fácil.
'When Gabriela arrives, everything will become easier.'

17.1.3 With verbs of perception

The infinitive construction with verbs of perception studied in section 16.2.3 has a parallel with the gerund, e.g.,

*O guarda viu o rapaz **pular** <u>a cerca</u>.*   [with the infinitive]
*O guarda viu o rapaz **pulando** <u>a cerca</u>.*   [with the gerund]
'The policeman saw the boy jump over the fence [or, jumping over the fence].'

With verbs of perception (*ver* 'to see,' *ouvir* 'to hear,' *sentir* 'to feel') both constructions are possible, and there is no difference in meaning between them—the same happens in English, as seen in the two glosses given above.

With verbs of suasion, however, only the infinitive is possible in this construction:

*A diretora mandou Maria **ficar** <u>no porão</u>.*
'The director told Maria to stay in the basement.'

but

** A diretora mandou Maria **ficando** <u>no porão</u>.*

17.1.4 With connectives

We saw in section 16.2.5 that the infinitive alternates freely with the subjunctive (or with the indicative) after certain connectives. Now, some connectives that occur before *que* + subjunctive can also occur (without *que*) with the gerund, without perceptible change in meaning:

> *Não vou à reunião mesmo que você insista.*　　**[subjunctive]**
> *Não vou à reunião mesmo você insistindo.*　　**[gerund]**
> '(I) am not going to the meeting, even if you insist.'

This alternation occurs with the connectives *mesmo* 'even if' and *nem* 'not even if':

> *Não vou à reunião nem que você insista.*　　**[subjunctive]**
> *Não vou à reunião nem você insistindo.*　　**[infinitive]**
> '(I) am not going to the meeting, not even if you insist.'

With *embora* 'although' (which occurs without *que*) the gerund alternates with the subjunctive only when the subordinate verb is understood to have the same subject as the main verb; thus, we may have

> *Embora desconfie de nós, ele vai nos ajudar.*
> *Embora desconfiando de nós, ele vai nos ajudar.*
> 'Although mistrusting us, he will help us.'

As can be seen, the gerund has no overt subject. Now, in the sentence below only the subjunctive, not the gerund, is possible:

> *Embora Patrícia desconfie de nós, vou pedir a ajuda dela.*
> 'Although Patrícia mistrusts us, (I) will ask for her help.'

The reason is that there is a subject in the subordinate clause (*Patrícia*).

17.2 Participle

17.2.1 With auxiliaries

The participle (*amado, vendido, partido*) corresponds closely to the English past participle: first, the participle is used with the auxiliary *ter* 'to have,' e.g.,

Muitos participantes tinham <u>chegado</u> antes da hora.
'Many participants had arrived ahead of time.'

The use of the participle with auxiliaries (*ter, haver*) is described in chapter 13.

Second, the participle is used (in both languages) to form the passive voice (with the auxiliary *ser*):

Este romance foi <u>escrito</u> por Machado de Assis.
'This novel was written by Machado de Assis.'

See chapter 21 for details about the formation of passive sentences.

In the two constructions given above, the Portuguese participle functions just like the English one, the only proviso being that it must agree with the subject when used in passive sentences; compare the passive given above with

Esta poesia foi <u>escrita</u> por Machado de Assis.
'This poem was written by Machado de Assis.'

In the first sentence, *escrito* is in the masculine because *romance* 'novel' is masculine; in the second, it is in the feminine in order to agree with the feminine *poesia* 'poem.'

When used with *ter, haver* the participle does not agree (in this Portuguese differs from French):

O bolo que eu tinha <u>feito</u> ficou horrível.
'The cake [**masculine singular**] that I had made was awful.'

As tortas que eu tinha <u>feito</u> ficaram horríveis.
'The pies [**feminine plural**] that I had made were awful.'

17.2.2 As a qualificative

The participle, apart from its use with auxiliaries, functions very much like a nominal—its traditional association with the verb being motivated by morphological considerations. Thus, a sequence like *foi escrita* 'was written' can be viewed as parallel, for agreement purposes, to *foi riquíssima* 'was very rich.' We find the participle in all the environments in which a nominal is used as a modifier or as a complement of verbs like *ser* 'to be,' *estar* 'to be,'[1] *ficar* 'to become,' etc.

Note

[1]For the difference between *ser* and *estar,* see chapter 22.

For example, we may say:

> *Esta porta está mal pintada.*
> 'This door is poorly painted.'

> *Vamos instalar uma porta pintada e uma envernizada.*
> '(We) are going to install a painted door and a varnished (one).'

Here again the two languages coincide, the only difference being the requirement in Portuguese that the participle agree.

17.2.3 Free participle

In the written language, one finds the participle used as an adjunct, meaning 'when . . . ,' or 'as soon as . . .' For instance,

> *Terminada a escavação, os operários foram dispensados.*
> 'As soon as the digging was finished [literally, finished the digging], the workers were dismissed.'

> *Resolvido o problema, ficamos sem ter o que fazer.*
> 'As soon as the problem was solved [literally, solved the problem], we had nothing else to do.'

When used in this construction, the participle always has a complement and cannot be used alone; and the whole construction sounds natural only when occurring at the beginning of the sentence.

17.3 Imperative

Formally, the imperative has its complexities (see chapter 11); but its use is very simple and parallels the use of the English imperative. It is used to convey orders, requests, or advice:

Sai daí imediatamente!   **SpBr** [*saia daí. . .* **Wr**]
'Get out of there immediately!'

Por favor, me passa o sal.   **SpBr** [*passe-me. . .* **Wr**]
'Pass me the salt, please.'

Toma uma aspirina que você vai se sentir melhor.   **SpBr** [*Tome. . .* **Wr**]
'Take an aspirin, you'll feel better.'

The imperative is most often used without a subject, as in the above examples; yet it can also take a subject, as in

Você lava o carro antes do almoço.   **SpBr** [*Você lave. . .*   **Wr**]
'(You) wash the car before lunch.'

O senhor vira à direita na próxima esquina.   **SpBr** [*O senhor vire. . .*   **Wr**]
'(You) turn right at the next corner.'

18

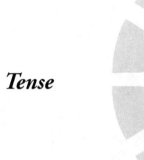

Tense

Tense has basically to do with the location of events in time. In Portuguese as in English, and in many other languages, the verb is enabled, through some special affixes and auxiliaries, to express time, as in

> *João trabalha aqui.* / *João trabalhava aqui.* / *João vai trabalhar aqui.*
> John works here.   /   John worked here.   /   John will work here.

As exemplified in these sentences, the basic tenses are the present, the past, and the future.

Upon this simple framework, each language builds a very rich system, including such complexities as expressing the relationship between two equally past events (one preceding the other); expressing immediate future as against a more remote future; depicting a past event as having occurred only once, or as occurring repeatedly, or during an extended period; viewing a present event as habitual or as simultaneous with the moment of speaking; and so on. Not all of these semantic ingredients are "tense," technically speaking (some of them are considered manifestations of "aspect"), but here they will be subsumed under the same label, which makes sense from a grammatical point of view—since aspect and tense are expressed by comparable devices in Portuguese.

Besides, tenses have a way of trespassing upon each other's territory, which contributes to complicate the general picture. Thus, in English one can express the future by using what is, morphologically, a present progressive tense, as in

I am calling her in a few minutes.

Likewise, Portuguese uses the present (in the simple form) to express an immediate future:

Eu te devolvo esse livro amanhã.
'I'll return this book to you tomorrow [literally, I return . . .].'

Portuguese and English do not differ too much as far as their resources for expressing tense are concerned. The main difference, and the main difficulty, is the fact that Portuguese, but not English, distinguishes two past tenses, perfect (here called the **preterit**) and imperfect.[1]

Note

[1]English reciprocates by distinguishing the simple past (*I did*) from the perfect past (*I have done*), a distinction that Portuguese speakers find difficult to grasp. As we will see, the formally similar opposition *eu fiz* vs. *eu tenho feito* is semantically very different.

18.1 Present

The **present tense** expresses, basically, ongoing events. We can distinguish two main forms, the **simple present:** *eu falo* 'I speak,' *eu vendo* 'I sell,' *eu durmo* 'I sleep,' and the **present progressive:** *eu estou falando* 'I am speaking,' *eu estou vendendo* 'I am selling,' *eu estou dormindo* 'I am sleeping.'[1]

Note

[1]**Progressive** is the traditional designation given to the sequence of the auxiliary *estar* plus a gerund. Thus, we may speak of the **present progressive** (*estou falando* '(I) am speaking'), **preterit progressive** (*estive falando* '(I) have been speaking'), **future progressive** (*estarei falando* '(I) will be speaking'), and so on.

18.1.1 The simple present

As in English,

> the simple present is used to express a habitual event, a permanent property, or a permanent state.

For example,

> *Os vizinhos sempre <u>fazem</u> barulho a esta hora.*
> 'The neighbors always make noise this time of the day.'

> *Carolina <u>toca</u> violão muito bem.*
> 'Carolina plays the guitar very well.'

> <u>*Chove*</u> *muito em Belém.*
> '(It) rains a lot in Belém.'

> *Minha filha <u>é</u> médica.*
> 'My daughter is (a) physician.'

> The simple present is also used to denote a general truth, which does not depend on time.

For example,

> *A água <u>ferve</u> a cem graus centígrados.*
> '(The) water boils at one hundred degrees Centigrade.'

In the above examples the event described is valid for the present moment, but also for a certain extension in the past and in the future. This is the basic meaning of the simple present. Note that the simple present in Portuguese is *not* used to express an event that is taking place at the moment of speaking; in this, Portuguese differs from French and is similar to English. Thus, a sentence like

> *Meu pai trabalha na garagem.*

does not mean 'My father is working in the garage (right now),' but rather 'My father (usually) works in the garage.' In order to express an event taking place at the moment of speaking one uses the present progressive, that is, *estar* + gerund, which exactly parallels English *be* + gerund:

> *Meu pai está trabalhando na garagem.*
> 'My father is working in the garage.'

Besides its main uses, described above, the simple present is also used in certain particular situations, namely,

To express the future

The simple present is commonly used to express futurity (usually along with a time expression that rules out ambiguity):

> *Amanhã bem cedo eu te telefono.*
> 'I'll call you tomorrow very early.'

The simple present cannot be used for events explicitly seen as very remote in the future. Thus, one says

> *O sol vai se extinguir* [or, *se extinguirá* **Wr**] *dentro de alguns bilhões de anos.*
> 'The sun will go out in a few billion years.'

but not

> ** O sol se extingue dentro de alguns bilhões de anos.*

Likewise, one says

> *Você vai morrer* [or *morrerá* **Wr**] *dentro de uns quarenta anos.*
> 'You will die in some forty years.'

but not

> ** Você <u>morre</u> dentro de uns quarenta anos.*

To express a past event

The simple present is sometimes used to express a past event (thus replacing the preterit tense). This happens, first, when one wishes to give the text a sense of lively action, as in

> *Entrei no quarto, e o que é que eu <u>vejo</u>? Anita rasgando todos os vestidos!*
> '(I) entered the bedroom, and what do I see? Anita tearing all the dresses!'

Second, the present is used in narrations of a historical character (this is sometimes termed the **historical present**); this use is found exclusively in the written language:

> *Em 1889 Dom Pedro <u>abdica</u> e é exilado.*   **Wr**
> 'In 1889 Dom Pedro abdicates and is exiled.'

As a polite way to ask for permission to do something

Here the present is used in situations where English usually has *shall*:

> *Te <u>trago</u> um cafezinho?*   **SpBr**
> 'Shall I bring you a coffee?'

After certain expressions

In sentences modified by a phrase indicating elapsed time, Portuguese uses the present if the condition described is still true, while English tends to use the present perfect:

> *Ele <u>é</u> uma pessoa doente desde 1995.*
> 'He has been a sick person since 1995.'

> *Desde que a mulher o abandonou, ele <u>vive</u> assim.*
> 'Since his wife left him, he has been living like that.'

> *Há doze dias que ele não <u>pára</u> de tossir.*
> 'He hasn't stopped coughing for twelve days [literally, There are twelve days . . .].'

> *Ele <u>mora</u> em Vitória há mais de dez anos.*
> 'He has lived in Vitória for more than ten years.'

With the verb *estar*

Finally, with the verb *estar* 'to be,' the simple present must be used to express a present condition, e.g.,

A porta <u>está</u> fechada.
'The door is closed.'

This is due, I suppose, to the impossibility of using *estar* as both an auxiliary and a main verb: * *A porta <u>está estando</u> fechada.*

18.1.2 The present progressive

> The present progressive is used to express an action or an event seen as
>
> simultaneous with the moment of speaking.

Examples are

Silêncio, porque os meninos <u>estão dormindo</u>.
'Silence, because the children are sleeping.'

Lucinha já <u>está fazendo</u> o almoço.
'Lucinha is already making lunch.'

Here Portuguese and English behave identically; in particular, use of the simple present in the above sentences would be totally inadequate.

The present progressive is also used to convey the idea of a transitory situation, as against the simple present, which, in the same contexts, expresses a permanent situation:

Eu <u>estou trabalhando</u> nessa escola.
'I am working in this school.'

Eu <u>trabalho</u> nessa escola.
'I work in this school.'

The first sentence means that I have just begun working in the school, or that I view my employment there as temporary; the second sentence means that I have a permanent job in the school.

The present progressive is also occasionally used to express an immediate future:

Amanhã eles <u>estão indo</u> ao Rio para um congresso.
'They are going to Rio tomorrow for a conference.'

Dentro de cinco minutos nós <u>estamos servindo</u> o jantar.
'In five minutes we'll be serving dinner.'

O céu está cada vez mais escuro; daqui a pouco <u>está chovendo</u>.
'The sky is getting darker; in a little while it will rain.'

The interpretation of the progressive as a future depends on the presence of contextualizing elements in the sentence (*amanhã* 'tomorrow,' *dentro de cinco minutos* 'in five minutes,' *daqui a pouco* 'in a little while' in the examples above).

18.2 Future

18.2.1 Simple futurity

The Portuguese verb has two main ways of expressing future events: the **future** tense and the sequence of the auxiliary *ir* (in the present) plus an infinitive. The future is almost exclusively used in the written language:

O presidente <u>falará</u> à nação hoje às nove horas.　　　　　　　　　**Wr**
'The president will address the nation tonight at nine.'

The sequence *ir* + infinitive can occur in all styles and is the only one found in informal speech:

O presidente <u>vai falar</u> à nação hoje às nove horas.
'id.'

These two constructions are synonymous in most cases. But only *ir* + infinitive can be used to express something that is about to happen, that is, a very immediate future. Thus, one can say

Entra depressa, que eles já <u>vão fechar</u> a porta!
'Come in quick, because they are going to close the door!'

Cuidado! A telha <u>vai cair</u>!
'Watch out! The tile is falling!'

The future in this context would sound very strange:

* *Entra depressa, que eles já <u>fecharão</u> a porta!*

* *Cuidado! A telha <u>cairá</u>!*

The safest road, therefore, is to use the compound form, *ir* + infinitive, whenever in doubt; and to use it exclusively when speaking (which is more or less what Brazilians themselves do).

Besides these two main ways of expressing futurity, it is also possible to use the simple present and the present progressive in a future sense, for which see 18.1.

18.2.2 The construction *terei feito*

English has a way of expressing future events that predate other future events; this is done by means of the sequence *will* + *have* + past participle, e.g.,

I *will have finished* my work by ten o'clock tomorrow.

Here the event denoted by *finished* is understood as previous to another moment in the future, expressed by *ten o'clock tomorrow*.

In Portuguese the same resource is available, and the structure conveying it is parallel to the English one, e.g.,

> *Eu <u>terei terminado</u> meu trabalho amanhã às dez horas.*   **Wr**
> *Eu <u>vou ter terminado</u> meu trabalho amanhã às dez horas.*
> 'I will have finished my work by ten o'clock tomorrow.'

Here the Portuguese and the English constructions are very similar both in form and in meaning, so that no lengthy explanations are needed. The only thing to note is that colloquial Portuguese has an alternate way to express anterior futurity, namely, by using the preterit tense, e.g.,

> *Quando você chegar amanhã de manhã eu já <u>terminei</u> meu trabalho.*   **SpBr**
> 'When you arrive tomorrow morning I'll have finished [literally, I have finished] my work.'

18.2.3 Conditional (future of the past)

The Portuguese **conditional** (*eu amaria* 'I would love,' *eu venderia* 'I would sell,' *eu partiria* 'I would leave') corresponds closely in use to the English conditional (auxiliary *would* + infinitive). The conditional, unlike the future, is still frequently used in the spoken language.

The main use of the conditional is to express something that might happen provided some (expressed or understood) condition is met. The conditional, in these cases, is generally interpreted as containing a contrary-to-fact assertion.

For instance,

> *A velhinha só <u>tocaria</u> se o piano fosse um Steinway.*
> 'The old woman would play only if the piano were a Steinway.'

> *Eu <u>sairia</u> com vocês, mas estou com gripe.*
> 'I would go out with you, but (I) have the flu.'

As can be seen, the condition itself is expressed by means of the imperfect subjunctive (*fosse*). In the second example, the condition is understood (= *se eu não <u>estivesse</u> com gripe* 'if I didn't have the flu'); and in this sentence it is understood that I am not going with you.

A second use of the conditional is to express futurity in relation to a past event.

For instance,

> *Naquele dia nós conhecemos o homem que anos depois <u>seria</u> eleito presidente.*
> 'That day we met the man who years later would be elected president.'

> *Cristiana me disse que <u>mandaria</u> um cartão.*
> 'Cristiana told me she would send a postcard.'

As can be seen by the glosses, English and Portuguese behave in parallel ways in both these uses of the conditional.

The conditional may also have other uses, listed below.

> With verbs of wishing, the conditional is used in order to express a polite request.

For example,

> *Eu <u>gostaria</u> de participar da exposição.*
> 'I would like to participate in the exhibit.'

> *Minha irmã <u>adoraria</u> conhecer a sua casa.*
> 'My sister would love to visit your house.'

> The conditional is also sometimes used to express a statement for which the speaker does not want to be held personally responsible.

For instance, the sentence

> *O porta-voz afirmou que o ministro <u>está</u> indisposto.*
> 'The spokesman alleged that the minister is ill.'

is neutral about the truth or falsity of the minister's illness. But if the speaker uses the conditional instead of the present indicative, e.g.,

> *O porta-voz afirmou que o ministro <u>estaria</u> indisposto.*   **Wr**
> 'The spokesman alleged that the minister is [literally, would be] ill.'

one gets the idea that the speaker does not want to share any responsibility as to the truth of the spokesman's statement; it may even be interpreted as intimating that the spokesman may be lying. This use of the conditional is not very frequent, and is mainly found in the written language.

There is a construction parallel to the future with *ir* (*vou cantar* '(I) will sing') for the conditional as well, in most of its uses. Thus, we may say the sentences below either with the conditional or with *ir* in the imperfect plus the infinitive:

> *A velhinha só <u>tocaria</u> se o piano fosse um Steinway.*
> *A velhinha só <u>ia tocar</u> se o piano fosse um Steinway.*
> 'The old woman would play only if the piano were a Steinway.'

> *Eu <u>sairia</u> com vocês, mas estou com gripe.*
> *Eu <u>ia sair</u> com vocês, mas estou com gripe.*
> 'I would go out with you, but (I) have the flu.'

In some cases, like the first of the above examples, no semantic difference can be perceived between the two versions. In other cases, as in the second example, the *ir* + infinitive construction seems to convey an idea of intentionality, so that *sairia* in that context means '(I) would go out,' but *ia sair* means rather '(I) was about to go out.' The difference is admittedly subtle and may be safely ignored in most cases. And, since the conditional is still in current use, the construction in question is much less frequent than the alternative future with *ir*.

Finally, we may note that the imperfect is sometimes substituted for the conditional; this is frequent in the spoken language, and one can say either

> *Cristiana me disse que <u>mandaria</u> um cartão.*
> 'Cristiana told me she would send a postcard.'

with the conditional, or

> *Cristiana me disse que <u>mandava</u> um cartão.*   **SpBr**
> 'id.'

Also:

> *Se eu tivesse tempo eu <u>faria</u> uma quiche para você.*
> *Se eu tivesse tempo eu <u>fazia</u> uma quiche para você.*   **SpBr**
> 'If I had time I would make a quiche for you.'

18.3 Past: Preterit vs. imperfect

There are two simple past tenses in Portuguese, termed **preterit** (*eu falei, eu vendi, eu dormi*) and **imperfect** (*eu falava, eu vendia, eu dormia*).[1]

Note

[1]Besides these, there is the **pluperfect** (*eu falara, eu vendera, eu dormira*), which is little used in writing and never in speaking.

The difference in use between the preterit and the imperfect past tenses is a traditional problem for English-speaking students of Romance languages. In this section I give some rules that account for most occurrences of these tenses; they should provide a good beginning and help the student get the "feel" for the use of the preterit vis-à-vis the imperfect. On the other hand, the phenomenon is not wholly understood even by linguists, and one must be prepared for occasional surprises.

This uncertainty refers only to the grammatical analysis of the phenomenon, of course; for the native speaker the difference between the preterit and the imperfect is very clear, and these forms are never confused in speech or in writing. Thus there certainly is a rule (more probably, a set of rules) still awaiting complete formulation. In the sections that follow I have refrained from attempting sweeping generalizations and have preferred instead to give a set of separate rules. This is, I think, prudent in view of our poor understanding of the phenomenon and makes better sense in a practical grammar like this one.

18.3.1 Temporal delimitation

The main difference between the preterit and the imperfect past tenses is that

with the **preterit** focus is on the temporal limits of the situation depicted whereas

with the **imperfect** the verb denotes a habitual state or action, or a quality considered as valid for an extended period in the past.

Take the examples

> Ele <u>viajou</u> para os Estados Unidos.
> Ele <u>viajava</u> para os Estados Unidos.

Both these sentences may be translated as 'He traveled to the U.S.,' yet they do not mean the same thing to the speaker of Portuguese. The first one describes a single trip, while the second describes a habitual event, which might be expressed in English as *He used to travel to the U.S.* With *viajou* the temporal limits of the event (its beginning and end) are defined; with *viajava* they are left open.

Another pair of examples is

> O senador <u>foi</u> grosseiro durante a entrevista.
> 'The senator was rude during the interview.'

> O senador <u>era</u> grosseiro durante as entrevistas.
> 'The senator was rude during the interviews.'

Here again we have a difference in temporal focus. The first sentence means that there was a specific interview during which the senator was rude. The second sentence leaves it pretty clear that there was an unspecified number of interviews and that the senator *used to* be rude during these interviews. Here again we have the imperfect denoting a habitual (that is, temporally nonpunctualized) event, and the preterit denoting a punctual, specific event.

Other examples are as follows:

> Ela <u>falou</u> inglês.
> 'She spoke English [say, during the interview].'

Ela falava inglês.
'She spoke English [i.e., she knew the language well enough to speak it].'

Os meninos aprenderam rápido.
'The boys learned fast [refers to a single, specific learning event].'

Os meninos aprendiam rápido.
'The boys learned fast [i.e., they were fast learners].'

Mamãe plantou um jardim (quando comprou a casa).
'Mom planted a garden (when she bought the house).'

Mamãe plantava um jardim (sempre que achava um lote vago).
'Mom planted a garden (whenever she found a vacant lot).'

In all of the above examples, the imperfect refers to a habitual event. The fact that its limits are not temporally delimited also results in the expression of states valid for extended periods, e.g.,

Renato foi muito bonito.
Renato era muito bonito.
'Renato was very handsome.'

The first sentence means that Renato was handsome for a relatively short period, and then he ceased to be handsome. The second one refers to an extended period, which may include even the whole of Renato's life.

18.3.2 The imperfect as a setting for other events

The second sentence given at the end of the previous section (but not the first one) may be used as a framework for another statement about Renato, as in

Renato era muito bonito quando nós casamos.
'Renato was very handsome when we got married.'

Here the imperfect *era muito bonito* 'was very handsome' depicts a temporal framework in which the preterit *nós casamos* 'we got married' is included. This is of course made possible by the fact that the imperfect is temporally indefinite, while the preterit is temporally delimited. The preterit would be unacceptable in this case:

* *Renato foi muito bonito quando nós casamos.*

Another example of a sentence in the imperfect acting as a temporal framework for a more punctual event is

Nós ainda <u>éramos</u> casados no final da guerra.
'We were still married at the end of the war.'

Here the punctual event is expressed by an adverbial phrase, *no final da guerra* 'at the end of the war.' Again, the preterit would be totally inadequate in this context:

* Nós ainda <u>fomos</u> casados no final da guerra.

Now take the following pair of sentences:

Meu pai <u>trabalhou</u> na alfândega.
Meu pai <u>trabalhava</u> na alfândega.
'My father worked in customs.'

Since the action expressed by *trabalhar* 'to work' is by nature an extended process (an employee is expected to hold his job for some time), the difference between the preterit and the imperfect in the two sentences above is attenuated, and there are many situations in which either sentence would be appropriate.

But this does not mean that they are entirely synonymous; there is a subtle, but perceptible, difference between the two tenses. The sentence with the imperfect,

Meu pai <u>trabalhava</u> na alfândega.

not only states that my father worked in customs during some past period, but it prepares the receptor for the possibility of some other event that took place during that period. That is, the imperfect provides a setting for some other event, and the sentence could be complemented as follows:

Meu pai <u>trabalhava</u> na alfândega quando houve o escândalo.
'My father worked in customs when the scandal broke out.'

Now, the version with the preterit states only the bare fact that my father worked in customs, and there is no expectation of any complementation; in fact, if we add the second clause to the preterit version the result sounds very strange:

* Meu pai <u>trabalhou</u> na alfândega quando houve o escândalo.

Thus, we can say that

> the use of the imperfect normally raises the expectation that another
>
> event will also be referred to; this second event is temporally contained
>
> in the period of time denoted by the imperfect, and when expressed is
>
> in the preterit.

Another example is

Ele <u>era</u> muito gordo (*quando morreu*).
'He was very fat (when he died).'

but

Ele <u>foi</u> muito gordo (* *quando morreu*).

Here again both the imperfect (*era*) and the preterit (*foi*) are acceptable; but only the former accepts the addition of another event, to be understood as temporally included in the extensions covered by the imperfect. This is in agreement with the "background" nature of the imperfect.

In some cases the imperfect can express a very short period of time, provided this period is taken as a background for some event; this happens in particular with the expression of the time of day, e.g.,

<u>*Eram*</u> *duas horas quando vovô telefonou.*
'(It) was two o'clock when Grandpa called.'

Since giving the time of day is practically always understood as a background for some other event, the imperfect is always used.

18.3.3 Finished vs. unfinished processes

Another effect of the use of the imperfect (which may or may not be related to its other semantic features) is that

> the imperfect often brings in the notion of an unfinished process, as
>
> against the preterit, which expresses a completed event.

The following pair of sentences exemplifies this opposition:

Foi um erro vender a casa.
'It was a mistake to sell the house.'

Era um erro vender a casa.
'It would be a mistake to sell the house.'

The difference in meaning between the two sentences is that the first (with the preterit *foi*) makes it clear that the house was, in fact, sold; the second (with the imperfect *era*) merely states that it would be a mistake to sell it, and leaves it open whether it was sold or not.

18.3.4 Continuous vs. discontinuous events

We saw in 18.3.1 that the imperfect presents an event or a state valid for an extended period of time; this is probably at the root of the following property:

> The imperfect tends to denote continuous events, as against the pret-
>
> erit, which is associated with discontinuous events.

Thus, one may say

Ele foi gordo duas vezes na sua vida.
'He was fat twice in his life.'

But not

> * *Ele <u>era</u> gordo duas vezes na sua vida.*

since the phrase *duas vezes na sua vida* 'twice in his life' presents the fact that he was fat as cut up into discrete, discontinuous episodes. Conversely, in the following examples only the imperfect is acceptable:

> *Joaquim não <u>gostava</u> de vinho.*
> 'Joaquim did not like wine.'
>
> * *Joaquim não <u>gostou</u> de vinho.*

The problem is that *vinho* 'wine' is taken as a generic reference (without article; see 26.1.4), and therefore *gostar de vinho* 'to like wine' refers to a generic situation, not to a discrete event. Correspondingly, the imperfect must be used. Now, if we use *esse vinho* 'this wine' instead, the event described by *gostar desse vinho* 'to like this wine' will be interpreted either as a discrete event or as a generic situation, and both the preterit and the imperfect will be appropriate:

> *Joaquim não <u>gostava</u> desse vinho.*
> 'Joaquim did not like this wine [he never liked it].'
>
> *Joaquim não <u>gostou</u> desse vinho.*
> 'Joaquim did not like this wine [when he tasted it].'

Another set of examples that exemplify this difference between the preterit and the imperfect is

> *Eu <u>estive</u> em todos os cômodos da casa.*
> * *Eu <u>estava</u> em todos os cômodos da casa.*
> 'I have been in every room in the house.'

The sentence is okay with the preterit because it means that I was in all the rooms, one by one, in separate visits. With the imperfect, however, it has the strange meaning that I was in all the rooms continuously, at the same time.

Now if we substitute the phrase *o cheiro* 'the smell' for *eu* 'I,' the situation is reversed: since it is easy to picture a smell as present all over the house, the imperfect is acceptable:

> *O cheiro <u>estava</u> em todos os cômodos da casa.*
> 'The smell was in every room in the house.'

Using the preterit yields a slightly odd result because it conveys the idea of a smell going from room to room:

> * *O cheiro <u>esteve</u> em todos os cômodos da casa.*

18.3.5 Conditional use of the imperfect

Finally, the imperfect is sometimes used as a synonym for the conditional, corresponding to the English conditional. This happens frequently in two situations: first, when the verb occurs in a complement to a contrary-to-fact clause, e.g.,

> *Se você quisesse, eu <u>fazia</u> isso para você.*
> 'If you wanted, I would do this for you.'

This sentence is a more colloquial synonym of

> *Se você quisesse, eu <u>faria</u> isso para você.*
> 'id.'

And, second, in complements to verbs expressing a promise, a supposition, or a piece of information, e.g.,

> *O cara prometeu que <u>pintava</u> (= <u>pintaria</u>) a casa em três dias.*
> 'The guy promised that he would paint the house in three days.'

> *Ela jurou que <u>pagava</u> (= <u>pagaria</u>) tudo em maio.*
> 'She swore that she would pay everything in May.'

> *Pensei que você nem <u>vinha</u> (= <u>viria</u>) .*
> '(I) thought you weren't even coming.'

> *Todos disseram que você <u>chegava</u> (= <u>chegaria</u>) às oito.*
> 'Everyone said that you were coming at eight.'

As we can see, in English also we may use the past tense in the last two cases.

Now, when the conditional expresses futurity in relation to a past event (as seen in 18.2.3 above) it is not replaceable by the imperfect:

> *Fui apresentado a Pereira, que mais tarde <u>seria</u> eleito senador.*
> '(I) was introduced to Pereira, who would later be elected senator.'

In this sentence the use of the imperfect, *era,* is unacceptable.

18.4 Past: The construction tenho feito

The Portuguese construction with the present indicative of *ter* followed by a past participle (*tenho feito*) presents a problem because, although it is formally similar to English *I have done* and to Spanish *he hecho,* it is different in meaning from either one.

The meaning of Portuguese *tenho feito* is close to that of English *I have been doing,* as in

> *Tem chovido horrores nos últimos dias.*
> '(It) has been raining cats and dogs these days.'

This sentence means not only that it has rained a lot, but also that the rainy season goes on. Likewise, in

> *Essa menina tem estudado demais.*
> 'This girl has been studying too much.'

we understand that she is still at it.

The construction **tenho feito** is used to indicate an event that began in

the past and has continued without interruption until the present.

One consequence is that *tenho feito* is incompatible with any indication that the event depicted is already complete. Thus, although in English we can say

> *I have already published my book.*

in Portuguese the following is unacceptable:

> * *Eu já tenho publicado meu livro.*

because the use of the *tenho feito* construction means that the event is not yet completed. Even without *já* the sentence is unacceptable,

> * *Eu tenho publicado meu livro.*
> * 'I have been publishing my book.'

because publishing a book is a punctual event. But we can say

> *Eu tenho publicado um livro por ano.*
> 'I have been publishing a book a year.'

since now we are envisaging the publication as a repeated event, covering a long extension of time.

If the event does not continue up to the present, the construction *tenho feito* is, of course, excluded; thus, one can say

> *Nós vivemos juntos de 1990 a 1997.*
> 'We lived together from 1990 to 1997.'

with the preterit, but not

> * *Nós temos vivido juntos de 1990 a 1997.*

If the event described is still in course, the past perfect *tenho feito* can be used:

> *Nós temos vivido juntos desde 1990.*
> 'We have been living together since 1990.'

The English construction with *have* plus the past participle is in most cases translated as the (simple) preterit in Portuguese:

> *A universidade contratou cinco novos professores.*
> 'The university has hired five new teachers.'

> *O nosso professor publicou seis livros até agora.*
> 'Our teacher has published six books to date.'

18.5 The pluperfect

Portuguese has a **simple pluperfect** form: *eu falara* 'I had spoken,' *eu vendera* 'I had sold,' *eu mentira* 'I had lied.' This form is never used in speaking, and even in writing it is becoming rare; it is replaced by a compound form (past imperfect of *ter* + past participle) that has exactly the same meaning: *eu tinha falado, eu tinha vendido, eu tinha mentido:*

> *O candidato declarou que <u>lera</u> todos os livros do programa.* **Wr**
> 'The candidate declared that he had read every book in the syllabus.'

> *O candidato declarou que <u>tinha lido</u> todos os livros do programa.* **Wr ~ SpBr**
> 'id.'

As we can see, the compound form is also appropriate in the written style, so that a student does not really need to learn the simple pluperfect, except to recognize it in its occasional appearances in written texts.

18.6 Other compound forms with ter

Two of the compound forms with *ter* have already been discussed, namely, *tenho feito* in connection with the past tenses (18.4) and *tinha feito* as the normal way to express the pluperfect (18.5). Here I examine briefly the remaining *ter* constructions, which do not present serious problems for the English-speaking student, as they are semantically similar to their English counterparts; the student only has to compare them with the translations given in the examples below. Besides the two *ter*-constructions already seen, the following are in current use:

terei feito (future of *ter* + participle)   ~   ***vou ter feito:***

> *O jogo <u>terá acabado</u> quando você chegar.* **Wr**
> 'The game will have ended when you arrive.'

Of course, since it contains a future, this sentence is typical of the written language. Colloquially one would substitute *vai ter* for *terá:*

> *O jogo <u>vai ter acabado</u> quando você chegar.*
> 'id.'

teria feito (conditional + participle):

> *Se você demorasse mais, o jogo <u>teria começado</u> sem você.*
> 'If you had taken longer, the game would have begun without you.'

ter feito   (infinitive + participle):

> *A companhia devia <u>ter nos avisado</u> desse atraso.*
> 'The company should have told us about this delay.'

tendo feito   (gerund + participle):

> <u>*Tendo desmanchado*</u> *o noivado, eles nunca mais se falaram.*
> 'Having broken their engagement, they never spoke to each other again.'

There are also the subjunctive forms *tenha feito, tivesse feito, tiver feito,* but no *ter*-constructions with *ter* in the preterit or in the pluperfect. These compound forms with *ter* are frequent both in the spoken and in the written language.

18.7 Compound forms with haver

Some of the compound forms studied in this section have equivalents with *haver* as the auxiliary instead of *ter:* thus, *tinha feito* can appear as *havia feito,* and *tenha feito* as *haja feito.* Several of these alternatives with *haver* are definitely archaic, and none is really frequent: for instance, *tenho feito* does not have (nowadays) an equivalent * *hei feito,* and *terei feito* did not, to my knowledge, ever have an equivalent * *haverei feito.* The only *haver* constructions likely to occur in modern texts are the ones with the infinitive, *haver feito,* with the gerund, *havendo feito,* with the past imperfect, *havia feito,* and with the imperfect subjunctive, *houvesse feito.* Even so, they are rare, and *ter* forms are preferred in all cases.

18.8 Progressive forms

As we've seen, a progressive form is a sequence of *estar* plus a gerund. We have already met the construction *estou fazendo* as the normal way to express an ongoing event (section 18.1.2). As for the remaining progressive constructions, they share their main semantic features and may be considered together in this section.

All tenses of *estar* can be used in a progressive construction, e.g.,

> *Alguns meninos <u>estão fazendo</u> barulho lá fora.*
> 'Some boys are making noise outside.'

> *Alguns meninos <u>estavam fazendo</u> barulho lá fora.*
> 'Some boys were making noise outside.'

And so on with *estiveram fazendo* 'have been making,' *estarão fazendo* 'will be making' **Wr,** *estariam fazendo* 'would be making,' etc.

It is also possible to build progressive constructions with compound tenses, as in

Alguns meninos <u>tinham estado fazendo</u> barulho lá fora.
'Some boys had been making noise outside.'

but these longer sequences are not very natural and occur only sporadically.

The meaning of these constructions is not particularly difficult for an English speaker, as they parallel closely the meaning of the English progressives. In both languages, they express ongoing events in the present, in the past, or in the future.

19

Governed Tense

In chapter 18 we considered only the tenses of the indicative; in the present chapter I examine the use of tenses of the subjunctive mood. The reason we have to consider the tenses of the subjunctive separately is the following: when a verb is in the indicative its tense is **autonomous,** that is, it is determined by semantic ingredients like the expression of current events, or past states, etc., without consideration of the tense of any other verb that may occur in the same sentence. But when a verb is in the subjunctive, its tense may be determined by the tense of the main verb. For example, in the sentence

> *Catarina <u>queimou</u> o bolo.*
> 'Catarina burned the cake.'

the choice of the preterit *queimou* is determined by what the speaker wants to say: in this case, to express a past, punctual, finished event. If the speaker wanted to express a future event, the verb form would be *queimará,* or more probably *vai queimar* 'will burn.' This is an example of the use of autonomous verb tense.

Now take the sentence

> *Catarina tinha medo que eu   <u>queimasse</u>   o bolo.*
> **imperfect**   **imperfect**
> 'Catarina was afraid that I might burn the cake.'

The speaker chooses the tense of *ter:* in this case, *tinha.* But once this is done, there is no choice as to the tense (or mood) of *queimar:* it must be the imperfect subjunctive *queimasse,* not, say, the present subjunctive *queime* (nor, of course, any form of the indicative, since the governing nominal, *medo* 'fear,' requires the subjunctive; see chapter 15). Here we have a case of **governed tense:** whenever the main verb is in the past, the subordinate verb must also be in the past. Governed tense occurs only when the subordinate verb is in the subjunctive.

If we rephrase the sentence, putting the main verb in the present, the subordinate verb must go to the present subjunctive:

> *Catarina tem medo que eu* <u>*queime*</u> *o bolo.*
>   **present**   **present**
> 'Catarina is afraid that I will burn the cake.'

The same phenomenon occurs with some cases of clauses introduced by connectives: the main verb governs the tense of the subordinate verb. For instance, whenever a subordinate clause is introduced by *caso* 'in case,' the subordinate verb must be in the subjunctive and in a tense determined by the tense of the main clause:

> *Eu* <u>*lavo*</u> *o carro,* **caso** *ninguém mais* <u>*queira.*</u>
>   **present**   **present**
> 'I (will) wash the car, in case nobody else wants (to do it).'

> *Eu* <u>*lavaria*</u> *o carro,* **caso** *ninguém mais* <u>*quisesse.*</u>
>   **conditional**   **imperfect**
> 'I would wash the car, in case nobody else wanted (to do it).'

Here we are concerned with the effect of a verb or a nominal in the main clause on the tense of the verb in the subordinate (normally introduced by *que*).

In all cases of verb or nominal government the connective *que* is present. This *que* makes no requirements of its own, but "passes along" the requirements of the preceding nominal or verb. For instance, returning to the example given above,

> *Catarina tem medo que eu* <u>*queime*</u> *o bolo.*
>   **present**   **present**
> 'Catarina is afraid that I will burn the cake.'

if we change the tense of the main verb, *tem* (present), to *tinha* (past imperfect), the tense of the subordinate verb, *queime* (present subjunctive), will change to *queimasse* (imperfect subjunctive):

Catarina tinha medo que eu　queimasse　o bolo.
　　　　past　　　　　　**imperfect**
'Catarina was afraid that I might burn the cake.'

Other examples are as follows:

Catarina pediu que eu　comesse　o bolo.
　　　　past　　　**imperfect**
'Catarina asked me to eat the cake [literally, asked that I eat (**subjunctive**) . . .].'

Catarina vai querer que eu　coma　o bolo.
　　　　future　　　　**present**
'Catarina will want me to eat the cake [literally, will want that I eat . . .].'

Catarina exige que eu　coma　o bolo.
　　present　　　**present**
'Catarina demands that I eat the cake.'

This correlation is governed according to the following table:

Main verb	*Subordinate verb*
Present	**present subjunctive**
Ela exige que você saia.	'She demands that you leave.'
Past (perfect or imperfect)	**imperfect subjunctive**
Ela exigiu que você saísse.	'She demanded that you leave.'
Conditional	**imperfect subjunctive**
Ela exigiria que você saísse.	'She would demand that you leave.'
Future	**present subjunctive**
Ela vai exigir que você saia.	'She will demand that you leave.'

Observe that the correlate of the future in the main sentence is the *present* subjunctive in the subordinate (not the future subjunctive, which never apears in verb- and nominal-governed clauses; see 15.8 for the rules of use of the future subjunctive).

Tense correlation works for auxiliaries in sequences of auxiliaries + main verb as well, e.g.,

> *Guilherme tinha medo de que sua filha   tivesse   perdido o emprego.*
> **imperfect indicative   imperfect subjunctive**
> 'Guilherme was afraid that his daughter had lost her job.'

> *Guilherme tem medo de que sua filha   vá   perder o emprego.*
> **present indicative   present subjunctive**
> 'Guilherme is afraid that his daughter may lose her job.'

In the first example, we have the auxiliary *ter* plus the main verb *perder* 'to lose' in the subordinate; in the second one, we have the auxiliary *ir* plus *perder*. As seen, *ter* and *ir* must be in the required tense of the subjunctive, according to the rule given above: in the first case, the main verb is in the past (*tinha*), and the auxiliary, which functions as the subordinate verb, is in the imperfect subjunctive (*tivesse*). In the second case, the main verb is in the present (*tem*), and the subordinate auxiliary is in the present subjunctive (*vá*).

20

Person

The use of persons in Portuguese presents few problems for the English-speaking student because the two languages are very similar in this respect. The main difference resides in the use of honorifics, which is very restricted in English, being limited to such little-used forms as *Your Majesty, Your Honor,* and the like. In Portuguese, *o senhor* (and, in Portugal, *Vossa Excelência*) are still in wide use to address people with whom one has little intimacy; and *você* is the normal form of address in Brazil.

In this chapter I examine the use of persons in the sentence; in chapter 8 the reader will find a complete list of personal pronouns, as well as their complete inflection.

20.1 Você *and* o senhor

Você (plural, *vocês*) means 'you,' but takes a third person verb form: *você <u>vai</u> descascar as batatas* 'you will peel the potatoes,' *vocês <u>chegaram</u> muito tarde* 'you (pl.) have arrived too late.'

The apparent contradiction in the use of *você* comes actually from an inadequate use of the technical term **person,** which is traditionally used to refer to two very different notions. First, traditional grammar calls 'person' the real person (or thing) that speaks, is addressed, or is referred to in a speech act; and, second, it also calls 'person' a verb form, characterized by a particular suffix. But there is no one-to-one correspondence between the two entities: even in English, one can say something like *now baby is going to bed because*

Mom must do the dishes, where both the addressee (*baby*) and the speaker (*Mom*) are referred to by means of "third person" expressions.

The same happens in Portuguese, but on a wider scale. Thus, forms like *você* 'you,' *o senhor* 'you (honorific),' *Vossa Excelência* 'your Excellency' refer to the addressee but take third person verb forms. This is a near-universal phenomenon in most of Brazil, where second person pronouns (*tu, vós*) have fallen into disuse.

20.2 Reflexives

Reflexive pronouns (see chapter 8) are used in three situations.

20.2.1 Identical subjects and objects

First, as in English, reflexive pronouns are used whenever the object (direct or indirect) of a verb is to be understood as being identical with the subject, as in

> *Eu me olhei no espelho.*
> 'I looked at myself in the mirror.'

> *Luizinho se considera um gênio.*
> 'Luizinho considers himself a genius.'

As shown in the above examples, the reflexive pronoun must match the subject in person and number; this holds true whenever a reflexive pronoun is used. Syntactically speaking, this use of the reflexives is identical in Portuguese and in English and requires no special comment.

20.2.2 Reciprocals

Reflexives are also used in Portuguese to express **reciprocity,** which in English is expressed by *each other,* as in the example

> *Amélia e eu nos amamos loucamente.*
> 'Amélia and I love each other madly.'

This leads to occasional ambiguities that only context can solve, e.g.,

> *O rapaz e a moça se beliscaram.*
> 'The boy and the girl pinched each other'   **or**
> 'The boy and the girl pinched themselves.'

20.2.3 Reflexive verbs

The third use of the reflexive is when it must obligatorily occur (but see below) with certain verbs, so that one says

Carolina <u>se</u> arrependeu.
'Carolina repented.'

Nós <u>nos</u> despedimos de todo o mundo.
'We said goodbye to everybody.'

These verbs are called **reflexive,** and in the standard language they must appear with a reflexive (although they do not have identical subjects and objects). The list of reflexive verbs is long; among the most common are the following:

achar-se	'to be located'
arrepender-se	'to repent'
atrever-se	'to dare'
casar-se	'to get married'
chamar-se	'to be called' (*eu <u>me</u> chamo Leo* 'my name is Leo')
compor-se	'to be composed' (*a máquina <u>se</u> compõe de três partes* 'the engine is composed of three parts')
dar-se	'to happen'
despedir-se	'to say goodbye'
divertir-se	'to have fun, to amuse oneself'
divorciar-se	'to divorce'
esquecer-se	'to forget'
ir-se	'to go away'
lembrar-se	'to remember'
levantar-se	'to get up'
queixar-se	'to complain'
sentir-se	'to feel' (*eu <u>me</u> sinto bem aqui* 'I feel fine here')
suicidar-se	'to commit suicide'
surpreender-se	'to be surprised'

Reflexive verbs are always accompanied by the reflexive pronoun of the same person as the subject. As we saw in chapter 8, the reflexive pronouns for the first and second persons are the same forms used as objects, whereas for the third person the special form *se* is used. Thus, the conjugation of a reflexive verb in, say, the preterit is as follows:

eu me diverti	'I amused myself'
ele / ela se divertiu	'he/she amused him/herself'

nós nos divertimos   'we amused ourselves'
eles / elas se divertiram   'they amused themselves'

20.2.4 Reflexive verbs in the spoken language

The use of reflexive verbs tends to disappear in the spoken language, so that one normally says (and frequently writes) *eu <u>levantei</u> às seis horas* 'I got up at six,' instead of *eu <u>me levantei</u> às seis horas*. This happens with most verbs in the list, so that they become regular verbs:

Maria e Francisco divorciaram.   **SpBr [standard, . . . <u>se</u> divorciaram.]**
'Maria and Francisco divorced.'

Eu esqueci de telefonar.   **SpBr [standard, *Eu <u>me</u> esqueci* . . .]**
'I forgot to phone.'

With a few verbs, like *compor-se* 'to be composed,' the reflexive pronoun remains obligatory, so that one cannot say **A máquina compõe de três partes,* but always

A máquina <u>se</u> compõe de três partes.
'The engine is composed of three parts.'

Some reflexive verbs, finally, are used only in the written language, never in informal speech; these verbs, of course, retain their reflexive pronoun as an obligatory appendage. Examples are *ir-se* 'to go away' and *dar-se* 'to happen':

Eles <u>se</u> foram.   **Wr**
'They went away.'

Isso <u>se</u> deu no século XVII.   **Wr**
'That happened in the seventeenth century.'

21

Passive and Impersonal Sentences

21.1 Passive sentences

Traditional grammars of Portuguese distinguish two types of passive sentences: "analytic" passives, which are formed with the auxiliary *ser* 'to be,' as in

> *As rosas <u>foram destruídas</u> pelas formigas.*
> 'The roses were destroyed by the ants.'

and "synthetic" passives, formed with the particle *se*, for example,

> *Na Páscoa <u>come-se</u> muito chocolate.*
> 'At Easter one eats a lot of chocolate.'

In this section I will consider only the first type; the *se*-construction is examined in 21.2 below, under the heading **impersonal sentences.**[1]

❀

Note

**[1] Whether or not the *se*-construction is a true passive is in part a terminological issue and relates to the way one defines "passive." In my opinion, it is more similar to impersonal sentences than to regular passives: in particular, both impersonal and *se*-sentences have the particle *se,* with similar meaning and similar syntactic behavior.

Formally, the Portuguese passive sentence is basically similar to the English one; that is, it is composed of

---

—a subject (generally understood as the patient of an action), that is,

the person or thing undergoing its effect

—the verb *ser* 'to be'

—the past participle of the main verb;

and, optionally,

—a complement with *por* 'by,' understood as the agent of the action

---

An example with the *por*-complement is

As rosas foram destruídas pelas formigas.
'The roses were destroyed by the ants.'

And an example without the complement is

Meu carro foi depredado.
'My car was vandalized.'

As in English, the complement is omitted whenever one does not know who the agent of the action is, or when one does not want to mention it for some reason.

So far, then, there is not much to say about the passive, since it seems to be so similar in Portuguese and in English. There are, however, some differences, namely,

—First, one must observe that the past participle behaves like a nominal and therefore agrees in gender and number with the subject:

*As rosas foram destruí**das**.*
'The roses were destroyed   [**feminine plural**].'

A rosa foi destruída.
'The rose was destroyed   [**feminine singular**].'

O carro foi destruído.
'The car was destroyed   [**masculine singular**].'

—Second, there are two varieties of the passive construction that occur in English but not in Portuguese:

a. Portuguese never forms a passive by moving an indirect object to the subject position, as in English

Glenda was given a ticket.

This must be expressed in Portuguese by a different construction, such as

Glenda recebeu uma multa.
'Glenda got a ticket.'

b. There is no direct Portuguese correspondent to the English construction exemplified by

Bill is believed to have drunk the whiskey.

In this sentence *Bill* represents the agent of *drink,* not the goal of the expressed belief; in other words, the believed thing is not Bill, but rather the event 'Bill drank the whiskey.' In such cases the Portuguese speaker must resort to other turns, e.g.,

Acredita-se que Bill bebeu o uísque.
'People believe that Bill drank the whiskey.'

Now, the sentence

Bill was forced to drink the whiskey.

does have a literal correspondent in Portuguese, viz.,

Bill foi forçado a beber o uísque.

because *Bill* represents not only the agent of the drinking, but also the goal of the act of forcing: the forced entity is in fact Bill, and that is why Portuguese accepts *Bill* as the subject of the passive in the above sentence.

Passive sentences have the communicative function of topicalizing a noun phrase—that is, marking it as the focus of the utterance at a given moment—and also of omitting the agent when convenient. Thus, the difference between

> *As rosas foram destruídas pelas formigas.*
> 'The roses were destroyed by the ants.'

and

> *As formigas destruíram as rosas.*
> 'The ants destroyed the roses.'

is that in the first instance one is talking about the roses, and in the second instance one is talking about the ants (see chapter 39 for details about the topicalization process).

The auxiliary of the passive voice is *ser* 'to be.' Some grammars also give *estar* 'to be' and *ficar* 'to become' as possible auxiliaries, because of sentences like

> *As rosas estavam destruídas.*
> 'The roses were destroyed.'

> *As rosas ficaram destruídas.*
> 'The roses were (i.e., became) destroyed.'

Nevertheless, I prefer to analyze these sentences as structures with subjective complements parallel to

> *As rosas estavam bonitas.*
> 'The roses were beautiful.'

because they do not accept the addition of a *by*-phrase:

> ** As rosas estavam destruídas pelas formigas.*
> ** As rosas ficaram destruídas pelas formigas.*

21.2 Impersonal sentences

Impersonal sentences are essentially a way to omit the agent, calling attention to the action itself or to its other participants. For instance,

> *Isso não se aprende na escola.*
> 'One does not learn this in school.'

This sentence focuses on the learning process, without regard to the learner, whose identity is irrelevant for the intended message. All languages have ways of building such sentences; in English it is possible to use the pronoun *one,* as above; or to use a passive without an expressed agent, as in

> The top of the mountain was blown away.

or to use some special words that leave the identity of the agent indeterminate, such as *people* in

> In this region people raise chickens and cattle.

In Portuguese the main ways to express indetermination of the agent are through the use of agentless passives (discussed in the previous section), of *se*-constructions, of subjectless third person plural verb forms, and of certain nominals such as *a gente* 'people' and *você* 'you,' referring to an indeterminate person. These forms will be examined in the sections that follow.

21.2.1 The *se*-construction

The *se*-construction is an alternative to the agentless passive as a way to make the agent indeterminate. Its characteristics are

> —the presence of the particle *se,* contiguous to the verb;
>
> —the nonexpression of the agent (understood as being indeterminate);
>
> —the verb in the third person (normally singular, but see below).

For example,

> *Na Páscoa <u>come-se</u> muito chocolate.*   **Wr**
> *Na Páscoa <u>se come</u> muito chocolate.*
> 'At Easter one eats a lot of chocolate.'

Note that the particle comes before the verb in the spoken language, and after the verb, with a hyphen (or, also, before the verb) in the written language. This is so because the particle *se* is a clitic and follows the general rules of clitic placement (see chapter 29).

Other examples of the *se*-construction are

Dizem que <u>se vive</u> muito bem na Amazônia.
'It is said that one lives very well in the Amazon.'

Aqui <u>se almoça</u> muito cedo.
'Here people eat lunch very early.'

<u>*Vende-se*</u> *esta casa.*
'This house is for sale.'

21.2.1.1 Standard form of the se-construction

The *se*-construction often includes a noun phrase, which in other constructions would be a direct object, as in

No Brasil só <u>se fala</u> português.
'In Brazil people speak only Portuguese.'

Português may be the normal direct object of *falar,* as in *eu falo português* 'I speak Portuguese.' In these cases, the formal standard language requires that the verb agree with that NP (which becomes, by rights, the subject). Thus, if we have a plural, the verb will also go to the plural:

Na Índia <u>se falam</u> muitas línguas. **Wr**
'In India people speak many languages.'

Traditional grammarians and some teachers still insist on this construction, which nevertheless is losing ground even in the written language. Nowadays the most usual construction is without agreement, that is, the verb stays in the third person singular in all cases:

Na Índia <u>se fala</u> muitas línguas. **SpBr**
'id.'

21.2.1.2 Use of the se-construction in expositive style

The *se*-construction is very widely used in Portuguese in contexts in which English employs the agentless passive, e.g.,

Neste artigo <u>se demonstra</u> que a lua é de queijo.
'In this article it is shown that the moon is made of cheese.'

<u>Fez-se</u> um levantamento completo de todas as ocorrências.
'A complete survey of all occurrences was made.'

These sentences are frequent in technical and scientific discourse, in contexts in which the agentless passive can also be used; but the *se*-construction is the preferred turn and often sounds more natural than the passive.

21.2.2 Subjectless third person

21.2.2.1 Third person plural

A common way of omitting the agent in Portuguese is to use the verb in the third person plural, without a subject, e.g.,

<u>Bateram</u> na porta.
'Someone knocked on the door.'

<u>Mataram</u> meu gato ontem de noite.
'My cat was killed last night.'

<u>Dizem</u> que essa fruta é venenosa.
'(They) say this fruit is poisonous.'

Acho que <u>vão</u> derrubar esse edifício.
'(I) think that this building is going to be torn down.'

This construction is very common in the spoken language and is correct, if less frequent, in writing as well.

21.2.2.2 Third person singular

In the spoken language, there is another, semantically similar construction: the third person singular, without subject, as in

Para ir a Nova Lima <u>vira</u> à esquerda e <u>pega</u> a MG-30.   **SpBr**
'To go to Nova Lima (one) turns left and takes (route) MG-30.'

This construction is widely used in spontaneous speech as a way of omitting the agent, whenever its identification is irrelevant or easily recoverable from context. Other examples are as follows:

Dói aqui quando engole.   **SpBr**
'It hurts here when I swallow [literally, when swallows].'

Chegou.   **SpBr**
'We have arrived [literally, (it) arrived].'

The above sentence may be uttered by a driver to inform his passengers that they have arrived at the destination; in more formal style one might use *chegamos.*

Quando fazia biscoito a casa toda ficava cheirando.   **SpBr**
'When (someone) made cookies the whole house smelled.'

21.2.3 Indeterminate lexical items

Finally, reference to the agent can be avoided by using certain lexical items that may have indeterminate meaning, such as *a gente* 'people,' *alguém* 'someone,' *você* 'you,' e.g.,

A gente nunca usa essa palavra.
'One never uses this word.'

Alguém bateu na porta.
'Someone knocked on the door.'

De Itabirito você vai a Ouro Preto em menos de uma hora.
'From Itabirito one goes to Ouro Preto in less than one hour.'

Compare the last example with the indeterminate use of English *you,* usually pronounced [jə].

22

Notes on the Use of Certain Verbs

In this chapter I discuss some verbs that may pose a problem for the English-speaking student. I start with the dichotomy between *ser* and *estar*, both of which are translated in English as 'to be.'

22.1 Ser *vs.* estar

22.1.1 General rule

In this section I consider the use of *ser* and *estar* when not employed as auxiliaries; for their use as auxiliaries, see chapter 13 for the use of *estar* with the gerund, and chapter 21 for the use of *ser, estar* in the formation of the passive voice.

Both *ser* and *estar* typically occur with a subject (overt or understood) and a complement that denotes some kind of quality attributed to the subject. The main difference between *ser* and *estar* is the following:

> *Ser* introduces a quality seen as **essential, inherent** to the subject,
>
> whereas *estar* introduces a quality seen as **temporary, transitory, or**
>
> otherwise **nonessential**.

This rule is not absolute, and there are several contexts in which the two verbs are used idiosyncratically; but it works for most cases and should be learned first. Particular cases are listed in section 22.1.2. Some examples will help make the general rule clear. Suppose we say

> *Lívia é muito triste.*
> 'Lívia is very sad.'

Here the use of *ser* (*é*) carries the meaning that she is a sad person—essentially sad, we might say. This contrasts with

> *Lívia está muito triste.*
> 'Lívia is very sad.'

which means that she is sad now, like anyone who becomes sad from time to time, but there is no intimation that she is an inherently sad person. That is why we can say

> *Lívia está muito triste com a morte do avô.*
> 'Lívia is very sad because of (her) grandfather's death.'

Here the use of *ser* would be totally infelicitous because one does not usually assign a momentary cause to an essential quality.

This is *not* simply an opposition between temporary and permanent qualities, as is made clear by cases like

> *Esse gato está morto.*
> 'This cat is dead.'

Of course, being dead is a permanent quality of the cat, but the verb used is *estar* because one does not see being dead as an essential quality of a cat—unlike its color or its breed, e.g.,

> *Esse gato é branco.*
> 'This cat is white.'

> *Esse gato é siamês.*
> 'This cat is (a) Siamese.'

Here *ser* is the appropriate verb to use because in these sentences we are referring to essential qualities of the cat.

Further examples are

> *Seu filho é muito alto.*
> 'Your son is very tall.' [= is a very tall person]

This may be said of an adult; but the following is said only of growing children:

> *Seu filho está muito alto.*
> 'Your son is very tall.' [= has grown a lot lately]

> *Eu sou americano.*
> 'I am American.'

but not

> ** Eu estou americano.*

because being American is seen as an essential, permanent quality. Conversely,

> *Eu estou de férias.*
> 'I am on vacation.'

but, since to be on vacation is necessarily a temporary condition, one does not say

> ** Eu sou de férias.*

Ser must also be used in general, timeless statements such as

> *Verbo é uma palavra que se conjuga.*
> '(A) verb is a word you (can) conjugate.'

Essa doença é horrível.
'This disease is terrible.'

Não é possível cozinhar sem alho.
'(It) is not possible to cook without garlic.'

22.1.2 Particular cases

In some cases the use of *ser* and *estar* deviates from the general rule given in the preceding section. The first observation is that *estar* tends to have a more extended usage than the general rule strictly allows; therefore, in some contexts it may be used interchangeably with *ser*. For instance, the general rule applies with locational expressions: one uses *estar* to introduce a person's location:

Guilherme está em Londres.
'Guilherme is in London.'

but *ser* is used when referring to a city or a geographic accident:

Londres é na Inglaterra.
'London is in England.'

This makes sense in terms of the general rule, since the location of a city is something inherent to it, unlike the location of a person. But with geographic terms one can also use *estar,* and the following is perfectly acceptable:

Londres está na Inglaterra.
'London is in England.'

Likewise,

O Canadá é / está ao norte dos Estados Unidos.
'Canada is to the north of the United States.'

Minha casa é / está no final dessa rua.
'My house is at the end of this street.'

In all these cases *estar* is used where the general rule would predict that only *ser* is appropriate. The converse is not possible: *ser* is not used for nonessential, transitory qualities or states:

*Eles estão debaixo da cama. / * Eles são debaixo da cama.*
'They are under the bed.'

Only *ser* is used in the following contexts:
—when identifying oneself

    —Quem é?
    —Sou eu, o Marco.
    "Who is it?"
    "It is me, Marco."

—in the expression *era uma vez* 'once upon a time,' used as an introduction to children's tales
—when stating the time of day

    Já são quase oito horas.
    '(It) is almost eight o'clock.'

Ser and *estar* are used indifferently with certain complements:

    Eles estão casados há dez anos. / Eles são casados há dez anos.
    'They have been married for ten years.'

I suspect that in these cases it is not relevant whether the quality is seen as inherent or not, and correspondingly either verb can be used.

With *vivo* 'alive' and *morto* 'dead' the use of the two verbs is peculiar. We may use either verb with *vivo* when it means 'living':

    Meu avô ainda é vivo. / Meu avô ainda está vivo.
    'My grandfather is still living.'

In the meaning 'my grandfather is still alive,' (e.g., if he is expected to die soon) only *estar* is used:

    Meu avô ainda estava vivo quando chegou ao hospital.
    'My grandfather was still alive when he arrived at the hospital.'

With *morto* 'dead,' as we saw, *estar* is used, since being dead is not an inherent property; but one can occasionally find *morto* with *ser*, although this turn is old-fashioned:

Napoleão já era morto quando isso aconteceu.   **Arch**
'Napoleon was already dead when this happened.'

Finally, with *falecido* 'deceased, late' only *ser* is used:

Meu avô já é falecido. / * . . . *está falecido.*
'My grandfather is already deceased.'

22.2 Other peculiar verbs

Many other verbs are used in Portuguese in ways that differ sharply from their English translations; while it is not possible to study them all here (this being the business of a dictionary), I list below the most important ones, with their usage as compared with English.

22.2.1 *Ter* vs. *estar com* 'to have'

Ter means 'to have,' and in some of its uses it is similar to English *to have*:

Eu <u>tinha</u> um carrinho maravilhoso.
'I had a wonderful little car.'

Vovó <u>teve</u> uma gripe fortíssima.
'Granny had a very strong flu.'

Ela <u>tem</u> cabelo ruivo.
'She has red hair.'

Ter also occurs in many constructions that in English employ other verbs:

Eu sempre <u>tenho</u> pena de você.
'(I) always pity you [literally, (I) always have pity . . .].'

Tomás <u>tem</u> cinqüenta anos de idade.
'Tomás is fifty years old [literally, has fifty years of age].'

Nós <u>tínhamos</u> vontade de ficar aqui.
'We wished we could stay here [literally, had wish to stay].'

Other such constructions are *ter esperança* 'to hope,' *ter medo* 'to fear,' *ter sono* 'to be sleepy,' and many others.

In all these cases *ter* is used when the sentence denotes a permanent or habitual state; when one wants to express a momentary state, *ter* is replaced by *estar com*. Thus,

> *Meu gato sempre <u>tem</u> fome de noite.*
> 'My cat is always hungry at night [literally, has hunger].'

because this is a habitual state of the cat. But if we want to say that the cat is hungry right now, the sentence becomes

> *Vou pegar a ração porque meu gato <u>está com</u> fome.*
> '(I)'m getting the chow because my cat is hungry [literally, is with hunger].'

Similarly, the following sentences express momentary states:

> *<u>Estou com</u> pena de você.*
> '(I) pity you (right now).'

> *Nós <u>estávamos com</u> vontade de comer uma pizza.*
> 'We wanted (at that moment) to eat a pizza.'

Estar com also substitutes for *ter* in its nonidiomatic use, with the same meaning alteration. Compare the examples given at the beginning of this section with

> *Eu <u>estou com</u> um carrinho maravilhoso.*
> 'I have a wonderful little car (for the moment).'

> *Vovó <u>está com</u> uma gripe fortíssima.*
> 'Granny has a very strong flu (today).'

If we say

> *Ele <u>tem</u> uma camisa xadrez.*
> 'He has a checkered shirt.'

we mean that he owns a checkered shirt, perhaps at home. But

> *Ele <u>está com</u> uma camisa xadrez.*

means that he is wearing a checkered shirt. One can say even

> *Ela <u>está com</u> cabelo ruivo.*
> 'She has red hair (today).'

if she usually dyes her hair and varies the color frequently.

Ter can also be used to express a momentary state, but this use is not common and sounds literary or old-fashioned. Thus, the sentence

Ele <u>tem</u> dor de cabeça.

will normally be understood only as 'He is subject to headaches,' not as 'He has a headache (now).'

22.2.2 *Ficar* vs. *virar* 'to become'

Ficar and *virar* both translate into English as 'to become,' but they are used in different constructions. *Virar* always takes a noun phrase as its complement, e.g.,

Comendo desse jeito, você vai acabar virando <u>um elefante</u>.
'Eating like that, you will end up becoming an elephant.'

Depois de publicar um livro ele virou <u>aquele pedante que todos detestamos</u>.
'After he published a book he became that pedant we all hate.'

Ficar has the same meaning, but it is normally used with a qualificative nominal:

Vovó ficou <u>bonita</u> depois de velha.
'Granny became pretty after she got old.'

Ele toma Bovril para ficar <u>forte</u>.
'He takes Bovril in order to become strong.'

Virar cannot occur with a qualificative nominal:

* *Vovó virou <u>bonita</u>*

* *Ele virou <u>forte</u>*

On the other hand, *ficar* can occur with a noun phrase, but this is not the most usual construction:

Ele comeu demais e ficou <u>um elefante</u>.
'He ate too much and became an elephant.'

While this sentence is acceptable, it sounds more natural with *virar*.

Another verb for 'to become' is *tornar-se* (always reflexive; see chapter 20); *tornar-se* may be used in either of the environments described above:

Depois de publicar um livro ele se tornou <u>um pedante</u>.
'After he published a book he became a pedant.'

Vovó se tornou <u>bonita</u> depois de velha.
'Granny became pretty after she got old.'

While all three verbs can be used in all situations, *tornar-se* is preferred in writing, and *virar* and *ficar* are appropriate in all styles.

22.2.3 *Haver* and *ter* 'there to be'

The English construction *there to be,* as in the sentence

There is a fly in my soup.

is translated into Portuguese by means of the existential verbs *haver* or *ter.* Thus, the above sentence is translated as

Há uma mosca na minha sopa.	**Wr**
Tem uma mosca na minha sopa.	**SpBr**

Some comments are in order: First, as indicated above, *haver* is the standard written form, whereas *ter* is the one that occurs in the spoken language. The distinction here is pretty sharp, and *ter* is found in written texts only when it is necessary to reproduce spoken utterances (as in plays or dialogues), and *haver* is very rare in speech.

Second, unlike their English counterpart, these verbs do not agree (that is to say, they are subjectless), so that we have

<u>*Há*</u> *quatro moscas na minha sopa.*	**Wr**
<u>*Tem*</u> *quatro moscas na minha sopa.*	**SpBr**
'There are four flies in my soup.'	

As can be seen, the Portuguese verbs remain in the third person singular whatever the number of the accompanying noun phrase (cf. Spanish <u>*Hay*</u> *cuatro moscas en mi sopa*).

22.2.4 Light verbs

Light verbs are verbs that, apart from their use in regular constructions, appear in many sequences of verb + object or complement with a peculiar, unpredictable meaning. Portuguese has several such light verbs; in this section I list the most frequent of them, with the special constructions in which they occur (many of which, as noted below, are colloquial and in wide use). There is no way to give a complete list of such constructions here, as they are very numerous; the student will find a near-complete list in a good dictionary,[1] in the entries for *dar, fazer, bater, passar, tomar,* etc.

Note

[1]Such as Houaiss and Avery, or Michaelis (see bibliography for the complete references).

dar

By far the most frequent light verb is *dar,* which when "heavy" means 'to give.' It occurs in many constructions, of which the most important are listed below. Observe that some of them require a preposition after the complement, e.g., *dar andamento a*.

dar a louca	'to go wild, to make a foolish decision'	**SpBr**

Cristina deu a louca e mudou para São Paulo.   **SpBr**
'Cristina went wild and moved to São Paulo.'

dar andamento a   'to get going'

Preciso dar andamento a esses projetos.
'(I) have to get these projects going.'

dar as caras   'to show up'   **SpBr**

Dê as caras amanhã na festa!   **SpBr**
'Show up tomorrow at the party!'

dar a entender   'to hint'

A professora deu a entender que prefere trabalhos curtos.
'The teacher hinted that she prefers short essays.'

dar baixa   'to be mustered out'

Meu irmão deu baixa da Marinha em 1990.
'My brother was mustered out of the navy in 1990.'

dar bola para   'to pay attention, to flirt'   **SpBr**

Eu nunca dou bola para essas teorias.   **SpBr**
'I never pay attention to these theories.'

Ela vive dando bola para mim.   **SpBr**
'She is always flirting with me.'

dar o bolo em   'to stand someone up'

Francisco deu o bolo na menina.
'Francisco stood the girl up.'

dar certo   'to turn out well'

Acho que minha candidatura vai dar certo.
'(I) think my candidacy will turn out well.'

dar duro   'to work hard'

O rapaz nunca tinha dado duro na vida.
'The young man had never worked hard in his life.'

dar em   'to beat, to spank'

Ela deu no pobre cachorro até cansar.
'She beat the poor dog until she tired of it.'

dar em   'to result'

Todo o esforço deu em nada.
'All the effort resulted in nothing.'

dar em   'to lead to' (said of a road)

Essa rua dá na praia?
'Does this street lead to the beach?'

dar jeito de   'to be possible'   **SpBr**

Parece que não deu jeito de conseguir o aumento.   **SpBr**
'It seems that it was not possible to get the raise.'

dar de cima de / *dar em cima de*   'to harass sexually'   **SpBr**

    Esse cretino vive dando de cima das garotas.   **SpBr**
    'This idiot is always sweet-talking the girls.'

dar na vista   'to show'

    Está dando na vista que o casamento deles fracassou.
    '(It) shows that their marriage was a failure.'

dar para   'to be possible'   **SpBr**

    Não deu para te ligar ontem.   **SpBr**
    'It was not possible to call you yesterday.'

dar para   'to be enough'

    Essa mistura dá para vinte e quatro bolinhos.
    'This mix is enough for twenty-four cookies.'

dar para is a rather coarse way of expressing 'to agree to sexual intercourse':

    Ela dava para qualquer um.   **SpBr**
    'She made out with anyone.'

dar por   'to notice'

    Quando eu dei pela falsidade dele, era tarde.
    'When I noticed his duplicity, it was too late.'

dar sopa   'to be easily available'   **SpBr**

    Comi uns pastéis que estavam dando sopa em cima da mesa.   **SpBr**
    '(I) ate some pastries that were (available) on the table.'

dar na cara   'to be evident'   **SpBr**

    Dá na cara que eles não se suportam.   **SpBr**
    'It is evident that they can't stand each other.'

Dar is also used in connection with *uma* plus the participle of a verb (always in the feminine), e.g., *dar uma arrumada* 'to clean up a little.' This construction conveys the meaning of a hurried or not very important action:

Por falta de tempo vou só dar uma arrumada no quarto.
'Because of lack of time I'm only cleaning up the room a little.'

O médico vai dar uma passada aqui de tarde.
'The physician will drop by for a moment in the afternoon.'

See also

dar cabo de	'to do away with'	
dar com	'to find'	
dar conta de	'to account for'	
dar as costas para	'to turn one's back to'	
dar espetáculo	'to make oneself ridiculous'	
dar fé	'to certify'	
dar fim a	'to put an end to'	
dar importância a	'to heed'	
dar lugar a	'to yield'	
dar no pé	'to run away'	**SpBr**
dar o basta	'to say enough'	**SpBr**
dar o fora	'to run away'	**SpBr**
dar ouvidos a	'to pay heed to'	
dar para trás	'to be called off'	**SpBr**
dar patada em	'to speak rudely to'	**SpBr**
dar satisfação	'to make amends'	
dar sorte	'to be lucky'	
dar trela	'to lead on'	**SpBr**
dar uma gafe	'to make a social blunder'	
dar uma volta	'to go for a walk'	

and many others.

fazer

Fazer in its proper use means 'to make' or 'to do.' When followed by an infinitive it means 'to cause,' as in

Esse filme me fez chorar.
'This movie made me cry.'

Fazer also occurs as a light verb in sequences like the following:

fazer amizade com   'to strike a friendship with'

Júlio faz amizade com qualquer um.
'Júlio makes friends with anyone.'

fazer as pazes com   'to make peace with'

Eles brigaram, e agora fizeram as pazes de novo.
'They quarreled, and now they have made up again.'

fazer onda   'to make a fuss'   **SpBr**

Não sei por que fazem tanta onda com o Carnaval.   **SpBr**
'(I) don't know why people make such a fuss about Carnival.'

fazer de conta   'to make believe'

Faça de conta que hoje é amanhã.
'Make believe today is tomorrow.'

fazer gosto em   'to approve'   [used only for family events]

Dona Esquipéria não fez gosto no casamento de Guidinha.
'Dona Esquipéria did not approve of Guidinha's marriage.'

fazer jus a   'to earn, to deserve'

Eu já fiz jus a umas boas férias.
'I have earned the right to a good vacation.'

fazer o favor de   'to be so kind as'

Me faz o favor de passar o açúcar.   **SpBr**
'Will you pass me the sugar, please?'

fazer mal   'not to agree with [said of food]; to harm'

As enchiladas me fizeram mal.
'The enchiladas didn't agree with me.'

não fazer mal   [only in the negative] 'not to matter'

> *Não faz mal se o café vier frio.*
> 'It doesn't matter if the coffee arrives cold.'

And also

fazer água	'to leak [said of boats]'	
fazer (alguém) de bobo	'to make a fool (of someone)'	
fazer anos	'to have a birthday'	
fazer cera	'to delay'; 'to stall [in soccer]'	**SpBr**
fazer cerimônia	'to stand on ceremony'	
fazer por onde	'to act so as to deserve'	
fazer economia	'to save'	
fazer efeito	'to take effect, to result'	
fazer falta	'to be missed'	
fazer farol	'to show off'	**SpBr**
fazer fita	'to pretend not to want something one really wants'	**SpBr**
fazer força	'to make an effort'	
fazer graça	'to be cute'	
fazer hora	'to kill time'	**SpBr**
fazer (o) papel de	'to act a part'	
fazer parte de	'to belong to'	
fazer pouco de	'to slight'	
fazer questão de	'to make an issue of'	
fazer sucesso	'to succeed'	
fazer caso	'to pay heed' [usually in the negative]	

bater

Bater properly means 'to hit,' 'to defeat,' or 'to beat':

> *Eu bati na parede e me machuquei.*
> 'I hit the wall and hurt myself.'

> *O Atlético sempre bate no Cruzeiro.*
> 'The Atlético always beats the Cruzeiro [soccer teams].'

> *Dizem que o marido até batia nela.*
> 'They say that her husband even spanked her.'

> *Bater as claras com o açúcar.*
> 'Beat the egg whites with the sugar.'

Bater is also a light verb in some expressions, e.g.,

bater boca	'to argue heatedly'	**SpBr**

Os dois ficaram batendo boca até altas horas.   **SpBr**
'The two of them argued until late in the night.'

bater pino	'to be in a bad way [mentally]'	**SpBr**

Acho que nosso chefe está batendo pino.   **SpBr**
'(I) guess our boss is pooped.'

Also

bater as asas	'to run away'	
bater as botas	'to die'	
bater carteira	'to pick pockets'	
bater o pé	'to insist'	
bater papo	'to chew the fat'	**SpBr**

passar

Passar usually means 'to go by,' 'to pass,' or 'to press (clothes).' It appears as a light verb in

passar a perna em   'to outsmart, to cheat'

O verdureiro me passou a perna.
'The greengrocer cheated me.'

passar por   'to pretend to be'

Ele passava por milionário para impressionar as meninas.
'He pretended to be a millionaire in order to impress the girls.'

passar pito em   'to reprehend'

Não suporto quando me passam pito.
'(I) can't stand it when someone scolds me.'

passar por alto   'to skip'

Vamos passar por alto as infrações menores.
'Let us skip over the minor infractions.'

and some others.

tomar

Tomar means 'to take' (or, with a suitable object like *cerveja* 'beer,' 'to drink'). In the following sequences it functions as a light verb:

tomar conta   'to take care,' and also 'to take over'

> *Tome conta da minha menina.*
> 'Take care of my girl.'

> *As preocupações tomaram conta dela.*
> '(Her) worries took her over.'

tomar por   'to mistake for'

> *Você me toma por um moleque?*
> 'Do you take me for a scoundrel?'

tomar gosto por   'to acquire as a habit; to take to'

> *Ele tomou gosto pela bebida.*
> 'He learned to like drinking (alcohol).'

The examples given above are just the most common usages of the most frequent light verbs; the complete list is long and must be learned item by item, being in essence a lexical matter.

22.3 Modals

Modals are verbs that are added to a noninflected form of another verb (an infinitive or a gerund); the whole construction has only one subject, expressed in the first verb, and this subject is understood to be valid for the infinitive or gerund as well. What characterizes a modal, as against other verbs which take the infinitive, is that with the modal
   a. no subordinate clause in the indicative or subjunctive is possible;
   b. the following verb cannot have a subject (overt or understood) different from the subject of the modal.[1]

Note

   [1]By these criteria, auxiliaries are also modals; but auxiliaries are set apart as a separate category because of some other characteristics (see chapter 13).

Most modals may also occur as main verbs; but in general the meaning of the modal cannot be predicted from the meaning of the same verb when in its nonmodal use, so that it is important to learn each of them separately. Thus, *dever* as a main verb means 'to owe,' as in

> *Roberto me <u>deve</u> mais de mil reais.*
> 'Roberto owes me more than a thousand reals.'

But when used as a modal it conveys an idea of possibility:

> *Roberto <u>deve</u> chegar bem atrasado hoje.*
> 'Roberto will probably arrive pretty late today.'

The difference between a modal and a nonmodal verb is illustrated by the following examples:

> *<u>Posso</u> devolver o livro amanhã.*
> '(I) may return the book tomorrow.'

Posso is a modal since the following verb must be in the infinitive and its subject must be understood as identical to the subject of the main verb. But in

> *<u>Quero</u> devolver o livro amanhã.*
> '(I) want to return the book tomorrow.'

quero is not a modal, because we may say

> *<u>Quero</u> que você devolva o livro amanhã.*
> '(I) want you to return the book tomorrow.'

where the second verb is in the subjunctive, and furthermore the two subjects are different. Likewise, in

> *<u>Lamento</u> estar tão longe neste momento.*
> '(I) am sorry to be so far away at this moment.'

lamento is not a modal because we may add a subject to the infinitive (*estar*), and this subject may be different from the subject of the main verb:

> *<u>Lamento</u> você estar tão longe neste momento.*
> '(I) am sorry that you are so far away at this moment.'

Verbs like *poder* and *começar,* which do not require a preposition, are called **(simple) modals.** Some modals, like *chegar,* when used as modals require a preposition:

> *Ele <u>chegou</u> a bater nos meninos.*
> 'He came to the point of beating the children.'

and will be called **two-word modals**. All two-word modals occur with a following infinitive; simple modals may occur with an infinitive or with a gerund.

22.3.1 Simple modals

The most frequent simple modals are:

acabar **(+ gerund)**   'to end up'

> *Eles <u>acabaram concordando</u> conosco.*
> 'They ended up agreeing with us.'

começar **(+ gerund)**   'to start by'

> *Marcelo <u>começou telefonando</u>.*
> 'Marcelo started by calling.'

continuar **(+ gerund)**   'to go on'

> *Paulo <u>continua falando</u> por dois.*
> 'Paulo goes on speaking for two.'

dever **(+ infinitive)**   'must' or 'probably'

> *Às oito horas os hóspedes <u>devem descer</u> para o jantar.*
> 'At eight o'clock the guests must come down to dinner.'

> *<u>Devemos telefonar</u> lá pelas oito horas.*
> '(We)'ll probably phone around eight.'

poder **(+ infinitive)**   'may'

> *O teto <u>pode cair</u> a qualquer momento.*
> 'The roof may fall at any moment.'

22.3.2 Two-word modals

A two-word modal is formed by a verb plus an accompanying preposition (or, only in the case of *ter que* 'to have to,' a conjunction) that may be considered as a part of the whole expression; the latter usually means something different from the meaning of the verb when alone. For instance, the sequence *chegar a* means 'to come to the point of,' whereas *chegar,* when without *a,* is 'to arrive.' Semantically speaking, then, a two-word modal is more than the sum of its parts—which makes it necessary to learn it as a separate lexical item.

Following is a list of the most frequent two-word modals, with examples of their use:

acabar de   'to have just done'

> *Marcelo <u>acabou de telefonar</u>.*
> 'Marcelo has just called.'

acabar por   'to end up doing'

> *Marcelo <u>acabou por telefonar</u>.*
> 'Marcelo ended up calling.'

chegar a   'to come to the point of'

> *Ele <u>chegou a chorar</u>.*
> 'He came to the point of crying.'

deixar de   'to fail'

> *O candidato <u>deixou de levar</u> em conta a opinião das mulheres.*
> 'The candidate failed to take into account the women's opinion.'

haver de   'shall' (indicates strong intention of a future action) **Wr**

> *<u>Hei de vencer</u> esse jogo a qualquer custo.*   **Wr**
> '(I) shall win this game at any cost.'

ter que (or *ter de*)[1] 'to have to'

> *O cliente <u>tem que entrar</u> pela porta de trás.*
> 'The client has to enter by the back door.'

Note

[1] *Ter que* is the usual form; *ter de* is more formal, found primarily in the written language. By the way, this is probably the only example of *que* before an infinitive: *tenho que sair* '(I) have to go out.'

Modals may occur with auxiliaries:

Nós podíamos ter ajudado o pobre garoto.
      modal auxiliary
'We might have helped the poor boy.'

Agora ela deve estar almoçando.
      modal auxiliary
'Now she should be eating lunch.'

And they may also co-occur with each other:

Você tem que começar a estudar de noite.
'You have to start studying at night.'

Ricardo chegou a deixar de comer.
'Ricardo came to the point of failing to eat.'

22.3.3 Other modality markers

The same semantic features that characterize modals may be expressed by means of non-verbal elements, in particular by adverbs. Thus, the sentence

Os clientes têm que entrar pela porta de trás.
'Clients must enter by the back door.'

has a close synonym in

Os clientes entram obrigatoriamente pela porta de trás.
'Clients enter compulsorily by the back door.'

This way to express semantic modality does not require special study, since it is identical for Portuguese and for English, and furthermore the meaning of *entram obrigatoriamente* 'enter compulsorily' is readily derivable from the meaning of the separate words.

V The Noun Phrase

23

Structure of the Noun Phrase

23.1 Noun phrases

A **noun phrase** (abbreviated **NP**) is a sequence of one or more words with certain specific properties, namely,

—An NP can appear in certain syntactic functions, such as **subject**, **object**, or **complement of a preposition**, e.g.,

<u>Minha irmã</u> trabalha em um banco. **[subject]**
'My sister works in a bank.'

Eu adoro <u>esses biscoitos que você faz</u>. **[object]**
'I love these cookies you make.'

Marlene veio na chuva sem <u>sombrinha</u>. **[complement of the preposition** *sem*]
'Marlene came in the rain without (an) umbrella.'

The underlined sequences are all NPs; and only NPs can occur in the three functions shown above—that is, the subject of a clause is always an NP, and so on.

As the above examples show, the internal structure of the NP varies widely: an NP can be made up of a possessive + a nominal (*minha irmã*) or just a nominal (*sombrinha*), and it may even contain a whole clause (*esses biscoitos que você faz*); and these are only three of many possible ways of building an NP. What characterizes all NPs is their syntactic properties—the three functions listed above—and their semantic content (see below).

—Semantically speaking, an NP can *refer* to an entity of the world, which can be understood as a specific singularized object (*minha irmã* 'my sister'), as a general class (*os cachorros* 'the dogs'), or as an abstraction (*a sabedoria* '(the) wisdom'). In this particular an NP differs from say, a verb phrase, which never refers to an entity but rather denotes a process (*trabalha em um banco* 'works in a bank'), a state (*está triste* 'is sad'), or a quality (*dá muito trabalho* 'is a lot of trouble'). We say that an NP has **referential potential**, as against all other syntactic structures in the language. The referential nature of the NP is its basic semantic property and conditions the way it is internally built.

23.2 Heads and modifiers

23.2.1 Definitions

In a typical NP one can find a word that sums up its intended reference; this word is called the **head** of the NP. An example will make this clear; take the NP

> *Aquele passarinho azul*
> 'That blue bird'

Any person, upon hearing this NP, knows that the speaker intends to refer to a bird; not to any bird, for sure: *that* bird, and a *blue* bird. But it is clear that we are speaking about a bird (not, say, about the blue color). Now, if the NP were

> *Aquele azul berrante*
> 'That loud blue'

we would know that the speaker wants to refer to the blue color. We then say that in *aquele passarinho azul* the head of the NP is *passarinho;* in *aquele azul berrante* the head is *azul.* All other elements in the NP will be called **modifiers** (many words can occur as heads or as modifiers, as is the case with *azul* in the above examples).[1]

Note

**[1] How does a hearer know so surely which word in an NP is the head? This need not concern us here; I direct the interested reader to Perini et al., 1996 (75–106), where the question is discussed and answered in detail.

Some more examples will show that identifying the head of an NP is no great problem in practice:

NP	Head	Modifier(s)
minha irmã 'my sister'	*irmã*	*minha*
esses bolinhos de bacalhau 'these codfish cakes'	*bolinhos*	*esses; de bacalhau*
Alexandre (man's name)	*Alexandre*	—
o primeiro presidente do Brasil 'the first president of Brazil'	*presidente*	*o; primeiro; do Brasil*

The distinction between head and modifier is necessary for describing several important grammatical facts. A head is, semantically, the **reference center** of an NP, that is, it shows what the NP is referring to; for instance, in *esses bolinhos de bacalhau* 'these codfish cakes' the head *bolinhos* stipulates that the speaker is referring to cakes, not to codfish or to anything else.

Syntactically, the head determines:

—The conditions for agreement within the NP. In *meu carro amarelo* both *meu* and *amarelo* appear in the masculine singular because *carro* is masculine and is in the singular.

—The conditions for agreement in the sentence. In the sentence

Meu carro amarelo está na oficina.
'My yellow car is in the shop.'

the verb *está* 'is' is in the third person singular because the subject NP, *meu carro amarelo,* has a head, *carro,* which is third person and is in the singular. That is, the gender, person, and number of the head are the gender, person, and number of the NP.

—The starting point for describing most ordering relations within the NP. Thus, I will be speaking below about **prehead modifiers** and **posthead modifiers**, that is, modifiers are classified according to their position in the NP relative to the head.

Nominal agreement is considered in chapter 34. In this chapter we will be concerned primarily with the order of elements within an NP.

23.2.2 Elliptical heads

In some cases there is no word present in the NP that can be called the head; we can speak then of **elliptical heads**. This happens in two situations:

Anaphoric contexts

When part of an NP is repeated in the subsequent context, one understands the missing part in the second one to be identical to the corresponding part in the first. This is called an **anaphoric context** and may result in an NP that lacks an overt head, as in

Meu tio tem um <u>carro vermelho</u> e <u>um azul</u>.
'My uncle has a red car and a blue one.'

Since there is no word in Portuguese for English *one* in this context, the second of the two NPs referring to cars (*um azul*) does not contain the word *carro,* which is the head of the first NP (*um carro vermelho*), and is the understood head of the second one.

In such cases everything works in the second NP as if a head *carro* were present, in particular (a) the NP is understood as referring to a car; and (b) modifier agreement is in the masculine singular, following the gender and number of *carro.* For our purposes, then, we may say that the head of the NP *um azul* in the above sentence is *carro,* elliptical but unambiguously recoverable from the context.[1]

Note

**[1] This raises the serious theoretical question of how to establish the precise status of *carro* in the NP *um azul:* an underlying formal element, deleted by a transformation? An empty element provided with an index that refers to *carro* in the previous NP? A semantic rule that recovers the referent from the gap in the second NP? In spite of its theoretical import, this question is of no consequence for our purposes in this grammar and cannot be resolved here.

Nonanaphoric contexts

In a few well-defined cases, an NP occurs in nonanaphoric contexts without any word that could be called its head, and yet with a clear reference to an entity that is not directly mentioned. This happens when the NP is composed solely of the words *poucos, todos,* and *alguns* (all in the masculine plural). In these cases the entity referred to is always a set of human beings:

<u>Poucos</u> já leram as obras de Camões.
'Few (people) have read Camões's works.'

<u>Muitos</u> votaram em Cardoso sem o conhecerem.
'Many (people) voted for Cardoso without knowing him.'

<u>Alguns</u> acham que educação é escola.
'Some (people) think that education is the same as school.'

24

Ordering of Modifiers Relative to the Head

24.1 Ordering

In English, the order of elements in the NP is comparatively simple: modifiers made up of single words tend to come before the head, and modifiers introduced by prepositions come after the head:

The	*red*	<u>*roof*</u>	*of the house*
modifier	**modifier**	**head**	**modifier**

Of course, this is only a general rule because in sequences like *attorney general* and *president elect* the head comes before a single-word modifier; but these sequences are uncommon and may be considered exceptions (as can words like *afraid, awake, asleep,* which function as modifiers, yet come after the NP head).

Another complexity not covered by the general rule is the ordering constraints obtaining among modifiers; one can say *a nice red car,* but * *a red nice car* sounds positively odd. Portuguese has the latter complexity, so I will pay some attention to the ordering of modifiers. Furthermore, the ordering of modifiers in relation to the head also varies, so that it is normal (but not equivalent) to say *um <u>simples</u> dentista* 'a mere dentist' as well as *um dentista <u>simples</u>* 'a simpleminded dentist.' As for modifiers introduced by prepositions, they must come after the head as in English and require no special study: *o telhado <u>da casa</u>*. I start, then, with the problem of ordering the modifiers with relation to the head.

24.2 Prehead modifiers

24.2.1 General rule

The ordering of modifiers within the NP is determined basically in terms of their position relative to the head. To start with the items that (typically) occur *before* the head: these correspond in many cases to English items with similar meanings, e.g., articles and demonstratives like *o* 'the,' *um* 'a,' *aquele* 'that,' which in both languages always come before the head:

<u>a</u> *mesa   / <u>uma</u> mesa*
'the table / a table'

<u>aquela</u> *biblioteca*
'that library'

There may be more than one prehead modifier in an NP, and their ordering is also in most cases the same as in English, e.g.,

<u>alguns</u> <u>poucos</u> *centavos*
'some few cents'

<u>todos</u> <u>os</u> *avisos*
'all the warnings'

<u>esses</u> <u>dois</u> *rapazes*
'these two young men'

Items typically functioning as prehead modifiers are relatively few, and it is possible to give a complete list of them. Some of these items can also occur after the head, as we will see. These items are distinguished by subclasses (labeled I, II, and III) according to the order in which they appear with respect to each other. The following table shows how these items are ordered among themselves:

I	II		III	
Predeterminers	**Determiners**		**Quantifiers**	
todos 'all'	*o*	'the'	*quantos*	'how many'
ambos 'both'	*um*	'a'	*tantos*	'so many'
	este	'this'	*tal*	'such'
	esse	'this'	*poucos*	'few'
	aquele	'that'	*muitos*	'many'
	algum	'some'	*vários*	'several'
	nenhum	'no'	*qualquer*	'any'
	cada	'each'	*certo*	'certain'
	que	'what' [interrogative or exclamative]	**possessives**	
	qual	'which' [interrogative]	**numerals**	

Relative order of prehead modifiers

Whenever the items in the table occur **before the head,**[1] their ordering with respect to each other follows the rule below:

The basic order of the elements in the table is **I—II—III**, that is,

a. whenever an item of group I occurs in an NP it must be the first element of the NP;

(*continued*)

b. an item of group II is the second element if there is in the same NP

an item belonging to group I; otherwise, it is the first; and

c. items of group III always occur after item(s) of groups I or II (if any).

Note

[1]Several of these items can also occur after the head; see below.

This rule results in sequences like the following:

ambos aqueles gatos	'both those cats'
I II	
os poucos centavos	'the few cents'
II III	
todos os muitos problemas	'all the many problems'
I II III	

Comparison of the above phrases with their English translations shows that the two languages behave in basically parallel ways; there are a few differences, which are listed below.

The names given above to the three groups (**predeterminers, determiners, quantifiers**) are traditional. In the case of the quantifiers, this nomenclature reflects the fact that the group has a semantic feature in common, that is, most of its members denote quantity—with exceptions: the possessives, as well as *certo* and *qualquer*, do not indicate quantity.

24.2.2 Co-occurrence of items

Possessives
Syntactically speaking, group III is a much less coherent class than groups I or II, and its members are less homogeneous in behavior. For instance, there can be only one item of each of groups I or II per NP; but a noun phrase may contain two items of group III, e.g.,

meus muitos amigos 'my many friends'
 III III

muitos meus amigos 'many friends of mine'
 III III

meus dois amigos 'my two friends'
 III III

dois meus amigos 'two friends of mine'
 III III

These sequences usually involve possessives. We cannot put possessives into a fourth group, though, because, as we've seen, they may be the first or the second group III element in the sequence. For the moment, therefore, and pending further discussion, this will be considered an exception, in that they can occur with other members of group III in the same noun phrase.

As can be seen in the glosses, the position of the possessive has semantic consequences: when the possessive comes first in its group it is **nonrestrictive**, but when it occurs after some other item of group III it has a **restrictive** meaning, Thus, the phrase *meus muitos amigos* 'my many friends' refers to *all* my friends (which are many), whereas *muitos meus amigos* 'many friends of mine' refers to a *subset* of my friends.

what a / such a

In English, sequences of *what* + article are permissible, as in *what a fever!* In Portuguese, however, exclamative *que* and the article are mutually incompatible because they belong to the same group (II); exclamative expressions have no article:

> *Que febre!*
> 'What a fever!'

Similarly, we cannot have *tal* 'such' followed by the article in Portuguese (as in English *such a fever*) because the article belongs to group II, and *tal* belongs to group III:

> *Com tal febre você não deveria sair.*
> 'With such a fever you shouldn't go out.'

But the ordering **article** + *tal* does occur, as is to be expected:

> *Com uma tal febre você não deveria sair.*
> 'id.'

todo, todos

Todo(s) appears in three constructions, namely,

 — *Todo* in the singular, without article, meaning 'every, each':

> *Todo cidadão tem direitos.*
> 'Every citizen has rights.'

> *Ela vai todo dia ao shopping.*
> 'She goes to the mall every day.'

— *Todo* in the singular, followed by an article or a demonstrative like *esse, este, aquele,* meaning 'whole, all':

> *Ela passa todo o dia na cama.*
> 'She spends all day in bed.'

> *Toda a cidade foi inundada.*
> 'The whole town was flooded.'

> *Todo esse barulho por nada.*
> 'All that noise for nothing.'

> *Ele utilizou todo um arsenal de truques.*
> 'He used a whole armory of tricks.'

— *Todos* in the plural, followed by an article, a demonstrative, or a personal pronoun, meaning 'every, all':

> *Todos os cidadãos têm direitos.*
> 'All the citizens have rights.'

> *Todos nós votamos no senhor.*
> 'All of us voted for you.'

Todo(s) and *ambos* 'both,' as seen above, are the only two members of group I and have the privilege of appearing first in the NP. Remember that *ambos,* unlike English *both,* is a written form and is not used in common speech.

Note that the requirement that the article follow *todos* is not observed in the spoken language, and even in writing one frequently finds *todos* without an article:

> *Põe todos sacos naquela gaveta.*   **SpBr**
> 'Put all bags in that drawer.'

24.2.3 Posthead occurrence

Several of the items in the above list can also occur after the head, in most cases with a difference in meaning. For instance, one may say

<u>*Nenhum lingüista*</u> *aceitaria essa teoria.*
'No linguist would accept this theory.'

or

<u>*Lingüista nenhum*</u> *aceitaria essa teoria.*
'id.'

In the case of *nenhum* there is no semantic difference between the two orderings; but this is exceptional. In all other cases postposing the modifier entails some alteration in the meaning of the NP. The following items can occur after the head:

nenhum
algum, qualquer, certo
possessives
numerals (ordinals and cardinals)
este, esse[1]
todos, ambos

Note

[1]But not *aquele,* except in the regional speech of southern Brazil: *o professor aquele* 'that teacher.'

algum
Algum when preposed means 'some':

<u>*Alguma pessoa*</u> *vai me ajudar.*
'Some person will help me.'

but when it is postposed it means 'no,' that is, it becomes a synonym of *nenhum* (this use is confined to the written language):

<u>*Pessoa alguma*</u> *vai me ajudar.*   **Wr**
'No person will help me.'

Postposed *algum* is used when the speaker intends to put some emphasis on the negation: *pessoa alguma* corresponds approximately to 'no person at all.'

qualquer

Qualquer when preposed means 'any':

> *Qualquer idiota vê isso.*
> 'Any idiot can see that.'

In this sense, *qualquer* refers to the totality of entities mentioned, that is, *qualquer pessoa* is very close to *toda pessoa* 'any person.' When postposed it may have the same meaning:

> *Peça ajuda a uma pessoa qualquer.*
> 'Ask for help from anyone you want.'

Or it may mean 'common' with a derogatory connotation:

> *Ela casou com um sujeito qualquer.*
> 'She married a common fellow.'

certo

Certo when preposed means '(a) certain, one' and is normally preceded by an indefinite article:

> *Fui procurado por um certo Xavier Medeiros.*
> 'I was contacted by one Xavier Medeiros.'

The article may be omitted, and this is considered more correct by some, but it is not usual. When postposed, *certo* means 'correct':

> *Um exercício certo vale dez pontos.*
> 'A correct exercise is worth 10 points.'

Possessives

The **possessives** that concern us here are *meu* 'my,' *seu* 'your, his / her,' *nosso* 'our,' *teu* 'your,' *vosso* 'your (pl.).' Possessives formed with prepositions, like *dele* 'his,' *de vocês* 'your (pl.)' behave like normal prepositional phrases and always come **after the head of the NP** (see section 10.3 for a list of all these possessives, including conditions in which they are used).

Preposed possessives have a definite meaning:

> *Meu amigo me telefonou às quatro horas.*
> 'My friend called me at four o'clock.'

In this position it can be preceded by the definite article:

> <u>*O meu amigo*</u> *me telefonou às quatro horas.*
> 'id.'

The presence of the definite article makes no difference in meaning, and the two constructions are equivalent for all purposes—their use is largely a question of personal taste.[1]

Note

[1]Some grammars try to state the semantic and/or syntactic conditions under which the use of the definite article before a possessive is permissible. I think such an effort is misguided. The most one can say is that there is a tendency toward a wider use of the article in informal speech.

We can also have an indefinite article with the preposed possessive, and in this case the construction translates as English *a N of mine / yours,* etc.:

> <u>*Um meu amigo*</u> *ganhou o prêmio.*
> 'A friend of mine won the prize.'

Postposed possessives, without an article, have a generic meaning, that is, they refer to a general class, rather than to one or more particular individuals:

> <u>*Amigo meu*</u> *não passa necessidade.*
> 'Whoever is my friend will never be in need.'

With the indefinite article, it has the specific meaning:

> <u>*Um amigo meu*</u> *ganhou o prêmio.*
> 'A friend of mine won the prize.'

This means the same as

> <u>*Um meu amigo*</u> *ganhou o prêmio.*
> 'id.'

Postposed possessives never occur with the definite article; that is, we cannot say * *o amigo meu* (this does not apply to possessives formed with *de,* which, as I said, behave like prepositional phrases: *o amigo dele* 'his friend').

Possessives are less used in Portuguese than in English. For instance, the article is sometimes used to express a possessive, in expressions like *ele quebrou a perna* 'he broke his leg' (see section 26.1.1).

Numerals

Cardinal numerals normally occur before the head:

> *Os cinco candidatos estão esperando no saguão.*
> 'The five candidates are waiting in the hall.'

When postposed, they have the same meaning as their ordinal counterparts:

> *O capítulo cinco é o mais difícil.*
> 'Chapter five [that is, the fifth chapter] is the most difficult.'

> *Luís Quinze foi rei da França.*
> 'Louis the Fifteenth was the king of France.'

As we saw in chapter 9, with the numbering of kings, popes, and centuries, ordinals are used up to ten; from then on, postposed cardinals are used: *Dom João Sexto* 'Dom João the Sixth,' but *Luís Quinze* 'Louis XV,' *João Paulo Segundo* 'John Paul II,' but *João Vinte e Três* 'John XXIII.'

Ordinal numerals occur before the head:

> *Rodrigues Alves foi o quinto presidente do Brasil.*
> 'Rodrigues Alves was the fifth president of Brazil.'

They may occur postposed in rare cases, namely,

—In poetry, in a very few set phrases like *o amor primeiro* 'the first love' (also *o primeiro amor*).

—In the numbering of parts of a book:

> *O capítulo terceiro* (also *o capítulo três*)
> 'Chapter three'

> *Isso se encontra no Canto Sexto da Ilíada.* (also *no Sexto Canto . . . / no Canto Seis . . .*)
> 'This can be found in the sixth canto of the *Iliad*.'

este, esse

Este, esse 'this' (but not **aquele** 'that') can also appear after the head in one particular context: when repeating a nominal mentioned shortly before, e.g.,

O governo de um pequeno país, <u>país esse</u> afligido pela inflação . . .   **Wr**
'The government of a small country, (country this) distressed by inflation . . .'

This repetition of **esse, este** has the purpose of avoiding ambiguity; in the above sentence, it points clearly to the country (not the government) as the distressed entity. This use of **este, esse** is restricted to the written language.

The following table will help students visualize the behavior of these items:

Item	Meaning (preposed)	Meaning (postposed)
algum	'some'	no'
qualquer	'any'	'any'/'common'
certo	'(a) certain, one'	'correct'
possessives	**definite**	—(without article) **generic** —(with *um*) **definite**
cardinals	**quantity**	**order**
ordinals	**order**	**order**
este, esse	'this'	'this' (when recalling a recently mentioned nominal)

Items that can occur before or after the head

24.2.4 *Todo(s), ambos*

Todo(s) and *ambos* can appear after the head, in very peculiar ways. *Todo(s)* can appear within the NP immediately after the head, that is, in the same way as the preceding items: thus, one can say

<u>*Todos*</u> *os crocodilos fugiram do zoológico.*
'All the crocodiles fled from the zoo.'

or

Os crocodilos <u>todos</u> fugiram do zoológico.
'id.'

There is no difference in meaning between the two versions. So far, *todos* is not too different from items like *nenhum.* But there is more: first,

> *todo* without an article cannot be postposed

<u>*Todo*</u> *cidadão tem direitos.*   **but**   * *Cidadão <u>todo</u>* . . .
'Every citizen has rights.'

And, second,

> *todos* can also be postposed **outside** the NP, to certain positions in the sentence—in particular, it can occur after the verb, or at the end of the sentence

<u>*Os crocodilos*</u> *fugiram <u>todos</u> do zoológico.*
'The crocodiles fled all from the zoo.'

<u>*Os crocodilos*</u> *fugiram do zoológico <u>todos</u>.*[1]
'id.'

Again, postposition does not alter the meaning of *todos.*[2]

Notes

[1]Many speakers do not accept *todos* in this position, at the very end of the sentence.

[2]In English also, the quantifier *all* can be postposed, but a resumptive pronoun is required, as in *the crocodiles fled from the zoo, all of them.*

As for *ambos,* it seems to occur only preposed (*ambos os pais* 'both parents') or immediately after the verb:

Os pais ficaram ambos agradecidos.
'The parents became both grateful.'

24.3 Posthead modifiers

We saw in the previous section a list of items that usually occur before the head. Except for those items, the normal position of modifiers in the Portuguese NP is **after** the head—and in this, Portuguese differs from English, which almost invariably puts modifiers before the head, e.g.,

A casa nova
'The new house'

The items that occur typically after the head (unlike the ones listed in 24.2.1) are very numerous, numbering several thousands in the language, including most nominals. Many of them can also occur before the head, and, in this case, they have the property of occurring **after** any of the items of the list given in 24.2.1—that is, their position when preposed to the head is **after the position of group III**. In the phrase

Minha nova casa
'My new house'

one may observe that *nova* comes after *minha* 'my,' a member of group III. This ordering is obligatory: * *nova minha casa* is unacceptable. The same happens with other members of group III:

As cinco novas casas
'The five new houses'

Quantas <u>novas</u> casas?
'How many new houses?'

and so on. This, of course, results in an ordering similar to the English one, so there is no special learning problem here.

In many cases, Portuguese allows the same modifier to appear before or after the head, usually with a concomitant difference in meaning. For instance, *a casa nova* means 'the new house,' and this may mean that it is in effect new (recently built) or that it is a house someone has just bought; but *a nova casa* has only the latter meaning.

Furthermore, there are many nominals that can function as modifiers, but only postposed to the head; and there are a few that can appear only preposed. The precise conditions governing the position of modifiers are not well known, but from what *is* known some rules can be drawn, and these will be given in what follows.

Another question to consider in relation to posthead modifiers is their ordering relative to each other when an NP contains more than one modifier. Here, again, there are some rules that may be useful, although they do not cover the entirety of the cases. I will consider each of these questions in turn in the following sections.

24.3.1 Fixed-position items

There are a few items that can appear as modifiers only before the head: *mero* 'mere,' *pretenso* 'self-styled,' *reles* 'raffish, second-class,' *suposto* 'supposed,' *parco* 'meager,' *meio* 'half.' These cannot appear after the head:

Um <u>mero</u> subalterno
'A mere subordinate'

<u>Meia</u> melancia
'Half a watermelon'

O <u>suposto</u> vencedor
'The supposed winner'

Apparently, these items are restricted to prehead position by virtue of an idiosyncratic marking, that is, there is no known reason (semantic or otherwise) why they should not occur after the head. Most of them have a derogatory connotation, as *mero, pretenso, reles, suposto,* and *parco.* But *meio* has no such connotation, and there are many derogatory words that are not restricted in the way those few items are, for example, *falso* 'false, counterfeit,' *mau* 'bad, of poor quality,' *fraco* 'weak (also in quality),' and many others. Therefore, it is easier to learn the small list of words that function as modifiers only before the head than to attempt generalizations—this is what native speakers probably do when they learn the language.

To the above list we may add some items occurring in slang or in very colloquial language, such as *big* 'excellent'—pronounced, of course, ['bigi]—*puta* 'terrific,' *baita* 'big,' which always occur preposed (and also do not vary in gender or in number):

> *Um baita salário*   **SpBr**
> 'An excellent salary'

Similarly, some items are marked for the postposed position. First, there are some nominals that, when used as modifiers, do not vary for gender or number. Most of them denote colors: as *laranja* 'orange (color),' *rosa* 'pink,' *gelo* 'ice-colored, light grey,' *grená* 'purplish red,' to which we may add *alerta* 'alert':

> *Um vestido laranja | Três vestidos laranja*
> 'An orange dress   / three orange dresses'
>
> *Paredes gelo*
> 'Ice-colored walls'

Some of these items can appear as heads, and then they do vary in number:

> *Muitas laranjas*
> 'Many oranges'

Notice that variable color terms behave like normal modifiers, that is, they agree, and they can (under favorable circumstances) appear either preposed or postposed:

> *Um vestido branco | Três vestidos brancos*
> 'A white dress   / three white dresses'
>
> *O branco vestido da noiva*
> 'The bride's white dress'

It is only the invariable ones that are confined to postposed position.

Besides these, there are a few more items that can appear only postposed, for no known reason: *ruim* 'bad,' *comum* 'common,' *esnobe* 'snobbish,' *macho* 'male,' *fêmea* 'female':

> *Aquele livro ruim*
> 'That bad book'
>
> *O interesse comum*
> 'The common interest'

Uma cobra <u>macho</u>
'A male snake'

Comum appears preposed in the set phrase *comum acordo* 'mutual consent.'

The above categories exhaust the list of items marked for one of the two possible positions relative to the head of the NP.

24.4 Position rules

I now consider the problem of describing the conditions for preposing and postposing modifiers. When both positions are possible, there is always some difference in meaning or in use in discourse between the two versions; and in many cases when only one version is possible, there is a semantic explanation for that fact. In what follows I will give an overview of what has already been found about the problem.

Here we have to deal with a heterogeneous group of factors: a modifier can be ordered in a particular way with respect to its head because of the meaning it carries; or because of the way the whole NP fits into the discourse; or because of the fact that it is part of an idiom or a set phrase (as in *doce ilusão* 'sweet delusion,' which never occurs as * *ilusão doce*). Let's look at the semantic factors first.

24.4.1 Thematic roles

The position of a modifier with respect to its head often carries a semantic consequence. For instance, a modifier can express the **agent** of an action, as in

A invasão <u>japonesa</u>
'The Japanese invasion'

The modifier *japonesa* denotes the agent of the action of invading. It is a general fact in the language that whenever a modifier denotes the agent it must appear after the head; we then say that the meaning 'agent' (to use the technical designation, the **thematic role** 'agent') is available only to modifiers in postposed position. There are no cases in which an agentive modifier appears before the head. This allows us to state a rule to the effect that

Whenever a modifier means 'agent' it must be postposed.

As we shall see, there are several rules similar to this one.

Note that the above rule does *not* mean that whenever a modifier is postposed it must mean 'agent'; the rule works in one direction only. There are many meanings that can be expressed only by postposed modifiers; all the above rule says is that an agent cannot be expressed by a preposed modifier. That understood, we may proceed to list some of the semantic readings that are exclusive to postposed modifiers.

All the following meanings can be expressed by a modifier only if it is postposed:
—**Agent**, e.g.,

A invasão japonesa (never * *a japonesa invasão*)
'The Japanese invasion'

—**Patient**, e.g.,

Preservação ambiental
'Environmental preservation'

—**Possession**, e.g.,

O palácio presidencial
'The presidential palace'

—**Authorship**, e.g.,

As sonatas mozartianas
'The Mozartean sonatas'

—**Provenance** or **origin**, e.g.,

O café brasileiro
'(The) Brazilian coffee'

—**Classifier**, e.g.,

Um engenheiro mecânico
'A mechanical engineer'

"Classifier" is used here in a special meaning: one understands *engenheiro mecânico* 'mechanical engineer' as one of the natural subdivisions of the greater class of engineers.

Other subdivisions of the class of engineers are 'electrical,' 'nuclear,' 'chemical,' etc. These are "natural" classes of engineers as opposed to nice, tall, French, or competent engineers, which can also be regarded as subclasses but are not exclusive to the class of engineers: teachers, taxi drivers, and flutists can also be nice, tall, French, or competent (but never chemical, mechanical, or electrical in the sense that engineers can be). Further examples of classification in this meaning are

> *Lingüista histórico*
> 'Historical linguist' (that is, a professional who works on historical linguistics)

> *Cirurgião plástico*
> 'Plastic surgeon'

> *Agente secreto*
> 'Secret agent'

> **—Stereotyped behavior**, e.g.,

> *Um amigo cachorro*
> 'A treacherous friend [literally, a dog friend]'

> *Um cozinheiro porco*
> 'An unsanitary cook [literally, a pig cook]'

Here *cachorro* 'dog' and *porco* 'pig' are used not as a way to refer to the animals themselves, but as modifiers, attributing to the head some quality stereotypically attached to the animal.[1] Correspondingly, the meaning of the word when used as a modifier cannot be easily derived from its meaning when used as a head; we need additional information about cultural beliefs and stereotypes, as well as about more or less fanciful associations, as in the phrase *eleitor fantasma,* literally 'phantom voter,' used for names of nonexistent persons included in voter lists.

Note

[1] It is probably better not to comment on what these attachments reveal about the gratefulness or justice of human judgments about animals.

—Extensional qualification, e.g.,

Um filho médico
'A son (who is a) doctor'

Meu irmão deputado
'My congressman brother'

In these cases one may understand 'who is,' or something equivalent, before the modifier. Consequently, in *um filho médico* one understands that the person in question is both a son and a doctor; compare this with *um amigo cachorro* 'a treacherous friend,' where the person is a friend but not (literally) a dog. Of course, *um amigo cachorro can* be understood extensionally as 'a friend who is a dog,' that is, Fido. In any of these cases, the modifier comes after the head. There are a few exceptions, like

Um jovem pianista
'A young pianist'

who is both a young person and a pianist. This may have to do with the very concrete meaning of *jovem* 'young'; in any case such exceptions are infrequent.

24.4.2 Restrictiveness

A semantic feature that is connected with the position of the modifier is restrictiveness. Compare the following two cases:

O escritor famoso está no banheiro.
'The famous author is in the bathroom.'

O famoso escritor está no banheiro.
'id.'

Although the two underlined NPs translate similarly in English, they have different meanings in Portuguese. In the first case, *o escritor famoso,* we may be referring to one of several authors, and we single this one out by adding the quality 'famous'; it is understood that he is the only famous author present (this is the **restrictive** reading of the modifier). We may also, with the same phrase, refer to the only author present and volunteer the information that he is famous (this is the **nonrestrictive**, or **appositive**, reading).

But with *o famoso escritor* only the latter, nonrestrictive meaning is available: that is, here *famoso* is added for extra information, but it does not single out the intended author among other authors. This difference may be represented in English if we use restrictive vs. appositive clauses, viz.,

> *O escritor famoso*
> 'The writer who is famous' **or** 'the writer, who is famous'

> *O famoso escritor*
> **only** 'The writer, who is famous'

These data allow us to state a general rule (which has some exceptions; see below):

Preposed modifiers are interpreted as nonrestrictive; postposed modifiers can be interpreted as restrictive or nonrestrictive.

The main exceptions are:

—**Deictic** modifiers are always restrictive, even when they occur before the head. A deictic word is one that can be understood only in relation to the situation in which it is uttered, e.g., *today* (the precise day it refers to depends on the day it is uttered), *here, I, next,* etc. In Portuguese some deictic words can function as modifiers and can appear before the head:

> *O próximo mês*
> '(The) next month'

> *O atual presidente* [**or** *o presidente atual*]
> 'The current president'

Though preposed, they are restrictive: in *o próximo mês* the modifier *próximo* singles out the next month, as against the current or the past one; in *o atual presidente* the modifier *atual* 'current' singles out one president among several other presidents.

—**Relative superlatives** like *melhor* 'best,' *mais inteligente* 'most intelligent' are also restrictively interpreted, even when they are preposed:

O melhor aluno da escola
'The best student in the school'

O mais brilhante cientista do século [**or** *o cientista mais brilhante* . . .]
'The most brilliant scientist of the century'

This may have to do with the fact that relative superlatives are necessarily restrictive, by virtue of their basic meaning: their use presupposes a comparison between several candidates, which presupposes some kind of restriction.

—Items that *must* appear before the head[1]—either because they cannot appear after it, like *pretenso* 'self-styled,' or because they have a different meaning when postposed, like *grande* 'great' (when preposed) or 'large' (when postposed)—also can be restrictive even when preposed.

Note

[1] Here we are dealing with qualificative items, not with articles, quantifiers, or determiners like *aquele* 'that,' examined in section 24.2 above.

Thus, we can say

Só os pretensos heróis se candidatam; os verdadeiros salvam a pátria e voltam para casa.
'Self-styled heroes go into politics; true ones save the fatherland and go back home.'

Os grandes homens criam idéias; os pequenos ganham dinheiro com elas.
'Great men create ideas; small ones make money with them.'

In the above sentences we can see how preposed modifiers (*pretensos, grandes*) can be used restrictively (self-styled heroes are singled out among all heroes, great men are singled out among all men). This happens because *pretenso* can appear only before the head and because *grande* in the reading 'great' also can appear only in this position.

24.4.3 Changes in meaning

As just seen, the word *grande* can occur before or after the head, but with a particularly radical change in meaning: when preposed it means 'great,' when postposed it means 'large, big.' This happens with a few other items:

	When preposed	**When postposed**
simples	'mere'	'simple, naïve'
pobre	'poor, unhappy'	'poor, impecunious'
verdadeiro	'real'	'true'
antigo	'former'	'ancient'
certo	'certain'	'correct'
semelhante	'such'	'similar'
caro	'dear'	'expensive' (also 'dear')

Examples:

Uma simples criança
'A mere child'

Uma criança simples / um problema simples
'A naïve child'   / 'a simple (= easy) problem'

Um pobre refugiado
'A hapless refugee'

Um refugiado pobre
'A poor (= impecunious) refugee'

Uma verdadeira obra de arte
'A real work of art'

Uma obra de arte verdadeira
'A true work of art'

Interestingly, the phrase *uma verdadeira obra de arte* usually refers to something that is just as beautiful as a work of art but is not necessarily a work of art in the literal sense. So one can say *Eduardo é uma verdadeira dama* 'Eduardo is [as gentle as] a lady,' without saying that Eduardo *is* a lady.

> *Um <u>semelhante</u> indivíduo*
> 'Such an individual'

> *Um indivíduo <u>semelhante</u>*
> 'A similar individual'

The above items are exceptional in that they have totally different meanings according to their position relative to the head; for instance, *grande* after the head cannot mean 'great,' only 'large.'

In the case of *novo* 'new' and *velho* 'old' and *antigo* 'ancient' the change in meaning is just as great but not so strictly tied to ordering. *Novo* and *velho* have one meaning when postposed and another when preposed *or* postposed, so that the postposed modifier is ambiguous; for *antigo* the situation is reversed, so that it is ambiguous when preposed. For instance:

> *Uma <u>nova</u> casa*
> 'A new (recently acquired) house'

> *Uma casa <u>nova</u>*
> 'A new (recently acquired **or** recently built) house'

> *Um velho amigo*
> 'A long-standing friend'

> *Um amigo velho*
> 'An aged friend' **or** 'a long-standing friend'

> *Um <u>antigo</u> escritor*
> 'A former writer' **or** 'an ancient writer'

> *Um escritor <u>antigo</u>*
> **only** 'An ancient writer'

This is as far as one can go with general rules. Preposed modifiers tend to acquire set meanings together with their heads, so that one sometimes finds cases whose meaning is not amenable to generalization; thus, *um grande homem* is 'a great man,' not 'a large man'; but *uma grande cidade* is understood to be 'a large city' besides meaning 'a great city,' and *um grande edifício* is necessarily a large building.

This tendency explains the emergence of (sometimes subtly) different meanings in particular sequences of modifier + head even with items that do not, as a rule, change their meaning when preposed; for instance, *um funcionário alto* means 'a tall civil servant,' but *um alto funcionário* is 'a top civil servant.'

24.4.4 Evaluatives

It is often said that preposed modifiers carry a "subjective" meaning. Although this is a somewhat vague statement, it certainly contains some truth. We may focus it a little better by saying that preposed modifiers tend to express the speaker's personal evaluation of a quality. This can be seen in the pair

> *Salários <u>altos</u> / <u>altos</u> salários*
> 'High salaries'

The first phrase refers to high salaries, without any intimation of the speaker's opinion about them. The second one not only conveys the idea that the salaries are high, but also suggests that there is something that the speaker finds remarkable about it: perhaps they are higher than expected or unduly high for the particular job in question.

This may explain why many items that never appear preposed in their simple form do so when in the absolute superlative form, e.g., *final* 'final,' which is never preposed except in contexts like

> *Uma <u>finalíssima</u> decisão do Supremo*
> 'An absolutely final decision of the Supreme (Court)'

Also *burro,* which as a modifier means 'stupid,' only appears before the head when in the superlative:

> *Aquele <u>burríssimo</u> auxiliar arruinou meu trabalho.*
> 'That most stupid attendant ruined my work.'

24.4.5 Expectation of adequacy

Finally, there is a semantic feature that is very frequently found in preposed modifiers, namely, the **expectation that the quality expressed by the modifier is particularly adequate to the entity referred to by the head**; in short, **expectation of adequacy**. A good example is

> *Uma madrasta <u>cruel</u> / uma <u>cruel</u> madrasta*
> 'A cruel stepmother'

*Uma mãe <u>cruel</u> / * uma <u>cruel</u> mãe*
'A cruel mother'

Why can *cruel* co-occur with *madrasta* 'stepmother' in both the preposed and the postposed positions, but only in the postposed position with *mãe* 'mother'? The reason is that there is a culturally conditioned expectation that stepmothers be cruel, while mothers are expected to be loving and tender. Let one thing be clear: nobody really believes that stepmothers are cruel; but cruelty is part of the cultural stereotype of the concept of 'stepmother,' not of the concept of 'mother.' Therefore, *cruel* 'cruel' cannot appear preposed with *mãe* 'mother' because there is no expectation that the quality 'cruel' is particularly adequate to mothers. Similarly, one can say

Um brilhante <u>cientista</u>
'A brilliant scientist'

but the following is at least awkward:

* *Um <u>musculoso</u> cientista*
'A muscular scientist'

A scientist need not be brilliant and may be well-muscled; but brilliancy, not strong muscles, is culturally expected from a scientist. In Portuguese this is reflected in the order of the modifier: a modifier can be preposed when there is an expectation of adequacy linking it to its head; otherwise, preposing it gives awkward or unacceptable results.

It is also possible, up to a point, to manipulate the expectation of adequacy so as to cause its emergence even when there is no culturally established stereotype. This may be done by preposing an evaluative modifier, thus conveying to the receptor the idea that the speaker admits that there *is* such a culturally established stereotype—and, furthermore, that the speaker assumes it to be shared by the receptor, who is subliminally invited to participate in what, after all, is a lie. For example, I say

Os <u>intragáveis</u> pães de queijo
'The unpalatable cheese rolls'

and with this phrase I not only state that the cheese rolls in question are unpalatable, but I also hint that cheese rolls are normally unpalatable, and that this is a current assumption previously accepted by the receptors of my message.

24.5 Set phrases

In a number of set phrases the order is fixed without any discernible semantic or textual reason. These cannot properly be called idioms because the two elements preserve their normal meaning; only the order is fixed. Some examples are

<u>doce</u> ilusão	'sweet del
<u>alta</u> burguesia	'high bourgeoisie'
<u>santa</u> Igreja	'Holy Church'
<u>baixa</u> renda	'low income'
<u>triste</u> sina	'sad lot'

All of the above modifiers can also appear after the head, but not in those particular phrases; thus, one can say *uma cidade santa* 'a holy city,' but not * *Igreja Santa; uma palavra doce* 'a sweet word,' but not * *ilusão doce*.

24.6 Expanded modifiers

Finally, when a modifier is expanded (usually by means of an adverbial element or a prepositional phrase) it is normally postposed to the head, e.g.,

Comprei um vestido <u>lindo de morrer</u>.
'(I) bought a very beautiful dress [literally, beautiful to die (for)].'

Essa é uma marca <u>bem boa</u>.
'This is a pretty good brand.'

Preciso de batatas <u>boas para sopa</u>.
'(I) need potatoes good for (making) soup.'

Ele casou com uma mulher <u>linda como um anjo</u>.
'He married a woman (as) beautiful as an angel.'

A modifier expanded by the adverb *bem* 'well' can occur before the head if the speaker wants to call attention to the modifier, e.g.,

O policial montava um <u>bem treinado</u> cavalo branco.
'The policeman rode a well-trained white horse.'

This is frequent only with modifiers expanded by *bem*. In rare cases one finds preposed modifers expanded by other adverbs, but they always sound pedantic.

25

Ordering of Modifiers Relative to Each Other

A head may be followed by more than one modifier; and in many cases the ordering of these modifiers is not indifferent. In this section I will present the rules that describe the ordering constraints obtaining between two postposed modifiers (as far as such rules are known); sequences of more than two modifiers, which are rare, are not covered here.

25.1 Classifiers vs. qualifiers

Modifiers can, of course, express a number of different semantic relations; among these are **classification** and **qualification**. As we saw briefly above (section 24.4.1), a modifier is said to be a **classifier** when it singles out one class among several into which a greater class is usually divided. For instance, if one asks what kinds of engineers there are, people will mention electrical engineers, nuclear engineers, civil engineers, etc., and not nice engineers, fat engineers, and the like. Logically speaking, all of these are subdivisions of the class of engineers, but the former are felt to be the natural subclasses; in other words, the language treats the difference between fat and thin engineers (**qualifiers**) and the difference between electrical and civil engineers (classifiers) differently.

The main difference is that when both kinds of modifiers occur in a noun phrase, the classifier must be contiguous to the head (and always *after* it) and the qualifier must come after it:

Um engenheiro civil   simpático
classifier qualifier
'A nice civil engineer'

In English, the order is reversed: the qualifier comes first, then the classifier, which must occur contiguous to the head. That is why one cannot say *a civil nice engineer,* unless *civil* is taken in its qualifying reading (_ _ _ce' or 'nonmilitary'). Thus, *um engenheiro simpático civil* means a nice engineer who is not in the military. Another example:

Um poeta romântico francês
classifier qualifier
'A French romantic poet'

Here it is understood that the poet belongs to the romantic school. But in

Um poeta francês romântico

the most immediate interpretation is that the French poet in question is a sentimental person. Here again, *romântico* must be taken in its qualificative reading, since it is not contiguous with the head. Still, with *francês,* we have

Um pão francês delicioso
'A delicious French bread'

This noun phrase refers to French bread (a kind of white bread), whereas the following noun phrase

Um pão delicioso francês

refers to bread imported from France.
Other examples of the ordering classifier–qualifier are as follows:

Política externa inadequada
classifier qualifier
'Inadequate foreign policy'

Chapeleiro real   irritado
classifier qualifier
'Angry royal hatmaker'

Azul marinho horrível
   classifier qualifier
'Horrible dark blue'

Perito meteorológico desempregado
   classifier   qualifier
'Jobless meteorological expert'

Doente mental incurável
   classifier qualifier
'Incurable mentally sick person [literally, incurable mental sick (person)]'

Artista plástica genial
   classifier qualifier
'Brilliant plastic artist'

In all of these NPs the two modifiers must appear in the order given, if the classificative reading of the first one is to be preserved. The opposite order yields either an unacceptable sequence (**doente incurável mental*) or changes the classifier into a qualifier (*chapeleiro irritado real* 'true angry hatmaker').

Sequences of head + classifier can be considered as intermediate between "free" sequences of head + (qualificative) modifier, on one hand, and compound nominals, on the other. In a free sequence such as *engenheiro simpático* 'nice engineer,' *simpático* modifies *engenheiro* directly, and thus we can use the same word in a predicative construction: *esse engenheiro é simpático* 'this engineer is nice.' But in a sequence of head + classifier such as *engenheiro mecânico* the modifier applies to something else: the engineer himself is not mechanical. If we say *esse engenheiro é mecânico* 'this engineer is mechanical,' *mecânico* will refer to the engineer directly, and we must be referring to some kind of robot.

Sequences of head + classifier, unlike sequences of head + qualifier, are learned as set phrases, not spontaneously produced; on the other hand, most of them correspond to similar constructions in English, so that only a minority of classificative constructions present acquisition problems.

25.2 Informational load

Another factor governing the order of modifiers is the informational load of each modifier: the most informationally relevant modifier comes last. This is a discourse factor and can be fully exemplified only in the context of sequences larger than single noun phrases or even sentences. Take the NP

Uma moça alta maravilhosa
'A wonderful tall girl'

By themselves, the two modifiers, *alta* 'tall' and *maravilhosa* 'wonderful,' already have different potential informational loads. That is, other things being equal, *maravilhosa* will be taken as the most relevant modifier, because it is a (semantic) superlative. Therefore, the reverse order sounds odd:

* *Uma moça maravilhosa alta*

But this holds true only if other things are equal, as they often are not. Once this NP is inserted into a wider context, it may turn out that *alta* 'tall' becomes the most relevant piece of information, as in

Dizem que todas as moças bonitas são baixinhas.
Mas eu conheço <u>uma moça maravilhosa alta</u>.
'People say that all pretty girls are short. But I know a wonderful tall girl.'

Now the ordering *moça maravilhosa alta* sounds perfectly natural.

25.3 Increasing restrictiveness

A third factor governing the order of modifiers is the relative inclusiveness of the modifiers involved. As we know, a modifier typically restricts the extension of the head, so that the head plus the modifier refers to a smaller set than just the head. For example, when we say *cavalo* 'horse' we may be referring to any horse, but in *cavalo branco* 'white horse' only a subset of all horses is denoted. The restrictiveness increases as modifiers are added: *cavalo branco velho* 'old white horse' refers to a subset of all white horses, and so on.

In some cases, the order of the modifiers is indifferent; for instance, we may say

Um vestido novo importado
'An imported new dress'

or

Um vestido importado novo
'A new imported dress'

This happens when the two modifiers are not related in terms of inclusiveness, that is, an imported dress is not necessarily new, and a new dress is not necessarily imported. But in some cases there are relations of inclusiveness, e.g.,

> *Essa escola pública federal*
> 'This federal public school'

In the Brazilian system, a federal school is always public; in other words, federal schools are a subset of all public schools. Whenever this situation obtains, the most restrictive modifier must come last, so that * *escola federal pública* is not acceptable. We then say that modifiers must be ordered by **increasing restrictiveness.**

25.4 Prepositional phrases

All of the examples examined above have single-word modifiers. But a modifier can also be composed of a prepositional phrase, e.g.,

> *Uma casa <u>de tijolo</u>*
> 'A brick house'
>
> *A casa <u>de Pedro</u>*
> 'Pedro's house'

When an NP has two modifiers, and one of them is a prepositional phrase, the prepositional phrase regularly comes at the end:

> *As praias maravilhosas do Nordeste*
> 'The wonderful beaches of the northeast'
>
> *Uma casa nova de tijolos*
> 'A new brick house'

The converse ordering does occur in special cases. The factors that motivate the postposition of the single nominal after the prepositional phrase are, first, the presence of a particularly high informational load in the nominal (see 25.2 above):

> *Na rua só havia casas antigas; a exceção era <u>uma casa de tijolos nova</u>, bem na esquina.*
> 'The street had only ancient houses; the exception was a new brick house, right on the corner.'

Here *casa de tijolos nova* 'new brick house' is put into contrast with the preceding *casas antigas* 'ancient houses'; therefore, *nova* has a high informational load and can occur at the end of the NP.

The other situation in which the nominal may be postposed to the prepositional phrase is when the prepositional phrase is a classifier (see 25.1 above):

> *Um motorista de táxi idoso*
> 'An aged taxi driver'

Since *motorista de táxi* is felt to be one of the classes into which people normally distinguish drivers, *de táxi* is treated as a classifier and therefore stays contiguous to the head.

26

Use of the Article

Portuguese, like English, has two articles, the **definite** *o / a* 'the,' and the **indefinite** *um / uma* 'a.' The article must agree with the head in gender and number:

> *Um carro / uma casa*
> 'A car / a house'

> *O carro / os carros / a casa / as casas*
> 'The car / the cars / the house / the houses'

Um has a plural form, *uns / umas,* which translates as 'some' in English:

> *Eu trouxe uns presentes.*
> 'I have brought some presents.'

There are several important differences between Portuguese and English in the use of articles, so the matter requires some attention. There are some general rules, complemented by a host of particularities that (pending some more general analysis, still not available) must be listed individually. We start with the uses of the definite article.

26.1 The definite article

Although Portuguese and English differ in the use of the definite article, the general character of this item is the same in both languages; that is, the definite article (as opposed to the indefinite article or to the absence of article) is normally used to refer to an entity that was previously mentioned or is otherwise assumed to be present in the listener's mind, e.g.,

> *Comprei um carro usado. Ontem descobri que o carro estava cheio de ferrugem.*
> 'I bought a used car. Yesterday I found out that the car was full of rust.'

Or when two persons are looking at a picture, and one of them says

> *O pintor morreu há mais de trinta anos.*
> 'The painter died more than thirty years ago.'

the speaker assumes that just saying *o pintor* 'the painter' (instead of, say, *o pintor que fez este quadro* 'the painter who made this picture') is clear enough and that the idea of that particular painter must be present in the listener's mind because the listener is looking at the picture at that moment.

In this the two languages are similar, and no lengthy comment is needed. In what follows I concentrate on the points in which Portuguese differs from English in its use of the definite article.

26.1.1 When to use the definite article

The general rule of use of the definite article is the following:

> The definite article expresses the extension of the notion denoted by the head. Generally speaking, the definite article is used when one wants to refer to the ***totality*** of a class—including classes composed of only one member.

A few examples may clarify the application of the rule:

> *As aranhas têm oito pernas.*
> '(The) spiders have eight legs.'

We are referring to the entire class of spiders and therefore use the definite article (for an alternative way of expressing the same meaning, see section 26.1.4).

> *O cavalo é um mamífero.*
> 'The horse is a mammal.'

Here again we have a reference to the whole class, using the singular as in English.

> *A platina é um metal precioso.*
> '(The) platinum is a precious metal.'

Since we are speaking of platinum in general (that is, the statement is valid for all platinum), we use the definite article.

The general rule also applies when we refer to elements belonging to a single-member class—even when the reference is to an abstract entity, e.g.,

> *A natureza é cruel.*
> '(The) nature is cruel.'

> *O amor é cego.*
> '(The) love is blind.'

English often omits the article in such cases, but in Portuguese even abstract nominals take the article when in the context described by the general rule.

In other cases the definite article is used with unique entities, e.g.,

> *O sol é uma estrela.*
> 'The sun is a star.'

> *A Avenida Rio Branco tem mais de três quilômetros.*
> '(The) Rio Branco Avenue is more than three kilometers long.'

> *O monte Everest foi escalado nos anos cinqüenta.*
> '(The) Mount Everest was climbed in the fifties.'

> *A Sears é uma cadeia de lojas de departamentos.*
> '(The) Sears is a chain of department stores.'

In these examples Portuguese is more consistent than English (considering the general rule as stated above): whenever reference is made to the entire class, even if it is a single-member class, the definite article is used.

But in grammar consistency should not be expected to go very far; besides the general rule, there are several minor rules applying to particular sets of nominals or special contexts.

—Modified heads

> When an NP head is modified by a prepositional phrase, it usually takes the article.

Ela fala <u>o francês do Canadá</u>.[1]
'She speaks Canadian French.'

Os croatas jogam <u>o futebol do futuro</u>.
'The Croatians play the soccer of the future.'[2]

As we will see, in these contexts the article is usually omitted when the head is not modified: *ela fala <u>francês</u>* 'she speaks French,' *ele joga <u>futebol</u>* 'he plays soccer.'

Notes

[1] This is the preferred construction. With names of languages, the article is sometimes omitted: *ela fala francês do Canadá.*

[2] As can be seen in this example, English also requires the article when the NP head is modified by a prepositional phrase. But when the modifier is classificative (see 25.1), the requirement is relaxed: *eles jogam <u>futebol de salão</u>* 'they play indoor soccer.'

—Personal names

> Personal names, which designate unique entities, should, according to the general rule, take the definite article, and they often do.

O Manuel te ligou ontem.
'(The) Manuel called you yesterday.'

This is usual in the spoken language in Portugal and in many regions of Brazil (in particular in the large cities of the southeast: Rio, Belo Horizonte, São Paulo). In some other regions—the interior of Minas Gerais, for instance—and in formal written language, personal names do not take the article:

Manuel te ligou ontem.
'Manuel called you yesterday.'

In a personal name preceded by a title, the use of the article is, with a

few exceptions, mandatory:

O doutor Ferreira não atende hoje.
'(The) Dr. Ferreira is not working today.'

Aqui é a casa do padre Mello.
'Here is Father Mello's residence.'

The following titles, however, do not take the article: *Santo / São* 'Saint,' *Dom* (formerly used with names of kings and some high nobles of Portugal and currently with bishops, archbishops, and cardinals of the Catholic Church). With *dona* (before names of women, to show some degree of respect) and *frei* 'friar,' the use of the article is optional:

*Dom Pedro II foi imperador por meio século. / * O dom Pedro II . . .*
'Dom Pedro the Second was emperor for half a century.'

Dona Catarina / A dona Catarina mora no segundo andar.
'Dona Catarina lives on the second floor.'

We may note, finally, that in Portuguese (as in English) vocatives never have an article:

<u>*Manuel*</u>, *acho que o ônibus está chegando.*
'Manuel, (I) think the bus is coming.'

—Names of countries, continents, oceans, etc.

> With names of countries, continents, and oceans the article is generally
>
> used.

A França, a Alemanha e a Áustria ficam na Europa.
'(The) France, (the) Germany, and (the) Austria are in (the) Europe.'

O Atlântico está bravo hoje!
'The Atlantic (Ocean) is furious today!'

All names of continents and oceans take the article. But with names of countries there are several exceptions: the most important are *Portugal, Cuba, Israel, Honduras:*

Portugal tem dez milhões de habitantes.
'Portugal has ten million inhabitants.'

Some country names are always plural; these names take articles and other modifiers in the plural and are considered plural also for effects of verb agreement:

Os Estados Unidos (abbreviated *os EUA* or *os EEUU*)   'the United States'

Os Países Baixos   'the Netherlands'

Os Emirados Árabes Unidos   'the United Arab Emirates'

Of these, only *Estados Unidos* is common; the Netherlands are usually referred to as *a Holanda*. In the spoken language, *Estados Unidos* is often used as a singular:

Standard

Os Estados Unidos ficam perto do México.
'The United States are near Mexico.'

Colloquial

O Estados Unidos fica perto do México.   **SpBr**
'id.'

With names of **states and provinces**, there is no general rule. Some take the article:

O Paraná, o Rio Grande do Sul, a Paraíba, o Pará, o Espírito Santo, a Bahia, o Rio Grande do Norte, o Ceará, o Piauí, o Maranhão, o Pará, o Amazonas, o Acre, o Amapá, o Distrito Federal (states and territories of Brazil);

a Flórida, a Califórnia, o Novo México, o Arizona, o Texas, a Luisiana, a Geórgia, o Alasca, o Havaí, o Maine, a Pensilvânia.

Some are always used without the article:

Minas Gerais, Santa Catarina, Pernambuco, Goiás, São Paulo, Sergipe, Alagoas, Roraima, Rondônia (states of Brazil);

Nova York (**or** *Nova Iorque*), *Ohio, Nova Jérsei, Nevada, Montana.*

And some can be used with or without the article:

(o) Tocantins, (o) Mato Grosso, (states of Brazil).

With less-known foreign names the tendency seems to be not to use the article:

Ele morou dois anos em Jalisco.
'He lived in Jalisco [state of Mexico] for two years.'

Fui de carro de Vermont até Iowa.
'(I) went by car from Vermont to Iowa.'

—Names of cities and parts of cities

Unlike general geographic designations, names of cities usually take no article.

Belo Horizonte, São Paulo, Fortaleza, Lisboa, Nova York, Roma, Paris

Only the following are consistently used with the article:

o Rio de Janeiro	'Rio de Janeiro'
o Porto	'Oporto'
o Cairo	'Cairo'
a Cidade do México	'Mexico City'
a Cidade do Cabo	'Capetown'

Other city names are sometimes used with the article; the general tendency seems to be that the natives of these cities use the article, whereas strangers tend not to:

(o) Recife, (o) Crato (both the town in Portugal and the one in the state of Ceará, Brazil), *(o) Pará* (*Pará de Minas*), *o Brás* (*São Brás do Suaçuí*).

With these names, whenever in doubt, the best strategy is to omit the article.

With names of districts and neighborhoods within a city there is no general rule; some cannot take the article:

Copacabana, Ipanema, Bonsucesso, São Cristóvão	[in Rio]
Perdizes, Pinheiros	[in São Paulo]

Other district names regularly take the article:

a Glória, a Gávea, a Tijuca	[in Rio]
o Morumbi, a Mooca,[1] *os Jardins, o Brás*	[in São Paulo]
a Pampulha, a Barroca, o Caiçara	[in Belo Horizonte]

Note

[1] Pronounced *Moca* ['mokə].

The tendency seems to be to increase the use of the article and to make all district names masculine. Thus, traditionally no article is used with the district names *Santo Antônio, Lourdes,* and *Santa Efigênia;* but young people now normally say *o Santo Antônio, o Lourdes, o Santa Efigênia.* Also, the designations of recently created districts are all masculine and are used with the article: *o Belvedere, o Santa Mônica, o Tupi.*

—Designation of activities and skills

A word like *piano* 'piano' may be taken as naming a musical instrument and therefore as signifying a physical object. But it is also the designation of a particular skill, as in *Carli-*

nhos toca piano 'Carlinhos plays (the) piano.' The same ambiguity applies to several other groups of words, such as names of languages, sports, sciences, and academic subjects, etc. In all these cases,

---

—when used with verbs referring to the respective activity or skill, words designating languages, sports, sciences, and academic subjects are used generally **without** an article;

—when understood as referring to the respective physical objects, languages, and so on, these words are used regularly, that is, **with** the article.

For instance, we may say

Ela colocou <u>o piano</u> na sala.
'She placed the piano in the living-room.'

with an article before *piano,* since it is understood as the actual object. But we have no article in

Ninguém tocou <u>piano</u> melhor que Horowitz.
'Nobody played (the) piano better than Horowitz.'

because here we are referring to the piano not as a piece of furniture, but rather as the name of an activity. With verbs denoting activities or skills, these items are used without an article:

Ele fala perfeitamente <u>alemão</u>.[1]
'He speaks German perfectly.'

Eu toco <u>flauta</u>.
'I play (the) flute.'

Todos aqui jogam <u>tênis</u>.
'Everyone here plays tennis.'

Note

[1] With names of languages the article may be used: *ele fala perfeitamente <u>o alemão</u>;* this is not the most common construction, though.

The same applies to these items when used with a preposition (*de, para,* or *em*) to designate a medium or to modify words designating professionals, students, or scholarly subjects:

Machado só escrevia <u>em português</u>.
'Machado wrote only in Portuguese.'

Esta sonata é para <u>violino</u>.
'This sonata is for (the) violin.'

Marlene é aluna de <u>francês</u>.
'Marlene is a student of French.'

Perdi meu livro de <u>matemática</u>.
'I lost my math book.'

Meu instrutor de <u>tênis</u> está doente.
'My tennis instructor is sick.'

The same items take the article in the regular way in other situations, namely,

—When they refer to physical objects:

Ele bateu em Virgínia com <u>o violão</u>.
'He hit Virgínia with the guitar.'

—When referrring to activities not in relation to their actors:

<u>*O tênis*</u> *é muito popular na Europa.*
'(The) tennis is very popular in Europe.'

—When considered as a source or a goal (as in a translation, which is from one language into another):

Este livro foi traduzido do sueco para o português.
'This book was translated from (the) Swedish into (the) Portuguese.'

—When referring to selected aspects of an activity:

A sintaxe do chinês é difícil.
'The syntax of (the) Chinese is difficult.'

Meu irmão conhece profundamente as regras do futebol.
'My brother has a profound knowledge of the rules of (the) soccer.'

—Possessives

> With one-word possessives (*meu, seu, nosso, teu, vosso*), use of the article
>
> is optional.

*Meu pai (**or** o meu pai) tem uma fazenda.*
'My father has a farm.'

There is no difference in meaning, and both versions are equally correct (in spite of assertions to the contrary sometimes found in grammars). The spoken language tends to prefer use of the article.

With possessives composed of *de* + personal pronoun (*dele, dela, de vocês*), the head takes an article according to the general rules, the possessive being felt as a normal prepositional phrase:

A mãe dele é rica e bonita.
'His mother [literally, the mother of his] is rich and pretty.'

—The article used for the English possessive
Portuguese normally uses the definite article where English uses the possessive in the expression of inalienable possession—that is,

> When the possessed entity is a part of one's body or a personal relation, or something considered to be in a specially intimate relation with the possessor; and, furthermore, the possessor is the **subject** of the sentence, the definite article is normally used to denote possession.

For example,

> *A vítima perdeu o braço no desastre.*
> **possessor**
> 'The victim lost his [literally, the] arm in the accident.'

> *Carlinhos levou os filhos para a praia.*
> **possessor**
> 'Carlinhos took his [literally, the] children to the beach.'

The same use of the article also occurs frequently when the head denotes an object of personal use or when the context makes it clear that it belongs to the subject:

> *Ela deixou a bolsa no ônibus.*
> **possessor**
> 'She left her [literally, the] purse on the bus.'

> *O motorista voltou para o carro.*
> **possessor**
> 'The driver went back to his [literally, the] car.'

The possessive *can* be used in these cases, but it sounds much less natural than the definite article:

> *Ela deixou sua bolsa no ônibus.*
> 'She left her purse on the bus.'

—The article with infinitives
In Portuguese it is possible to use the definite article with an infinitive, as in

O pintar paisagens é uma atividade fora de moda.   **Wr**
'(The) painting landscapes is an old-fashioned activity.'

Acordávamos ouvindo o cantar dos pássaros.   **Wr**
'(We) woke up hearing the birds' singing.'

In the first example, we have an infinitive clause, including an object (*paisagens*); in the second example, the infinitive functions as a nominal, with a normal modifier introduced by a preposition (*dos pássaros*).

When used with an infinitive, the article is always in the masculine singular (that is, in the unmarked form). This construction is not usual in the spoken language, being regarded as somewhat literary.

—**Special cases**

The article is optionally used with names of **days of the week** without preposition; it is obligatory when a preposition precedes.

A sexta-feira / sexta-feira é o dia mais ocupado para mim.
'(The) Friday is the busiest day for me.'

Fui na casa dele na sexta-feira (not ** em sexta-feira*).
'I went to his home on Friday.'

The article is omitted before the word *casa* meaning 'home,' in the expressions *em casa* '(at) home,' *de casa* 'from home,' and *para casa* '(to) home':

Eu acho que vou ficar <u>em casa</u> hoje à noite.
'I think I'll stay home tonight.'

É melhor ir direto de casa para o trabalho.
'It is better to go straight from home to work.'

26.1.2 Anaphoric use of the definite article

> The definite article is found **without** an accompanying nominal in
> anaphoric contexts, e.g.,

Ele me mostrou dez caminhonetes, e eu comprei <u>a</u> pior.
'He showed me ten pickup trucks, and I bought <u>the</u> worst (one).'

Since there is no exact correlate of English *one* in this context, Portuguese simply omits the second occurrence of *carro* 'car,' keeping the article as a sort of a reminder. This is called the **anaphoric** use of the article (in most traditional grammars, the article is called a "pronoun" in such cases, but there is no good reason for this difference in nomenclature). Other examples are

Guarde os livros no porão, exceto <u>os</u> que estiverem mofados.
'Store the books in the basement, except for those that are moldy.'

Jogamos fora tanto as frutas verdes quanto <u>as</u> podres.
'(We) threw away both the unripe fruits and the rotten (ones).'

26.1.3 "Neuter" *o*

> The form **o** (invariable in gender and number) is also used as a "neuter"
>
> article, corresponding to Spanish *lo*:

Ele só teve o melhor da vida.
'He had only the best in life.' [Spanish: *lo mejor de la vida*]

In particular, *o* is found before the relative pronoun *que,* in so-called **headless relatives** (see chapter 36), corresponding to English *what, whatever:*

Em São Paulo você encontra o que quiser.
'In São Paulo you find whatever you want.'

Ela trouxe o que vocês pediram.
'She has brought what you had asked for.'

26.1.4 Use of the article with generic heads

In English, reference to a generic entity is most commonly made with a plural nominal, without an article, as in

Foxes eat meat.

> In Portuguese reference to a generic entity can be expressed with or without the definite article, and the nominal can be in the singular or the plural.

The subject in the example given above, then, may be expressed in Portuguese as a nominal without an article:

Raposa come principalmente carne.
literally, 'Fox eats mainly meat.'

or as a nominal in the singular, with the definite article:

A raposa come principalmente carne.
literally, 'The fox eats mainly meat.'

or as a nominal in the plural, with the definite article:

> *As raposas comem principalmente carne.*
> literally, 'The foxes eat mainly meat.'

or as a nominal in the plural, without an article:

> *Raposas comem principalmente carne.*   **Wr**
> literally, 'Foxes eat mainly meat.'

The last version, which is the one that most closely parallels the usual English one, is the least common and tends to appear in formal texts. By far the preferred construction in the spoken language is the first one, and it deserves some comment.

A generic head expressed by means of the singular, not preceded by any article, is extremely common in informal speaking. This construction occurs most frequently in sentences that convey a habitual or generic meaning like

> *Criança dá muito trabalho.*
> 'Children are a lot of trouble [literally, Child gives a lot of trouble].'

> *Ninguém aqui gosta de manga.*
> 'Nobody here likes mangoes [literally, mango].'

> *O marido dela planta banana para exportação.*
> 'Her husband plants bananas [literally, banana] for export.'

This may be considered the normal way of expressing this kind of meaning in the spoken language. In the formal written variety the other possibilities are preferred:

> *As crianças dão muito trabalho.*
> '(The) children are a lot of trouble.'

> *Ninguém aqui gosta de mangas.*
> 'Nobody here likes mangoes.'

On the other hand, the singular head without an article often sounds awkward when the sentence expresses a punctual phenomenon that is incompatible with a generic meaning. Thus, one can say

> *As raposas destruíram meu galinheiro.*
> 'The foxes destroyed my chicken coop.'

but not

* <u>*Raposa*</u> *destruiu meu galinheiro.*
'id.'

which sounds very awkward.

26.2 The indefinite article

Like English, Portuguese has an indefinite article, *um / uma,* which corresponds roughly in meaning and use to English *a.* Now, besides this parallel behavior, in a certain number of situations the use of Portuguese *um* differs from English *a;* as we will see, unlike what happens with the definite article, English tends to use the indefinite article more extensively than Portuguese.[1]

Note

**[1]The indefinite article has the same form as the numeral *um* 'one.' It is traditionally analyzed as a different item, though, and there are good reasons to keep this analysis. One reason is that there are cases in which interpretation as an article does not correspond to interpretation as a numeral, e.g.,

    Só <u>um</u> gênio nos tirará deste aperto.

This sentence may mean 'Only a genius can get us out of this jam,' or 'There is only one genius who can get us out of this jam.' In the first case, we have an article, in the second, a numeral.

um

Um corresponds approximately to English *a,* and it is used primarily to refer to an entity not previously mentioned, that is, to introduce a new concept:

    Ele comprou <u>um</u> carro novinho.
    'He bought a brand-new car.'

    Tem <u>uma</u> dentista que mora no apartamento de cima . . .
    'There is a dentist who lives in the apartment above . . .'

Sometimes the best translation for *um* is *some* (when used with a singular):

    <u>*Um*</u> *dia eu te mato.*
    '<u>Some</u> day I'll kill you.'

uns

Portuguese also has a plural indefinite article, *uns*. Since English *a* has no plural of its own, *uns* is normally translated as *some* or *a few:*

> *Faz <u>uns</u> dias que ele não aparece.*
> 'He hasn't shown up for a few days.'

> *Vê se você faz <u>uns</u> pāezinhos pra nós.*
> 'See if you can make us some rolls.'

Uns is also used to express an approximate quantity, and then it may be translated as the English preposition *about:*

> *Ele ganha <u>uns</u> oito mil por mês.*
> 'He earns about eight thousand a month.'

26.2.1 Anaphoric use of the indefinite article

The indefinite article can also be used in anaphoric contexts, in a situation parallel to the one seen in 26.1.2 for the definite article:

> *Ele me mostrou várias caminhonetes, e eu escolhi <u>uma</u> azul.*
> 'He showed me several pickup trucks, and I chose a blue (one).'

Here again, there is no Portuguese word to translate English *one,* the second mention of *caminhonete* 'pickup truck' being simply omitted. Another example is

> *Não me basta encontrar um sócio; quero <u>um</u> que trabalhe duro.*
> 'It is not enough for me to find a partner; I want one who works hard.'

26.3 Omission of the article

The article is omitted in some special cases:

> —First, the article may be omitted when reference is made to a generic entity, as in

> <u>*Raposa*</u> *é um perigo para os galinheiros.*
> literally, 'Fox is a danger to the chicken coops.'

> *Eu detesto <u>manga</u>.*
> literally, 'I hate mango.'

This case of omission of the article was studied in 26.1.4 above, in connection with the ways of expressing generic nominals.

—Second, the article is omitted when a nominal expresses an **attribute**, rather than **referring** to an entity. This is the difference between **attributive** and **referential** nominals (see section 7.2).

One important characteristic of nominals used referentially is that they usually convey complex concepts; a referential nominal like *carro* 'car' evokes in the mind of the receptor the general idea not only of a car, but also of an object that has size, weight, color, brand, and so on.

Now, attributively used nominals convey impoverished concepts, usually reduced to one main feature. This can be seen clearly with items that can be used in either capacity (these include a majority of nominals in the language). Take for instance *amigo,* which when used referentially means 'friend' and when used attributively means 'friendly.' It is referential in

> *Meu melhor amigo*
> 'My best friend'

Here, of course, we are speaking of something referred to by the word *amigo,* which is endowed with a name, has presumably an address and a phone number, and, being a physical object, has some weight, a particular shape, etc.

We may also take the same word attributively, as in

> *Um gesto amigo*
> 'A friendly gesture'

Here the word *amigo* plays a different role: it no longer evokes in the mind of the listener the concept of a person (with a name, an address, etc.). Rather, it *adds* to the central idea evoked by the phrase (the idea of 'gesture') a quality, so that one is not speaking merely of a 'gesture,' but of a 'friendly gesture.'

Returning now to the use of the article, we may say that the absence of an article before a nominal is a way to signal that that nominal is to be understood attributively.

The difference appears very clearly in the pair

> *O bebê é homem.*
> 'The baby is male.'

> * *O bebê é um homem.*
> 'The baby is a man.'

The second sentence is odd because it asserts that the baby is everything a man is—including being an adult. Now, the first sentence only adds a quality to the baby, that is, its sex, and therefore is totally acceptable, being a normal way of saying that the baby is male.

—Third, no article is usual in appositions:

O chefe do governo, <u>general Carmona</u>, se recusa a dar entrevistas.
'The head of the government, General Carmona, refuses to give interviews.'

O padre Macedo, <u>vigário de Santa Rita</u>, mora aqui há quarenta anos.
'Father Macedo, parson of Santa Rita, has been living here for forty years.'

But the article normally appears when the apposition contains a modifier:

Sérgio Silva, <u>o melhor vereador da cidade</u>, vai falar na TV hoje.
'Sérgio Silva, the best councilman of the city, speaks today on television.'

27

Other Nominal Constructions

In chapter 24 we studied the ordering properties of a set of modifiers (termed predeterminers, determiners, and quantifiers) that characteristically occur before the head of the noun phrase. And in chapter 26 we examined the semantic and syntactic behavior of the articles. In this chapter I examine some remaining constructions involving nominals: in section 27.1, those that show important grammatical differences when compared with their English counterparts; in section 27.2, the English double-noun construction (*wood fence, color television,* and the like) and the ways it translates into Portuguese; and in section 27.3, the uses of the singular and the plural.

27.1 Use of determiners and quantifiers

Some determiners and quantifiers present no problems: for instance, *poucos* and *muitos* are used in a way that closely parallels their respective English correlates, *few* and *many:*

Poucos autores ganham dinheiro com seus livros.
'Few authors make money with their books.'

Essa lei só beneficia uns poucos.
'This law benefits only a few.'

> *Os descontentes são <u>muitos</u>.*
> 'The dissatisfied are many.'

For other items some comment is necessary.

27.1.1 *Este, esse, aquele*

The difference between *este* 'this' and *esse* 'id.' is ignored by most users of Portuguese, who tend to use exclusively *esse*—in speaking and, more and more, in writing. On the other hand, formal texts are expected to respect the difference, according to the following rules:

—*Este* is used to refer to objects close to the speaker, *esse* to refer to objects close to the receptor:

> <u>Esta</u> *Universidade tem o prazer de convidar V. Exa. . . .*   **Wr**
> 'This university [that is, our university] has the pleasure of inviting Your Excellency . . .'

> *Gostaríamos de saber se <u>essa</u> Universidade se interessa . . .*   **Wr**
> 'We would like to know if this university [that is, your university] is interested . . .'

—*Este* is used to refer to present time units, *esse* to future or past time units:

> <u>Este</u> *ano nossas atividades aumentaram.*   **Wr**
> 'This year our activities increased.'

> *Cheguei a Belém em 1998; <u>nessa</u> época, eu estava desempregado.*
> 'I came to Belém in 1998; at that time I was unemployed.'

—*Este* refers to what follows in a text, *esse* to what precedes:

> *Ele agradeceu com <u>estas</u> palavras: . . .*   **Wr**
> 'He expressed gratitude with these words: . . .'

> *Depois de dizer <u>essas</u> palavras, ele se assentou.*
> 'After saying these words, he sat down.'

—*Este* also means 'the latter' and contrasts with *aquele,* which stands for 'the former':

> *Os operários e os industriais se odeiam; aqueles se sentem explorados por estes.*   **Wr**
> 'Workers and industrialists hate each other; the former feel exploited by the latter.'

This use of *este* and *aquele* is limited to written texts.[1]

Note

[1]And, besides, makes the text less readable; I, for one, always have to read the preceding context once more in order to get the anaphoras right.

—*Este* is sometimes used in formal texts as an equivalent to the personal pronoun *ele:*

Puseram a rainha num calabouço. Esta só saiu dali para ser guilhotinada.   **Wr**
'The queen was thrown into a dungeon. She only came out to be guillotined.'

In informal speech, and in most written texts as well, the only existing opposition is *esse* vs. *aquele*. *Esse* replaces *este* in all its uses, and *aquele* is used to refer to objects relatively far away (not close to the speaker or to the receptor) and to distant periods of time, thus corresponding to English *that:*

Olha lá aquela nuvem!
'Just look at that cloud!'

Naquele tempo ninguém tinha computador.
'At that time nobody had a computer.'

Finally, I want to mention again a peculiar use of *este* and *esse* (but not *aquele*) occurring after the head, when resuming a recently mentioned word:

O país está cheio de problemas, problemas esses que vêm desde o século passado.   **Wr**
'The country is plagued by problems, [problems these] that go back to the last century.'

This use is limited to the written language.

27.1.2 *Algum, nenhum*

In its most common use, *algum* means 'some,' followed by a singular or a plural head; it agrees with the head in gender and number:

Algum menino / alguma menina / alguns meninos / algumas meninas
'Some boy   / some girl   / some boys   / some girls'

It has two basic meanings: first, it denotes an element randomly selected from a set, and in this reading it corresponds closely to the indefinite article *um:*

> <u>*Algum*</u> *menino vai acabar comendo esses bombons.*
> 'Some boy will end up eating these bonbons.'

Or it may denote a relatively small quantity; this meaning arises when *algum* is used in the plural or in the singular with uncountable (mass) nominals:

> <u>*Algumas*</u> *meninas estavam brincando de roda.*
> 'Some [= a few] girls were playing ring-around-a-rosy.'

> *Acrescente* <u>*alguma*</u> *manteiga.*
> 'Add some butter.'

As we saw in chapter 24, *algum* can also be used as a negative word; this happens when it occurs in a negative sentence after the verb:

> *Ele nunca escreveu livro* <u>*algum*</u>.   **Wr**
> 'He never wrote any book.'

If *algum* occurs in a negative sentence before the verb, it keeps its normal meaning:

> <u>*Algumas*</u> *professoras não aceitaram a decisão.*
> 'Some teachers didn't accept the decision.'

Nenhum means 'no,' or 'any' (in negative sentences), and it is never used in the plural:

> <u>*Nenhum*</u> *profissional revela seus segredos.*
> 'No professional discloses his secrets.'

> *Ele nunca escreveu livro* <u>*nenhum*</u>.
> 'He never wrote any book.'

In this last use, *nenhum* and *algum* are synonyms. But the negative use of *algum* is infrequent and tends to be limited to the written language, *nenhum* being preferred in informal speech.

27.1.3 *Cada*

Cada means 'each' or 'every' in most contexts. It is always used with the singular (except, rarely, when referring to periodic events; see below) and does not vary in gender:

Cada participante recebe cinqüenta reais.
'Each participant gets fifty reais.'

Cada cabeça tem suas idéias.
'Every head has its ideas.'

Os participantes recebem cinqüenta reais cada.
'The participants get fifty reais each.'

When not used in connection with a nominal (as in the last example), *cada* may be followed by *um(a):*

Os participantes recebem cinqüenta reais cada um.
'The participants get fifty reais each.'

Cada is sometimes used like English *every* to denote periodic events (and then it occurs before a plural, always preceded by a numeral):

Ela me visita cada duas semanas.
'She visits me every two weeks.'

This construction, however, is not the most common one. The same idea can be expressed more naturally by

Ela me visita de duas em duas semanas.
'id.'

With a singular, *todo* is preferred:

Temos eleições todo ano / todos os anos.
'We have elections every year.'

Sometimes one hears *cada ano* for 'every year,' but it does not sound very natural, except in the expression *cada ano que passa* 'every year that goes by.'

Finally, *cada* is used in exclamative sentences in order to express amazement at something:

Você tem cada idéia!
'You have such (crazy) ideas!'

Em Minas tem cada montanha!
'In Minas there are such (big) mountains!'

27.1.4 *Que? qual? quanto? etc.*

Que corresponds to English *what* or *which* and is a general interrogative/exclamative particle. It is invariable in gender and number:

Que rapazes simpáticos!
'What nice young men!'

Que cidades você visitou?
'Which towns did you visit?'

Qual translates as *which* and is used to single out an element among several others of the same kind (in these cases, as seen above, *que* is also appropriate). *Qual* is used only as an interrogative, never as an exclamative, and varies in number: singular *qual*, plural *quais*:

Quais cidades você visitou?
'Which towns did you visit?'

Você vai usar qual casaco?
'Which coat are you going to wear?'

Quanto means 'how much,' and its plural *quantos* 'how many.' It may be used as an interrogative or an exclamative and varies in number and gender: *quanto, quantos, quanta, quantas*:

Quanta cerveja você bebeu?
'How much beer did you drink?'

Nossa, quantos pernilongos que tem aqui!   **SpBr**
'Gee, what an awful lot of mosquitoes there are here!'

Tanto means 'so much,' and its plural *tantos* 'so many'; it is used in exclamative or comparative contexts and varies in number and gender:

Tantas mulheres procuram emprego hoje em dia!
'So many women are looking for jobs nowadays!'

Ele tinha tanto dinheiro que não sabia o que fazer com ele.
'He had so much money that he didn't know what to do with it.'

Tal, plural *tais*, is frequently used in connection with the indefinite article *um*, and in this case it means 'a certain':

Uma tal Doutora Alice telefonou hoje.
'A certain Dr. Alice phoned today.'

A sonata foi publicada por um tal José da Silva Freitas.
'The sonata was published by one José da Silva Freitas.'

Without the article, *tal* is used in the written language as English *such (a):*

Como ele foi fazer tal coisa?   **Wr**
'How could he do such a thing?'

Tais idéias podem nos levar a uma guerra.   **Wr**
'Such ideas can lead us to a war.'

In less formal language, the same idea is normally expressed differently, e.g.,

Como ele foi fazer uma coisa dessas?
'How could he do such a thing?

Umas idéias assim podem nos levar a uma guerra.
'Such ideas can lead us to a war.'

Tal can also be used in connection with *que* + a subordinate clause, and in this case it corresponds to English *such . . . that.* In this use, *tal* may come before or after the NP head:

Ela fez um barulho tal que todo mundo acordou.
'She made such a noise that everyone woke up.'

Ela fez um tal barulho que todo mundo acordou.
'id.'

The presence of the article *um* in these cases is optional.

Tamanho means 'so big, so great' and is used only in the written language:[1]

Nunca toleraríamos tamanho insulto.   **Wr**
'We would never stand so great an insult.'

Note

[1] *Tamanho* is also a nominal, meaning 'size,' and in this usage it is common to the written and spoken languages: *quero um tênis tamanho 39* '(I) want tennis shoes size 39.'

27.1.5 Determiners and quantifiers used as heads

Some of the items studied above can appear alone in the NP, in which case they function as heads; for instance,

> *Poucos acreditam no que o governo diz.*
> 'Few (people) believe what the government says.'

The following quantifiers can occur as heads: **poucos** 'few (people); **muitos** 'many (people)'; **alguns** 'some (people)'; **todos** 'everyone'; and **tantos** 'so many (people)'; also the interrogative / exclamative **quantos** 'how many, so many.' In this function they always occur in the masculine plural and always refer to people:

> *Muitos se desiludiram com o novo presidente.*
> 'Many people became disillusioned with the new president.'

> *Alguns acham que educação é escola.*
> 'Some people think that education means schools.'

> *Tantos já tentaram encontrar esse tesouro!*
> 'So many have already attempted to find this treasure!'

> *Todos têm o direito de falar.*
> 'Everyone has the right to speak.'

> *Quantos já tentaram, sem conseguir!*
> 'So many have already tried, without success!'

Besides these items, there are also some that can appear *only* as heads of NPs. The following items refer to inanimate objects:

isto, isso	'this'	[= 'this thing']
aquilo	'that'	[= 'that thing']
tudo	'everything'	
nada	'nothing'	
algo	'something'	

These are sometimes called the **neutral** forms of *este, esse, aquele, todos, algum*, respectively. They are used as heads, most often alone in the NP, and they always refer to inanimate objects:

> *Isso é um bolo de aniversário.*
> 'This is a birthday cake.'

Aquilo parece uma nuvem de chuva.
'That looks like a rain cloud.'

Tudo tem seu lado bom.
'Everything has its good side.'

Você vai querer algo para beber?　　　　**Wr**
'Are you going to want something to drink?'

Algo and *isto* are little used in the spoken language; speakers prefer *alguma coisa* 'something' and *isso*, respectively. *Tudo* can be used in combination with *isto, isso, aquilo:*

Tudo isso um dia vai ser seu.
'All this will be yours one day.'

Nada 'nothing' can also be used with *isto, isso, aquilo* but always joined to them by the preposition *de:*

Nada disso me interessa.
'Nothing of this interests me.'

Now we have some items that necessarily refer to persons: **alguém** 'someone,' **ninguém** 'no one,' and the interrogative **quem?** 'who?' For instance,

Alguém precisa me ajudar.
'Someone must help me.'

Ela não gosta de ninguém.
'She loves no one.'

Você estava falando de quem?
'Whom were you speaking about?'

The general interrogative 'what' is rendered by **que?** or **o que?** when alone in its NP:

O que você vai comer?
'What are you going to eat?'

Que é isso?
'What is this?'

The form *o que?* is probably the most usual.

Finally, we may mention ***outrem***[1] 'someone else,' an almost completely obsolete word used in very formal contexts, such as in legal texts.

Note

[1]The only correct form is *outrem,* stressed on the first syllable, not *outrém,* as found in some grammars.

27.2 The double-noun construction and prepositional phrases

The English double-noun construction exemplified by *wood fence, snowfall,* etc. is rendered in Portuguese in most cases by a sequence of **nominal + prepositional phrase:** *cerca de madeira* 'wood fence,' *queda de neve* 'snowfall.' In some cases we find two nominals, without preposition, and written with or without a hyphen, as in *homem-rã* 'frogman,' *navio fantasma* 'ghost ship.'

Translating the double-noun construction into Portuguese presents two difficulties: first, is it to be translated as a double nominal (*homem-rã*) or as a nominal + prepositional phrase (*cerca de madeira*)? second, in the latter case, which preposition is to be used? Many cases are not amenable to generalization and must be learned individually; on the other hand, there are some rules of thumb worth learning, as long as it remains clear that they are only approximations.

27.2.1 *Cerca de madeira* 'wood fence'

The first rule of thumb is the following:

The most usual Portuguese correlate of the English double-noun construction is a head complemented by a prepositional phrase with the preposition *de.*

That is, *cerca de madeira* represents the normal, unmarked case; other examples include

um manual de geologia	'a geology handbook'
roupa de couro	'leather clothing'
esse funcionário do governo	'this government employee'
dor de cabeça	'headache'
alguns romances de mistério	'some mystery novels'
tênis de mesa	'table tennis'
coronel do exército	'army colonel'
Departamento de Lingüística	'Linguistics Department'

In the above examples one can find several different semantic relations between the two nominals: subject (*manual de geologia*), material (*roupa de couro*), location (*dor de cabeça*), etc. This is to be expected, since the use of *de* is the general case.

27.2.2 *Tiro ao alvo* 'target shooting'

[handwritten: Sp. Something white, or dawn / in Sp. say Tiro al blanco]

> When the relation is one of location, in most cases the preposition is
>
> *em* (for "the location where") or *a* (for "the location to where").[1]

tiro ao alvo	'target shooting'
a expedição a Marte	'the Mars expedition'
um tumor no cérebro	'a brain tumor'
o trabalho na fazenda	'farmwork'
um perito em Física	'a physics expert'[2]

Notes

[1]In the case of "location from where," the preposition is *de,* as in the general case: *laranja da Bahia* 'Bahia orange [that is, navel orange].' This is so because one of the meanings of *de* is 'from': *eles chegaram da Europa* 'they arrived from Europe.'

[2]As seen in this example, "location" may be understood metaphorically.

Dor de cabeça 'headache' is an exception to this rule, as are a few other phrases with the word *dor* 'pain.' One can also say *dor na cabeça*, but this is not a synonym of *dor de cabeça*: *dor na cabeça* means 'a pain in the head'—which may have been caused by a cut, or a blow. The same is true of *dor de barriga* 'bellyache, diarrhea' versus *dor na barriga* 'a pain in the belly'. *Dor de cotovelo*, literally 'elbow-ache,' and *dor de corno*, literally 'horn-ache,' both mean 'jealousy.'

27.2.3 *Rabisco a lápis* 'pencil doodle'

> When the second nominal expresses a medium, the preposition *a* is
>
> used.

rabisco a lápis	'pencil doodle'
desenho a pincel	'brush drawing'
quadro a óleo	'oil picture'
fogão a gás	'gas stove'
motor a diesel	'diesel engine'
lavagem a seco	'dry cleaning'

27.2.4 *Televisão a cores* 'color television'

Besides these rules, useful generalizations are hard to find, and each case will have to be learned individually as a lexical item. Here is a list of some of the frequent cases in which prepositions other than *de* are used:

televisão a cores	'color TV'
adoração ao diabo	'devil worship'
pagamento por hora	'hourly pay'
mistura para bolo	'cake mix'
creme para a pele	'skin cream'

Thus, the prepositions that can appear in this construction are *de, a, por, em,* and *para* (*ao* is a contraction of the preposition *a* plus the article *o*).

27.2.5 *Navio fantasma* 'ghost ship'

The cases in which Portuguese translates double nouns with a sequence of nominals, without preposition, can be distinguished into two kinds of constructions. First is a sequence in which the two nominals do not agree with each other, being merely placed next to each other:

navio fantasma	'ghost ship'
navio-escola	'school ship'
mulher-macaco	'apewoman'

Note that in *navio-escola* and *mulher-macaco* the two elements belong to different genders. Also, the plural in these examples is made by adding *-s* to only one element: *navios-escola, navios fantasma, mulheres-macaco*. These sequences might properly be considered as compound nominals (even when written without a hyphen).

27.2.6 *Vontade férrea* 'iron will'

In the second case, one of the elements (normally the second one) agrees with the first; we then have the normal "adjective" construction, as in

vontade férrea	'iron will'
poema amoroso	'love poem'
cultura invernal	'winter culture'
jornal nova-iorquino	'New York newspaper'
proteção ambiental	'environmental protection'
corrida armamentista	'arms race'
conselho municipal	'city council'

This construction is dependent upon the existence in the lexicon of a suitable qualifier; thus, we may speak of the *polícia londrina* 'London police' because the qualifier *londrino* is available; but 'Amsterdam police' must be translated as *polícia de Amsterdam* because there is no qualifier corresponding to *Amsterdam*. Of course, *polícia de Londres* is also correct.

In almost all cases it is also correct to use the normal *de* construction:

vontade de ferro	'iron will'
poema de amor	'love poem'
cultura de inverno	'winter culture'
jornal de Nova York	'New York newspaper'
proteção do ambiente	
(**or** *ao ambiente*)	'environmental protection'
etc.	

In a few cases the adjective construction has become part of the lexicon, so that the construction with *de,* although understandable, is never used, e.g.,

> ** corrida de armas*   'arms race'
> ** conselho da cidade*   'city council'

In these cases the adjective construction should be used.

27.2.7 *Homem de um braço só* 'one-armed man,' and *vara de pesca* 'fishing rod'

Two other frequent English constructions are likewise translated by the *de* construction in Portuguese:

The English construction instanced by *one-armed man* is also expressed in Portuguese with *de:*

> *homem de um braço só*
> 'one-armed man [literally, 'man of one arm only']'

> *bicho de sete cabeças*
> 'seven-headed beast'

> *menina de olhos azuis*
> 'blue-eyed girl'

Finally, English gerunds when used as modifiers normally correspond to prepositional phrases with *de:*

> *vara de pesca* (**or** *vara de pescar*)   'fishing rod'
>
> *máquina de costura*   'sewing machine'
>
> *cão de caça*   'hunting dog'

27.3 Use of the singular vs. the plural

Although Portuguese nominals have singular and plural forms just like English ones, the use of the numbers is not totally identical. In particular, as we will see, there is a growing tendency in the spoken language to avoid the use of plurals. Thus, whenever a quantifier is used (and therefore there is no doubt about the number of the NP head) the singular is preferentially used in speech, although the plural is also possible and tends to occur in writing:

Tem <u>muita criança abandonada</u> no Brasil.	**SpBr**
Há <u>muitas crianças abandonadas</u> no Brasil.	**Wr**
'There are many abandoned children in Brazil.'	

O governo está levando <u>muito profissional</u> ao desespero.	**SpBr**
O governo está levando <u>muitos profissionais</u> ao desespero.	**Wr**
'The government is leading many professionals to despair.'	

Ela tem <u>sobrinho demais</u>.	**SpBr**
Ela tem <u>sobrinhos demais</u>.	**Wr**
'She has too many nephews.'	

Sometimes the singular is used even without the quantifier, if the number is obvious from the context or if it is felt to be irrelevant, e.g.,

O rapaz está cheio de <u>espinha</u>.	**SpBr**
O rapaz está cheio de <u>espinhas</u>.	**Wr**
'The boy is full of pimples.'	

Vou para Manaus porque tenho <u>amigo</u> lá.	**SpBr**
Vou para Manaus porque tenho <u>amigos</u> lá.	**Wr**
'(I) am going to Manaus because I have friends there.'	

Quem foi que fritou <u>a batata</u>?	**SpBr**
Quem foi que fritou <u>as batatas</u>?	**Wr**
'Who was it that fried the potatoes?'	

Esse muro é de <u>tijolo</u>.	**SpBr ~ Wr**
Esse muro é de <u>tijolos</u>.	**Wr**
'This wall is (made) of bricks.'	

Another context in which Portuguese prefers the singular (as against the plural in English) is when referring to generic entities. This use of the singular also has a colloquial flavor, perhaps less strong than the singular in the sentences just examined. We saw some examples in chapter 26 above, and here are some more:

<u>Gato</u> requer muito cuidado.
'Cats require a lot of care.'

Você precisa comer mais <u>verdura</u>.
'You must eat more vegetables.'

Eu não suporto <u>intelectual pretensioso</u>.
'I cannot stand pretentious intellectuals.'

A few words were formerly used only in the plural, even when referring to only one object (like English *pants*); some of them are now used in the singular, in all styles: *calça* (formerly *calças*) 'pants,' *olheira* (formerly *olheiras*) 'dark circles under the eyes.' These words are used in the plural only when they refer to more than one object, as in

> *Comprei quatro <u>calças</u> na ponta-de-estoque.*
> '(I) bought four (pairs of) pants at the outlet.'

Some words are still used only in the plural: *férias* 'vacations,' *víveres* 'foodstuffs,' *parabéns* 'congratulations,' *pêsames* 'sympathy,' *fezes* 'feces,' *costas* 'back (part of the body),' and a few others that are rare or archaic nowadays.

As for *óculos* 'eyeglasses,' it is used sometimes in the plural, but most often in the singular, keeping its -*s:*

> *Esse óculos me custou mais de trezentos reais.*   **SpBr**
> *Esses óculos me custaram mais de trezentos reais.*   **SpBr ~ Wr**
> 'These eyeglasses cost me more than three hundred reals.'

VI The Sentence

28

The Simple Sentence

28.1 Grammatical functions

A **sentence** is a structure that typically (although not necessarily) contains a subject, a verb, and often one or more complements. Each of these elements is said to have a **grammatical function**; **subject, direct object, indirect object,** and the like are labels for the various grammatical functions within the sentence. The importance of these functions for our purposes is that they must be used to describe word order within the sentence as well as the requirements verbs and nominals demand of their complements (some are preceded by prepositions, for instance, while some are not). Therefore, I start this chapter with a quick look at the main grammatical functions found in the Portuguese sentence (this section may be skipped by those who already have basic grammatical training).

The subject is the element that has an agreement relation with the verb (as we saw previously, only noun phrases can function as subjects). In the sentence

<u>Nós</u> comp<u>ramos</u> um computador novo.
'We bought a new computer.'

the subject is *nós,* and this is clearly shown by the verb form, *compramos.* If we change the subject, the verb may have to change in agreement with it:

Ele comprou um computador novo.
'He bought a new computer.'

Eu comprei um computador novo.
'I bought a new computer.'

Subject-verb agreement is discussed in chapter 35; it exists in English as well (as in *I am, you are*), with the difference that in Portuguese verbs are much richer in forms, and agreement is consequently more "visible" than in English.

Besides the subject and the verb, a sentence may include several other elements, including the **direct object,** the **indirect object,** the **subjective complement,**[1] the **predicative,** and various **adjuncts.**[2]

Notes

[1]The subjective complement is called **predicative of the subject** (*predicativo do sujeito*) in traditional Portuguese grammars: it is the function of *verde* 'green' in *meu carro é verde* 'my car is green.'

**[2]The precise definition of these functions is still under discussion. Most linguists start from the traditional definitions, which to my mind is dangerous since such definitions are far from clear; others have tried to improve on them, so far, I believe, without much success (for example, see Perini 1995). Here I will run the risks of the first option rather than go into lengthy and possibly inconclusive theoretical discussions.

A direct object is also a noun phrase but has no agreement relation with the verb:

Ele comprou   um computador novo.
  subject   **direct object**
'He bought a new computer.'

Ele comprou   vários computadores novos.
  subject   **direct object**
'He bought several new computers.'

The above examples show that selecting a plural direct object has no effect on the verb, which stays in the singular in order to agree with the singular subject *ele* 'he.'

The indirect object is distinguished from the direct object by requiring a preposition (that is, it is always composed of preposition + NP):[1]

Eu sempre penso   em você.
              indirect object
'I always think of you.'

Note

*[1]This definition of "indirect object" is far from precise, of course. I will not try to elaborate it, however, because I am not sure that the so-called indirect object is syntactically distinguishable from other prepositional complements, normally termed "adverbial complements" or "adverbial adjuncts." While being of some theoretical import, this omission is not crucial for our purposes in this grammar.

The subjective complement is an element used in connection with so-called **copulative verbs** (*verbos de ligação*), of which the most important are *ser* 'to be,' *estar* 'to be,' *ficar* 'to become,' *tornar-se* 'to become,' *permanecer* 'to stay,' *andar* 'to be,'[1] *continuar* 'to go on':[2]

> *Essa tia era <u>um problema</u>.*
> 'This aunt was <u>a problem</u>.'

Notes

[1] *Andar* means 'to be' when followed by a qualificative, as in *ela anda triste* 'she has been sad (lately)'; *andar* also means 'to walk.'

*[2]The subjective complement, unlike the direct object, bears some relationship to the subject, e.g., the two agree in many cases:

> *Essa tia era <u>rica.</u> / Esse tio era <u>rico</u>.*
> 'This aunt was rich [**feminine**]. / This uncle was rich [**masculine**].'

This is the main reason the subjective complement must be distinguished from the direct object, which never agrees with the subject.

About direct and indirect objects two observations may be useful:

—First, unlike Spanish, Portuguese does not add a preposition before direct objects with animate nouns; thus, Spanish has

> *Yo encontré <u>a</u> Manuel en la calle.*
> 'I met Manuel on the street.'

but in Portuguese the same meaning is conveyed by

> *Eu encontrei Manuel na rua.*
> 'id.'

The preposition is still used in very formal style before some particular nouns like *Deus* 'God' in set phrases like *amar a Deus* 'to love God'—but not in nonstereotyped sentences like *você devia procurar Deus* 'you should look for God.'

—Second, in Portuguese it is not usual to add a pleonastic, or redundant, object pronoun as in Spanish

> *A mí no <u>me</u> gustó la película.*
> 'I did not enjoy the film.'

In Portuguese one says simply,

> *O filme não me agradou.*
> 'id.'

In both these points, Portuguese and English are similar, so there should be no problem in using these structures correctly.

The predicative is a qualifying element that may modify the subject or an object but does not belong to the same noun phrase. For instance,

> *Manuel entrou na sala <u>furioso</u>.*
> 'Manuel came into the room furious.'

> *Nós todos consideramos Cardoso <u>um espertalhão</u>.*
> 'We all consider Cardoso a wise guy.'

The predicative can be a modifying nominal (*furioso*) or a whole noun phrase (*um espertalhão*). Whenever represented by a single nominal, it agrees in gender and number with its antecedent (the subject or the object of the sentence).

Finally, the simple sentence may include adjuncts, of which the most important are several kinds of **adverbial adjuncts**. These are a pretty heterogenous lot, but their differences need not concern us here. Suffice it to say that they convey several kinds of additional information, such as:

Time

> *Ela começou a trabalhar aqui <u>há dois anos</u>.*
> 'She started working here two years ago.'

Location

> *Eu conheci minha namorada <u>em Guarapari</u>.*
> 'I met my girlfriend in Guarapari.'

Cause

> *Meu tio se arruinou <u>por causa do jogo</u>.*
> 'My uncle went broke because of gambling.'

Manner

> *<u>Lentamente</u>, o cachorro começou a reagir.*
> 'Slowly, the dog began to react.'

The speaker's opinion

> *<u>Francamente</u>, esse seu amigo não me agrada.*
> 'To be frank, I don't like this friend of yours.'

and some others. In this grammar, adverbial adjuncts will be referred to simply as **adverbials**.

28.2 Simple vs. complex sentences

A sentence may contain other sentences. For example,

> [*Vovó sonhou que* [*eu perdi o emprego*]]
> 'Granny dreamed that I had lost my job.'

is a sentence (*vovó sonhou que eu perdi o emprego*) that contains, as a part of itself, another sentence (*eu perdi o emprego*). It has two verbs, *sonhou* and *perdi,* each with its subject, respectively, *vovó* and *eu,* and so on. In this case we have a **complex sentence** (complex sentences are studied in chapter 36). In this chapter we will be concerned only with sentences like

> *Vovó sonha toda noite.*
> 'Granny dreams every night.'

Eu perdi o emprego.
'I have lost my job.'

These **simple sentences** include at most one subject and one verb apiece. In this chapter I discuss them in connection with the way words are ordered within them.

28.3 *Word order in the simple declarative sentence*

A sentence is termed **declarative** when it does not bear the formal marks of an **interrogative** (presence of final '**?**,' and often also presence of question words like *que?* 'what?,' *quando?* 'when?,' *como?* 'how?,' etc.) or of an **exclamative** (presence of final '**!**,' and often also presence of such exclamative words as *que!* 'what (a)!,' *como!* 'how!,' etc). In Portuguese (as in English) the normal, unmarked order of terms in a declarative sentence is **subject + verb + complement.**[1]

Note

[1]Strictly speaking, **subject + *predicate head* **+ complement.** 'Verb' is the designation of a word **class**, and here we are dealing with syntactic (and semantic) **functions**; but since the class of verbs always occurs in the sentence as the predicate head, I decided to keep the traditional ambiguity of 'verb' as the designation of both a class and a function. I do so in order not to overload the text with terminological novelties, however justified they may be.

Thus, a typical sentence will follow the model of

Nós compramos um computador novo.
subject   verb   complement
'We bought a new computer.'

A sentence may lack a complement:

César ronca.
subject verb
'César snores.'

or it may lack an overt subject:[1]

Cheguei de São Paulo hoje.
'(I) arrived from São Paulo today.'

Note

**[1]Traditionally, a sentence like *Cheguei de São Paulo hoje* is analyzed as having an elliptical subject. But this is not the best way to analyze such cases; treating them as subjectless sentences provides a more simple and coherent description.

The unmarked order may, however, occur in reverse sequence, as in

Chegou meu irmão.
'My brother arrived [literally, Arrived my brother].'

Here the subject occurs after the verb. Such inversions, extremely common in Portuguese and less so in English, are discussed in what follows.

28.3.1 Ordering of subject and verb

Subject-verb inversion is not fully understood, but it is possible to state some rules that will be useful to the student. The first thing to note is that

subject-verb inversion typically occurs **in the absence of an object.**

In this, Portuguese differs from Spanish to a certain extent; whereas Spanish likes to make inversion in such sentences as

Delante de ella voceaban sus mercancías <u>dos mujeres</u>.
'Before her two women were calling out their wares.'
[from Butt and Benjamin 1995]

in Portuguese the presence of a direct object usually blocks inversion. The above sentence would be translated as

> *Diante dela <u>duas mulheres</u> apregoavam suas mercadorias.*
> 'id.'

because of the presence of the object *suas mercadorias* 'their wares.' In such cases inversion may be found, but it is rare, has an obsolete flavor, and is not to be encouraged.

Inversion is avoided with verbs that can have an object even when no object actually appears in the sentence; thus, one cannot say

> * *Come demais <u>meu cachorro</u>.*
> 'My dog eats too much.'

> * *Grita muito criança.*
> 'Children shout a lot.'

Although *comer* and *gritar* occur in the above sentences without objects, these verbs appear frequently with objects, as in

> *Meu cachorro come banana.*
> 'My dog eats bananas.'

> *Os manifestantes gritavam palavras de ordem.*
> 'The protesters shouted slogans.'

Therefore, the subjects of *comer* and *gritar* cannot be postposed.
On the other hand,

> a subject can be postposed when it is strongly emphasized (typically when it refers to some entity contrasted with another) in imperative utterances.

This is the only case in which inversion occurs in the presence of an object, e.g.,

*Limpa **você** esse chão!*   **SpBr**
'**You** clean this floor!'

This sentence implies that there are other possible candidates for cleaning the floor, and the speaker wants to strongly assert that *you* should do the task.

Furthermore,

inversion is normal with verbs that never take objects.

With such verbs, the order **verb + subject** is preferred in the situations described below:

—**When one wants to call special attention to the subject, or when the subject is particularly long**

Acabou o tempo dos cavalheiros educados.
'The age of polite gentlemen is gone.'

Nasceu meu primeiro filho.
'My first child was born.'

Chegaram aqueles pacotes que você tinha encomendado.
'Those parcels you had ordered have arrived.'

Existem cisnes de duas cores.
'There are [literally, there exist] two-colored swans.'

Sobrou um pouco do arroz de ontem.
'A little of yesterday's rice was left over.'

Surgiu um novo problema.
'A new problem emerged.'

Falta a assinatura do diretor.
'The director's signature is missing.'

Desapareceu a maior parte do dinheiro.
'Most of the money disappeared.'

In these sentences, inversion is not compulsory, but it is more natural than the direct order. The latter is preferred only when special attention is to be directed toward the verb:

—*Mas onde está o dinheiro?*
—<u>*A maior parte do dinheiro*</u> *desapareceu!*
"But where is the money?"
"Most of the money disappeared!"

Here attention is called not to the money, but to the fact that it disappeared. Therefore, one follows the general rule that places the element with the higher information load (*desapareceu* 'disappeared') at the end of the sentence.

—Very often, when the sentence begins with an adverbial

Em 1808 *chegou* <u>*Dom João*</u> *ao Rio de Janeiro.*
adverbial
'In 1808 Dom João arrived in Rio de Janeiro.'

Aqui *estão* <u>*as cenouras.*</u>
adverbial
'Here are the carrots.'

Naquele ano *morreu* <u>*Chiquinha Gonzaga.*</u>
adverbial
'That year Chiquinha Gonzaga died.'

Lá *vem* <u>*aquele idiota.*</u>
adverbial
'There comes that idiot.'

—In sequences of causative verb + infinitive

In these cases, inversion of the subject of the infinitive is very frequent (but not compulsory) when the subject is composed of several words:

Frederico fez entrar <u>*o grupo todo*</u>.
'Frederico let the whole group come in.'

This sentence is just as acceptable without inversion:

Frederico fez <u>*o grupo todo*</u> *entrar.*
'id.'

Verbs participating in this construction are *fazer* 'to make, to let'; *deixar* 'to allow'; *mandar* 'to order'; *pedir (para)* 'to ask.' In this construction (as will be seen in chapter 35) agreement of the infinitive with the subject is optional when the subject is postposed:

Frederico fez entrar <u>as crianças</u>. **or**
Frederico fez entrarem <u>as crianças.</u>
'Frederico let the children come in.'

Here the preferred version is the first one, *without* agreement. But when the subject precedes, the situation is reversed, and agreement is usually applied (at least in the written language):

Frederico fez <u>as crianças</u> entrarem.
'id.'

When the subject is short, composed only of a nominal with or without an article, inversion is less frequent, and the order subject-verb is preferred:

Frederico fez <u>Maria</u> entrar.
'Frederico let Maria come in.'

Inversion in this case is somewhat unnatural:

* Frederico fez entrar <u>Maria</u>.
'id.'

unless one wants to strongly emphasize the subject of *entrar, Maria.*

—In impersonal sentences with *se*

With impersonal sentences with *se* inversion is the rule:

Vendem-se <u>verduras</u>. **Wr**
'Vegetables are for sale.'

But in these sentences the status of the subject is somewhat questionable. In the above sentence, *verduras* 'vegetables' is the subject, as shown by the agreement on the verb (*vendem*, third person plural). Nevertheless, the sentence is felt to be parallel to ones like

Ele vende <u>verduras</u>.
'He sells vegetables.'

where *verduras* also comes after the verb and also refers to the patient of the action (the thing that is being sold). As a result, one more frequently says

Vende-se <u>verduras</u>. **SpBr**
'Vegetables are for sale.'

Here *verduras* is not a subject, since the verb does not agree with it, and of course we can no longer speak of subject-verb inversion. *Verduras* here is the object, and its position after the verb is regular.

This is the usual situation with impersonal sentences with *se* (see chapter 21 for details); and one can say that the subject comes after the verb only in relation to sentences like *vendem-se verduras,* which are more and more neglected in favor of *vende-se verduras.*

—In parenthetic sentences marking turn-taking in reported conversations

—Entretanto—disse <u>ele</u>—ninguém viu o crime.
"However—he said—nobody saw the crime."

Inversion in parenthetics is usual in Portuguese; the direct order is also possible but not very frequent.

—With the verb *ser* in short answers composed only of verb + subject

—Quem limpou a parede?
—Foi <u>a empregada</u>.
"Who cleaned the wall?"
"(It) was <u>the maid</u>."

—Quem dá as ordens aqui?
—Sou <u>eu</u>.
"Who gives orders here?"
"I do [literally, am <u>I</u>]."

—After *ao* meaning 'when'

Ao chegarem <u>os policiais</u>, a quadrilha se dispersou.
'When the policemen arrived, the gang dispersed.'

Ela começa a trabalhar ao terminar <u>a festa</u>.
'She starts working when the party ends.'

28.3.2 Objects

The normal order is **subject + verb + direct object;** the **indirect object** occurs most often at the end, but it can also occur before the direct object, in particular when it is short, e.g.,

Carla comprou um boné novo para o meu menino.
 subject   direct object   indirect object
'Carla bought a new cap for my boy.'

> *Carla comprou   para mim   um boné novo.*
> **subject   indirect object direct object**
> 'Carla bought me a new cap.'

In standard Portuguese a preposition must precede the indirect object (except when it is a clitic; see chapter 29), so there is no exact correspondent to the English construction instanced by

> Carla bought Daniel a new cap.
>   **indirect object**

which must be rendered as

> *Carla comprou um boné novo <u>para o Daniel</u>.*
>   **indirect object**

or

> *Carla comprou <u>para o Daniel</u>   um boné novo.*
>   **indirect object**

In the spoken language, however, there is a tendency to omit the preposition, at least in some conditions:

> *Por favor, pede <u>o Luís Henrique</u> para descer.*   **SpBr**
> 'Please, ask Luís Henrique to come down.'

Here one would expect *ao Luís Henrique*. This seems to occur preferably with some verbs, but the phenomenon is too poorly known to be treated in detail here.

Both the direct and the indirect object frequently occur preposed, usually to the beginning of the sentence, and often separated by a comma:

> <u>*Esse boné*</u> *Carla comprou para o meu menino.*
> **direct object**
> 'This cap Carla bought for my boy.'

> <u>*Para o meu menino*</u>, *Carla comprou esse boné.*
>   **indirect object**
> 'For my boy, Carla bought this cap.'

These are cases of **topicalization**, in which the preposed element is understood as the main topic of the utterance (see chapter 39 for a study of topicalization processes).

The direct object in the modern language must appear either **after the verb** or, when topicalized, **at the head of the sentence.**[1] Thus, the following sentence is *not* ambiguous:

> *O rato, o gato matou.*
> 'The rat, the cat killed.'

It means that the cat killed the rat, not the other way around. No other position is acceptable for the direct object, except occasionally in traditional poetry up to the 1920s.

Note

[1]Always excepting clitics, which follow their own ordering rules (see chapter 29).

28.4 Vocatives

Vocatives (used to call the attention of the listener) present no special problem, being very similar in Portuguese and in English. In both languages they may appear in any one of several positions within the sentence but usually occur at the head of the utterance, e.g.,

> *Neide, por favor me traz um pano de prato limpo.*   **SpBr**
> *Por favor me traz um pano de prato limpo, Neide.*   **SpBr**
> 'Neide, please bring me a clean dishcloth.'

A vocative may occur by itself, as above; or it may be introduced by a particle. The particle *ó*, pronounced [ɔ], is used nowadays almost exclusively in formulas of religious discourse:

> *Ó Maria, mãe de Deus!*
> 'O Mary, mother of God!'

In current speech the particle is *ô*, pronounced [o]:

> *Ô Neide, por favor me traz um pano de prato limpo.*   **SpBr**
> 'Neide, please bring me a clean dishcloth.'

29

![Decorative sunburst/wheel ornament]

Use of Oblique Pronouns

29.1 Pronominal objects

Oblique pronouns are, basically, the objective forms of the personal pronouns. Thus, 'I' is rendered in Portuguese as *eu,* but 'me' is *me.* So far, in this particular Portuguese and English are parallel, e.g.,

> <u>Eu</u> cumprimentei a professora. / A professora <u>me</u> cumprimentou.
> 'I greeted the teacher.   / The teacher greeted me.'

Similarly, *te* is used as the objective form of *você* 'you' (or of *tu,* when used), *nos* [nus] 'us' as the objective form of *nós* ['nɔs] 'we,' *a* 'her' as the objective form of *ela* 'she,' and so on (see table 8.1).

In fact, as we saw in chapter 8 and shall see again below, the spoken language has largely subverted this schema, mainly through the extensive use of third person non-oblique forms as objects, as in

> *Encontrei <u>ela</u> no supermercado.*   **SpBr**
> '(I) met her [literally, I met she] in the supermarket.'

In what follows I start by describing the standard written use of the oblique pronouns; then, I describe the points in which the spoken language differs from written usage.

Oblique pronouns are used contiguous to the verb and are positioned as shown in 29.3 below. The direct object is expressed by the pronouns *me* 'me,' *te* 'you,' *o / a* 'him/her, you,' *nos* 'us,' and *os / as* 'them, you (pl.)':

> *O diretor <u>me</u> chamou.*
> 'The director called me.'

And similarly

> *O diretor <u>te</u> chamou.*
> 'The director called you.'

> *O diretor <u>a</u> chamou.*   **Wr**
> 'The director called her.'

> *O diretor <u>nos</u> chamou.*
> 'The director called us.'

> *O diretor <u>os</u> chamou.*   **Wr**
> 'The director called them.'

Note that third person oblique pronouns—current only in the written language—may refer to a third party (corresponding to *ele / ela* 'he / she'), but also to the addressed person (corresponding to *você* 'you,' and other forms). Thus, *o diretor a chamou* may mean, according to context, 'the director called her' or 'the director called you' (when addressing a woman).

When postposed, these pronouns are connected to the verb by means of a hyphen:

> *Chamei-<u>a</u>.*   **Wr**
> '(I) called her.'

> *O diretor chamou-<u>nos</u>.*   **Wr**
> 'The director called us.'

In the formal written language, *o / a* are the pronouns to be used as the oblique forms of both *ele / ela* 'he / she' and *você, o senhor,* etc. 'you.' *Te* is the oblique form of *tu* 'you' and in principle should not occur when other pronouns are substituted for *tu* (see chapter 8 for the use of these different words for 'you'). This is just a grammatical injunction, of course, one that is obeyed only as much as such injunctions usually are. In the spoken language, *te* is the oblique form of *você* 'you':

Eu te chamei, mas você não respondeu.   **SpBr**
'I called you, but you didn't answer.'

29.2 Clitics

See 8.1.5 for a definition of "clitic." Many grammars of Portuguese present the position of clitic pronouns within the sentence as an extremely complex phenomenon; yet, when we take into account current Brazilian usage (both spoken and written) this is not a particularly difficult point and can be described with the help of a few simple rules. The real difficulty lies not in the rules involved, but in the interference of the European written standard, which is still taught (although not consistently followed). The result is that speakers tend to be less secure in their judgments than they should, considering the relative simplicity of the modern Brazilian system.

The items in question are the objective forms of the personal pronouns, namely,

me	'me'	[clitic form of *eu* 'I']	
te	'you'	[clitic form of *você* 'you']	
o, a	'him /her'	[nonreflexive clitic forms of *ele* 'he' and *ela* 'she,' respectively]	**Wr**
os, as	'them'	[nonreflexive clitic forms of *eles* 'they' and *elas* 'they (fem.)']	**Wr**
lhe	'him /her'	[indirect object form of *ele, ela*]	**Wr**
lhes	'them'	[indirect object form of *eles, elas*]	**Wr**
nos	'us'	[clitic form of *nós* 'we']	
vos	'you (pl.)'	[clitic form of *vós* 'you (pl.)']	**Arch**
se	'himself / herself / themselves / yourself / yourselves' [reflexive form of all third-person pronouns]		

Lhe(s) is very little used in the spoken language (at least in the variety here described). *Vos,* like its nonclitic form *vós,* has virtually disappeared from Brazilian Portuguese. As for *o, a, os, as,* they are largely confined to the written language, being replaced in speech by nonclitic forms, respectively, *ele, ela, eles, elas.* In other words, the only clitics still in general use are *me, te* (as the clitic form of *você* 'you'), *nos,* and the reflexive *se.*

The following tables will help the reader visualize the pronominal system of written and spoken Portuguese:

Written language

Subject		Direct object	Indirect object	After preposition[1]	Reflexive
eu	'I'	*me*	*me*	*mim*	*me*
tu	'you (sing.)'	*te*	*te*	*ti*	*te*
você	'you'[2]	*o/a*	*lhe*	*você*	*se*
ele/ela	'he/she'	*o/a*	*lhe*	*ele/ela*	*se*
nós	'we'	*nos*	*nos*	*nós*	*nos*
vós	'you (pl.)' **Arch**	*vos*	*vos*	*vós*	*vos*
vocês	'you (pl.)'	*os/as*	*lhes*	*vocês*	*se*
eles/elas	'they'	*os/as*	*lhes*	*eles/elas*	*se*

Spoken language

Subject		Direct/Indirect object[3]	After preposition[1]	Reflexive
eu	'I'	*me*	*mim*	*me*
você	'you'[2]	*te ~ você*[4]	*você*	*se*
ele/ela	'he/she'	*ele/ela*	*ele/ela*	*se*

(continued)

Subject		Direct/Indirect object[3]	After preposition[1]	Reflexive
nós	'we'	*nos*	*nós*	*nos*
vocês	'you (pl.)'	*vocês*	*vocês*	*se*
eles/elas	'they'	*eles/elas*	*eles/elas*	*se*

Notes

[1]After the preposition *com* 'with,' some pronouns have special forms, which are agglutinated with the preposition as one word:

comigo	'with me'	
contigo	'with you'	**Wr**
consigo	'with him/herself'	**Wr**
conosco	'with us'	
convosco	'with you (pl.)'	**Arch**

Consigo is not common in the spoken language, which prefers the use of nonreflexive pronouns + *mesmo / próprio,* which may be translated as 'self': *ele fala com ele mesmo* 'he speaks to himself.'

[2]All honorific pronouns, such as *o senhor/ a senhora* 'you (respectful),' as well as *Vossa Majestade* 'Your Majesty,' *Vossa Excelência* 'Your Excellence,' etc., pattern like *você.*

[3]In the spoken language the same forms are used for direct and indirect objects.

[4] *Você* is placed in the sentence as a regular, nonpronominal object—which means normally after the verb: *ela não viu você* 'she did not see you'; *te* behaves like a clitic and occurs normally before the verb: *ela não te viu* 'id.' The two pronouns are used interchangeably, with no difference in meaning or degree of formality.

29.2.1 When *o* becomes *-lo* and *-no*

As we saw in chapter 8, *o, a,* and their plurals undergo certain changes in particular positions. After an infinitive[1] they become *-lo, -la, -los, -las,* and the infinitive loses its final *-r;* an accent is added when the truncated infinitive ends in *-a* or *-e,* to keep the stress on the last syllable. For example,

amá-lo	[= *amar* + *-o*]	**Wr**
vendê-la	[= *vender* + *-a*]	**Wr**
senti-los	[= *sentir* + *-os*] etc.	**Wr**

Note

[1]In the classical language, this occurred after any verb form ending in *-r* or *-s;* thus, *queres* plus *-a* became *quere-la, quer* plus *-os* became *qué-los,* and *puser* plus *-as* becomes *pusé-las.* These sequences are not used nowadays, partly because with these verb forms it is normal to place the clitic *before* the verb: *ele a quer* 'he wants her,' *se você o puser na mesa* 'if you put it on the table,' etc. Now, with the infinitive, the *l-* forms are very common in writing and are sometimes even heard in speech in set expressions like *muito prazer em conhecê-la* 'very glad to meet you' (an alternative, more common form is *muito prazer em conhecer você / a senhora*). One finds today *-lo,* etc. after the presentative word *eis* 'here is': *Você estava procurando um alfinete? Ei-lo.* **Wr** 'You were looking for a pin? Here it is.' (The word *eis* is used almost exclusively in writing.)

The same change occurs when the pronoun occurs after the first part of a split future or conditional (in the construction called **mesoclisis**; see below):

amá-lo-ei	[= *amarei* + *-o*]	**Wr**

After any form ending in a nasal sound, the same pronouns add an initial *n-:*

amam-na	[= *amam* + *-a*]	**Wr**
peguem-nos	[= *peguem* + *-os*]	**Wr**
põe-nas	[= *põe* + *-as*]	**Wr**

29.3 Positions of clitics in the sentence

29.3.1 General rules

Clitics appear in peculiar positions; for instance, although the normal place for (nonclitic) objects is after the verb,

*Fernando **ajudou** a mulher.*
'Fernando helped (his) wife.'

*Fernando **deu** um carro novo para sua filha.*
'Fernando gave a new car to his daughter.'

when the object is a clitic pronoun, it normally appears before the verb:

> *Fernando <u>nos</u> **ajudou**.*
> 'Fernando helped us.'

> *Fernando <u>me</u> **deu** um carro novo.*
> 'Fernando gave me a new car.'

The position after the verb, with a hyphen, is also possible, but less and less preferred:

> *Fernando **ajudou**-<u>nos</u>.*   **Wr**
> *Fernando **deu**-<u>me</u> um carro novo.*   **Wr**

In order to describe the ordering of the clitics with respect to the verb one must start by distinguishing two possibilities: the pronoun is **proclitic** when it appears immediately before the verb (before the auxiliary, if any) and **enclitic** when it appears immediately after the verb or auxiliary—as in the examples, always with a hyphen.[1] Clitics always appear contiguous to the verb and cannot be separated even by the negative particle:

> *Fernando não <u>nos</u> ajudou.*
> 'Fernando didn't help us.'

Note

[1]There is a third possibility, termed **mesoclitic**, when the clitic appears between the radical and the ending of the future or of the conditional, as in *ele ajudar-nos-ia* 'he would help us.' Yet this is only a special case of an enclitic pronoun because it cannot be attached to the end of these verb forms: **ajudaria-nos;* therefore, the rules governing the placing of enclitics are also valid for mesoclitics. Mesoclitic pronouns have all but disappeared from even the written language, except in extremely formal styles, and most Brazilians have difficulty in using them.

The rule for ordering clitic pronouns is very simple:

Clitic pronouns in spoken Brazilian Portuguese are always placed before the main verb.

Instances of the application of this rule are as follows:

<u>Me</u> *empresta esse livro, por favor.*   **SpBr**
'Lend me that book, please.'

Ele vai <u>nos</u> *levar até o aeroporto.*
'He is going to take us to the airport.'

Seu filho tem <u>se</u> *sentido mal.*
'Your son has been feeling unwell.'

O médico <u>me</u> *receitou esses comprimidos.*
'The doctor prescribed (to me) these pills.'

Observe that clitic pronouns may appear at the beginning of an utterance; and they do not occur before the auxiliary but rather before the main verb.

In the written language, the situation is more complex, although not as complex as the one described in traditional grammars, which corresponds to nineteenth-century usage. The following rules apply:

Restriction to proclitic placement

No clitic may appear at the beginning of a main clause or immediately

after a topicalized element.

Restrictions to enclitic placement

No clitic may appear after a participle or after a gerund preceded by *em*;

no clitic may appear after the verb if the clause begins with:

(continued)

—a relative or interrogative pronoun;

—any of the items in the following list:

não	'do not'	*tudo*	'everything'
nunca	'never'	*nadá*	'nothing'
só	'only'	*alguim*	'someone'
mesmo	'even'	*ninguém*	'nobody'
também	'also'	*que*	'that'

Otherwise, the clitic may be placed after or before the verb, indifferently.

Some grammarians give a longer list of items requiring proclitic placement. I have decided to give the short list because, first, the facts are not well known, since no detailed survey on the subject is available; and, second, because even educated speakers tend to be insecure about their judgments in many cases. The above rules, which are still usually followed in written texts, should be sufficient for a general orientation, and by following them the student will avoid any really serious errors.

These rules disallow the following sentence, which as we saw is correct in the spoken language:

> *<u>Me</u> empresta esse livro, por favor.*   **SpBr**
> 'Lend me that book, please.'

In the written language, the clitic must be placed after the verb (following the first rule); besides, the written form of the imperative must be substituted:

> *Empreste-<u>me</u> esse livro, por favor.*   **Wr**
> 'id.'

Other examples of the application of the rules are

*O motorista disse **que** <u>me</u> empresta o carro.*
'The driver said that he'll lend me the car.'

In this sentence the clitic *me* cannot occur after the verb *empresta* because of the presence of *que* at the beginning of the clause. Similar cases are as follows:

Ninguém <u>me</u> *compreende.*
'Nobody understands me.'

Quem <u>te</u> *deu esse relógio?*
'Who gave you that watch?'

*Catarina **não** <u>me</u> telefonou.*
'Catarina did not call me.'

Finally, the clitic must precede a participle:

Elvira tem <u>se</u> destacado em sua profissão. [not ** tem destacado-se*]
'Elvira has distinguished herself in her profession.'

When in doubt about where to place a clitic in a written sentence, the safest approach is to put it before the main verb, unless it is sentence-initial.

29.3.2 Final notes on clitic placement

The account of clitic placement given in this section leaves out some relatively infrequent usages; I will mention them here because the student may find them in old or particularly formal written texts. The main case is the occurrence of clitics before the auxiliary or a modal, as in *ela <u>se</u> tem destacado em sua profissão* 'she has distinguished herself in her profession,' a sentence that is considered correct, but that is becoming rare in writing. Compare *Elvira <u>se</u> ha destacado en su profesión,* the usual construction in Spanish.

The rule is that the preposed clitic may be placed before an auxiliary, a modal, or a sequence of modal + auxiliary, as in

O governador não <u>os</u> devia ter nomeado.   **Wr**
'The governor should not have appointed them.'

Such extreme preposing of the clitic is not obligatory, and there is always an alternate position, which is the preferred one nowadays. Thus, the two examples given above are more likely to appear as

Ela tem se destacado em sua profissão.
'She has distinguished herself in her profession.'

O governador não devia tê-los nomeado.   **Wr**
'The governor should not have appointed them.'

Another detail is that when the clitic occurs between an auxiliary and the main verb it is traditionally considered to be enclitic to the auxiliary, so that a hyphen would be necessary; thus, instead of *Elvira tem se destacado* 'Elvira has distinguished herself' one should write *Elvira tem-se destacado.* This rule is still often followed in writing, but I suspect that most people would accept, and preferably use, the nonhyphenated version (which is preferred, for one, by *Folha de São Paulo,* one of the most prestigious of Brazilian newspapers).

Finally, there are sequences of two clitics, attached to the same verb, and often contracted with each other; examples are *dê-mo* 'give it to me' and *ela no-lo entregou* 'she delivered it to us'; these sequences are never found in the spoken language and are very infrequent even in writing.

29.3.3 Special rules

When modified by certain items such as *só* 'only,' *todos* 'all,' *mesmo* 'self,' and some others, third person object pronouns as well as *você, o senhor,* etc. remain in their subject forms (and in the written language are often preceded by the preposition *a*), so that one says

O diretor queria chamar só ela.
O diretor queria chamar só a ela.   **Wr**
'The director wanted to call only her.'

As for first person pronouns and *tu,* when used in writing they take the preposition *a* when modified and correspondingly appear in the special form used with prepositions, e.g.,

O diretor queria chamar só a mim.   **Wr**
'The director wanted to call only me.'

O diretor queria chamar só a ti.   **Wr**
'The director wanted to call only you.'

But in the spoken language *eu, nós* is used, without preposition (that is, first person pronouns pattern like *ele*):

O diretor queria chamar só eu.   **SpBr**
'The director wanted to call only me.'

> *A televisão vai mostrar <u>nós</u> todos.*   **SpBr**
> 'The television will show us all.'

The use of *eu* or *nós* as an object is permissible only in this case. Otherwise, it is felt to be substandard.

The preposition *a* is also used before personal pronouns as a mark of emphasis or contrastivity:

> *Ronaldo não te odeia; ele odeia <u>a mim</u>.*   **Wr**
> 'Ronaldo doesn't hate you; he hates <u>me</u>.'

This is a rare case of the use of the preposition *a* in a construction similar to Spanish *odio a tu mujer* '(I) hate your wife.' As noted, it occurs primarily in writing; in speech one finds sometimes the subject form of the pronoun in this context:

> *O Ronaldo não te odeia; ele odeia <u>eu</u>.*   **SpBr**
> 'id.'

29.4 Object pronouns in the spoken language: A summary

The different system used in the spoken language (and increasingly in less formal varieties of writing) can be summarized as follows:
  —First, *te* is freely used as the oblique form of *você*:

> *Você não sabe quanto eu <u>te</u> amo.*   **SpBr**
> 'You don't know how much I love you.'

  —Second, *você* (as well as *o senhor*) can be used in lieu of *te* as an alternative objective form:

> *Todos aqui <u>te</u> admiram muitíssimo.*
> *Todos aqui admiram <u>você</u> muitíssimo.*   **SpBr**
> 'Everyone here admires you very much.'

The use of either of these two forms as an object is free and carries no difference in meaning or degree of formality.
  —Third, *ele* 'he,' *ela* 'she,' *eles* 'they (masc.),' and *elas* 'they (fem.)' are used as objects, so that *o, a, os, as* have entirely dropped from current use, except in a very few fixed expressions. Thus, one says

Encontrei <u>ela</u> no supermercado.   **SpBr**
'(I) met her in the supermarket.'

Acho que vou convidar <u>eles</u> também.   **SpBr**
'(I) think that I am going to invite them too.'

The use of object pronouns described above is universal and not, as is sometimes said, restricted to so-called substandard or uncultured language. No Brazilian, of any social class, region, or degree of education, routinely says a sentence like *eu a vi* 'I saw her,' although they will employ it in writing.

——For first person pronouns, the oblique forms remain in general use: *ela <u>me</u> viu* 'she saw me,' *ela <u>nos</u> viu* 'she saw us' are entirely correct and natural in speech. Use of *eu* and *nós* as objects is common but is consistently avoided by even minimally educated people.

——Finally, it may be noted that in some regions (northeast, the Amazon, and Rio) the pronoun *lhe* is used in speech as an oblique form of *você* 'you' (but not of *ele/ela* 'he/she'). In such areas speakers tend to use it both as an indirect object (its standard use) and as a direct object, so that one hears sentences like

Eu <u>lhe</u> vi no supermercado.   **Regional**
'I saw you in the supermarket.'

This phenomenon is not universal, and many speakers prefer the general colloquial forms *você, te.* In other areas (like Minas Gerais, São Paulo, and the south in general) this use of *lhe* is rare or unknown.

29.5 Possessive use of oblique pronouns

Portuguese shares with other Romance languages the possibility of expressing a possessive meaning by means of oblique pronouns, as in

Ele <u>me</u> quebrou o nariz.
'He broke my nose [literally, He broke me the nose].'

This construction is used exclusively with the personal pronouns *me, te, nos,* and *lhe(s),* the last only in the written language. It is always possible to express exactly the same idea by using a possessive, as shown in the following examples (both Portuguese versions given below have the same meaning):

O gato <u>te</u> arranhou a canela?   [cf. *O gato arranhou a <u>sua</u> canela?*]
'Did the cat scratch your shin?'

> *Ela <u>nos</u> passou na frente.*   [cf. *Ela passou na <u>nossa</u> frente.*]
> 'She stepped ahead of us.'

> *Você <u>me</u> amassou o carro!*   [cf. *Você amassou <u>meu</u> carro!*]
> 'You have dented my car!'

The oblique construction is possible when the possession expressed is inalienable, that is, when the possessed object is seen as intimately connected to the possessor, in particular when one refers to body parts; and also when the possessive is part of certain expressions (where it has in fact no concrete possessive meaning), such as *na minha frente* 'in front of me,' *atrás de mim* 'behind me,' *ao meu encontro* 'in my direction.'

> *O inimigo <u>lhe</u> veio ao encontro.*   **Wr**   [**cf.** *O inimigo veio ao encontro <u>dele</u>.*]
> 'The enemy came in his direction.'

> *Um elefante <u>me</u> passou na frente.*   [**cf.** *Um elefante passou na <u>minha</u> frente.*]
> 'An elephant stepped in front of me.'

When the possessor is expressed by a nonpronominal noun phrase or by a third person pronoun in the spoken language, the oblique construction is not possible, and the normal possessive construction must be used, e.g.,

> *O gato arranhou a canela <u>da menina</u>.*
> 'The cat scratched the girl's shin.'

> *O gato arranhou a canela <u>dela</u>.*
> 'The cat scratched her shin.'

The latter sentence is correct both in writing and in speaking, but its version with *lhe*,

> *O gato <u>lhe</u> arranhou a canela.*   **Wr**
> 'id.'

is exclusive of the written language (as are any sentences including *lhe*).

    Contrary to what is asserted in some grammars, the oblique construction with possessive meaning described above is fairly frequent, even in the spoken language.

29.6 Use of me, nos *in complaints*

The oblique *me* and *nos* can be used in emphatic sentences expressing a complaint, to refer to the complaining person, e.g.,

Ele <u>nos</u> arrumou uma confusão . . .
'He made such a mess (on us) . . .'

Os alunos <u>me</u> vieram com umas perguntas impossíveis.
'The students came (on me) with some unanswerable questions.'

This construction is sometimes called, rather misleadingly, dative of interest. It is not the same as the one exemplified in Spanish *la niña <u>se</u> comió los pasteles* 'the girl ate the cakes,' where the pronoun in fact denotes the interested person; the Spanish dative of interest has no correspondent in Portuguese.

29.7 Sequences of oblique pronouns

Sentences with two oblique pronouns of the type commonly found in Spanish, e.g.,

<u>Me lo</u> dijeron hoy.
'(They) said it to me today.'

are not found in current Brazilian Portuguese. Rather, other turns of phrase are employed, mainly the following:
a. Substitute a nonclitic pronoun or a nonpronominal phrase for one of the pronouns. Thus, the Spanish sentence given above might be translated as

Me disseram isso hoje.   **SpBr**
Disseram-me isso hoje.   **Wr**
'(They) said it to me today.'

or

Disseram isso para mim hoje.   **SpBr**
'id.'

b. Omit one of the pronouns (whenever context is sufficient to allow recovering its referent):

—*Você sabia que o Francisco morreu?*
—*Me disseram hoje.*   **SpBr**
"Did you know that Francisco died?"
"(They) said (it) to me today."

Sequences of oblique pronouns did occur in the older language and still may be found occasionally in texts written up to the early 1900s (in Portugal they are still used, at least in writing). In many of these sequences the pronouns are agglutinated, as in *mo* (= *me* + *o*). Today, the only combinations still used (very rarely and only in writing) are those composed of *se* followed by an indirect object pronoun, i.e., *me, te, lhe, nos, lhes*, e.g.,

> *Quando os revoltosos foram às ruas, juntaram-se-lhes muitos*
> *comerciantes descontentes.*   **Wr**
> 'When the rebels went to the streets, many dissatisfied merchants joined them.'

Such sentences look rather pedantic nowadays. A more idiomatic way of expressing the same idea is

> *Quando os revoltosos foram às ruas, muitos comerciantes descontentes se juntaram a eles.*
> 'id.'

One can also find a pronominal sequence in the idiom *pouco se me dá*, which means 'I don't care.' But this is a set phrase, unanalyzable in the modern language.

29.8 Oblique pronouns after prepositions

As we saw in chapter 8, personal pronouns have special forms when used after prepositions, as shown in the table below (pronominal forms are given in the table together with a sample preposition):

	After *com*	After other prepositions
1st singular	*comigo*	*para mim*
[2nd singular	*contigo*	*para ti*][1]
3rd singular	*com você*	*para você*
	com ele	*para ele*
3rd singular reflexive	*consigo*	*para si*

(continued)

	After *com*	After other prepositions
1st plural	*conosco*	*para nós*
[2nd plural	*convosco*	*para vós*][1]
3rd plural	*com vocês*	*para vocês*
	com eles	*para eles*
3rd plural reflexive	*consigo*	*para si*

Personal pronouns (forms used after prepositions)

Note

[1] These forms, as we saw in chapter 8, are archaic in Brazilian Portuguese.

With the preposition *entre* 'between, among,' which often introduces more than one NP, subject forms of the pronoun may be used. The first pronoun is found in the subject form or, more rarely, in the oblique form; as for the second (and third, if any), the subject form is normally used, although grammatical tradition insists on the use of the oblique:

Entre <u>eu</u> e <u>você</u> não deve haver segredos.
Entre <u>mim</u> e <u>você</u> não deve haver segredos.
'Between me and you there should be no secrets.'

Entre <u>você</u> e <u>eu</u> não deve haver segredos.
'Between you and me there should be no secrets.'

The use of *mim* in the last example, although recommended, yields a very strange result:

* *Entre <u>você</u> e <u>mim</u> . . .*

Most Brazilians will reject this construction as ill-formed, even in writing.

In comparative constructions Portuguese requires subject forms, even when the oblique is used in English, e.g.,

Ela canta como <u>eu</u>.
'She sings like me.'

Ninguém sofreu mais do que <u>eu</u>.
'Nobody suffered more than I (did).'

30

Adverbs and Adverbials

The traditional designation **adverb** covers a widely (not to say wildly) heterogeneous group of items. These items do not constitute a coherent class and do not all behave in the same way. Both in Portuguese and in English grammars, adverbs are subclassified according to meaning categories, such as place, manner, time, etc., which are syntactically no more coherent than the greater category adverb. Nevertheless, and in spite of some good scholarship available on the subject,[1] the label "adverb" is still in universal use and will be retained here, with the warning that it does not have to stand for anything more specific than "noninflecting word not classifiable as a conjunction or as a preposition." One word of comfort, though: the traditional labeling is the same for English and for Portuguese, so that the Portuguese translation of an English adverb is always called an adverb in Portuguese as well.

When describing their syntactic positions, I will be speaking of **adverbials,** rather than of adverbs because whatever is said about the ordering possibilities of single words like *apressadamente* 'hastily' may also be said of phrases like *com pressa* 'in haste.' That is, these two forms are not different from the point of view of their syntactic behavior, and they may be lumped together under the label adverbials.[2]

Notes

**[1] For instance, Greenbaum (1969); Nøjgaard (1995); Pecoraro and Pisacane (1984).

[2]In this section I do not discuss particles like *não* 'no, do not' and *sim* 'yes,' which are not properly adverbials. For these, see section 31.3.3.

Morphologically speaking, adverbs can be distinguished into two main groups: adverbs derived from nominals through the suffix *–mente* '-ly,' and other adverbs. I consider them in turn in the following sections.

30.1 Adverbs in -mente

The suffix *-mente* functions similarly to English *-ly,* forming adverbs from nominals, e.g.,

lento	'slow'	*lentamente*	'slowly'

The only observation to be made is that in Portuguese the nominal base for adverbs in *-mente* is the feminine form of the nominal, as seen in the above example (*lenta* + *mente*). Other examples:

cuidadoso	'careful'	*cuidadosamente*	'carefully'
completo	'complete'	*completamente*	'completely'
imenso	'huge'	*imensamente*	'hugely'

The feminine character of the base, of course, does not show when the nominal has only one form for both genders, e.g.,

cortês	'polite'	*cortesmente*	'politely'[1]
infeliz	'unfortunate'	*infelizmente*	'unfortunately'
só	'alone, lonely'	*somente*	'only'[1]

Note

[1]The accent on *cortês* and on *só* disappears in the adverb by virtue of the general accent rules (see 6.1).

It is possible to form an adverb from the superlative form of the nominal; thus, we have *cuidadosíssimo* 'most careful,' formed on *cuidadoso* 'careful' by means of the suffix *-íssimo;* from this base we derive the adverb *cuidadosissimamente* [*cuidados-* + *-issima* + *-mente*] 'most carefully' (for superlative formation, see chapter 41).

As we saw in 3.1.2, *-mente* adverbs keep the stress of the original nominal as a secondary stress:

rápido	['hapidu]
rapidamente	[ˌhapida'mẽtʃi]

In the adverb, the syllable *ra* [ha] gets secondary stress, as a reminder of its status as the (primarily) stressed syllable in *rápido*.

When two adverbs in *-mente* are coordinated by means of the conjunction *e* 'and,' and sometimes *mas* 'but,' the suffix may be omitted in the first adverb:

Ele trabalha <u>demorada e pacientemente</u>. **Wr**
'He works slowly and patiently.'

As indicated, this rule applies only in the written language. If the adverbs are coordinated without a conjunction, both suffixes must appear:

Ele trabalha <u>demoradamente, pacientemente</u>.
'He works slowly, patiently.'

As for the meaning of these adverbs, it is sometimes straightforwardly related to the original nominal, expressing a manner, as in *lentamente,* which means 'in a slow manner.' But in other cases, as in English, the semantic relation is idiosyncratic, as for instance in *somente* (from *só* 'lonely'), which does not mean 'in a lonely manner,' but rather 'only'; *imensamente* (from *imenso* 'huge'), not 'in a huge manner,' but rather 'very much'; *absolutamente,* from *absoluto,* which does not mean 'in an absolute manner,' but 'by no means'; *antigamente,* from *antigo* 'ancient,' which means 'formerly.' In these cases, the fact that the adverb is derived from the nominal is not relevant for learning purposes, and the adverbs should probably be learned as independent, individual items. Also, *-mente* cannot be added to any qualificative nominal, either because it would not make sense (* *louramente** 'blondly') or for no known reason (* *mamente,* from *mau* 'bad'; instead, one says *mal* 'badly').

30.2 Nonderived adverbs

Besides adverbs in *-mente,* Portuguese has many other words that are traditionally called adverbs, for example, *mal* 'badly, poorly,' *bem* 'well,' *depressa* 'quickly,' *devagar* 'slowly,' *aqui* 'here,' and so on. Since these words are in very frequent use, I give below a list of the most important ones, following a rough semantic classification as found in traditional grammars.

30.2.1 Adverbs of manner

Most adverbs of manner are derived by means of the suffix *-mente;* a few are nonderived, viz.,

bem	'well'
mal	'badly, poorly'[1]

and their comparatives

melhor	'better'
pior	'worse'[2]

Notes

[1] *Bem* is also used as an intensifier, as in *bem rico* 'quite rich'; and *mal* is also used as a preverbal particle, meaning 'hardly': *ele mal fala com ela* 'he hardly speaks to her.' In these uses, they have no comparative form.

[2] *Melhor* and *pior* are also comparatives of the nominals *bom* 'good' and *mau* 'bad,' respectively: *este uísque é bom, mas aquele é melhor* 'this whiskey is good, but that (one) is better.'

Plus the following:

depressa	'quickly'
devagar	'slowly'
assim	'thus, like this, like that'

Assim is a deictic, that is, it refers to some manner inferable from context, e.g.,

Eu nunca vou conseguir trabalhar <u>assim</u>.
'I'll never be able to work like that.'

For the use of *assim* as a discourse marker, see chapter 40.

30.2.2 Adverbs of place

The most important adverbs of place are as follows:

aqui	'here'
aí	'there'
ali	'there'
lá	'there'

The difference between *aá* and *lá* is that *aí* is used to refer to a place near the addressee, and *lá* to a place far from both the speaker and the addressee:

> *Sai logo daí, menino!*   **SpBr**
> 'Get out of there right now, kid!'

> *Ele quer ficar lá para sempre.*
> 'He wants to stay there forever.'

Ali is used like *lá*, to refer to a place not near either the speaker or the addressee, but not very far away—whereas *lá* can refer to very distant places:

> *Põe esse sapato ali no banco.*   **SpBr**
> 'Put this shoe there on the stool.'

This sentence implies that the stool is not very far away. Now, one could never use *ali* in the sentence

> *A NASA mandou uma sonda lá em Marte.*   **SpBr**
> 'NASA sent a probe (there) to Mars.'

These adverbs are very often used in speech to reinforce the determiners *esse* 'this' (reinforced by *aqui* or *aí*) and *aquele* 'that' (reinforced by *lá*), e.g.,

> *Eu vou ficar com esse sapato aqui.*   **SpBr**
> 'I am keeping this shoe (here).'

> *Me dá esse lápis aí.*   **SpBr**
> 'Give me that pencil (there).'

Aquela montanha *lá* às vezes fica coberta de neve.   **SpBr**
'That mountain (over there) sometimes gets covered with snow.'

Cá 'here' is used nowadays only in certain fixed expressions. First, it occurs as a complement of verbs of movement:

Vem cá.   **SpBr**
'Come here.'

Dá cá um beijo.   **SpBr**
'Give me (here) a kiss.'

Ele veio cá ontem.
'He came here yesterday.'

Cá is used after the preposition *para* 'to':

Meu namorado prometeu mudar para cá ainda este ano.
'My boyfriend promised to move (to) here still this year.'

It also occurs after *de* 'from,' but only in the expression *de cá para lá* (and its variant *de lá para cá*) 'back and forth, from here to there':

As galinhas estavam correndo de cá para lá.
'The chickens were running back and forth.'

Cá also occurs in the idiom *cá entre nós* 'just between us.' *Cá* is also used (less frequently) as a reinforcement of locational phrases, e.g.,

Cá na minha casa essas coisas nunca acontecem.
'Here in my home such things never happen.'[1]

Note

[1] In European Portuguese *cá* is much more frequently used, as an alternative to *aqui;* compare European *ele já cá não vive* with Brazilian *ele não mora mais aqui* 'he doesn't live here any more.'

Other important adverbs of place are *longe* 'far (away)' and *perto* 'close (by)':

Ele mora muito <u>longe</u>.
'He lives far away.'

The other adverbs of place are normally used in conjunction with *aqui, aí,* and *lá* or as the first part of compound prepositions. Thus, *dentro* 'inside' and *fora* 'outside' may appear alone as in

Eles estão <u>dentro</u>.
'They are inside.'

But it is more natural to add a reinforcement:

Eles estão <u>lá fora</u>   /   <u>aqui fora</u>   /   <u>aí fora</u>.
'They are out there /   out here /   out there.'

Their use as part of compound prepositions is instanced in

Os parafusos ficam <u>fora da</u> caixa.
'The screws go outside the box.'

<u>Dentro de</u> casa está muito calor.
'Inside the house it is very hot.'

The following adverbs of place function like *dentro* and *fora*:

atrás	'behind'
debaixo	'under'
detrás	'behind'
diante	'in front (of), ahead'
em cima	'above, on top (of)'
na frente	'in front of'

and some others.

Adverbs of place are never preceded by purely reinforcing prepositions, as in English *in here, over there*. A last adverb of place, *acolá* (a synonym of *lá* 'there') may be found occasionally in old texts but is no longer used nowadays.

30.2.3 Adverbs of time

These items present no particular problems because they behave in much the same way as their English counterparts. The most frequent are the following:

agora	'now'
ainda	'still'
amanhã	'tomorrow'
antes	'before'
cedo	'early'
depois	'later'
hoje	'today'
já	'already'
logo	'immediately, right away'
nunca	'never'
ontem	'yesterday'
outrora	'in ancient times' **Wr**
sempre	'always'
tarde	'late'

Então is usually given as an adverb of time meaning 'at that time,' but in this use it is rare, except in archaic texts; nowadays it is used exclusively as a discourse marker, 'then':

Carolina não vai aparecer; <u>então</u>, você fica no lugar dela.
'Carolina is not going to show up; then, you may take her place.'

30.2.4 Other types of adverbs

Other ideas expressed by adverbs are:

doubt

> *<u>Talvez</u> alguém possa nos ajudar.*
> 'Perhaps someone can help us.'

The other adverbs of doubt are archaic: *quiçá, porventura,* both meaning 'perhaps.'

degree

> *Elias trabalha <u>menos</u> do que os outros.*
> 'Elias works less than the others.'

Adverbs of degree are usually complemented by a comparative expression (*do que os outros* 'than the others' in the above example). With *menos* 'less' and *mais* 'more' the comparative expression is introduced by *que* or *do que* (both forms are equally frequent):

> *Elias trabalha <u>mais</u> (do) que os outros.*
> 'Elias works more than the others.'

With *tanto* 'as much as,' the comparative expression is introduced by *quanto:*

> *Elias trabalha <u>tanto</u> quanto os outros.*
> 'Elias works as much as the others.'

The same adverbs may modify nominals; in such cases *tão* is used instead of *tanto:*

> *Ela é <u>mais</u> bonita (do) que um anjo.*
> 'She is more beautiful than an angel.'

> *Ela é <u>tão</u> bonita quanto um anjo.*
> 'She is as beautiful as an angel.'

inclusion

> *Ele odeia todo mundo—<u>inclusive</u> a própria mãe.*
> 'He hates everybody—including his own mother.'

Ele odeia todo mundo—até a própria mãe.
'id.'

30.3 Position and scope

From a positional point of view, adverbials may be **free,** that is, when they can appear in all or most interstices between the major constituents of the sentence; or **bound,** when they are restricted to occurrence next to a particular constituent, be it the verb, an NP modifier, an NP, or a prepositional phrase. The degree of freedom an adverbial enjoys within a sentence depends, on one hand, on its grammatical function—in particular, its status as an **adjunct** or a **complement;** and, on the other hand, on its **scope.**

30.3.1 Complements vs. adjuncts

Let's examine each one of these notions in turn. An adverbial is a complement when its occurrence with a particular verb is obligatory, it being so to speak required by the verb.[1] For instance, one can say

Tomás morava em Campinas.
'Tomás lived in Campinas.'

but not

* Tomás morava.

Note

**[1]Strictly speaking, it is not the verb as a word that requires the complement, but rather its meaning, that is, the concept it conveys. Thus, the verb *viver* means (as in English) 'to be alive' or 'to dwell'; and only when it occurs in the latter meaning does it require an adverbial complement; thus, we can say: *pelo menos, ele ainda está vivendo* 'at least, he is still alive [literally, he is still living],' where *viver* occurs without a complement (and means 'to be alive').

The adverbial, *em Campinas,* is then taken to be obligatory, required by the verb *morar* 'to live (= dwell),' and is therefore a complement. An adverbial complement may denote location (as above), time, manner, company, or destination:

A reunião durou <u>uma hora</u>. [**cf.** **A reunião durou.*]
'The meeting lasted one hour.'

Eles já estavam se sentindo <u>bem</u>.
'They were already feeling well.'

Tomás mora <u>com seus quatro filhos</u>.
'Tomás lives with his four children.'

O casaco é <u>para Laurinha</u>.
'The coat is for Laurinha.'

An adverbial is an adjunct when it represents additional information, which may very well be important but is not required by the verb, which can occur without it, e.g.,

Tomás abriu uma loja <u>em Campinas</u>.
'Tomás opened a store in Campinas.'

We may very well dispense with the adjunct, and say

Tomás abriu uma loja.
'Tomás opened a store.'

Adverbial complements obey the following ordering rule:

> An adverbial functioning as a complement must occur immediately af-
>
> ter the verb.

It can be moved to the head of the sentence only in very special (and rare) situations in order to convey a very strong emphasis, usually involving contrast with some parallel expression. And it can occupy no other position in the sentence:

<u>Em Campinas</u>, Tomás morava.
'In Campinas, Tomás lived.'

This sentence can be used, for instance, to correct the mistaken impression that Tomás both lived and worked in Campinas, to which the speaker answers something like '<u>In Campinas</u>, Tomás lived; but he worked in São Paulo.' No other position is acceptable for the adverbial complement, as shown by the following example:

> * *Tomás <u>em Campinas</u> morava.*[1]

Note

[1]Such inversions, unacceptable nowadays, were widely used in verse up to the 1920s.

30.3.2 Scope

When an adverbial functions as an adjunct, it sometimes has wide freedom of occurrence and sometimes is bound to a fixed position. This depends mainly on its **scope.** In order to define this notion, let us take some examples, starting with the following sentences, in which the adverbial can occur at the beginning or at the end as well as between the major constituents:

> <u>*Às três horas*</u>, *a professora passou a palavra ao visitante.*
> 'At three o'clock, the teacher gave the floor to the visitor.'

> *A professora, <u>às três horas</u>, passou a palavra ao visitante.*
> *A professora passou, <u>às três horas</u>, a palavra ao visitante.*
> *A professora passou a palavra, <u>às três horas</u>, ao visitante.*
> *A professora passou a palavra ao visitante, <u>às três horas</u>.*
> 'id.'

Here, the adverbial is normally separated by a comma. In other cases the comma is not necessary (at least not in all positions):

> <u>*Somente*</u> *a professora passou a palavra ao visitante.*
> 'Only the teacher gave the floor to the visitor.'

> *A professora <u>somente</u> passou a palavra ao visitante.*
> 'The teacher only gave the floor to the visitor.'

> *A professora passou <u>somente</u> a palavra ao visitante.*
> 'The teacher gave only the floor to the visitor.'

A professora passou a palavra <u>somente</u> ao visitante.
'The teacher gave the floor only to the visitor.'

A professora passou a palavra ao visitante, <u>somente</u>.
'The teacher gave the floor to the visitor only.'

From the point of view of their positions, the only difference between *às três horas* 'at three o'clock' and *somente* 'only' is that the former (like its English translation) requires a comma in all cases. But there is an important difference in meaning, as can be seen by the English glosses: with *às três horas* the difference in position does not affect the meaning relationship betweeen the adverbial and the sentence and its parts; but with *somente* (as with English *only*) position is relevant to meaning: the first sentence means that the teacher, nobody else, gave the floor to the visitor; the second sentence means that the teacher gave the floor to the visitor, but did nothing else; the third sentence means that she gave only the floor, nothing else; and the two remaining sentences mean that she gave the floor only to the visitor, to nobody else.

This is called a difference in scope: we say that *às três horas* has as its scope the verb (that is, the process or action expressed by the verb), regardless of position, whereas the scope of *somente* is the following constituent (except when it comes last, in which case the scope is the preceding constituent). The question of determining the possible positions of adverbials is comparatively simple, but the question of determining their scope is a highly complex matter, for which no really satisfactory description is available in the literature. On the other hand, the scope depends on meaning features of each particular item, plus the intended meaning of the sentence, so that it is usually similar in Portuguese and in English. For instance, *muito* in its meaning of 'very' takes a nominal as its scope in both languages:

Um músico <u>muito</u> brilhante
'A very brilliant musician'

and *às vezes* 'sometimes' has the verb as its scope in both languages:

Ela <u>às vezes</u> ronca.
'She sometimes snores.'

Some adverbials are specialized (for instance, *infelizmente* 'unfortunately' always takes the whole sentence as its scope); but most adverbials can take more than one scope, depending on the intended meaning.[1] Thus, *muito* can intensify a nominal, as above in *um músico muito brilhante* 'a very brilliant musician,' but it can also intensify a verb, as in

Meu pai trabalhava <u>muito</u>.
'My father worked a lot.'

Note

1An adverbial can have as its scope the whole **sentence, the **verb** (or, perhaps more accurately, the **verb phrase**), or a **nominal**—usually one in modifying function, as in *muito forte* 'very strong,' but also sometimes a nominal functioning as an NP head, as in *somente Maria telefonou* 'only Maria called.' Finally, it is said in traditional grammars that an adverbial can also have as its scope another adverbial (as for example in *muito lentamente* 'very slowly'). This strange property is, however, an illusion created by the fact that we are used to calling **adverb(ials)** a set of words that do not in fact constitute a grammatical class. In *muito lentamente* we do not have an adverbial modifying another adverbial, but rather a word of one class (*muito*) modifying a word of another class (*lentamente*). I repeat, my use of the term "adverb(ial)" in this grammar reflects not any conviction of the adequacy of traditional taxonomy, but only an inevitable consequence of our current ignorance of the best way of classifying these items.

30.3.3 Position rules for adverbial adjuncts

We can now return to the main question, the position of adverbials in the sentence. The first rule is as follows:

> Whenever an adverbial adjunct has the sentence as its scope, its occurrence is free.

This means that it may occur anywhere in the sentence (except, of course, inside the major constituents, for instance, inside a noun phrase). And in this case the adverbial is more often than not separated by a comma. An example is *felizmente* 'fortunately,' which always takes the sentence as its scope:

Felizmente, a inundação não atingiu a biblioteca.
'Fortunately, the flood did not reach the library.'

This sentence has the following variants, all acceptable:

A inundação, <u>felizmente</u>, não atingiu a biblioteca.
A inundação não atingiu, <u>felizmente</u>, a biblioteca.
A inundação não atingiu a biblioteca, <u>felizmente</u>.
'id.'

Observe that, unlike English, Portuguese does not allow an adverbial to occur between the negative particle *não* and the verb.[1] Compare the above variants with the English sentence

The flood did not, <u>fortunately</u>, reach the library.

Note

[1] Only a clitic pronoun can occur between *não* and the verb.

The second rule is this:

> Whenever an adverbial adjunct has as its scope a noun phrase or a prepositional phrase, it must occur next to the modified phrase: usually before it, but sometimes after it, when the adverbial comes last in the sentence (or when intonation interferes; see below).

An instance is the sentence

<u>Somente</u> *a professora passou a palavra ao visitante.*
'Only the teacher gave the floor to the visitor.'

Here the scope of *somente* 'only' is the noun phrase *a professora* 'the teacher,' and the adverbial must occur immediately before the noun phrase. In the sentence

A professora passou a palavra <u>somente</u> ao visitante.
'The teacher gave the floor only to the visitor.'

somente refers to the prepositional phrase *ao visitante* 'to the visitor' and correspondingly occurs next to the modified phrase (as shown by the glosses, Portuguese is parallel to English in this particular).

In speech the scope can be manipulated to a certain degree by using intonation; thus, for example, in

> *A professora <u>somente</u> passou a palavra ao visitante.*
> 'The teacher only gave the floor to the visitor.'

the scope of *somente* is, as we have seen, the verb. But if the sentence is pronounced in a certain way—with a rising contour on *somente,* followed by an intonational break—the scope of *somente* will be understood to be *a professora,* so that the sentence will mean 'only the teacher gave the floor to the visitor.'

The third rule is as follows:

> Whenever an adverbial adjunct has as its scope an NP modifier, it must occur before it if it is composed of only one word; otherwise, it occurs after the NP modifier.

The first part of the rule is exemplified by

> <u>excessivamente</u> *gordo*
> 'excessively fat'
>
> <u>muito</u> *gordo*
> 'very fat'
>
> <u>mais</u> *gordo*
> 'fatter'

where the modifying adverbial occurs before the modified element, that is, *gordo* 'fat.' This rule has at least one exception, the word *demais* 'too,' which, although written as one word, occurs after the modified element:

gordo <u>demais</u>
'too fat'

When the adverbial is compound (preposition + noun phrase), it occurs after the modified element:

gordo <u>em demasia</u>
'fat in excess'

gordo <u>de espantar</u>
'amazingly fat'

The adverbials *um pouco* 'a little' and *um tanto* 'somewhat' occur before the modified nominal, although they are composed of more than one word:

<u>*um pouco*</u> *gordo*
'a little fat'

We are left with one last case, that is, when the scope is the verb. Here the situation is complex, and adverbials behave in several different ways:
—With many, ordering is free:

<u>*Amanhã*</u> *a loja vai fechar por causa do feriado.*
'Tomorrow the store will close on account of the holiday.'

A loja <u>amanhã</u> vai fechar por causa do feriado.
A loja vai fechar <u>amanhã</u> por causa do feriado.
A loja vai fechar por causa do feriado, <u>amanhã</u>.
'id.'

The only position where the adverbial does not occur is between the auxiliary and the main verb; and when sentence-final, it usually requires a comma. Adverbials behaving like *amanhã* include

na reunião   'in the meeting'   (and adverbials of place in general)

sempre   'always'

(continued)

dentro em breve	'shortly'	
às três horas	'at three o'clock'	
depois	'afterwards'	
enquanto isso	'meanwhile'	
por acaso	'by chance'	
agora	'now'	(and adverbials of time in general)
inutilmente	'in vain'	(and many, but not all, adverbs in -*mente*)

—Other adverbials must occur immediately before the verb (or before the auxiliary) if they are to have the verb as their scope; an example is *quase* 'almost':

> *Eu quase estava caindo em cima dela por causa do gelo.*
> 'I was almost falling on her because of the ice.'

> *Eu estava quase caindo em cima dela por causa do gelo.*
> 'id.'

If we place *quase* after the verb, the scope will be not the verb, but the following phrase:

> *Eu estava caindo quase em cima dela por causa do gelo.*
> 'I was falling almost on her because of the ice.'

As can be seen by the gloss, the same happens with English *almost*.
Adverbials that behave like *quase* are

só	'only'
somente	'only'
principalmente	'chiefly'
pelo menos	'at least'
até mesmo	'even'
também	'also'
exclusivamente	'exclusively'

—Some adverbials must occur in any position after the verb in order to modify it:

Carolina conversou <u>gentilmente</u> com todos os participantes.
'Carolina talked kindly to all participants.'

Gentilmente here expresses the manner in which Carolina talked to the participants. The same word can also express the speaker's opinion about Carolina's behavior (in which case its scope is the sentence); the latter reading arises when *gentilmente* appears at the head of the sentence:

<u>*Gentilmente*</u>*, Carolina conversou com todos os participantes.*
'Kindly, Carolina talked to all participants.'

Adverbials that behave like *gentilmente* (when modifying the verb) include the following:

muito	'a lot'
bastante	'enough'

(continued)

um pouco	'a little'
alto	'loud'

These adverbs, unlike *gentilmente,* cannot take the sentence as their scope. This derives from their meaning, which prevents them from qualifying an event. They belong to two well-defined semantic classes: *muito, bastante,* and some others are **quantifiers,** whereas *alto* is an example of a word that can also modify an NP head:

um homem <u>alto</u>	**vs.**	*Ele fala <u>alto</u>.*
'a tall man'		'He speaks loud.'

Other examples are

um homem <u>baixo</u>	**vs.**	*Ele fala <u>baixo</u>.*
'a short man'		'He speaks softly.'
O rio é <u>fundo</u>.	**vs.**	*Iremos <u>fundo</u> nessa questão.*
'The river is deep.'		'We shall go deep into this question.'
uma viagem <u>rápida</u>	**vs.**	*Ela escreveu <u>rápido</u>.*
'a quick trip'		'She wrote rapidly.'
a <u>primeira</u> aluna da turma	**vs.**	*Ele quer ser servido <u>primeiro</u>.*
'the first student in the class'		'He wants to be served first.'
uma canção <u>bonita</u>	**vs.**	*Ela canta <u>bonito</u>.*
'a beautiful song'		'She sings beautifully.'

Note that when used as adverbials these words do not vary in gender or number.

The above lists are not exhaustive; as noted, scope possibilities depend on the semantics of each item, and it is hardly possible to list all cases in a grammar. On the other hand, in most cases English and Portuguese adverbials work in similar ways.

30.4 English and Portuguese adverbials

In general, the behavior of Portuguese adverbials is similar to that of English ones: as we saw above, in English the scope of *at three o'clock* stays the same as we move the adverb around the sentence, whereas the scope of *only* changes, thus paralleling the behavior of *às três horas* and *somente,* respectively. Also, when an English adverbial modifies a nominal, it cannot be moved, e.g.,

My cousin is fat <u>in excess</u>.
* My cousin is <u>in excess</u> fat.
* <u>In excess</u> my cousin is fat.
etc.

In these respects the two languages are similar. But there are also some differences, since Portuguese free adverbials, when occurring between the major constituents of the sentence, have more freedom of movement than English ones. For instance, the adverbial in English is usually placed between the auxiliary and the main verb, whereas in Portuguese it may also occur after the verb or before the auxiliary:

Alice estava <u>realmente</u> fazendo uma dieta.　　**or**
Alice estava fazendo <u>realmente</u> uma dieta.　　**or**
Alice <u>realmente</u> estava fazendo uma dieta.
'Alice was really following a diet.'

Alice tinha <u>realmente</u> feito uma dieta.　　**or**
Alice tinha feito <u>realmente</u> uma dieta.　　**or**
Alice <u>realmente</u> tinha feito uma dieta.
'Alice had really followed a diet.'

31

Interrogation, Exclamation, Negation

31.1 Interrogation

There are two main types of questions: **yes-no questions** and **wh- questions,** and each of them corresponds to a particular syntactic structure. A yes-no question is one that can be answered simply yes or no, e.g.,

Have you finished dinner?

Syntactically, yes-no questions are characterized, in English, by inversion and the presence of the sign **?**. In Portuguese, inversion is not used, and only the sign **?** marks these sentences as interrogative:

Você terminou de jantar?
'Have you finished dinner?'

A wh- question, on the other hand, is open-ended and requires independent information that goes beyond mere truth-value, e.g.,

Where do you live?

Here yes or no would be an entirely inadequate answer. Wh- questions have at their head one of a small set of words that, in English, begin with *wh-* (or *how*) and in Portuguese generally with *qu-*. The syntactic structures conveying each of these two types of questions differ and will be discussed separately in the sections that follow.[1]

Note

[1]Rigorously speaking, there is a clear difference between an **interrogative sentence, which refers to a particular syntactic structure, and a **question,** which is a type of utterance, having as its function the request of a piece of information. As we know, it is possible to utter a question without the use of an interrogative sentence, as when someone says *I have forgotten your name,* but is in fact asking for that information. Here, however, I will employ the terms "yes-no question" and "wh- question" rather loosely to refer both to the type of utterance and to the syntactic structure that usually expresses it; this causes no inconvenience in the context of this grammar and allows me to avoid burdening the exposition with terminological distinctions that, however correct, are not relevant for our purposes.

31.1.1 Yes-no questions

The way to express a yes-no question in Portuguese is simply to add **?** to the end of the sentence. This corresponds, in pronunciation, to a rising intonation contour not unlike the one found in English yes-no questions:

> *Você acabou de jantar?*
> 'Have you finished dinner?'

Subject-verb inversion as a mark of yes-no questions does not occur in Portuguese except in extremely artificial language or in (wrong) translations from English. It should not be used. Whenever inversion is found, it has nothing to do with the interrogative character of the sentence, that is, it occurs in cases in which inversion is found in the declarative version of the sentence, e.g.,

> *Já chegaram os jogadores?*
> 'Have the players already arrived?'

The declarative version of this sentence is also inverted:

> *Já chegaram os jogadores.*
> 'The players have already arrived.'

31.1.2 Wh- questions

A wh- question includes a wh- word (not necessarily at the beginning; see below). Its intonational contour differs from both yes-no questions and assertions. It is characterized by a higher pitch, falling immediately, on the wh- phrase, whether the latter comes at the beginning or at the end of the utterance. With the wh- word at the beginning, the result sounds very similar to English utterances like

Which CD are you going to take?

As in English, wh- questions can also be pronounced without any distinguishing intonation, that is, with the same intonation as assertive utterances.

31.1.2.1 Interrogative words

The interrogative words that appear in wh- questions are as follows:

que?	'what? / which?'
qual?	'which?'
quanto? quantos?	'how much? / how many?'

These three interrogative words always precede a nominal (except when used in anaphoric context), e.g.,

Que besteira ele disse agora?
'What nonsense did he say now?'

Qual CD você vai levar?
'Which CD are you going to take?'

Quantos alunos tem a sua turma?
'How many students are there in your class?'

The remaining interrogative words are used independently, that is, without an attached nominal:

would have Stress in Sp. (which has stress on interrogatives)

como?	'how?'
quem?	'who?'
o que?	'what?'
onde?	'where?'
aonde?	'where to? / where?'[1]
por que?	'why?'
quando?	'when?'

Note

[1]Most speakers make no distinction in use between *onde* and *aonde;* both may mean either 'where to?' or 'where?'

To this list we may add

cadê?	**SpBr**	'where is?'

The use of *cadê* is described in 31.1.2.5.

As in English, many of these items may appear with a preposition, which in Portuguese always precedes: *para quê?* 'what for?' *de onde?* 'where from?' etc.

These words, which in English appear almost always at the head of the sentence, in Portuguese may also remain in the place reserved for their function in the sentence. Thus, if we have a direct object, as in

Which piano did you buy?

in Portuguese it is possible to prepose the interrogative word, as in

Que piano você comprou?
'Which piano did you buy?'

or to leave it after the verb, which is the typical position for a direct object:

> *Você comprou que piano?*
> 'id.'

It is important to note that this sentence is not (necessarily) an 'echo-question' as in English

> You bought *which piano?*

as when someone cannot believe what he or she has just heard. *Você comprou que piano?* is a normal, nonemphatic question in Portuguese, and it is equivalent to *Que piano você comprou?*—unless the last phrase is pronounced with a sharp rising intonation, in which case it *is* an echo-question.

31.1.2.2 Use of é que

Wh- questions are very frequently also marked in the spoken language by means of the element *é que,* placed immediately after the preposed element. Thus, the sentence

> *Que piano você prefere?*
> 'Which piano do you prefer?'

sounds slightly stilted. The more natural way to ask this question in speaking is

> *Que piano <u>é que</u> você prefere?*   **SpBr**
> 'id.'

The use of *é que* is particularly frequent when the preposed element is only the interrogative word, so that a sentence like

> *Quem sua mãe vai chamar para a festa?*
> 'Whom is your mother going to invite to the party?'

is comparatively rare, and speakers will rather say

> *Quem <u>é que</u> sua mãe vai chamar para a festa?*   **SpBr**
> 'id.'

É que optionally becomes *foi que* if the main verb is in the preterit tense, e.g.,

Quem <u>foi que</u> sua mãe convidou para a festa?   **SpBr**   **or**
Quem <u>é que</u> sua mãe convidou para a festa?   **SpBr**
'Whom has your mother invited to the party?'

Curiously, *é que* must be used with the imperfect:

Quem <u>é que</u> ela mais odiava?   **SpBr**
'Whom did she hate most?'

Further examples of the use of *é que* are

Para onde <u>é que</u> ela foi?   **SpBr**
'Where did she go?'

Quando <u>é que</u> vamos ter um governo honesto?   **SpBr**
'When will we have an honest government?'

Para que <u>é que</u> você fez esse barulho todo?   **SpBr**
'Why did you make all this noise?'

In informal speech the form of *ser* is often omitted, so that one hears sentences like

Quem <u>que</u> ela mais odiava?   **SpBr**
'Whom did she hate most?'

Para que <u>que</u> você fez esse barulho todo?   **SpBr**
'What did you do all this noise for?'

31.1.2.3 Inversion in wh- questions

Subject-verb inversion, which as we saw does not occur in yes-no questions, does happen in wh- questions, but only in certain circumstances, not always, as in English. For instance, there is no inversion in

Onde você encontrou essas xícaras lindas?
'Where did you find these beautiful teacups?'

Here the subject (*você* 'you') is in its normal place before the verb *encontrou* 'found.'

Inversion takes place only when the interrogative word is at the head of the sentence. The exact circumstances leading to inversion are not known, but it is possible to single out some contexts that favor it.

—First, when the verb *disallows* any object or accepts only a restricted set of possible objects (see chapter 33 about such requirements made by verbs about their objects). With such verbs, inversion—always optional—occurs also in declarative sentences, but it is particularly frequent in wh- questions. An example is *morrer* 'to die':

> *Quando morreu seu avô?*   **or**
> *Quando foi que morreu seu avô?*   **SpBr**
> 'When did your grandfather die?'

As seen, inversion also occurs when the element *é que / foi que* is used. Inversion is frequent in these cases but not mandatory; the following versions are perfectly acceptable:

> *Quando seu avô morreu?*
> *Quando foi que seu avô morreu?*   **SpBr**
> 'id.'

—The second context that favors inversion in wh- questions is with **unaccusative** verbs (see chapter 33), when occurring without an object, e.g.,

> *Por que acabou a festa?*   **or**
> *Por que foi que acabou a festa?*   **SpBr**
> 'Why did the party end?'

With unaccusatives, reflexive pronouns are often used (especially in the written language) and inversion remains possible:

> *Como se chama a sua namorada?*   **Wr**
> *Como chama a sua namorada?*   **SpBr**
> 'What is your girlfriend's name?'

Here, again, inversion is optional:

> *Por que a festa acabou?*   **or**
> *Por que foi que a festa acabou?*   **SpBr**
> 'id.'

—Then, we have inversion when the verb is *ser* or *estar,* both meaning 'to be' (see chapter 22 for the semantic difference between them), and also with *ter* 'to have':

> *Quem é Paulina?*   **or**

Quem é que é Paulina?   **SpBr**
'Who is Paulina?'

Onde está Paulina?   **or**
Onde é que está Paulina?   **SpBr**
'Where is Paulina?'

In this case inversion is **obligatory** if the verb is *ser:*

    * Quem Paulina é?
    * Quem é que Paulina é?

With *estar,* inversion apparently may be dispensed with when *é que* is used; otherwise, it is obligatory, or at least preferred:[1]

    ? * Onde Paulina está?
    Onde é que Paulina está?   **SpBr**
    'Where is Paulina?'

Note

[1]I marked the first of these sentences with '?*' because it sounds better than the ones with *ser,* yet it is not totally acceptable.

Examples of inversion with *ter* are as follows:

    Quantos alunos tem a sua turma?
    'How many students are there in your class? [literally, How many students does your class have?]'

    O que é que tem esse menino?   **SpBr**
    'What is the matter with this child? [literally, What does this child have?]'

—Finally, inversion is frequent when the sentence begins with an interrogative adverbial—*como* 'how' or *onde* 'where'—and this word acts as a complement of the verb, e.g.,

    Como vai seu pai?
    'How is your father?'

Onde fica a Praça Tiradentes?
'Where is Tiradentes Square?'

31.1.2.4 Indirect questions

As in English, interrogative sentences can appear as subordinate clauses and are then usually called **indirect questions,** as in

Quero saber quem comeu as salsichas todas.
'(I) want to know who ate all the sausages.'

Subject-verb inversion is possible in indirect questions, under the same conditions obtaining for wh- questions in general:

Quero saber onde está Paulina.
'(I) want to know where is Paulina.'

Quero saber por que acabou a festa.
'(I) want to know why the party ended.'

As for yes-no questions, they occur as subordinate clauses with the conjunction *se* 'if, whether':

Quero saber se você acabou de jantar.
'(I) want to know if you have finished dinner.'

Quero saber se já chegaram os jogadores.
'(I) want to know if the players have already arrived.'

Here the facts of Portuguese are very similar to those of English and require no special comment.

31.1.2.5 Cadê?

The interrogative word *cadê* is typical of the spoken language; it means 'where is' and is always used before a noun phrase, and the sequence is a complete utterance:

Cadê aquele caderno amarelo?   **SpBr**
'Where is that yellow notebook?'

A *cadê*-phrase can be subordinated to a verb accepting an indirect question:

Não sei <u>cadê o caderno amarelo</u>. **SpBr**
'(I) don't know where the yellow copybook is.'

Cadê has a variant, *quede* or *que é de,* pronounced [ˈkɛdʒi], still used nowadays by older speakers.

31.1.3 Echo-questions

Finally, I want to mention a third category of interrogative sentences, usually termed **echo-questions.** These may have the structure of a yes-no question or of a wh- question; in the latter case, both in English and in Portuguese, the interrogative word is not pre-posed, remaining in its original place in the sentence.

Echo-questions have a peculiar intonation pattern, with a sharp rise at the end (sometimes represented as **?!** or **??**), and they express incredulity or sometimes a request for confirmation:

Você foi com a Cláudia no cinema?? **SpBr**
'Did you go to the movies with Claudia? [I can hardly believe my ears!]'

*Você foi ao cinema com **quem**??*
'You went to the movies with **whom**? [please repeat what you just said]'

31.1.4 Tag-questions

In Portuguese it is possible to build tag-questions much the same way as in English, e.g.,

Ela comprou um carro novo, não comprou?
'She bought a new car, didn't she?'

Ela não entendeu nada, entendeu?
'She didn't understand a thing, did she?'

Of course, since Portuguese lacks a semantically empty verb like *to do,* the tag-question repeats the preceding verb. Except for that, the Portuguese and English constructions are similar. Yet, tag-questions including repetition of the verb are not very frequent. Portuguese speakers prefer to use the all-purpose tag *não é?,* frequently abbreviated as *né?,* e.g.,

Ela comprou um carro novo, não é?
'She bought a new car, didn't she?'

Ela não entendeu nada, né?
'She didn't understand a thing, did she?'

31.2 Exclamations

Two exclamatory constructions require some comment because they differ in Portuguese and in English.

—First, English exclamatory phrases or sentences beginning with *what a* are rendered in Portuguese by sentences beginning with *que,* without an article:

> *Que resposta estúpida!*
> 'What a stupid answer!'

> *Que bolo ótimo ela faz!*
> 'What a delicious cake she makes!'

As can be seen, the exclamatory construction may be only a phrase or a complete sentence. When the exclamation is a complete sentence (as in the second example above), it is customary to add a *que* immediately after the exclamatory noun phrase:

> *Que bolo ótimo <u>que</u> ela faz!*   **SpBr**
> 'id.'

As in English, the exclamatory phrase is obligatorily preposed.

—The second construction to be noted corresponds to English exclamations beginning with *how,* e.g.,

> How clever he is!
> How well he plays!

These constructions may be translated in Portuguese in two ways. In the first one, the exclamatory element is preposed, as in English, and the construction is introduced by *que:*

> *Que sabido ele é!*
> 'How clever he is!'

> *Que bem ele toca!*
> 'How well he plays!'

[handwritten note: Sp. que bien toca / como toca de bien]

Here, too, the colloquial language usually inserts *que* after the exclamatory phrase:

Que sabido que ele é!   **SpBr**
'How clever he is!'

Que bem que ele toca!   **SpBr**
'How well he plays!'

Que is also used in nonsentential exclamations like

Que bonito!
'How beautiful!'

The second construction corresponding to English exclamations with *how* is introduced by *como,* plus the whole sentence **without preposing any element,** that is, in its
normal declarative form. The English sentences seen above may, then, be translated as

Como ele é sabido!
'How clever he is!'

Como ele toca bem!
'How well he plays!'

Como is not used in nonsentential exclamations, which always employ *que.*
These two constructions, exclamatory *que* and *como,* are synonymous and equally
natural and frequent.[1]

Note

[1]There is still an exclamatory word *quão,* sometimes found in sentences like *quão bem ele toca!*
'how well he plays!' but its use nowadays is confined to poor translations from English. No one, in
speaking or writing, employs *quão* spontaneously, and its use is not to be encouraged.

The item *mas,* usually a coordinator meaning 'but' (see chapter 37), is often used as
a sort of reinforcement before exclamatory words, e.g.,

Mas que frio!
'What cold (weather)!'

Mas como essa mulher sabe dançar!
'How (well) this woman can dance!'

Finally, *cada,* which normally means 'each, every,' can be used as an exclamatory, corresponding approximately in meaning to English *such:*

> *Comprei umas laranjas; cada laranja!*
> '(I) bought some oranges; such oranges!'

Cada in this construction has a strong appreciative content, either favorable or unfavorable. In the sentence above, the speaker tries to convey a sense of amazement at the size or quality of the oranges. In the following,

> *Eles me deram cada incumbência!*
> 'They have assigned me such duties!'

the idea is primarily of highly difficult or unpleasant duties.

31.3 Negation

Negation in Portuguese is very different from negation in English and deserves careful examination. I will first consider verb negation and then nominal negation.

31.3.1 Verb negation

31.3.1.1 Negative before the verb

Negating a verb in Portuguese is, in principle, very simple: all one has to do is to prepose a negative particle (typically *não*) to the verb:

> *Eugênio não trabalha mais aqui.*
> 'Eugênio does not work here any longer.'

> *Sua mãe não vai encontrar o sofá que ela está procurando.*
> 'Your mother will not find the sofa she is looking for.'

There are other negative words: *nada* 'nothing,' *ninguém* 'no one,' *nunca* 'never,' *jamais* 'never,' *nem* 'not even,' and *nenhum* 'no.' *Nenhum* always occurs before nominals (*nenhuma razão* 'no reason'), and the others can appear by themselves. These words function basically like *não:*

> *Eugênio nunca trabalhou aqui.*
> 'Eugênio has never worked here.'

Nenhuma pessoa telefonou para a gente.
'No person called us up.'

Nada vai desanimar o rapaz.
'Nothing will discourage the young man.'

There is one difference, though: *não,* when negating a verb, *must* come immediately before it (except for clitic pronouns, which may intervene):

Eugênio não me telefonou.
'Eugênio did not call me up.'

whereas the other negative words can be separated from the verb by certain elements in the sentence:

Eugênio nunca, que eu saiba, trabalhou aqui.
'Eugênio has never, to my knowledge, worked here.'

Nada, nem essa má notícia, vai desanimar o rapaz.
'Nothing, not even that bad news, will discourage the young man.'

31.3.1.2 Negative after the verb

The negative words seen above can also appear after the verb; in such case, the presence of *não* before the verb is obligatory. Thus, the sentence

Eugênio nunca trabalhou aqui.
'Eugênio has never worked here.'

can also be said, with the same meaning,

Eugênio não trabalhou aqui nunca.
'id.'

A professora não ajudou ninguém.
'The teacher didn't help anyone [literally, didn't help no one].'

It is a general principle in Portuguese that several negatives in the same sentence reinforce each other, instead of canceling each other, as in English; thus, there may be even more than two, as in

[handwritten: Sp. ella nunce le pídio a nadie que le ayudera/se en nada]

Ela <u>nunca</u> pediu que <u>ninguém</u> a ajudasse em <u>nada</u>.
'She never asked anyone to help her in anything [literally, She never asked no one to help her in nothing].'

31.3.1.3 Double negative in the spoken language

In the spoken language, verb negation may be expressed the same way as in the written language, that is, by simply preposing *não* to the verb. But it is more common to add a second occurrence of *não,* e.g.,

Eu <u>não</u> vou lá <u>não</u>.   **SpBr**
'I'm not going there.'

The positioning of the second *não* follows these rules:

---

1. The second *não* occurs at the end of the sentence (except in coordinated structures; see below).

2. It negates the main clause, never the subordinate one, <u>except</u> for objective clauses, which may be independently negated (if last in the sentence).

3. In coordinated sentences with *e* and just one subject for both, the second *não* occurs at the end of the whole structure or at the end of the first sentence; it negates whatever precedes it.

Rules for the placement of the second negative

Following is an example of each of these rules:

Rule 1.

> *Eu <u>não</u> vou lá <u>não</u>.*   **SpBr**
> 'I'm not going there.'

Here, the second negative goes right at the end of the sentence. The same happens even with long sentences, e.g.,

> *Eu <u>não</u> vou lá na casa de campo daquele idiota <u>não</u>.*   **SpBr**
> 'I'm not going to that idiot's country house.'

Rule 2.

When the sentence includes subordinate clauses, they are not included in the negation:

> *O Ferreira <u>não</u> sai de casa quando está chovendo <u>não</u>.*   **SpBr**
> 'Ferreira does not go out when it's raining.'

Although the second negative comes at the end of the sentence, the subordinate, *quando está chovendo,* is not itself negated. If the subordinate is negated, it cannot take a second negative:

> *O Ferreira sai de casa quando <u>não</u> está chovendo.* / **. . . <u>não</u> está chovendo <u>não</u>.*
> 'Ferreira goes out when it is not raining.'

The same happens with relative clauses:

> *Zélia é o nome da moça que <u>não</u> me reconheceu.* / **. . . <u>não</u> me reconheceu <u>não</u>.*
> 'Zélia is the name of the girl who did not recognize me.'

But objective clauses *can* be independently negated, as in

> *Eu desconfio que ela <u>não</u> gosta de você <u>não</u>.*   **SpBr**
> 'I suspect she does not like you.'

The second negative is acceptable, although only the subordinate (*ela não gosta de você não*) is negated; this is possible because the subordinate clause is an object.

Rule 3.

In coordinate structures with *e,* the second negative may appear after the first or after the second member of the coordination, but not indifferently. It can appear at the end of the second member only when the negative applies to the whole structure, as in

> *Você não vai pegar o carro e só devolver amanhã não.*   **SpBr**
> 'You are not going to borrow the car and return it only tomorrow.'

Here the whole portion comprised between the two negatives is negated: you will *not* borrow the car, and (consequently) you will *not* return it tomorrow. But in

> *Você não vai pegar o carro não e seu pai vai saber disso.*   **SpBr**
> 'You are not going to borrow the car, and your father will know about it.'

Here the negated portion is only the first member of the coordination; the second member (*seu pai vai saber disso* 'your father will know about it') is affirmative. Accordingly, the second negative appears at the end of the first member.

In spite of some complexity, the double negative must be learned, because it is one of the important patterns of the language and is extremely common in Brazilian speech.

In very informal speech, the first part of the negation may be omitted, so that the second *não* becomes the sole marker of negation:

> *Vou lá não.*   **SpBr**
> 'I'm not going there.'

> *O barco precisa de pintura não.*   **SpBr**
> 'The boat doesn't need painting.'

31.3.2 Nominal and adverb negation

Nominals and adverbs can also be negated, with the help of the same particles. For instance, we may say

> *Os candidatos não aprovados serão notificados por telefone.*
> 'The candidates who did not pass will be notified by phone.'

> *Você pode tocar bateria, mas nunca aqui.*
> 'You can play the drums, but never here.'

In particular, English "unpassives" are translated by *não* plus a participle:

> *Ele deixou muitos livros não lidos.*
> 'He left many unread books.'

Another possibility is to use *sem* plus an infinitive (which in this case is understood as a passive):

Ele deixou muitos livros <u>sem</u> ler.
'id.'

When used with a nominal, the negative particle always precedes. But with most adverbs the negative may occur before or after the adverb, e.g.,

Você pode tocar bateria, mas <u>não</u> aqui. / . . . aqui <u>não</u>.
'You can play the drums, but not here.'

—O diretor está livre?
—<u>Não</u> hoje. / Hoje <u>não</u>.
"Is the director free?"
"Not today."

Some adverbs must be negated by *nem* instead of *não: nem sempre* 'not always,' *nem tanto* 'not so much,' *nem todos* 'not all,' *nem sequer* 'not even.' *Nem* always occurs before the adverb.

With other adverbs, the negative must follow:

—A sua banda vai tocar?
—Talvez <u>não</u>.
"Is your band playing?"
"Perhaps not."

This difference in behavior is due to the fact that an adverb like *aqui* 'here' *is modified* by the negative, whereas an adverb like *talvez* 'perhaps' *modifies* the negative. In both cases, the modifying element comes first. Adverbs that modify the negative and therefore come before it are, besides *talvez, também* 'also,' *certamente* 'certainly,' *provavelmente* 'probably,' and some others.

Também não corresponds to English *neither,* or *either* in a negative sentence:

Minha banda não tocou, e a sua <u>também não</u>.
'My band didn't play, and neither did yours. / . . . and yours didn't either.'

Tampouco is an older word for *também não:*

Minha banda não tocou, e a sua <u>tampouco</u>.　　　　**Arch**
'id.'

31.3.3 Independent negation and affirmation

The word used for independent negation, corresponding to English *no,* is again *não:*

> —*Você já resolveu se compra esse vestido?*
> —*Não.*
> "Did you already decide whether you're buying this dress?"
> "No."

The word for *yes* is *sim;* but affirmation in Portuguese differs from affirmation in English and requires some comment. When directly questioned and intending to give a simple affirmation as an answer, a Brazilian will almost never use *sim.* Instead, the most common way to answer affirmatively is *by repeating the verb used in the question,* duly changed for person if necessary:

> —*Você comprou o vestido?*
> —*Comprei.*
> "Did you buy the dress?"
> "Yes [literally, (I) bought]."

> —*O Eurico chegou de Goiânia?*
> —*Chegou.*
> "Did Eurico arrive from Goiânia?"
> "Yes [literally, (he) arrived]."

In the answer the speaker may repeat, instead of the verb, some particularly salient word found in the question, e.g.,

> —*Seu orientador já viajou?*
> —*Já.*
> "Has your adviser already left?"
> "Yes [literally, already]."

Sim may be used, along with the repeated word, as a reinforcing element:

> —*O Eurico chegou de Goiânia?*
> —*Chegou <u>sim</u>.*
> "Did Eurico arrive from Goiânia?"
> "Yes [literally, (he) arrived, yes]."

> —*Seu orientador já viajou?*
> —*Já <u>sim</u>.*

"Has your adviser already left?"
"Yes [literally, already, yes]."

Finally, the answer may be built as it is in English, only with *sim;* but this is exceptional and usually sounds strange—it may even identify the speaker as a foreigner. *Sim,* used alone, sounds natural only in cases of emphasis.

31.3.4 A note on the pronunciation of *não*

The particle *não* is normally pronounced [nũ] when negating a verb; in all other positions—alone, when used as a second negative, or when negating a nominal or an adverb—it is pronounced regularly, [nãw]. The latter pronunciation is also acceptable before a verb, but it is rare except in careful speech. For instance,

> *Ela não vai não.*　　　　　**SpBr**
> 'She is not going.'

is pronounced ['ɛlə nũ 'vaj nãw] or, in careful, deliberate speech, ['ɛlə nãw 'vaj nãw]. In fast, relaxed speech, before a verb form beginning with a vowel, *não* may be reduced to just [n], as in *ele não é amigo de ninguém,* pronounced ['eli nɛ a'migu . . .], 'he is a friend to no one.'

32

Prepositions

32.1 Autonomous vs. governed prepositions

Prepositions have two main functions. The first is to precede noun phrases in such a way that the resulting sequence (**preposition + NP**) is either an **adjective phrase** or an **adverbial phrase**—no longer a noun phrase. For example, take the sequence *minha avó* 'my grandmother': being a noun phrase, it can be the subject or the object of a sentence, as in

> *Minha avó telefonou.*
> 'My grandmother called.'

> *Encontrei minha avó no teatro.*
> '(I) met my grandmother in the theater.'

Now, if we add a preposition, say *de*, the resulting sequence, *de minha avó*, is no longer a noun phrase; rather, it functions as an adjective phrase and can occur as a modifier—but never as a subject or an object:

> *A casa de minha avó fica na esquina.*   [**cf.** *a casa amarela* . . .]
> 'My grandmother's house is on the corner.'   [**cf.** the yellow house . . .].'

Now, take the noun phrase *essa casa* 'this house': if we add the preposition *em* 'in,' the resulting sequence, *nessa casa,* will be an adverbial phrase:

Mônica mora <u>nessa casa</u>.   [**cf.** . . .*mora <u>aqui</u>*.]
'Monica lives <u>in this house</u>.'   [**cf.** . . . lives <u>here</u>.]

Whenever a preposition occurs with the function of building an adverbial or an adjective phrase out of a noun phrase, we speak of **autonomous prepositions.** Autonomous prepositions often have a discernible meaning in themselves; for instance, one can say that *em* in the preceding sentence means 'location,' and so on.

The second function of prepositions is to connect complements to verbs, nominals, and sometimes to adverbs. For instance, the verb *gostar* 'to like' always takes the preposition *de* before its complement:

Ninguém aqui gosta <u>de</u> carne de porco.
'Nobody here likes pork.'

Likewise, the nominal *amor* takes a complement with the preposition *por* (sometimes *a*):

O meu amor <u>por</u> você
'My love for you'

Some adverbs also take complements, like *longe* 'far,' which takes *de:*

Eu morava muito longe <u>de</u> Belo Horizonte.
'I lived very far from Belo Horizonte.'

Most verbs take complements without a preposition (that is, direct object or subjective complements), but all nominals and adverbs taking complements require a preposition. In all these cases we speak of **governed prepositions.** An important feature of governed prepositions is that they have no clear meaning in themselves—their function is purely structural, that is, they work as connecting elements between larger portions of the sentence.[1]

Note

[1]Some prepositions can be governed or autonomous, according to context. Thus, *em* is autonomous in *moro em Curitiba* '(I) live in Curitiba,' and governed (required by the verb) in *pensei em você* '(I) thought of you.' That is, the opposition autonomous vs. governed is an opposition of functions, not of classes.

Consequently, governed prepositions present a particularly thorny problem to students because it is very difficult to justify the presence of individual prepositions in semantic terms. For instance, there is no known reason why *gostar* requires *de,* while *adorar* 'to love' requires no preposition at all and *pensar* 'to think' requires *em.* Therefore, learning to use governed prepositions is largely a matter of memorizing individual cases.

In this chapter we will be concerned with the autonomous use of prepositions; governed prepositions, which are a special case of valency, are covered in chapter 33.

Prepositions can be **simple** (like *de, para, a, em*) or **compound** (like *ao lado de* 'besides,' *em cima de* 'on,' *para com* 'towards,' etc.). Syntactically speaking, simple and compound prepositions behave in the same way, so that they may be studied together without inconvenience.

32.2 Autonomous prepositions

There is not much to say about autonomous prepositions in general; on the other hand, there is a lot to be learned about each one in particular. Some prepositions are semantically complex and very poorly understood; to convince oneself of this all one has to do is try to list the possible meanings of the word "of" in English. The most one can do is list the most frequent meanings of each preposition and warn the student about the surprises along the way.

Accordingly, I give below a list of the Portuguese prepositions with their most frequent readings. In the most favorable—and, luckily, the most numerous—cases the meaning is fairly concrete and does not vary (as, for example, *exceto* 'except,' *contra* 'against'); in the least favorable cases, it is impossible even to single out a basic meaning— as for *de,* which may correspond to English "of," "to," "from," "by" . . . In what follows I consider each preposition in turn; as indicated, some prepositions, or some readings of certain prepositions, are specific to the written or to the spoken language. I limit the exemplification to the most difficult cases; for the easier prepositions an English translation is sufficient. I start with the prepositions that present some difficulty.

32.2.1 Preposition *a*

The preposition *a* has several meanings. I list below its uses, starting with the most frequent ones:

—'place': indicates direction or distance:

> *Ela já foi a̲ Miami mais de dez vezes.*
> 'She has already gone to Miami more than ten times.'

> *De Mariana a̲ Ouro Preto são doze quilômetros.*
> 'From Mariana to Ouro Preto it is twelve kilometers.'

In this sense *para* is also very frequently used instead of *a*. In the formal standard, *a* denotes a temporary dislocation, *para* a permanent one:

> *Ele foi a̱ Mariana e volta amanhã.*
> 'He went to Mariana and will be back tomorrow.'

> *Ele se mudou pa̱ra̱ Mariana.*
> 'He moved to Mariana.'

In the spoken language *para* may be used in both senses, *a* only when the dislocation is temporary.

—'indirect object': the entity (usually a person) that is the goal of some transference of literal or metaphorical possession:

> *O governador entregou uma medalha a̱os jogadores.*
> 'The governor gave a medal to the players.'

> *A Universidade explicou sua política a̱os docentes.*
> 'The university explained its policies to the instructors.'

In this use, *a* is usually replaced by *para* in the spoken language:

> *O governador entregou uma medalha pa̱ra̱ os jogadores.*   **SpBr**
> 'id.'

—'time': with times of the day:

> *À̱s oito horas bate o sino.*
> 'At eight o'clock the bell tolls.'

A is used to introduce times of the day, and in the expressions *à̱ noite* 'at night,' *à̱ tarde* 'in the afternoon'—but not with *dia* 'day' and *manhã* 'morning,' which make *de dia* 'by day,' and *de manhã* 'in the morning.'

It is also used with days of the week, but only in the plural, to indicate the time of a habitual event:

> *A faxineira vem à̱s quintas-feiras.*
> 'The maid comes every Thursday.'

But in the singular *em* is used:

> *A faxineira vem na̱ quinta-feira.*
> 'The maid comes on Thursday.'[1]

Note

[1]When the phrase denotes a unique event, another possibility is to use no preposition at all: *a faxineira veio quinta-feira* 'the maid came on Thursday,' *a faxineira veio dia 16* 'the maid came on the 16th.'

—before *Deus* 'God' and some other nominals, with verbs that normally take direct objects, in religious or otherwise solemn style:

> *Todos devem amar <u>a</u> Deus e respeitar <u>ao</u> próximo.*　　**Wr**
> 'Everyone must love God and respect his neighbor.'

—in the written language, before object pronouns when modified or when emphasized, as described in chapter 29:

> *O diretor queria chamar só a <u>ela</u>.*　　　　　　**Wr**
> 'The director wanted to call only her.'
>
> *O diretor queria chamar só a <u>mim</u>.*　　　　　　**Wr**
> 'The director wanted to call only me.'
>
> *Ronaldo não te odeia; ele odeia <u>a mim</u>.*　　　　**Wr**
> 'Ronaldo doesn't hate you; he hates me.'

—to denote a location, instead of *em,* in certain expressions:

à mesa	'at table'
à porta	'at the door'
à sombra	'in the shade' [**or** *na sombra,* with the same meaning]
à época **Wr**	'at the time' [**or** *na época,* with the same meaning]

—*a* is also used in many set adverbial phrases, e.g.,

à americana	'in American style'
à Shakespeare	'in Shakespearean style'
a cavalo	'on horseback'
(**but** *de bicicleta* 'by bicycle,' *de carro* 'by car,' etc.)	
a curto / médio / longo prazo	'in the short / medium / long term'
à força	'by force'
a lápis	'with pencil'
à mão	'at hand'
a meu ver	'in my opinion'
a prazo	'in installments'
a torto e a direito	'left and right'
ao acaso	'at random'
aos arrancos	'in jerks'
aos tapas	'by slapping'
aos trancos e barrancos	'in jerks and starts'
às pressas	'in a hurry'
às toneladas	'by the ton'
às vezes	'sometimes'

and many others.[1]

Note

[1]For the use of the accent in *à*, see 32.5 below.

32.2.2 Use of the preposition *a* in the spoken language

There is a strong tendency in the spoken language to limit the use of the preposition *a*. It is still used in some of the contexts described in the preceding section: in fixed expressions and set phrases (*a prazo* 'in installments,' *à força* 'by force,' etc.); in the indication of distances (*de Mariana a Ouro Preto* 'from Mariana to Ouro Preto'); and to indicate times of the day (*às cinco horas* 'at five o'clock'). In all other cases another preposition tends to be substituted, viz.,

—with direction, the preposition used is *em:*

> *Ela já foi em Miami mais de dez vezes.*   **SpBr**
> 'She has already gone to Miami more than ten times.'

—with indirect objects, the preposition used is *para:*

> *O governador entregou uma medalha para os jogadores.*   **SpBr**
> 'The governor gave a medal to the players.'

—with days of the week, *em:*

> *A faxineira vem nas quintas-feiras.*   **SpBr**
> 'The maid comes every Thursday.'

—in expressions like *à mesa* 'at table,' *em:*

na mesa	'at table'	**SpBr**
na porta	'at the door'	**SpBr**

> (*continued*)
>
> *na sombra*   'in the shade'
>
> *na época*   'at the time'

As seen above, in some cases (like the two last examples) *em* is also acceptable in writing.

32.2.3 Other prepositions

até   'until'

> *Aqui a gente trabalha <u>até</u> as cinco.*
> 'Here we work until five.'

> 'even'

> *<u>Até</u> o comandante estava insatisfeito.*
> 'Even the commander was dissatisfied.'

Até, like English *even*, can also be used in adverbial contexts, as in *Ela <u>até</u> tentou fugir de casa* 'She even attempted to leave home.'

com   'with'
Com corresponds to 'with,' expressing both company and instrument:

> *Eu sempre vou ao cinema <u>com</u> um amigo.*
> 'I always go to the movies with a friend.'

> *Sandra chegou <u>com</u> um vestido lindíssimo.*
> 'Sandra came in a beautiful dress.'

> *Minervina entortou o arame <u>com</u> o alicate.*
> 'Minervina bent the wire with the pliers.'

—*com* introduces several very common expressions expressing bodily and psychic conditions; these correspond to English adjectives, viz.

com fome	'hungry'
com medo	'afraid'
com preguiça	'lazy'
com raiva	'angry'
com sede	'thirsty'
com sono	'sleepy'
com vontade	'willing'

—see chapter 22 on the role of *estar com* to express transitory states and situations.

de

De is the most common—and therefore the most complex—preposition in Portuguese. In what follows I try to catalogue its most frequent uses.

—in many cases *de* corresponds to *of* or to the genitive ending *'s*, in their various meanings:

A capital <u>do</u> Canadá é Ottawa.
'The capital of Canada is Ottawa.'

O carro <u>de</u> Daniel é aquele branco ali.
'Daniel's car is that white one over there.'

A invasão <u>da</u> Normandia foi em 1944.
'The invasion of Normandy was in 1944.'

A irritação <u>do</u> chefe era contagiosa.
'The boss's irritation was contagious.'

Esse lugar não é <u>de</u> ninguém.
'This is nobody's seat.'

—*de* is also used to express *from:*

Acabei de chegar <u>da</u> Inglaterra.
'(I) have just arrived from (the) England.'

Minha amiga é de Lisboa.
'My friend is from Lisbon.'

Unlike Spanish *desde*, Portuguese *desde* is not normally used to translate *from*, being restricted to the meaning of *since*. Thus, we have in Spanish

Desde mi ventana ves el volcán.
'From my window you can see the volcano.'

but in Portuguese *de* is used:

Da minha janela você vê o vulcão.
'id.'

—*de* expresses the material out of which something is made:

Comprei uma flauta de prata.
'(I) have bought a silver flute.'

—or the subject matter of a book:

Joguei no lixo todos os meus livros de Física.
'(I) have thrown into the garbage can all my physics books.'

Besides these general uses, *de* appears in many constructions as a sort of all-purpose preposition; here all I can do is list the most important among these constructions.

—*de* is often used like English *with*, except when *with* denotes company:

Ele veio de terno azul.
'He came in a blue suit.'

Ela me bateu de martelo.
'She hit me with a hammer.'

This use of *de* is not possible if the following nominal is preceded by an article:

Ela me bateu com um martelo [**not** * *de um martelo*]
'She hit me with a hammer.'

—*de* is used to introduce the words *maneira* 'manner, way,' *jeito* 'id.,' *lado* 'side,' *vez* 'time,' which in English often occur without a preposition:

Dessa vez eu te pego.
'This time I'll catch you.'

Meu pai mora desse lado do rio.
'My father lives this side of the river.'

De que jeito eu posso te ajudar?
'How [which way] can I help you?'

—*de* may denote the goal or finality of an object:

sala de reuniões / cão de caça / máquina de escrever
'meeting room / hunting dog / typewriter [literally, writing machine].'

—*de* may express a cause (in particular with designations of emotions and bodily conditions):

Os pobres exploradores morreram de fome.
'The poor explorers died of hunger.'

O coitadinho sofre do coração.
'The poor thing has heart trouble [literally, suffers from the heart].'

—*do* (*de* + *o*) may appear, optionally, before *que* in the second member of a comparison or in a superlative expression:

Todo mundo é mais elegante (do) que eu.
'Everyone is more elegant than I (am).'

Esse edifício é o mais alto do mundo.
'This building is the tallest in the world.'

De appears, obligatorily, before the complement of *mais* 'more' and *menos* 'less' when preceding a measure, corresponding to English *than:*

Meu filho pesa mais de quatro quilos.
'My son weighs more than four kilos.'

—*de* corresponds to English *by* before passive participles, when the verb *ser* 'to be' is not present:

A prefeita compareceu acompanhada do marido.
'The mayor attended, escorted by her husband.'

In this context, *por* can also be used.

—English *by* is also translated as *de* (not as *por*) when it expresses authorship:

> *Ouvimos uma abertura de Mozart.*
> 'We heard an overture by Mozart.'

—*de* is used with means of transportation:

> *Ele só viaja de avião.*
> 'He only travels by plane.'

But note: *a cavalo* 'on horseback,' *a pé* 'on foot.'

—*de* also introduces a measurement:

> *um menino de um ano* / *uma casa de dois milhões de dólares*
> 'A one-year-old boy / a million-dollar house'

—*de* is used in a curious construction, after an insulting or commiserating qualifier:[1]

> *O idiota do meu vizinho.*
> 'The idiot of my neighbor.'

> *O coitado do Chico pegou uma gripe.*
> 'Poor Chico caught the flu.'

Note

**[1]This construction is particularly interesting because it is the only known example in which the element governed by a preposition is, semantically, the head of the noun phrase; thus, *o cachorro do vizinho* 'that dog of my neighbor' refers to the neighbor, not to his dog. Compare English *a scarecrow of a woman*.

—with divisions of the day, the use of prepositions is complex: *de* may introduce any divisions, but *a* and *por* occur only with some:

> *de madrugada* **à madrugada* *pela madrugada* 'early in the morning'

(continued)			
de manhã	**à manhã*	*pela manhã*	'in the morning'
de dia	**ao dia*	**pelo dia*	'by day'
de tarde	*à tarde*	**pela tarde*	'in the afternoon'
de noite	*à noite*	**pela noite*	'by night'

—*de* also occurs in partitive constructions, as in the examples

> *Me dá um pouco mais desse vinho branco.*   **SpBr**
> 'Give me some more of that white wine.'

> *Ela já viu de tudo na vida.*
> 'She has seen (a bit) of everything in her life.'

—*de* is also used to reinforce a modifier:

> *Ele levou um tapa dos bons.*
> 'He got a good slap [literally, a slap of the good (ones)].'

> *Seu tio é um corrupto dos piores.*
> 'Your uncle is an awful embezzler [literally, an embezzler of the worst (ones)].'

—*de* introduces a personal condition (in particular, an occupation), corresponding to English *as:*

> *Ele trabalhou atè de estivador.*
> 'He worked even as a stevedore.'

Here *como* can also be used.

—finally, *de* occurs in a number of fixed expressions, for example,

de propósito	'on purpose'

(continued)

de bem (com)	'on good terms with'
de boa vontade	'willingly'
de fato	'in fact, indeed'
de má vontade	'unwillingly'
de mal (com)	'not on speaking terms'
de mentira	'pretend' [**as in** *a pretend solution*]
de repente	'suddenly'
de vez	'once and for all'
de vez em quando	'from time to time'
de verdade	'for real'
de passagem	'by the by'
etc.	

See chapter 27 for the important role played by the preposition *de* in expressions corresponding to the English double-noun construction, as, for example, *cerca de madeira* 'wood fence,' *jogador de tênis* 'tennis player,' *saída de emergência* 'emergency exit,' and the like.

em

—*em* is the general preposition indicating location and may correspond to English 'in,' 'on,' 'at,' 'into,' and 'onto.' It expresses location or the goal of a motion (but not the source of a motion, which is expressed by *de*):

Eu nunca morei em Curitiba.
'I have never lived in Curitiba.'

Vou deixar um recado na porta.
'(I)'ll leave a message on the door.'

Cuspir <u>no</u> chão é feio.
'Spitting on the floor is bad manners.'

Os meninos estão <u>na</u> escola.
'The children are at school.'

Jogue tudo isso <u>na</u> gaveta de baixo.
'Throw all this into the bottom drawer.'

Besides, *em* appears in several other meanings, e.g.,
—'in' [period of time]

Rossini escreveu sua obra-prima <u>em</u> quarenta dias.
'Rossini wrote his masterwork in forty days.'

—'to'   [direction]   **SpBr**

As we saw in 32.2.2 above, *em* is used in the spoken language to express the goal of a motion without implying a permanent displacement (in which case *para* is used):

Nós vamos <u>no</u> restaurante e depois <u>no</u> clube.   **SpBr**
'We are going to the restaurant, and afterwards to the club.'

When expressing a permanent displacement, *em* cannot be used:

*Carlito mudou <u>para</u> Lavras.   /   * <u>em</u> Lavras.*
'Carlito moved to Lavras.'

—'in' [situation or manner]

Os espectadores fugiram <u>em</u> pânico.
'The onlookers fled in panic.'

Vamos ficar <u>em</u> silêncio durante um minuto.
'Let us be silent [literally, in silence] for one minute.'

Em is also used in fixed expressions, such as:

em compensação	'on the other hand'

(*continued*)

em pé	'standing'
em vez (de)	'instead of'
na verdade	'actually'

etc.

entre
—'between'

> *Barbacena fica <u>entre</u> Belo Horizonte e o Rio.*
> 'Barbacena is between Belo Horizonte and Rio.'

—'among'

> *Quero morrer <u>entre</u> os meus.*
> '(I) want to die among my dear ones.'

para
—'to' [location]

> *Eu gostaria de me mudar <u>para</u> uma cidade pequena.*
> 'I would like to move to a small town.'

—'to, until' [time]

> *A reunião fica adiada <u>para</u> quinta-feira.*
> 'The meeting is postponed until Thursday.'

—'to' [indirect object]

> *O governador entregou uma medalha <u>para</u> os jogadores.*   **SpBr**
> 'The governor handed a medal to the players.'

> *Foi só isso que ela falou <u>para</u> mim.*   **SpBr**
> 'That was all she told me.'

—'(in order) to' [purpose]

> *Ele só aceitou o cargo <u>para</u> se aproveitar.*
> 'He only accepted the office in order to profit.'

—'for' [agent]
Para introduces the agent, when expressed, in the construction exemplified by

> *<u>Para</u> nós é difícil explicar essas coisas.*
> 'It is difficult for us to explain these things.'

or

> *<u>Para</u> nós essas coisas são difíceis de explicar.*
> 'These things are difficult for us to explain.'

—'about to' [+ infinitive]

> *O telhado está <u>para</u> cair.*
> 'The roof is about to fall.'

—*para* is used in a few idioms, e.g.,

para a frente / para frente	'ahead'
para lá (de)	'beyond; more than'
para sempre	'forever'
pra burro **SpBr**	'very much'[1]
pra chuchu **SpBr**	'very much'[1]

Note

[1]In these expressions the preposition is usually written in its shortened form, *pra*, which is its normal pronunciation.

para com 'toward' [expressing a personal relationship, not direction]

> *O professor de Física era totalmente injusto para com os alunos.*
> 'The physics teacher was totally unfair toward (his) students.'

por 'by' [location]

> *A gente passa por Santa Rita para ir à fazenda.*
> 'We go by Santa Rita to go to the plantation.'

> *A resposta veio por e-mail.*[1]
> 'The answer came by e-mail.'

Note

[1]Pronounced [iˈmeju].

—[agent of the passive voice]

> *Essas árvores foram plantadas pela Prefeitura.*
> 'These trees were planted by the city.'

—'around, near' [approximate time or location (usually preceded by *lá*)]

> *A banda começou a tocar lá pelas oito horas.*
> 'The band started to play around eight.'

> *Ele morava lá pelos lados de Caeté.*
> 'He lived near Caeté.'

—[extension in time]

> *Vou te amar por toda a vida.*
> '(I)'ll love you all (my) life.'

—'for' [cause]

> *O réu foi condenado por homicídio.*
> 'The defendant was sentenced for murder.'

O Rio é famoso por sua beleza natural.
'Rio is famous for its natural beauty.'

—'per, each' [distribution]

A entrada é dez reais por pessoa.
'The admission is ten reals per person.'

Eles passaram a cem por hora.
'They rushed by at a hundred (kilometers) per hour.'

Dou quatro aulas por semana.
'(I) teach four classes each week.'

—'for' [price]

Vendi meu carro por cinco mil reais.
'(I) sold my car for five thousand reals.'

Por is not used to denote place like English *by* in *a house by the lake;* in this meaning Portuguese employs *junto a, ao lado de,* or *perto de: uma casa junto ao lago / perto do lago / ao lado do lago*.

sob   **Wr**   'under'
Sob is very rarely used nowadays in a locative sense; it is replaced by *embaixo de* or *debaixo de*:

O cachorro estava embaixo da cama. [. . . *sob a cama.*   **Arch**]
'The dog was under the bed.'

But it is still used when it means 'under the domination of,' as in

Escrevi a história de Portugal sob o domínio espanhol.   **Wr**
'(I) have written the history of Portugal under Spanish rule.'

or in other nonlocative meanings, e.g.,

Isso é interessante sob vários aspectos.
'This is interesting under several points of view.'

Não gosto de trabalhar sob pressão.
'(I) do not like to work under pressure.'

> *Essa camisa parece feita <u>sob</u> medida para você.*
> 'That shirt looks custom-made for you.'

sobre   **Wr**   'on'

> *Coloque tudo <u>sobre</u> a mesa.*   **Wr**
> 'Put everything on the table.'

In this reading, 'on' is colloquially rendered by *em cima de:*

> *Coloque tudo <u>em cima da</u> mesa.*
> 'id.'

—'about'

> *Preciso de um livro <u>sobre</u> criação de canários.*
> 'I need a book about canary raising.'

In the meaning of 'about,' *sobre* is current in all registers.

The following list includes all common prepositions that require no special comment:

a despeito de	'in spite of'
a favor de	'in favor of'
a fim de	'in order to'
a respeito de	'about'
abaixo de	'below'
acerca de	'about'
acima de	'above'
antes de	'before'

(*continued*)

ao lado de	'at the side of'
ao redor de	'around'
apesar de	'in spite of'
após **Wr**	'after'
atrás de	'behind'
através de	'through'
conforme	'according to'
contra	'against'
de acordo com	'according to'
debaixo de	'under'
dentro de	'inside'
depois de	'after' [time]
desde	'since' [time]
diante de	'in front of'
durante	'during'
em cima de	'on' [location]
em frente de	'in front of'
em vez de	'instead of'
embaixo de	'under'
exceto	'except'

(*continued*)

fora	'except'
fora de	'outside'
graças a	'thanks to'
junto de / junto a	'next to'
para cá de	'on this side of'
para lá de	'beyond; more than'
perto de	'near' [location]
por causa de	'because of'
por intermédio de	'with the help of'
por meio de	'by means of'
quanto a	'as for'
salvo **Wr**	'except'
segundo	'according to'
sem	'without'

32.3 Omission and duplication of prepositions

32.3.1 Omission

In some cases the preposition may be omitted, being recoverable from context. This happens in four situations:

—before sentential noun phrases

In many cases a verb requires a preposition before its complement, but not if the complement contains a clause, e.g.,

> *Eu preciso de você.*
> 'I need you.'

Here the preposition must be present, and ** Eu preciso você* is totally unacceptable; but if the complement contains a clause, the preposition is normally omitted:

> *Eu preciso sair mais cedo.*
> 'I need to leave earlier.'

> *Eu preciso que você saia mais cedo.*
> 'I need you to leave earlier.'

This happens only when the preposition is governed, that is, when it is required by the verb—and therefore carries no independent meaning. Autonomous prepositions must be kept, lest information be lost, as in

> *Nós trabalhamos para que vocês descansem.*
> 'We work so that you may rest.'

Here the preposition *para* cannot be omitted.

—in relative clauses

Relative constructions present certain special problems, dealt with in chapter 36. One of these is the positioning, and eventual omission, of prepositions.

In English, a relative pronoun may be preceded by a preposition, as in

> The town *in* which we live

As we know, in the spoken language it is more usual to place the preposition after the verb (while omitting the relative pronoun), as in

> *The town we live in*

Portuguese has a relative construction parallel to the first English one:

> *A cidade na qual nós moramos*   **Wr**
> *A cidade em que moramos*   **Wr**
> 'The town in which we live'

Like English speakers, Portuguese speakers tend to avoid this construction, which is almost exclusively found in writing. But the solution employed by Portuguese is different from the English one. In the spoken language, the preposition may simply be omitted (and the relative pronoun must be *que,* never *o qual*), as in

> *A cidade que nós moramos*   **SpBr**
> 'id.'

This applies when omitting the preposition causes no loss of information.[1]

Note

[1]The omission of the preposition in such cases is attested in writing, the oldest example as far as I know being *o samba que você me convidou* 'the samba-party you invited me to,' in a song by Noel Rosa (1910–37).

Otherwise, the preposition is kept, but not before the relative pronoun as in the written standard—rather, it is kept in its place after the verb, and a personal pronoun is added, e.g.,

> *O empresário que eu trabalho <u>para ele</u> é libanês.*   **SpBr**
> 'The businessman I work for (him) is Lebanese.'

The latter construction is properly described in chapter 36; here we are concerned only with preposition deletion in these contexts. The preposition is omitted, as I said, when there is no danger of information loss, which means when it is governed by the verb. Thus, in the above example, *morar* 'to live' requires a complement with the preposition *em* 'in.' Since this is the only possibility, omitting the preposition does not lead to ambiguity or vagueness; correspondingly, the preposition is omitted. It can also be kept, but it is not the most frequent option:

> *A cidade que nós moramos fica em Illinois.*   **SpBr**
> *A cidade que nós moramos <u>nela</u> fica em Illinois.*   **SpBr**
> 'The town we live in (it) is in Illinois.'

Other examples of preposition deletion with relatives are as follows:

> *O carro que eu falei é aquele ali.*   **SpBr**
> 'The car I talked (about) is that one.'

Written version:

> *O carro do qual / de que eu falei é aquele ali.*　　**Wr**
> 'id.'

> *Você sempre gosta das coisas que eu gosto.*　　**SpBr**
> 'You always like the things I like.'

Written version:

> *Você sempre gosta das coisas das quais / de que eu gosto.* **Wr**
> 'id.'

In this last example, the *de* which precedes *as coisas* 'the things' is obligatory, since it is not followed by a sentential noun phrase; but the second one (before *que eu gosto* 'which I like) is usually omitted.

—in anaphoric contexts

When the same preposition occurs before two noun phrases in the same sentence, the second one can be omitted:

> *Minha irmã detesta falar de comida e (de) crianças.*
> 'My sister hates speaking about food and (about) children.'

The preferred version is the full one, with both prepositions; but the reduced one is also correct and occurs with some frequency. Another example is

> *O governo é cruel para com os professores e (para com) os funcionários.*
> 'The government is ruthless toward the teachers and (toward) the civil servants.'

Here, perhaps because the preposition is a long one, the shorter version of the sentence sounds slightly better; in any case, both are acceptable.

—with *ir* and *vir*

The preposition *para* is often omitted after the verbs *ir* 'to go' and *vir* 'to come,' when followed by a clause of purpose, e.g.,

> *Eu fui lá tirar umas fotos.*　　[**or:** . . . *para tirar umas fotos.*]
> 'I went there to take some pictures.'

> *O rapaz veio limpar a casa.*　　[**or:** . . . *para limpar a casa.*]
> 'The boy came to clean the house.'

32.3.2 Duplication

—*de* and *para* plus *aqui*, *aí*, and *lá*

When used in connection with the adverbs of place *aqui* 'here,' *cá* 'here,' *aí* 'there,' and *lá* 'there,' the prepositions *de* and *para* may be optionally repeated before the adverb; thus, either of the sentences in each pair below is correct, the second one being more colloquial:

> *Ele veio <u>lá do Rio</u>.*
> *Ele veio <u>de lá do Rio</u>.*   **SpBr**
> 'He came from Rio.'

> *Nós chamamos nossa prima <u>cá para a fazenda</u>.*
> *Nós chamamos nossa prima <u>para cá para a fazenda</u>.*   **SpBr**
> 'We called our cousin here to the farm.'

For the use of *lá* and *aqui* as a reinforcement of adverbials of place, see chapter 42.

32.4 Dangling prepositions

Portuguese has no cases of "dangling prepositions" in the English style, such as
>   Where is the library <u>at</u>?

But there is one context in which one finds Portuguese prepositions at the end of a sentence, without a following noun phrase. When two prepositions are used contrastively, that is, a preposition with a noun phrase followed by the semantic opposite of the preposition with the same noun phrase, the second noun phrase may be omitted in certain cases, leaving the second preposition at the end of the sentence:

> *Márcio foi ao jogo <u>de</u> boné e eu fui <u>sem</u>.*
> 'Márcio went to the game with a cap and I went without (a cap).'

> *Alguns são <u>a favor do</u> governo, outros são <u>contra</u>.*
> 'Some people are in favor of the government, and some are against (it).'

Among the simple prepositions, *sem* and *contra* are the only ones found with any frequency at the end of a sentence.

Compound prepositions are freely used in this construction, provided they have an opposite to be set in contrast:

> *As telhas ficam <u>em cima das</u> ripas, e as vigas <u>embaixo</u>.*[1]
> 'The tiles go on top of the slats, and the beams go under (them).'

Observe that the simple preposition that usually is the last part of a compound is omitted in this position; thus, *embaixo de* 'under' becomes simply *embaixo*. An alternative analysis would be that compound prepositions like *embaixo*, etc., are adverbials, thus not requiring a following noun phrase—which would reduce the cases of dangling prepositions to *contra, sem,* and the very occasional occurrences of other sentence-final simple prepositions.[2]

Notes

[1]The traditional spelling is *em cima* as two words, *embaixo* as one word.

**[2]Or, even better, *embaixo*, etc. belong to a third category, which has a total distribution equal to the sum of the distributions of prepositions + adverbs.

32.5 A note on the contraction à

We saw in chapter 5 that some prepositions contract with articles, personal pronouns, and some demonstratives, so that *de + ele* becomes *dele*, *em + o* becomes *no*, etc. (a complete list of contractions may be found in appendix 3). Most of these contractions present no difficulty once their component parts are recognized; thus, we say *a casa de Maurício* 'Maurício's house,' and *a casa dele* 'his house,' where *ele* is substituted for *Maurício*, and *de* becomes *d-;* we can say simply that *dele* stands for *de + ele*.

But one case requires some comment, namely, the contraction of the preposition *a* with the feminine article *a*, yielding *à*. This contraction has the disadvantage of being pronounced in the same way as either of its parts, that is, a simple [a]; this fact gives rise to many uncertainties on the part of native speakers, who rarely know when to put the accent that marks the contraction. Besides, the contraction *à* has shown a tendency to become a word in its own right, so that it occurs where one would definitely not expect a sequence of preposition + article.

Curiously, the use of *à* may be easier for English speakers, who in most cases only have to put the accent whenever English has a preposition (*to* or *at*, more often than not) followed by an article, e.g.,

Dei uma blusa nova à menina.
'(I) gave a new blouse to the girl.'

Havia alguém à porta.   **Wr**
'There was someone at the door.'

On the other hand, *à* is used in some environments where its presence is difficult to explain, as for instance in the expression *pagamento à vista* 'cash payment,' where one would expect only the preposition (hence simply *a*), because with a masculine noun we have not *ao,* but *a: pagamento a prazo* 'payment in installments'; or *filé à Chateaubriand* 'Chateaubriand-style steak,' where *à* occurs before a masculine nominal. Here the only thing to do—for a native as for a foreign student—is to memorize a few expressions like

à vista	'cash (payment)'
à Luís Quinze	'Louis XV-style'
às voltas com	'tied up with'
às mil maravilhas	'marvelously'
às avessas	'backwards'
etc.	

When in doubt, go for the accent; you may be wrong, but most Brazilians, being equally doubtful, will not notice your mistake.

33

Valency

33.1. Verb valency and nominal valency

In Portuguese, as in English, the verb functions as a sort of main axis of the sentence; to quote Allerton (1982), "One aspect of this centrality of the verb in the sentence is that the kind of verb that is selected for a particular sentence determines the basic structure of that sentence." For instance, if a sentence contains *tropeçar* 'to stumble' as its main verb, it cannot have a direct object; if the main verb is *fazer* 'to make,' it must have a direct object;[1] and if the main verb is *comer* 'to eat,' it may or may not have a direct object:

> *O cavalo tropeçou.*
> 'The horse stumbled.'

> * *O cavalo tropeçou uma pedra.*
> * 'The horse stumbled a stone.'

> * *Ele sempre faz.*
> * 'He always makes.'

> *Ele sempre faz um café excelente.*
> 'He always makes excellent coffee.'

O gato já comeu o queijo.
'The cat has already eaten the cheese.'

O gato já comeu.
'The cat has already eaten.'

Note

[1]This is true for nonanaphoric contexts; in anaphoric contexts, the object can be omitted, e.g., *Eu o proibi de fazer café, mas ele sempre faz.* 'I have forbidden him to make coffee, but he always makes (some).' In English, as seen in the translation, the object appears, here as the pronoun *some,* but in Portuguese it is simply omitted.

Learning a language includes, then, learning the valency of its verbs—with particular attention, of course, to those points where it differs from the learner's own language. Portuguese and English, being after all relatively close languages, do not differ greatly in this respect; but there are differences, and these are the subject of this chapter.

As a learning problem, verb valency has two main aspects: first, the list of **complements** a verb may take—for instance, the verb *tropeçar* 'to stumble' does not take any complement, the verb *fazer* 'to make' takes a direct object, and so on; and, second, for the particular case of verbs taking complements preceded by prepositions, the list of **prepositions** each verb requires with its complement—for instance, the verb *gostar* 'to be fond of' requires the preposition *de* before its complement, e.g.,

Eu gosto muito de você.
'I am very fond of you.'

The second problem (choice of preposition with each verb) is the most difficult because it differs markedly from language to language and is not usually predictable from the meaning of the verb.

Speaking of the valency of a *verb* is somewhat misleading. Valencies apply, strictly speaking, to associations of particular verbs with particular meanings; for instance, *pensar* 'to think' requires the preposition *em:*

Eu penso muito em você.
'I think a lot of you.'

But this is true of *pensar* only in the meaning 'to bring to mind'; if we take the same verb with the meaning 'to reflect,' it can be used without any complement, e.g.,

Os animais não pensam.
'Animals don't think.'

Another example is the verb *sonhar,* which takes the preposition *com* when it means 'to dream of (while sleeping),' but takes a direct object in the meaning 'to fancy, to imagine,' e.g.,

Sonhei <u>com meu avô</u> esta noite.
'(I) dreamed of my grandfather last night.'

Gandhi sonhou <u>um mundo sem violência</u>.
'Gandhi dreamed a world free of violence.'

It is important to keep this in mind when describing a highly versatile verb like *dar,* which has as its basic meaning 'to give.' *Dar* may occur with a direct object; with a direct and an indirect object; with the preposition *em;* with the preposition *para;* with the preposition *por;* and with several other prepositions. But the occurrence of *dar* in each of these environments is not random, but rather semantically systematic. Thus,

—*dar* with a direct and an indirect object means 'to give':

Meu pai deu um carro para meu irmão.
'My father gave my brother a car.'

—*dar* with a direct object only means 'to produce':

Essa árvore dá umas frutas excelentes.
'This tree yields excellent fruit.'

—*dar em* means 'to beat, to spank':

Ela deu no pobre cachorro até cansar.
'She beat the poor dog until she grew tired of it.'

and so on.[1]

Note

[1]A fuller list of the possible meanings of *dar* + preposition can be found in section 22.2.4.

Therefore, it should be understood that an expression like "the valency of verb X" is short for "the valency of verb X in reading Y."

33.2 Complements and the valency of verbs

From the point of view of valency we can distinguish several kinds of verbs, according to the complements they require, disallow, or freely allow. Some of the elements of the sentence are relevant to this classification, and some are not. The ones that are relevant are the **direct object,** the **indirect object,** the **predicative,** the **subjective complement,** and some of the **adverbials.**[1]

Note

[1]For the definitions of these functions, see chapter 28. As for the vagueness in the reference to adverbials, it is inevitable at present because we still lack a really accurate analysis of such elements. Note that the subject need not be included in the list because any verb can quite freely occur with or without a (overt) subject, the only exception being *haver* in the reading 'there to be' (for which see chapter 22).

For each of these functions, a verb is marked in one of three possible ways: the verb may **require** the presence of a phrase in that function; or it may **disallow** it; or it may freely **allow** it. Some examples will make this clear. Take the verb *comer* 'to eat': this verb may occur with or without a direct object:

> *O gato já comeu o queijo.*
> 'The cat has already eaten the cheese.'

> *O gato já comeu.*
> 'The cat has already eaten.'

On the other hand, *comer* disallows the presence of an indirect object or a subjective complement. The verb *estar* 'to be,' on the other hand, requires the presence either of a subjective complement or of an adverbial:

> *O canário está <u>doente</u>.*
> 'The canary is <u>sick</u>.'

> *O canário está <u>na gaiola</u>.*
> 'The canary is in his cage.'

When we consider the list of Portuguese verbs, the list of relevant grammatical functions, and the three requirement possibilities (requires, disallows, allows) we come to a truly astronomical quantity of items to be learned. But in fact the problem is not so serious for the student because the vast majority of cases are identical in English and in Portuguese. What needs to be learned is a set of situations in which the two languages differ. For instance, no one has to teach the English-speaking student that *empurrar* 'to push' allows a direct object (*empurramos o carro ladeira acima* 'we pushed the car uphill'), and that *desmaiar* 'to faint' disallows a direct object. This comes automatically from the student's knowledge of English.

The differences that do exist are of two types: grammatically conditioned structures and lexical idiosyncrasies. An example of the first category is the possibility of omitting the direct object in Portuguese in contexts in which English requires a pronominal object to be present, e.g.,

> *Nós levantamos o carro e eles empurraram.*
> 'We lifted the car and they pushed (it).'

These cases are studied below in section 33.3.

Examples of the second category are cases of verbs that require the presence of specific prepositions before their complements, e.g., the verb *precisar* 'to need' requires the preposition *de,* whereas its English counterpart requires a direct object (without preposition):

> *Estou precisando de um martelo.*
> '(I) need a hammer.'

These cases are numerous and cannot all be included in a grammar; dictionaries list all such cases.[1]

Note

[1] Of which the best is still Fernandes (1957).

33.3 Some important valency patterns

33.3.1 Omission of required complements

A complement may be required by the verb, which means that it must occur if the sentence is to be accepted as correct, e.g.,

Ele sempre <u>faz</u> um café excelente.
'He always makes excellent coffee.'

* *Ele sempre <u>faz</u>.*
* 'He always makes.'

In anaphoric contexts, however, the complement, being easily recoverable from the context, may be simply omitted in Portuguese, whereas in English a pronoun must occupy its place, e.g.,

Nós pedimos café, e ele <u>fez</u> para nós.
'We asked for coffee, and he made (some) for us.'

João lixou a porta e Maria <u>pintou</u>.
'João sanded the door, and Maria painted (it).'

33.3.2 Acceptance of designated complements

In some cases a verb disallows a complement, unless it is one of a small set of nominals, and this nominal must occur modified. Thus, *morrer,* in Portuguese as in English, occurs without a complement. But it may accept a direct object if this object has as its head the nominal *morte* 'death,' plus some kind of modifier. Thus, we may say

Ele <u>morreu</u> uma morte heróica.
'He died a heroic death.'

Without the modifier the sentence is not acceptable (presumably because it is redundant):

* *Ele <u>morreu</u> uma morte.*

We find this phenomenon with *dormir* 'to sleep':

A menina <u>dormiu</u> um sono profundo.
'The girl slept a deep slumber.'

but not with *falecer* 'to decease,' *desmaiar* 'to faint,' or *adormecer* 'to fall asleep.'

In some cases a complement may be omitted if it is typically used with a verb (or with a verb plus some other complement). That is, the omission is allowed by virtue of the general context, not by some grammatical rule. Thus, *pôr* 'to put, to place' usually requires a direct object *and* an adverbial of place:

O velhinho pôs   o peixe   na geladeira.
                  object   adverbial
'The old man put the fish in the refrigerator.'

But if we are talking of a hat, for instance, it is not necessary to include the adverbial of place if the hat is placed on someone's head (which is the expected place to put a hat):

O velhinho pôs o chapéu e foi embora.
'The old man put his hat on and went away.'

Now, if the hat is placed in some unexpected place, the adverb must be present:

O velhinho pôs o chapéu no bolso e foi embora.
'The old man put his hat in his pocket and went away.'

33.3.3 Unaccusatives

Unaccusatives are verbs that typically can occur
a. with a subject expressing the agent and a direct object expressing the patient, and
b. with a subject expressing the patient, and no object (but not in the passive form).
An example is *quebrar* in

O gato quebrou o jarro.
'The cat broke the vase.'

O jarro quebrou.
'The vase broke.'

In the first sentence, which has a direct object (*o jarro*), this object is the patient and the subject (*o gato*) is the agent. In the second sentence, without object, the subject (*o jarro*) is the patient.
     With other (nonunaccusative) verbs the subject keeps its thematic role regardless of the presence of an object, e.g.,

O gato comeu o queijo.
'The cat ate the cheese.'

O gato comeu.
'The cat ate.'

Here *o gato* 'the cat' is understood as the agent in both sentences.

As the glosses show, the facts of Portuguese are similar to the facts of English in this particular. In both languages the class of unaccusatives is large; in Portuguese it includes *estragar* 'to spoil,' *esquentar* 'to heat,' *animar* 'to stimulate / to be stimulated,' *virar* 'to turn over,' *levantar* 'to raise / to rise,' *abaixar* 'to lower / to drop,' *entortar* 'to twist,' *derramar* 'to spill,' *rasgar* 'to tear,' and many others.

What is peculiar to Portuguese is that the class of unaccusatives tends to grow, especially in the spoken language, so that there are many verbs that are transitive, intransitive, or reflexive in the written language, but unaccusative in the spoken one.[1]

Note

[1]Or in the spoken language of certain regions. For instance, I have noticed that speakers from Paraná and other southern states tend to use fewer unaccusatives than speakers from Minas or Rio; in Minas one says *a vidraça quebrou* 'the windowpane broke,' but many southerners say *a vidraça se quebrou,* keeping the reflexive. The geographical distribution of unaccusatives has not been studied, to my knowledge at least.

Thus, some unaccusatives that are usual in speaking have found their way into the written language, for example, *quebrar* 'to break,' *esquentar* 'to warm,' as in

> *Sandrinha esquentou o leite.*
> 'Sandrinha heated the milk.'
>
> *O leite esquentou.*
> 'The milk heated [= became hot].'

Then, some that are characteristic of informal speech tend to become generally used, such as *doer* 'to hurt' in

> *Esse sapato dói o meu pé.* **SpBr**
> 'This shoe hurts my foot.'
>
> *Meu pé está doendo.*
> 'My foot is hurting.'

In more formal speech one substitutes *machucar* for *doer* when there is a direct object:

> *Esse sapato machuca o meu pé.*
> 'This shoe hurts my foot.'

This sentence is also perfectly acceptable in the spoken language, which has therefore two ways to express the same idea.

33.3.4 Indirect causatives

The English verb *to have* is used to express indirect causation, as in

I had my hair cut yesterday.

In Portuguese, it is possible to express the same thing by means of *mandar:*

Mandei cortar meu cabelo ontem.
'I had my hair cut yesterday.'

but this is not the most favored option. More frequently, *mandar* is omitted, so that the sentence may be understood as denoting a direct or an indirect causation—ambiguity being solved by context, e.g.,

Cortei meu cabelo ontem.
'I cut my hair yesterday.'   **or**   'I had my hair cut yesterday.'

Other examples are

Ronaldo operou o joelho.
'Ronaldo operated on his knee.'   **or**   'Ronaldo had his knee operated.'

Vou reformar minha casa.
'(I)'m going to remodel my house.' **or**   '(I)'m going to have my house remodeled.'

33.4 Nominal and adverbial valency

Valency is not an exclusive characteristic of verbs. Nominals and adverbs also often require complements (always with a preposition); for instance, the nominal *amor* 'love' requires the preposition *por* (more rarely *a*) before its complement:

Eles demonstram um grande amor <u>pela escola</u>.
'They show a great love for the school.'

The nominal *medo* 'fear,' on the other hand, requires *de:*

Todos aqui têm medo <u>das enchentes</u>.
'Everyone here is afraid of the floods [literally, have fear of the floods].'

Another example is *favorável* 'favorable,' which takes the preposition *a*, e.g.,

A decisão final foi favorável <u>ao marido</u>.
'The final decision was favorable to the husband.'

And an adverbial like *favoravelmente* also takes *a:*

O tribunal decidiu favoravelmente <u>ao marido</u>.
'The court decided favorably to the husband.'

The complete list of nominals and adverbials requiring a prepositional complement is too long to be included in a grammar. Here, just as with verb valency, the student will have to resort to a nominal valency dictionary, of which the best is Fernandes (1958).

34

Nominal Agreement

34.1 Agreement

As we saw in chapter 7, every nominal when used referentially (that is, when referring to a concrete or abstract object) must belong to a specific gender and number; thus, *carro* 'car' is masculine and singular, *luzes* 'lights' is feminine and plural, and so on. On the other hand, modifiers like *vermelho* 'red,' *um* 'a, some,' and *o* 'the' normally must agree, that is, *be in* the same gender and number as the head. Consequently, words that can function as modifiers usually come in four forms: *vermelho, vermelha, vermelhos, vermelhas; um, uma, uns, umas; o, a, os, as.*

For example, taking the words *carro* 'car,' which is masculine, *luz* 'light,' which is feminine, and *vermelho* 'red,' which is used here as a modifier, we have four possible combinations:

carro <u>vermelho</u>	**[masculine, singular]**	'red car'
luz <u>vermelha</u>	**[feminine, singular]**	'red light'
carros <u>vermelhos</u>	**[masculine, plural]**	'red cars'
luzes <u>vermelhas</u>	**[feminine, plural]**	'red lights'

Agreement between a head nominal and its modifier is a very limited phenomenon in English, occurring only with the words *this* and *that*, which agree in number with their heads: *this* computer, *that* computer [singular]; *these* computers, *those* computers [plural]. Portuguese has the same basic process, but generalized for most nominals (that is, except some, like *cada,* which do not vary) and extended to gender as well as number.

In this chapter I examine the syntactic conditions that govern agreement between nominals. We may distinguish two main cases: first, agreement within the noun phrase between the head and its modifiers, and, second, agreement within the sentence between a subject or object noun phrase and a nominal functioning as a subjective complement or as a predicative.

Note that the spoken and written varieties of Brazilian Portuguese differ markedly as concerns number agreement, and, consequently, both in this chapter and in the one treating subject-verb agreement, we will have to consider separately the rules for each variety. In what follows I first describe the situation in the written (and formal spoken) language, and then I turn to the spoken language.

34.2 Agreement within the noun phrase

34.2.1 General rule

The general rule is very simple:

In a noun phrase, modifiers not introduced by prepositions must be in the same gender and number as the head.

General rule for nominal agreement

For example,

Aqueles	*maravilhosos*	*vestidos*	*vermelhos*
modifier	**modifier**	**head**	**modifier**

'Those beautiful red dresses'

Here the head is *vestidos* 'dresses,' which is masculine and plural; correspondingly, the modifiers *aqueles* 'those,' *maravilhosos* 'beautiful,' and *vermelhos* 'red' are also in the

masculine plural. If we had, say, a feminine singular head, all modifiers would have to follow:

> *Aquela maravilhosa blusa vermelha*
> 'That beautiful red blouse'

This applies only to modifiers not introduced by a preposition; whenever a preposition in-
tervenes, a new noun phrase begins, and the rule applies separately to it, e.g.,

> *Aquela maravilhosa blusa [de algodão vermelho]*
> 'That beautiful red cotton blouse'

Here, *aquela* and *maravilhosa* modify *blusa* and must be feminine; but *vermelho* belongs to
another noun phrase, part of the larger one, *algodão vermelho,* and agrees with its head, *algodão,* which is masculine.

34.2.2 Particular cases

The above rule has properly speaking no exceptions; yet there are some situations in which
its application is not clear, and these must be examined.

34.2.2.1 Invariable nominals

The first situation has to do with nominals that appear as modifiers yet show no variation
in gender, number, or both. This is usually due to phonological reasons, so they are said to
vary regularly, although this does not show in their overt forms. An example is *forte*
'strong,' which does not vary for gender: *um homem forte* 'a strong man,' *uma mulher forte*
'a strong woman.' Another is *simples* 'simple, naive,' which does not vary at all: *o homem
simples* 'the naive man,' *os homens simples* 'the naive men,' *a mulher simples* 'the naive
woman,' *as mulheres simples* 'the naive women.' In these cases we can say (following traditional analysis) that *forte* has masculine and feminine forms and *simples* has all four forms,
but that they are pronounced and written identically (see chapter 7 for details of the inflection of these nominals).

A similar case is *cada* 'each,' which does not vary in gender or number and consequently does not agree: *cada moça e cada rapaz* 'each girl and each boy.' *Cada* occurs only
with nominals in the singular.

Finally, there are several nominals that do not vary for idiosyncratic reasons. These
include *laranja* 'orange(-colored),' *baita* 'big,' etc.—see list in chapter 7. Thus, one says
carro laranja 'orange car,' *carros laranja* 'orange cars,' *luz laranja* 'orange light,' and *luzes
laranja* 'orange lights.'

34.2.2.2 One modifier, several heads

The second situation in which the application of the rule is doubtful involves a modifier that applies to more than one head, as in English *strong men and women*. In Portuguese, the modifier may come before or after the heads; in the first case, the following rule applies:

> When a modifier precedes two or more heads, agreement is made with the first head.

For instance,

> <u>Novos</u>   *métodos* *e* *técnicas*
> **masculine masculine**   **feminine**
> 'New methods and techniques'

> <u>Novas</u>   *técnicas* *e* *métodos*
> **feminine** **feminine**   **masculine**
> 'New techniques and methods'

In the second case, the rule is

> When the modifier comes after the heads, it may
>
> a. agree in gender and number with the last head; **or, optionally,**
>
> b. be in the plural—and in the masculine[1] if the heads are of different genders.

Note

[1]That is, in the *unmarked form,* which occurs by default if no factor determines otherwise.

Instances are as follows:

Método   e   técnica   <u>nova</u>
masculine   feminine   feminine
singular   singular   singular

or

Método   e   técnica   <u>novos</u>   **Wr**
masculine   feminine   masculine
singular   singular   plural
        'New method and techique'

The second alternative is preferred in writing; the first one occurs both in speech and in writing.

34.3 Nominal agreement in the sentence

Nominals can also occur as subjective complements; that is, they modify a noun phrase by means of a copulative verb such as *ser* 'to be,' *estar* 'to be,' *parecer* 'to look like,' *ficar* 'to become, to stay,' etc.; nominals can also occur as predicatives, modifying a noun phrase that is the subject or the object of certain verbs, like *considerar* 'to believe (something/someone) to be,' *chamar* 'to call (someone),' and some others. In these cases, the modifying nominal also agrees with the head of the noun phrase it modifies. Examples with copulative verbs are as follows:

Estela é <u>bonita</u>.
'Estela is pretty [**feminine**].'

Marcos é <u>bonito</u>.
'Marcos is handsome [**masculine**].'

Essas bananas parecem estragadas.
These bananas [**feminine plural**] look rotten [**feminine plural**].'

Esses ovos parecem estragados.
'These eggs [**masculine plural**] look rotten [**masculine plural**].'

With verbs accepting a predicative:

O chefe considera João desonesto.
'The boss believes João to be dishonest [**masculine**].'

O chefe considera Elza desonesta.
'The boss believes Elza do be dishonest [**feminine**].'

Ela chamou João (de) cretino.
'She called João stupid [**masculine singular**].'

In all these cases,

> the modifying nominal agrees with a specific noun phrase head, namely,
>
> the one it is semantically connected with.

Thus, in the last sentence *cretino* 'cretin' clearly refers to *João,* not to *ela;* accordingly, *cretino* must be in the masculine. If the student keeps this rule in mind, correct agreement will prove easy enough.

In the spoken language there is a curious exception to this rule: when the subject is *a gente,* which, as we saw in chapter 8, is an alternative form for *nós* 'we,' the nominal in question agrees in gender, but not in number, e.g.,

A gente é professor.   /   *A gente é professores.
'We are teachers.'

A gente está cansada.   /   *A gente está cansadas.
'We are tired [**feminine**].'

This has to do with the fact that *a gente* is formally singular (although semantically plural) and agrees with a verb equally in the singular.

There are a few cases in which the application of this rule is not clear, so we need to supplement it with some notes. The main problem concerns nominals that modify more than one head at the same time. In these cases,

---

when a nominal modifies more than one head, it must be in the plural;

and it must be in the feminine if all heads are feminine; or in the masculine if at least one head is masculine.

Some examples follow:

> **Estela**   *e*   **Marcos**   *são*   <u>*bonitos*</u>.
> **feminine**   **masculine**   **masculine**
> **singular**   **singular**   **plural**
> 'Estela and Marcos are handsome.'

> *O chefe considera*   **Sara**   *e*   **Antônia**   <u>*desonestas*</u>.
> **feminine**   **feminine**   **feminine**
> **singular**   **singular**   **plural**
> 'The boss believes Sara and Antônia to be dishonest.'

34.4 Marked and unmarked forms

As we saw in the preceding sections, the masculine form is used in items that modify heads belonging to both genders; this is so because the form traditionally called masculine is in fact the **unmarked** form, valid for all cases in which the feminine (or **marked**) form is not mandatory. This explains why the masculine is used when there is no basis for agreement at all, as in

> *Está* <u>*cheio*</u> *de crianças na praia.*
> 'The beach is full of children [literally, It is full [**masculine**] of children in the beach].'

Dirigir sem cinto de segurança é <u>perigoso</u>.
'Driving without (a) safety belt is dangerous [**masculine**].'

In the first example, *cheio* is not syntactically connected to any noun phrase; in the second one, *perigoso* is connected to a sentential noun phrase, *dirigir sem cinto de segurança* 'driving without a safety belt,' which does not belong to any gender. In both cases, the modifier is in the masculine, that is, the unmarked, form.

For the same reason, *eles* is the personal pronoun used to refer to several heads belonging to both genders:

A televisão e o computador estão ali; <u>eles</u> custaram mais do que o esperado.
'The television [**feminine**] and the computer [**masculine**] are there; they [**masculine**] cost more than expected.'

Convidei Manuela e Tiago, mas <u>eles</u> não puderam vir.
'(I) have invited Manuela and Tiago, but they [**masculine**] could not come.'

By the same token, the masculine is used for nominals qualifying heads of both genders:

Manuela e Tiago estão <u>enganados</u>.
'Manuela and Tiago are mistaken [**masculine plural**].'

34.5 Number agreement in the spoken language

The situation as described above is valid for the written language and for the most formal varieties of the spoken language (such as speaking in public or giving an interview on television). There are certain people who really speak like that all the time, but, first, it is a very rare phenomenon, and, second, this way of speaking tends to mark the speaker as a formal, somewhat pompous individual. The overwhelming majority of Brazilians use a more economical system, as described in this section.

To start with an example, take the phrase

As casas vermelhas
'The red houses'

Since *casas* is feminine and plural, both the article *as* and the nominal *vermelhas* are in the feminine plural, thus following the general rule.

As far as gender agreement is concerned, the general rule works without alteration for spontaneous speech as well; but number agreement differs. When speaking, Brazilians will normally say

> *As casa vermelha*   **SpBr**
> 'The red houses'

That is,

---

in casual speech the plural mark is present *only* in the first element of the phrase; all other elements remain in the singular, which is the un-marked number.

Thus, we hear (although we never read) sentences like

> *Aqueles menino malandro ainda não arrumaram as cama.*   **SpBr**
> 'Those lazy boys didn't yet make their beds.'

As stated in the rule, the first element in the phrase is the only one consistently marked for number; this happens when the first element is the article (as above) and also when several other terms are used, e.g.,

> *Aquelas menina danada*   **SpBr**
> 'Those wicked girls'

> *Uns bolinho muito gostoso*   **SpBr**
> 'Some very tasty cakes'

> *Cinco disquete*   **SpBr**
> 'Five diskettes'

In the last example, the semantics of *cinco* 'five' is sufficient to mark the phrase as plural, no overt plural morpheme being necessary.[1]

Note

[1]Many speakers flatly deny that they use phrases like *cinco disquete* and the like; yet they do, as is easily discerned by just listening to them for a couple of minutes. There is probably no one in Brazil who, when speaking, consistently applies the "official" number agreement rule to all phrases, all the time.

But when the phrase begins with a **nominal**—whether the head or a modifier—the preferred turn is not to mark the first element as a plural, but rather to leave all elements in the singular:

Menino levado dá muito trabalho.
'Naughty children are a lot of trouble.'

Eu detesto manga.
'I hate mangoes [literally, I hate mango].'

The singular is possible because a plural noun phrase without a determiner and a singular one without a determiner are synonymous; that is, what is expressed in the written language as *meninos levados, mangas*—namely, reference to a generic entity—is expressed in the spoken language as *menino levado* and *manga,* respectively.

Now, the usage just described is the normal way of speaking for most Brazilians of all classes, regions, and levels of schooling; it is *not* a characteristic of substandard or uncultured speech. At most, educated speakers may add some *-s*'s at strategic points, especially when speaking carefully; but practically no one uses all *-s*'s in their standard positions all the time. Naturally, the incidence of standard versus colloquial forms varies according to social and educational factors; but colloquial forms are by far the most numerous, and often the only ones, found in any given stretch of speech.

34.6 A note on obrigado

The word *obrigado* 'thank you' is supposed to agree with the gender of the speaker, so that men say *obrigado,* and women say *obrigada.* This rule is still frequently applied, but it is losing ground to the tendency to say *obrigado* regardless of sex.

35

Subject-Verb Agreement

In Portuguese, as in English, verbs agree with one of the terms of the sentence, namely, the **subject.** The basic phenomenon is the same in the two languages: English has *I am, you are, he is,* Portuguese has *eu sou, você é, ele é.* The difference is that the Portuguese verb is richer in forms, so that agreement is apparent in many cases in which in English it does not show—as for instance in past tenses, in the future, etc.

On the other hand, in practically all cases there is a simple correlation between subjects in the two languages, so that determining which term the verb should agree with is never a problem. That is, when translating into Portuguese the sentence *my brothers arrived from New York,* the element with which the verb is to agree is *meus irmãos* 'my brothers,' which is the subject in both languages. This parallelism frees us from broaching the vexed question of defining the subject; we may proceed to state the agreement rules.

35.1 Basic agreement rule

The basic agreement rule is as follows:

> The verb agrees with its subject in number and person.[1]

Note

**[1] This is in accordance with the way verb paradigms are presented: first person singular, third person plural, and so on. It has been remarked, though, that here "number" is taken in a rather loose manner, since of course *nós* 'we' is not the plural of *eu* 'I' in the usual sense—that is, *nós* does not designate more than one *eu*. That understood, however, we may go on employing the traditional terminology, which has no serious drawbacks as regards our eminently practical point of view.

For instance,

> *Eu saí do bar.* / *Léia saiu do bar.* / *Nós saímos do bar.* / *Ivan e Léia saíram do bar.*
> 'I left the pub.' / 'Léia left the pub.' / 'We left the pub.' / 'Ivan and Léia left the pub.'

As can be seen, when the subject noun phrase has more than one head, it counts as a plural, just as in English.

On the other hand, subject-verb agreement in Portuguese is more strictly grammatical than in English, and it is very rare to find cases of a verb in the plural agreeing with a formally singular subject (that is, without the plural suffix -*s*), as in English *the police are worried about the thefts;* in Portuguese one says *a polícia está* [**singular**] *preocupada com os roubos.*

35.2 Particular cases

The basic rule is simple enough, but there are some special cases in which secondary rules apply, either because the application of the basic rule is not clear or because they are exceptions.

35.2.1 Compound subjects

The first such situation is when we have a subject with more than one head (traditionally called a **compound subject**), for instance,

> *Camilo e Cláudio saíram do bar.*
> 'Camilo and Cláudio left the pub.'

Here we must distinguish cases in which the subject occurs before the verb, as in the above example, and cases in which the subject follows the verb, as in

> <u>*Chegaram*</u> *Camilo e Cláudio.*
> 'Camilo and Cláudio have arrived.'

The rule as found in traditional grammars is as follows:

The verb agrees with a compound subject in the following manner:

—if the subject precedes, the verb must be in the plural; as for person, it must be in the first person if any of the heads of the subject is a first-person item; in the second person if any head is a second-person item and there is no first-person item; and in the third person otherwise.

—if the subject follows, the verb may agree according to the preceding rule, or, optionally, agree with the first head of the subject.

Rule for agreement with compound subjects

Some observations on the rule: First, the part of the rule dealing with the second person is relevant only for those persons (very rare in Brazil) who employ second person forms according to the standard, either when speaking or when writing.

Second, the tendency both in speaking and in writing is to make the verb agree with the first head of a postposed compound subject; thus, the second of the following versions is highly favored at the expense of the first one:[1]

> *Morreram o pai, a mãe e vários irmãos.*
> 'The father, the mother, and several brothers died.'

> *Morreu o pai, a mãe e vários irmãos.*
> 'id.'

Note

**¹This may have something to do with the tendency, described below, not to agree at all when the subject comes after the verb.

Now, for person agreement, we have

Camilo e eu <u>fomos</u> ao circo.
'Camilo and I went to the circus.'

Since the subject includes a first-person item (*eu*), the verb must be in the first person plural.

35.2.2 Agreement with relative or topicalizing *que*

In English, a verb following a relative pronoun (*which, who, that,* etc.) agrees with the antecedent of the pronoun, that is, in general the immediately preceding noun phrase:

The men who <u>were</u> making noise downstairs have left.
The man who <u>was</u> making noise downstairs has left.

In Portuguese the same rule applies, with the advantage that the antecedent must *always* occur immediately before the pronoun:

Os homens *que <u>estavam</u> fazendo barulho embaixo foram embora.*
'The men who <u>were</u> making noise downstairs have left.'

O homem *que <u>estava</u> fazendo barulho embaixo foi embora.*
'The man who <u>was</u> making noise downstairs has left.'

The same rule is valid for *que* as part of the topicalizing expression *ser . . . que:*

*Foi **aquele homem** que <u>fez</u> o barulho.*
'It was that man who made the noise.'

*Foram **aqueles homens** que <u>fizeram</u> o barulho.*
'It was those men who made the noise.'

As can be seen, the initial form of *ser* 'to be'—that is, *foi* and *foram*—also agrees; topicalizing expressions like this one are studied in chapter 39.

35.2.3 Agreement with the verb *ser* 'to be'

The rules governing agreement in sentences with *ser* 'to be' are curiously complex and determine not agreement proper (which is regular) but rather the location of the subject—that is, which noun phrase the verb is to agree with. Some grammars give a long list of rules, but only three of them are in use in the modern language.

These rules apply to the choice of subject among two noun phrases connected by *ser,* as in

> *Raquel é a minha irmã mais querida.*
> 'Raquel is my dearest sister.'

In this sentence no doubt is possible, since both noun phrases are third person singular, and neither of them is a pronoun. But

---

if one of two noun phrases connected by *ser* is a personal pronoun, the

verb agrees with it, regardless of position.

For example,

> *Raquel sou eu.*
> 'I'm Raquel.'

> *Eu sou Raquel.*
> 'id.'

> *Vocês são o meu maior problema.*
> 'You are my greatest problem.'

> *O meu maior problema são vocês.*
> 'id.'

When one of the noun phrases is represented by *tudo* 'everything,' *isto, isso* 'this,' *aquilo* 'that,' or the interrogatives *quem* 'who' and *(o) que* 'what,' agreement is made with the other noun phrase, regardless of position.

For example,

> *Isso são bolinhos de bacalhau.*
> 'This is codfish cakes.'

> *Bolinhos de bacalhau são isso.*   **Wr**[1]
> 'Codfish cakes are these.'

> *Quem eram os Templários?*
> 'Who were the Templars?'

Note

[1]Many speakers reject this sentence as odd; and, in fact, it is much more common to say *bolinho de bacalhau é isso,* with both members in the singular.

Finally,

when one of the noun phrases is singular and the other is plural (all third person), agreement is made with the plural phrase.

Thus,

> *A vida <u>são</u> sofrimentos sem fim.*
> 'Life is endless sufferings.'

> *Essas crianças <u>são</u> meu grande problema.*
> * *Essas crianças <u>é</u> meu grande problema.*
> 'These children are my great problem.'

These rules work also for the spoken language, and all of the above sentences can be used in speech. There is a tendency to simplify the system, resulting in sentences like *Raquel é eu* **SpBr** 'I am Raquel'; but such forms are not used by schooled persons and should be avoided.

35.2.4 Indication of times of the day and days of the month

Here, again, the standard use differs from the spoken one. Traditionally, the verb *ser* 'to be' used with times of the day or with days of the month should agree with the time or day indicated:

> *<u>São</u> oito horas da noite.*
> 'It is eight P.M.'

> *Hoje <u>são</u> treze de junho.*   **Wr**
> 'Today is June thirteenth.'

In the spoken language, agreement is frequently (but not always) made with times of the day, but never with days of the month:

> *Hoje <u>é</u> treze de junho.*   **SpBr**
> 'Today is June thirteenth.'

35.2.5 Infinitive agreement (use of the personal infinitive)

Portuguese differs from most languages in that it allows infinitives to agree with their subjects in certain cases. One example is

> *Eu trouxe uns aparelhos para vocês <u>consertarem</u>.*
> 'I have brought some appliances for you (pl.) to fix.'

In this sentence *consertarem* is the third plural form of the infinitive of *consertar*, 'to fix,' and agrees with the subject *vocês* 'you (pl.).' We then say that the language contains a **per-**

sonal (that is, inflected) **infinitive.** The personal infinitive is comparatively little used in the spoken language, but it is frequent in all styles of writing. In this section I examine the rules governing agreement of the infinitive.

—With an overt subject

> The infinitive agrees whenever it has an overt subject (but see below the
>
> case of verbs of perception and suasion).

For instance,

> *Eu trouxe uns aparelhos para* **vocês** <u>*consertarem*</u>.
> **subject**
> 'I have brought some appliances for you (pl.) to fix.'

> *Eu lamento profundamente* **tantos engenheiros** <u>*estarem*</u> *desempregados.*
> **subject**
> 'I deeply regret that so many engineers are unemployed.'

—With verbs of perception and of suasion

There is a particular environment in which the presence of an overt subject is doubtful; it is as if the language itself were uncertain about it, and agreement is optional. This happens with the verbs studied in section 16.2.3, that is, **verbs of perception** like *ver* 'to see,' *ouvir* 'to hear,' *sentir* 'to feel,' and also with some **verbs of suasion,** like *mandar* 'to order,' *deixar* 'to let,' and *fazer* when meaning 'to compel.'

As we saw in chapter 16, these verbs may be followed by a sequence of a noun phrase plus an infinitive, e.g.,

> *Eu nunca ouvi Mariana   tocar.*
> **NP   infinitive**
> 'I have never heard Mariana play.'

The uncertainty is about the grammatical function of *Mariana:* is it the object of *ouvir* 'to hear' or the subject of *tocar* 'to play'? In a sense it is both, and this is what some older grammarians said.[1]

Note

**1 Modern grammarians have been repeating the same thing, under different disguises: raising, subject deletion, rule fluctuation, exceptional case-marking, and other labels that, to my mind, have added little to our understanding of the construction.

In English there is little doubt that *Mariana* is the object of *heard* (for instance, it can be replaced by an object pronoun, *her*). But in Portuguese there is a complicating factor: not only can the noun phrase in question be replaced by an object pronoun, as in English,

> *Eu nunca **a** ouvi <u>tocar</u>.*   **Wr**
> 'I have never heard her play.'

but the infinitive, *tocar,* can also agree with it, which can be seen in

> *Eu nunca ouvi **Mariana e Leo** <u>tocarem</u>.*
> 'I have never heard Mariana and Leo play [**third plural**].'

The first fact seems to show that the noun phrase is the object of the main verb; but the second suggests that it is the subject of the infinitive. To my knowledge, no one has managed to analyze this construction as a regular case of agreement, so we might as well treat it as an exception:

> In constructions of the type *ver* + *NP* + *infinitive,* the infinitive **optionally agrees** with the NP.

That is, we can also say

> *Eu nunca ouvi **Mariana e Leo** <u>tocar</u>.*
> 'id.'

This construction also occurs both in the written and in the spoken language. Agreement of the infinitive is the general rule in writing, whereas in speech it is more usual *not* to agree.

When the NP in question is a personal pronoun in its objective form, though, agreement is not possible:

> *Eu nunca **os** ouvi <u>tocar</u>.* / *<u>*tocarem</u>.*
> 'I have never heard them play [**third singular**].'

—Without an overt subject

When no subject is explicit in the sentence, agreement of the infinitive is governed by the following rules:

> The infinitive is inflected when it is necessary to mark its (understood)
>
> subject as different from the subject of the main verb.[1]

Note

[1]In practice, this only happens when the infinitive is to inflect for the first person plural; the third person plural—which would be the other possibility—is practically never used without an overt subject.

An example is

> *Tadeu lamenta profundamente <u>estarmos</u> desempregados.*   **Wr**
> 'Tadeu deeply regrets that we are unemployed.'

This construction is typical of the the written language. In speech an overt subject is used, which brings the sentence under the first rule:

> *Tadeu lamenta profundamente **nós** <u>estarmos</u> desempregados.*
> 'id.'

> The infinitive without an overt subject optionally agrees:
>
> a. when the main clause has a **factive** verb; or
>
> b. when governed by a preposition.

Factive verbs have a special semantic feature, namely, when they are used **there is an understanding between the speaker and the hearer that the subordinate clause is true.** Compare the following sentences:

The president regrets that inflation is high.
The president said that inflation is high.

In the first case, it is understood that inflation is, in fact, high; the second sentence lays the statement that inflation is high on the president's responsibility, with no commitment on the part of the speaker. This is due to the use of a factive verb (*regret*) in the first sentence, and a nonfactive one (*say*) in the second. Examples of factive verbs are *lamentar* 'to regret,' *revelar* 'to disclose,' *esconder* 'to conceal,' *perceber* 'to realize.'

In Portuguese, factive verbs have the syntactic effect of allowing optional agreement of the infinitive:

Os deputados lamentaram profundamente <u>terem</u> / <u>ter</u> que revogar essa lei.
'The congressmen deeply regretted having to repeal this law.'

Here, agreement is avoided when the two verbs are contiguous:

*Os deputados lamentaram <u>revogar</u> / * <u>revogarem</u> essa lei.*
'The congressmen regretted repealing this law.'

Finally, we have optional agreement when the infinitive is governed by a preposition:

Muitos turistas trazem matulas para <u>comer</u> / <u>comerem</u> na viagem.
'Many tourists bring provisions to eat during the trip.'

With prepositions the tendency seems to be *not* to agree; and with some very common prepositions agreement is not used, e.g.,

Elas gostavam de <u>jogar</u> / *<u>jogarem</u> tênis na praia.
'They enjoyed playing tennis on the beach.'

Therefore, when in doubt, it is better to avoid the personal infinitive after prepositions.

35.3 *Impersonal verbs* haver, ter, *and* fazer

Haver and *ter* both may mean 'there to be,' and when meaning this they are impersonal, that is, they occur only in the third person singular; in other words, they do not agree. The difference between them is that *haver* is used almost exclusively in writing, and *ter* preferably in speaking—although *ter* nowadays appears in writing as well, especially in texts like theater plays, publicity, and novels. Unlike English *there to be,* they do not agree, e.g.,

<u>Há</u> *mais de vinte galinhas no quintal.*	**Wr**
<u>Tem</u> *mais de vinte galinhas no quintal.*	**SpBr**
'There are more than twenty chickens in the backyard.'	

<u>Havia</u> *alguns problemas.*	**Wr**
<u>Tinha</u> *alguns problemas.*	**SpBr**
'There were some problems.'	

Fazer, preceding an expression of time, may refer to past events, continuing or not into the present (this is indicated by context), and in this case it is equally impersonal, as in

<u>Faz</u> *dez anos que eu vendi o sítio.*
'It's been ten years since I sold (my) country house.'

Ela está gripada <u>faz</u> vários dias.
'She has had the flu for several days.'

In this context, *haver* may be used as a synonym of *fazer:*

<u>Há</u> *dez anos que eu vendi o sítio.*
'It's been ten years since I sold (my) country house.'

Ela está gripada <u>há</u> vários dias.
'She has had the flu for several days.'

In this usage, *haver* is common also in the spoken language. *Fazer* is also impersonal when used to express natural events, as in

Fez umas noites muito frias em julho.
'There were some very cold nights in July.'

35.4 Impersonal sentences with se

This construction was discussed in chapter 21; here it will be enough to mention its main characteristics. The particle *se* is one of the resources used in Portuguese to omit the agent, thus calling attention to the event itself or to the patient, as in

> *Vende-se este lote.*
> 'This lot is for sale   [literally, One sells this lot].'

> *Para fazer vatapá, usa-se pimenta malagueta.*
> 'When making vatapá, one uses malagueta pepper.'

In the spoken language, the verb does not agree and stays in the third person singular regardless of what follows; thus, if we had a plural in the first sentence above, it would be

> *Vende-se esses lotes.*   **SpBr**
> 'These lots for sale.'

In some more traditional forms of the written language, however, the verb agrees with the following noun phrase (which therefore becomes the subject):

> *Vendem-se esses lotes.*   **Wr**
> 'id.'   *Impersonal subj*

As noted in chapter 21, agreement in this construction tends to disappear even in the written language.

35.5 Use and omission of subject pronouns

The Portuguese verb is more informative about its subject than its English counterpart; thus, we have *trabalho* '(I) work,' *trabalhamos* '(we) work,' *trabalham* '(they) work,' all of which correspond to the single English form *work*. One consequence is that in many cases the subject pronoun does not have to appear in the sentence:

> *Detesto café ralo.*
> '(I) hate weak coffee.'

This sentence is a synonym of

> *Eu detesto café ralo.*
> 'id.'

and they may be used interchangeably in all cases.[1] Yet sometimes omission of the subject is not allowed, and in some other cases one of the versions may be preferred.

Note

[1]The presence of the pronoun does not necessarily mean that it is emphatic; emphasis is indicated in speech by extra stress and higher pitch, and in writing it is sometimes represented by boldface, underlining, or some equivalent mark.

35.5.1 Obligatory vs. optional subject pronouns

Subject pronouns are obligatory when their absence would result in ambiguity. The most frequent case is represented by third person pronouns, which are particularly ambiguous. Thus, one may say

> *A companhia está em má situação; provavelmente vai perder o prédio.*
> 'The company is in poor shape; (it) will probably lose its building.'

The second verb, *vai,* has no overt subject because it is readily recoverable from context and can only be *ela* 'it [that is, the company].' But in

> *Você está totalmente enganado.*
> 'You are totally wrong.'

the subject pronoun *você* cannot be dispensed with because it would not be recoverable, and third person forms are not sufficiently explicit as to their subject: the subject of *está* might be not only *você,* but also *o senhor* 'you (respectful),' *ele* 'he,' *ela* 'she,' not to mention nonpronominal subjects. Thus, the following sentence, out of context, is not acceptable:

> * *Está totalmente enganado.*
> * 'Are totally wrong'

In invitations, like

> *Quer mais chá?*
> 'Do (you) want more tea?'

the subject may be omitted since it is clear enough; but even here the tendency is to keep it:

> *Você quer mais chá?*
> 'id.'

In all other cases a third person pronominal subject must be present:

> *Ela comprou um tapete caríssimo.*
> 'She bought a most expensive carpet.'

> *O senhor só sabe reclamar.*
> 'You (respectful) do nothing but complain.'

First person singular pronouns are obligatory when the first person of the verb is identical to the third person, which happens in the imperfect, pluperfect, conditional, in all tenses of the subjunctive, and in the personal infinitive:

> *Eu dizia sempre que isso era perigoso.*
> 'I always said that this was dangerous.'

Here *eu* must appear because the form *dizia* is identical to the third singular form; therefore, *dizia sempre que isso era perigoso* is ambiguous and can occur only in anaphoric contexts.

Apart from this situation, first person subject pronouns (and second person, when used), may be freely used or omitted; in the spoken language there is a tendency to use them, but omission, if slightly less frequent, is also perfectly acceptable. Even in contexts where omission would cause no ambiguity, use of subject pronouns with all verbs is often found, e.g.,

> *Meu marido chegou tarde; ele tinha trabalhado demais, e ele estava esgotado.*   **SpBr**
> 'My husband arrived late; he had worked too much, and he was exhausted.'

35.5.2 Subjectless verbs

In certain cases English has an obligatory "formal" subject, *it* or *there;* in such cases Portuguese shows no subject at all. This happens, first, with some verbs that indicate natural phenomena, as in

> *Choveu ontem.*
> '(It) rained yesterday.'

Está nevando.
'(It) is snowing.'

Fez muito calor ontem.
'(It) was very warm yesterday.'

The formal subject represented by English *it* does not have a correspondent in Portuguese, the verb alone being used (in its unmarked form, that is, the third person singular).

The same thing happens with the verbs *ser* 'to be,' *tornar-se* 'to become,' *ficar* 'to become' when introducing a qualifier; here, English also has *it,* e.g.,

É importante fundamentar cada teoria com dados suficientes.
'(It) is important to base each theory on sufficient data.'

Foi ótimo que a multidão se dispersasse antes da chuva.
'(It) was good that the crowd dispersed before the rain.'

Tornou-se indispensável comprar mais um carro.   **Wr**
'(It) became indispensable to buy another car.'

In general, this happens whenever English *it* is used nonanaphorically, that is, without a clear antecedent. Of course, if there is an antecedent, it may be necessary to include a pronoun also in Portuguese, e.g.,

O pernilongo estava no quarto; <u>ele</u> me impediu de dormir.
'The mosquito was in the room; <u>it</u> kept me from sleeping.'

Here the antecedent of *ele* is *o pernilongo* 'the mosquito.'

Finally, in some cases English has *there* as a formal subject, and Portuguese leaves the verb subjectless, e.g.,

Há sete dias na semana.   **Wr**
'(There) are seven days in the week.'

Não tem ninguém no pátio.   **SpBr**
'(There) is nobody in the patio.'

35.6 Subject-verb agreement in the spoken language

35.6.1 Variation

The use of subject-verb agreement in spoken Brazilian is not uniform. For all speakers, no matter how little schooled, the verb agrees with the subject in some situations. For instance, no one fails to make the distinction between the first person singular and the other persons; but some speakers do not go beyond that and say *nós ficou* 'we stayed,' *elas ficou* 'they stayed,' etc. This is extreme, and such forms are never used by even minimally educated persons.

On the other hand, probably no speaker, no matter how schooled, consistently obeys the same rules that are valid for writing. I give below a compromise description that may be followed without risk of sounding either pedantic or uncultured.

Most people frequently fail to distinguish between the third person singular and the third person plural for most forms; thus, one hears

> *Então os rapazinho <u>sobe</u> lá no alto da torre.*   **SpBr (unguarded)**
> 'Then the boys go up the tower.'

If asked to repeat, most speakers will restore the proper endings, saying *os rapazinhos* and *sobem;* but sentences like this occur all the time in the unguarded speech of every Brazilian. The student should not be surprised when hearing such constructions.

This phenomenon is more frequent in cases like *sobe / sobem,* in which the phonological difference between the forms is minimal. In cases like *é / são,* or *vai / vão,* where the difference is phonologically salient, the distinction is usually maintained:

> *As estrada por aqui <u>são</u> muito ruim.*   **SpBr (unguarded)**
> 'Roads around here are very bad.'

The opposition is equally maintained in the preterit, for the same reasons: *ficou* '(he/she) became' is not used for *ficaram* '(they) became':

> *Esses aluno <u>ficaram</u> muito motivado.*   **SpBr (unguarded)**
> 'These students became highly motivated.'

As for the first person plural, it is normally distinguished from all other persons, except in uncultured speech. But this does not mean that the ending *-mos* is universally used the way it is prescribed by grammars; in fluent speech one finds both a reduced form of the ending and an alternate form. The reduced form is *-mo,* often further reduced to *-m',* e.g.,

> *Eu e Chico <u>chegamo</u> / <u>chegam'</u> de manhã.*   **SpBr**[1]
> 'I and Chico arrived this morning.'[2]

Notes

[1]The form I represent here as *chegam'* is pronounced [ʃeˈgɐ̃m], with a perceptible final [m].
[2]The politeness rule requiring the first person to come last is not valid for Portuguese.

Alternatively, it is possible to substitute *a gente* for *nós* 'we'; *a gente* is a third person item, and the verb goes correspondingly to the third person singular form:

> *A gente <u>chegou</u> de manhã.*   **SpBr**
> 'We arrived this morning.'

The use of *a gente* or *nós* for 'we' (in speaking) is free and depends mainly on personal taste; *a gente* seems to be gaining ground in recent years and is preferred by younger speakers.

35.6.2 Postposed subjects

There is also a tendency in the spoken language to avoid agreement when the subject comes after the verb. Conditions vary, and agreement with first person subjects is normally made:

> *<u>Caí</u> eu lá em baixo.*
> 'I fell down there.'

> *Mais tarde <u>chegamos</u> nós com os salgadinhos.*
> 'Later on we arrived with the snacks.'

Use of the third person singular in these cases is substandard and does not occur in the speech of educated speakers. With third person subjects, however, even educated speakers often fail to agree:

> *<u>Apareceu</u> uns rapazes de Diamantina.*   **SpBr**
> 'Some young men from Diamantina showed up.'

The standard form, of course, would be

> *<u>Apareceram</u> uns rapazes de Diamantina.*
> 'id.'

which *can* also appear in the spoken language (and is not, therefore, marked '**Wr**').

36

Complex Sentences

36.1 Kinds of subordinate clauses

Complex sentences are those made up of more than one clause: either a main clause plus one or more subordinates or a set of coordinate clauses. Here we will be concerned with complex sentences of the first kind, which are the ones that may present learning problems. As for the difference between main and subordinate clauses and how to tell them apart, see chapter 14 above.

A subordinate clause has a syntactic function within the main clause; for instance, a subordinate can be an **object,** as in

> *A moça disse que você estava bêbado.*
> 'The girl said that you were drunk.'

The clause *que você estava bêbado*[1] is a direct object, and the same verb might have a nonsentential noun phrase in its place:

> *A moça disse um monte de asneiras.*
> 'The girl said a lot of nonsense.'

This kind of subordinate is called a **nominal clause.**

Note

**¹In fact, the subordinate clause is only *você estava bêbado.* This sequence, when preceded by *que,* becomes a noun phrase, with all the distributional properties of a noun phrase: it can be an object or a subject, and it can be governed by a preposition. Here, however, I will speak loosely of *que você estava bêbado* as being a clause, since the distinction is not relevant for our immediate purposes.

A subordinate can also function as a **modifier,** as in

O carro <u>que você comprou</u> não vai durar muito.
'The car you have bought won't last long.'

Here the subordinate *que você comprou* is a modifier and functions as a qualifying nominal:

O carro <u>vermelho</u> não vai durar muito.
'The red car won't last long.'

This kind of subordinate is called a **relative clause.**
And a subordinate can function as an **adverbial,** e.g.,

<u>*Quando você telefonou*</u> *eu estava no banho.*
'<u>When you called</u> I was in the bath.'

The subordinate may be replaced by an adverbial:

<u>*Às onze horas*</u> *eu estava no banho.*
'<u>At eleven</u> I was in the bath.'

This kind of subordinate is called an **adverbial clause.**
Nominal and adverbial clauses in Portuguese are relatively easy for English-speaking students because they closely parallel the corresponding English structures. The main points one should call attention to are the following: first, the greater freedom of movement of adverbial clauses, which, like adverbials in general, can occur in more positions in the sentence in Portuguese than in English (this difference between the two languages is covered in chapter 30). And, second, the use of mood in each kind of clause (see chapter

14). Relative clauses have a more complex structure and require some study; they are examined in the next section.

36.2 Relative clauses

36.2.1 Preliminary notions

Relative clauses are those that function as modifiers. Before studying their internal structure, we may define two preliminary notions: the notions of **antecedent** and of **restrictive vs. nonrestrictive** clauses.

The **antecedent** is the nominal that is modified by the relative clause; in Portuguese it must come always immediately before the relative pronoun (with its preposition, if any):

> *Aquele* **piano**   *que*   *você tinha*
>   **antecedent relative pronoun**
> 'That piano which you had'

There are no exceptions to the rule of placement of the antecedent before the pronoun, so that an English sentence like

> A   man   arrived   <u>who</u>   was limping badly.
> **antecedent   relative pronoun**

must be translated into Portuguese with the relative pronoun immediately following the antecedent, here *homem* 'man':

> *Um* **homem** *<u>que</u> mancava muito chegou.*

Some relative clauses lack an antecedent, and these are called **free relative clauses;** for instance,

> *<u>Quem</u> quiser pode entrar.*
> 'Whoever wants may go in.'

> *Só aceito <u>o que</u> me oferecem.*
> '(I) accept only what people offer me.'

Relative clauses are of two kinds: restrictive and nonrestrictive. The semantic difference between them is that restrictive clauses help single out an object among other similar objects, as in

O apartamento <u>que eu comprei</u> é muito pequeno.
'The apartment I bought is very small.'

Here the relative clause *que eu comprei* helps the receptor to identify which apartment I am talking about. Now, nonrestrictive clauses just add a quality (or whatever it is that the clause expresses) to a concept that is taken as already identified, as in

O apartamento, <u>que é muito pequeno</u>, fica em Ipanema.
'The apartment, which is very small, is in Ipanema.'

This sentence is uttered by someone who believes the hearer knows beforehand which apartment he or she is talking about. Nonrestrictive relative clauses, in Portuguese as in English, are normally separated by commas. The distinction between restrictive and nonrestrictive relative clauses is important because the relative pronouns used with each are not exactly the same, as shown in the next section.

36.2.2 Relative pronouns

Relative clauses (in Portuguese and in English) are introduced by specific items called **relative pronouns.** There are seven of these pronouns,[1] namely, *que* 'which,' *o qual* 'which,' *cujo* 'whose,' *onde* 'where,' *como* 'how,' *quem* 'who,' and *o que* 'what.' Unlike English, Portuguese does not allow omission of the relative pronoun, so that all relative clauses are marked by the presence of one of these items. Each of them has its peculiar features, which I examine in turn in what follows.

Note

**[1]In most grammars *onde* and *como* are classified not as pronouns, but as adverbs; we might be speaking of relative words, instead of pronouns. However, this distinction is not crucial for our purposes and need not be kept here.

que
Que is the generic relative pronoun, used in most cases in which a preposition is not present (and also with prepositions in the spoken language, as will be seen). Examples of its use are as follows:

O aluno <u>que</u> me telefonou
'The student who called me'

O aluno que você entrevistou
'The student that you have interviewed'

O velho que Colombo era em 1500
'The old man that Columbus was in 1500'

Que is also used with prepositions, mostly in the written language, and even then it is usually avoided in favor of *o qual:*

A reunião de que eu falei	**Wr**
'The meeting about which I talked'	

A companhia para que eu trabalhava	**Wr**
'The company for which I worked'	

As for the extended use of *que* in the spoken language, see 36.2.3 below.

o qual

O qual, which agrees in number and gender with its antecedent, has the same meaning as *que* but is used in partially different contexts. First, *o qual* is the preferred pronoun to use after prepositions in the written language:

A reunião da qual eu falei	**Wr**
'The meeting about which I talked'	

O casaco com o qual você apareceu na festa	**Wr**
'The coat with which you showed up at the party'	

This is the only context in which *o qual* is more frequent than *que*.

    O qual appears without a preposition only in nonrestrictive clauses (where *que* is also correct and more frequently used, being the only possibility in the spoken language):

O apartamento, o qual é muito pequeno, fica em Ipanema.	**Wr**
O apartamento, que é muito pequeno, fica em Ipanema.	
'The apartment, which is very small, is in Ipanema.'	

O qual is not used in restrictive clauses without a preposition, except, infrequently, to avoid ambiguity, since it is marked for gender and number and *que* is not:

A mãe do menino, a qual os policiais estão tentando localizar, . . .	**Wr**
'The boy's mother, whom [**feminine**] the policemen are trying to locate . . .'	

Here *a qual* is used to make it clear that it is the mother, not the boy, that the policemen are searching for.

cujo

Cujo corresponds to English *whose* and is likewise confined to the written language. But, unlike *whose,* it can refer to any antecedent, not only to human ones:

> *A professora <u>cujos</u> alunos me procuraram*   **Wr**
> 'The teacher whose students have contacted me'

> *O livro <u>cuja</u> capa está rasgada*   **Wr**
> 'The book the cover of which is torn'

As can be seen in the above examples, *cujo* agrees in number and gender with the following nominal.

Unlike English *whose,* *cujo* cannot be used as an interrogative; instead, Portuguese uses *de quem:*

> *<u>De quem</u> é esse livro?*
> 'Whose is this book?'

For the way to express *whose* in the spoken language, see 36.2.3 below.

onde

Onde is used like English *where,* to indicate location:

> *O apartamento <u>onde</u> o corpo foi encontrado*
> 'The apartment where the body was found'

Onde may be preceded by a preposition:

> *O sítio para <u>onde</u> você mandou as suas crianças*
> 'The country house you sent your children to [literally, the country house to where . . .]'

> *A cidade de <u>onde</u> a sua família veio*
> 'The city your family came from [literally, the city from where . . .]'

como

Como may be used as a relative when the antecedent denotes a manner, e.g.,

> *A maneira <u>como</u> ele me tratou*
> 'The way that he treated me'

> *O jeito <u>como</u> Dindinha fala*
> 'The way Dindinha speaks'

In these cases *como* corresponds to a sequence of a preposition + *o qual* and may be replaced by it (especially in writing):

> *A maneira <u>pela qual</u> ele me tratou*   **Wr**
>
> *O jeito <u>do qual</u> Dindinha fala*   **Wr**

In the spoken language, one finds *que* in these contexts:

> *A maneira <u>que</u> ele me tratou*   **SpBr**
>
> *O jeito <u>que</u> Dindinha fala*   **SpBr**

quem

Quem, unlike English *who* and Spanish *quien,* is used only in free relatives, that is, without an antecedent, unless it is preceded by a preposition (in which case it may have an antecedent or not):

> *Eu aprecio <u>quem</u> reconhece seus erros.*   [**free relative**]
> 'I value whoever recognizes his mistakes.'
>
> *O patrão <u>para quem</u> eu trabalho*   **Wr**   [**with preposition and antecedent**]
> 'The boss for whom I work'
>
> *Eu sei <u>com quem</u> você anda saindo.*   [**free, with preposition**]
> 'I know whom you are going out with.'

Clauses with *who* with an antecedent and no preposition have *que* or *o qual* in Portuguese:

> *O mecânico <u>que</u> consertou seu carro*
> 'The mechanic who fixed your car'

Quem can be translated as *who(m)* or *whoever,* according to the context.

o que

O que, like its English correlate *what,* most often occurs without an antecedent:

> *Guarde <u>o que</u> sobrar na geladeira.*
> 'Put what is left in the refrigerator.'

O que can have an antecedent when the latter is a whole clause, corresponding to English *which,* as in

Daniel chegou na hora, o que me surpreendeu.
'Daniel arrived on time, which surprised me.'

The antecedent of *o que* (the thing that surprised me) is the clause *Daniel chegou na hora* 'Daniel arrived on time.'

Tudo o que means 'everything (that)':

Tudo o que ela faz é bem feito.
'Everything she does is well done.'

36.2.3 Relative clauses in the spoken language

Just as English speakers try to avoid sequences like *with which, for whom,* and the like, Portuguese speakers avoid *de quem, para o qual,* and any construction in which a preposition precedes a relative pronoun. There are alternate constructions for preposition + relative pronoun in spoken Brazilian. Take the example

O patrão para quem eu trabalho   **Wr**
'The boss for whom I work'

The way to avoid the preposition before the relative pronoun is to leave the preposition in its normal place (here, after the verb), with a personal pronoun after it; the relative pronoun in this case is simply *que:*

O patrão que eu trabalho para ele   **SpBr**
'The boss I work for [literally, the boss that I work for him]'

The Portuguese solution is similar to the English one; the main difference is that English leaves the preposition dangling at the end of the sentence, whereas Portuguese adds a personal pronoun.

Whose is normally expressed by the same construction described above, with the preposition *de:*

O motorista que eu estou namorando com a irmã dele   **SpBr**
'The driver whose sister I am dating [literally, the driver that I am dating his sister]'

This turn replaces the pronoun *cujo* 'whose,' which is so rare nowadays that many speakers have some trouble understanding it.

Keeping the preposition in the above sentences is important because otherwise ambiguity might result. For instance,

O médico que eu trabalho <u>com ele</u>   **SpBr**
'The physician I work with'

Here we need the preposition because we might have, say, *para:*

O médico que eu trabalho <u>para</u> ele   **SpBr**
'The physician I work for'

The preposition (with its following pronoun) may be omitted if context or the features of the verb are sufficient to avoid ambiguity:

A rua que eu moro   **SpBr**
'The street I live (on)'

O livro que eu te falei é aquele amarelo ali.   **SpBr**
'The book I spoke to you (about) is that yellow one.'

In these cases, it is also possible to keep the preposition plus the pronoun, as a less favored alternative:

A rua que eu moro <u>nela</u>   **SpBr**
O livro que eu te falei <u>dele</u> é aquele amarelo ali.   **SpBr**

37

Conjunctions and Coordinators

Conjunctions are a traditional word-class that might more adequately be distinguished into two classes: conjunctions proper and coordinators. Conjunctions have the function of turning a clause into a noun phrase or an adverbial phrase; they thus join two clauses by subordinating one to the other—that is, by causing one of the clauses to be part of the other. For instance, *que* 'that' when preceding a clause makes up a noun phrase—which, like all noun phrases, can be a subject or an object or it can come after a preposition:

> *Ninguém sabe que a fazenda foi vendida.*
> 'Nobody knows that the farm was sold.'

Here, *que a fazenda foi vendida* (*que* + a clause) is the direct object of *sabe* 'knows.' And in

> *Você só vai sair quando eu deixar.* — future subjunctive
> 'You'll leave only when I let (you).'

quando eu deixar is an adverbial phrase, adding a circumstance of time to the sentence.

Coordinators also join sentences, but in a different way: they do not subordinate one to the other, but rather express some kind of semantic relationship while keeping the two sentences syntactically independent—that is, none of them is a term of the other. The most typical coordinator is *e* 'and,' e.g.,

Ela me chamou e eu fui.
'She called me and I went (there).'

Although the sequence expresses a temporal relationship (I went there after she called me), this is not reflected in the syntax: *eu fui* has no syntactic function inside the first sentence.

In addition, unlike conjunctions, coordinators also join nonsentential elements, like noun phrases (*João e Maria* 'João and Maria'), nominals (*forte e corajoso* 'strong and brave'), adverbials (*hoje e amanhã* 'today and tomorrow'), etc. And some coordinators can also join independent sentences, often separated by a period, e.g.,

Ninguém se ofereceu para me ajudar. Entretanto, vou tentar.
'No one offered to help me. However, I am going to try.'

The main characteristic of coordinators (when joining phrases or clauses) is that they join constituents **of the same class,** placing them side by side; and the resulting sequence belongs to the **same class** as each of the conjoined elements. Thus, *João e Maria* is itself a noun phrase, and *hoje e amanhã* behaves like an adverbial.

There are no major problems connected with learning coordinators or conjunctions, as their grammatical behavior is very similar in Portuguese and in English. The one complication is that conjunctions often require a particular mood for the verb they govern (see chapter 15). In what follows, accordingly, I list the main coordinators and conjunctions, with examples and occasional notes.

37.1 Coordinators

37.1.1 Simple coordinators

e 'and'

João e Maria
'João and Maria'

César chegou e venceu.
'César came and won.'

mas 'but'

Telefonei mas você não estava.
'(I) called but you were not (home).'

For the use of *mas* as a reinforcement in exclamative sentences, see 31.2.

ou 'or'

> *Por favor, compre um litro de leite <u>ou</u> uma lata de leite em pó.*
> 'Please buy a liter of milk or a can of powdered milk.'

nem 'neither, nor'
Portuguese *nem* is used for both English *neither* and *nor:*

> <u>*Nem*</u> *você <u>nem</u> sua quadrilha vão conseguir nada por aqui.*
> 'Neither you nor your gang are going to get anything around here.'
>
> *jendille · quadrilla*

Nem is also used as a sort of emphatic negative:

> *Ela <u>nem</u> me cumprimentou.*
> 'She didn't even greet me.'

> — *Você quer trabalhar comigo?*
> —<u>*Nem*</u> *! . . .* [pronounced long, with a rising intonation]
> "Do you want to work with me?"
> "No way!"

porém 'however, but'
Porém is a more emphatic form of *mas* 'but,' used preferably in writing; in the older language it could not occur at the beginning of a clause, but nowadays this restriction has disappeared:

> *Chamei, toquei a campainha, <u>porém</u> ninguém respondeu.*   **Wr**
> '(I) called, (I) rang the bell, but no one answered.'

Todavia, contudo, no entanto are near synonyms of **porém;** they are little used in the spoken language.

pois means 'since' in a causal sense:

> *Ela teve que ir sozinha, <u>pois</u> ninguém se prontificou a acompanhá-la.*   **Wr**
> 'She had to go alone, since no one offered to escort her.'

assim 'thus'

Sp. Así que

> *O vizinho está viajando. <u>Assim</u>, podemos fazer barulho à vontade.*
> 'The neighbor is out of town. Thus, we can make noise to our heart's content.'

logo 'therefore'
Logo is the prototypical coordinator used to introduce logical and mathematical conclusions, e.g.,

> *Penso, <u>logo</u> existo.*
> '(I) think, therefore (I) am.'

portanto	'therefore,'	***por conseguinte***	'therefore'
entretanto	'however'		
no entanto	'nevertheless'		
não obstante	'despite'		
apesar disso	'in spite of that'		

    Coordinated sentences can be separated by punctuation marks, including full stops; with some coordinators this is more common than with others. With *assim, apesar disso, entretanto, no entanto, todavia, portanto, por conseguinte,* and *não obstante* separation is normal:

> *Seu salário aumentou. <u>Portanto</u>, espera-se que você trabalhe mais.*
> 'Your salary was raised. Therefore, you are expected to work harder.'

With other coordinators the possibility of separation by a full stop varies; it occurs sometimes with *e* 'and,' but this is felt to be in poor taste by many.

37.1.2 Paired coordinators

Some coordinators come in pairs and are preposed to each of the coordinated elements, e.g.,

> *Essa menina <u>não só</u> toca <u>como também</u> dança.*
> 'This girl not only plays but (she) also dances.'

The most important paired coordinators are the following:

não só . . . mas também / não só . . . mas ainda   'not only . . . but also'
ou . . . ou   'either . . . or'

> *<u>Ou</u> você se comporta <u>ou</u> eu te mando para o diretor.*
> 'Either you behave or I'll send you to the director.'

quer . . . quer   'whether . . . or' [**used with the subjunctive**]
(Some speakers also use *quer . . . ou,* with the same meaning.)

> *Quer chova quer faça sol, o jogo vai prosseguir.*
> 'Whether it rains or the sun shines, the game will go on.'

> *Vamos sair mais cedo, quer o chefe permita quer não.*
> 'We are leaving earlier, whether or not the boss permits it.'

seja . . . seja 'be it . . . or'
(*Seja . . . ou* is used by some speakers.)

> *Eu sempre como bem, seja em casa seja em algum restaurante.*
> 'I always eat well, be it at home or in some restaurant.'

ora . . . ora 'sometimes . . . sometimes'

> *Ela ora trabalha como louca, ora fica só vendo televisão.*
> 'She sometimes works like mad, sometimes just watches TV.'

The following paired coordinators are used in comparative structures:

tão . . . como / tão . . . quanto 'as . . . as'

> *Ele é tão forte quanto você.*
> 'He is as strong as you.'

Quanto is the more usual option for the second part of the coordinator.

tanto quanto 'as much as'
In this case, as in English, the two parts are contiguous:

> *Minha mulher trabalha tanto quanto eu.*
> 'My wife works as much as I (do).'

quanto mais . . . mais	'the more . . . the more'
quanto menos . . . menos	'the less . . . the less'
quanto mais . . . menos	'the more . . . the less'
quanto menos . . . mais	'the less . . . the more'

> *Quanto mais eu trabalho, menos realizo.*
> 'The more I work, the less (I) accomplish.'

37.2 Conjunctions

Conjunctions may be classified according to the kind of constituent they help construct: noun phrase–building conjunctions (traditionally called **integrating conjunctions)** and adverbial phrase–building conjunctions (**adverbial conjunctions**). Conjunctions govern the **mood** of the verb in the introduced clause; in the following lists, I give in brackets the mood(s) required by each conjunction; for details, especially in cases of conjunctions that allow both moods, see chapter 15.

37.2.1 NP-building conjunctions

que 'that' [**subjunctive or indicative**]
The prototypical noun phrase–building conjunction is *que* 'that':

> *A imprensa descobriu que a princesa pretende casar com um fotógrafo.*
> 'The press found out that the princess intends to marry a photographer.'

Que as an integrating conjunction is very similar in use to English *that;* the only observation to be made is that *que,* unlike *that,* cannot be omitted:

> *Eu acho que ele está bêbado.*
> 'I think he is drunk.'

se 'if, whether' [**subjunctive or indicative**]
Se is used with negated verbs, with inherently negative verbs like *ignorar* 'not to know,' or with verbs expressing a question, when the truth of the subordinate clause is questioned, not asserted:

> *Perguntaram aí se você fica em casa de noite.*
> 'People have asked if you stay home at night.'

> *Ninguém sabe se o governador é honesto.*
> 'No one knows if the governor is honest.'

Here the speaker has no commitment as to the truth of the subordinate clause; compare the same sentence with *que,* where the truth of the subordinate is asserted:

> *Ninguém sabe que o governador é honesto.*
> 'No one knows that the governor is honest.'

In all these uses, *se* corresponds to English *if* or *whether.*

como 'that' [**indicative**]
Como is sometimes used as a synonym of *that* after certain verbs expressing a certainty on the part of the speaker:

Aposto <u>como</u> você não tem dinheiro.
'(I) bet that you have no money.'

37.2.2 Adverbial-building conjunctions

Most conjunctions are added to sentences in order to build adverbial phrases; accordingly, they express the several notions commonly found associated with adverbials: time, cause, mode, condition, etc. They do not present many problems, and in most cases an example is sufficient to illustrate their use. Most adverbial-building conjunctions require the indicative, *embora* 'although' and *caso* 'if' being the main exceptions. The most frequent ones are:

quando   'when' [**indicative**]

> *<u>Quando</u> ela termina esse serviço, sempre fica com os braços doendo.*
> 'When she finishes this job, she always has aching arms.'

enquanto   'while' [**indicative**]

> *Só posso ficar <u>enquanto</u> não escurecer.*
> '(I) can stay only while it doesn't get dark.'

porque   'because' [**indicative**]
Like English *because, porque* may express the cause of the event reported in the main clause, as in

> *Ele não tem emprego <u>porque</u> não procura.*
> 'He has no job because he doesn't look for (one).'

or the reason the speaker utters the main clause, as in

> *Está chovendo, <u>porque</u> o chão está todo molhado.*
> 'It must be raining, because the ground is all wet.'

In the latter case, the clause beginning with *porque* is usually preceded by a comma and can never appear at the beginning of the sentence.

embora   'although' [**subjunctive**]

> *<u>Embora</u> eles se amem, vivem brigando.*
> 'Although they love each other, they are always arguing.'

como 'as' [**indicative**]

> *Nenhum artista pinta <u>como</u> Vincent.*
> 'No artist paints as Vincent does.'

> *Ela agora vive <u>como</u> quer.*
> 'She now lives as she wishes.'

> *Você pode se vestir <u>como</u> quiser.*
> 'You can dress any way you please.'

—'since' [**indicative**]

> <u>*Como*</u> *vocês não me ajudaram, agora não vão comer.*
> 'Since you didn't help me, you won't eat now.'

se 'if ' [**indicative**]
Se—like English *if*—is mainly used to express a condition:

> *Você terá o emprego <u>se</u> defender a tese primeiro.*
> 'You'll have the job if you present your thesis first'

caso 'if' [**subjunctive**]
As we saw in chapter 15, *caso* is a synonym of *se* but requires a present or imperfect subjunctive:

> *Você terá o emprego <u>caso</u> defenda a tese primeiro.*
> 'You'll have the job if you present your thesis first.'

mal 'as soon as' [**indicative**]
Mal is used as a conjunction in the written language, in sentences like

> <u>*Mal*</u> *começou o concerto, o pianista se sentiu mal.*   **Wr**
> 'As soon as the concert began, the pianist felt unwell.'

37.2.3 Compound conjunctions

Many compound expressions function as conjunctions (all of the adverbial-building kind). Some are composed of a preposition followed by *que,* and these are listed in the next section; several other compound conjunctions are listed in section 37.2.3.2.

37.2.3.1 Conjunctions composed of preposition + que

These conjunctions have the same meaning as the prepositions they are composed of; they represent the particular case in which the noun phrase that always follows a preposition is composed of *que* plus a clause and usually require the subjunctive in the subordinate clause. For instance,

> *O inimigo entrou na cidade sem que ninguém o atacasse.*
> 'The enemy entered the city without anyone attacking him.'

> *Deixe ferver até que a água se reduza à metade.*
> 'Let boil until the water reduces to half.'

> *Trabalho para que meus filhos tenham uma vida boa.*
> '(I) work so that my children have a good life.'

With *desde que* the subjunctive is used in the meaning 'provided that'; in the temporal meaning 'since,' the indicative is used:

> *Podemos terminar isso rapidamente, desde que todos colaborem.*
> **subjunctive**
> 'We can finish this quickly, provided that everyone collaborates.'

> *A região está em decadência desde que as minas de ouro se esgotaram.*
> **indicative**
> 'The region is deteriorating since the gold mines gave out.'

37.2.3.2 Other compound conjunctions

There are other compound conjunctions, some of them (but not all) formed with an adverb + *que;* below is a list of the most frequent, with some examples:

uma vez que 'as soon as' [**subjunctive**]; 'as long as' [**indicative**]

> *Uma vez que vocês terminem o almoço, podemos sair.*
> 'As soon as you finish lunch, we'll be able to leave.'

> *Uma vez que ninguém se apresenta, eu mesmo tenho que ir.*
> 'As long as nobody volunteers, I have to go myself.'

Here, the conjunction has a different meaning according to the mood employed.

assim que 'as soon as' [**subjunctive or indicative**]

> *Fomos para a praia assim que acabou de chover.*
> 'We went to the beach as soon as it stopped raining.'

> *Íamos para a praia __assim que__ acabasse de chover.*
> 'id.'

sempre que   'whenever' [**subjunctive or indicative**]

> *__Sempre que__ Betânia cantava, eu chorava.*
> 'Whenever Betânia sang, I cried.'

> *__Sempre que__ Betânia cantasse, eu chorava.*
> 'id.'

With *assim que* and *sempre que* the mood employed causes a change in meaning, which the English glosses do not show. With the indicative, it is understood that the event described in the subordinate clause did (or does) in fact happen, but with the subjunctive it is understood only as a condition for the event described in the main clause. For instance, the first sentence with *sempre que* (with the indicative) means that Betânia did sing on several occasions; the second sentence (with the subjunctive) means that if Betânia sang I would cry, but there is no commitment as to any specific occasions in which this did happen.

se bem que   'even though' [**subjunctive or indicative**]
With *se bem que* the two moods are used interchangeably, without any semantic difference:

> *Vamos usar o meu carro, __se bem que__ ele **continua** falhando.*   [**indicative**]
> *Vamos usar o meu carro, __se bem que__ ele **continue** falhando.*   [**subjunctive**]
> 'We'll use my car, even though it is still misfiring.'

mesmo que   'even if' [**subjunctive**]

> *__Mesmo que__ chova, o jogo sempre se realiza.*
> 'Even if it rains, the game always takes place.'

mesmo se   'even if' [**indicative**]

> *__Mesmo se__ chove, o jogo sempre se realiza.*
> 'id.'

As we can see, *mesmo que* and *mesmo se* are synonymous; but *mesmo que* is used with the subjunctive and *mesmo se* with the indicative.

Other important compound conjunctions are as follows:

ainda que	'even if'	[**subjunctive**]
a menos que	'unless'	[**subjunctive**]

de modo que	'in such a way that'	**[subjunctive]**
de maneira que	'in such a way that'	**[subjunctive]**
de forma que	'in such a way that'	**[subjunctive]**
logo que	'as soon as'	**[subjunctive]**
já que	'since [causal]'	**[indicative]**
como se	'as if'	**[subjunctive]**
a fim de que	'in order to'	**[subjunctive]**

37.2.4 Polyvalent *que*

The word *que* is a versatile item: it can be an interrogative/exclamatory, a relative pronoun, or a conjunction. It also occurs in some environments in which its analysis is not very clear. I list below some examples of such uses, and when possible I suggest an analysis; as will be seen, several of these uses of *que* are specific to the spoken language.

—In some cases, *que* functions as a normal conjunction, and it may substitute for *porque* 'because,' as in

> *Volta amanhã que hoje eu não tenho tempo.*   **SpBr**
> 'Come back tomorrow, because I have no time today.'

or for *senão* 'or else,' as in

> *Não faz isso que eu te dou uma palmada.*   **SpBr**
> 'Don't do that, or else I'll slap you.'

—In other cases *que* seems to be what is left of a topicalizing *ser . . . que* (see chapter 39), after deletion of the first part:

> *Hoje que eu consegui falar com ela.*   **SpBr**
> '(It was) today that I managed to talk to her.'

—*Que* is also used to reinforce an interrogatory or exclamatory element:

> *Por que que eu não posso comer uma banana?*   **SpBr**
> 'Why can't I eat a banana?'

In cases with two consecutive *que*'s, the first one is pronounced ['ke], stressed, and the second one is pronounced [ki], unstressed.

> *Que carro que o Ricardo tem!*   **SpBr**
> 'What a car Ricardo has!'

—*Que* sometimes introduces what looks like a reduced objective clause:

Eles disseram que não.
'They said (that) no.'

Here *não* may be interpreted as an anaphorically reduced form of a previously mentioned clause. Similarly, we have

Eles disseram que sim / que nunca / que de jeito nenhum.
'They said (that) yes / never   / no way.'

—*Que* is also used in some other structures, which I am unable to analyze even tentatively:

Ela canta que dá gosto.   **SpBr**
'She sings (so well that) it is good to hear.'

Faz quase um mês que não chove.
'It hasn't rained for almost a month.'

38

Pronominalization and Anaphora

38.1 Anaphora, deixis, ellipsis, and pro-forms

All languages have ways of making utterances more economical, avoiding excessive repetition—like, for instance, the use of personal pronouns and the omission of easily recoverable material. The resources used in Portuguese are very similar to those used in English; but there are differences in detail. I describe them in this chapter, but first I shall define a few technical terms.

Anaphora is the general term covering the phenomenon of omission of an element, or its reduction to a pronoun, when it is recoverable from the linguistic context. Thus, we say in English

The old man decided to close the shop.

Here *the old man* is the subject of *decided; close* has no overt subject, but we understand that it too refers to the old man. The subjectless verb is in a syntactic position such that the rules of the language allow a receptor to understand its subject as being identical to the subject of the preceding verb. This is called an **anaphoric context.**

A different case is shown by

Sheila found out that I hate her.

The object of *hate* is understood to be 'Sheila,' but the word is not present after the verb; rather, we find a pronoun, *her*. Here, again, the language provides rules to recover the intended referent, which is overtly mentioned in the main sentence.

Portuguese is similar to English as regards the examples just given; thus, we say

O velho resolveu fechar a loja.
'The old man decided to close the shop.'

Sheila descobriu que eu a odeio.	**Wr**
Sheila descobriu que eu odeio ela.	**SpBr**
'Sheila found out that I hate her.'	

The absence of subject for *fechar* 'to close,' and the presence of the pronoun *a* 'her' (*ela* in the spoken version) are analogous to the use of the corresponding resources in English.

Deixis is basically the same phenomenon as anaphora, with one difference: the basis for recovering the omitted or reduced element is not in the text, but in the extralinguistic context. For instance, we may say

Ela me odeia.
'She hates me.'

while at the same time pointing at Sheila, thus making clear what the reference of the pronoun *ela* is. The linguistic resources used for expressing deixis are also used for anaphora.[1]

Note

[1]If we except some lexical items that are normally deictic, such as *eu* 'I,' which refers to whoever is speaking at the moment, or *hoje* 'today,' which refers to the present day, etc.

Ellipsis is one of the two main ways to signal anaphoras, and means the omission of recoverable elements in particular contexts; we saw an example in the sentence

O velho resolveu fechar a loja.
'The old man decided to close the shop.'

where the subject of *fechar* 'to close' is understood to be *o velho* 'the old man,' but is omitted.

Pro-forms are special items endowed with shifting reference, used to recover other elements in anaphoric contexts; pro-forms are the second major way of signaling anaphoras. Some pronouns are also pro-forms,[1] as are some verbs like English *to do* and Portuguese *fazer* in

> *O governo prometeu eliminar a corrupção, mas não o fez.*　　　　　**Wr**
> 'The government promised to wipe out corruption, but <u>did not</u>.'

Note

[1]And some are not. From this point of view, as from several others, words traditionally called pronouns do not constitute a real grammatical class; they are rather a bunch of items that grammarians have had trouble classifying.

38.2 Use of personal pronouns

Personal pronouns are used in very similar ways in English and Portuguese; here we only need to be concerned with the few points in which the two languages differ.

Personal pronouns have a deictic use, as seen above in connection with the sentence

> *Ela me odeia.*
> 'She hates me.'

used by a speaker who at the same time points at Sheila. In this particular English and Portuguese are identical, and no special comment is necessary.

There is also an anaphoric use of personal pronouns, as instanced in

> <u>*Sheila*</u> *descobriu que Márcia <u>a</u> odeia.*　　　　**Wr**
> 'Sheila found out that Márcia hates her.'

in which the two underlined elements (*Sheila* and *a*) refer to the same person. Among anaphoric personal pronouns, we may distinguish **reflexives** and **nonreflexives.** In the above sentence, *a* is nonreflexive. We may substitute *se,* which is a reflexive, with a corresponding change in reference:

> *Sheila descobriu que <u>Márcia</u> <u>se</u> odeia.*
> 'Sheila found out that Márcia hates herself.'

Now, as shown in the gloss, the pronoun (*se*) refers to Márcia, not to Sheila. This has to do with the property of reflexives to refer to a noun phrase in the same clause, whereas a non-reflexive typically refers to a noun phrase in another clause.[1]

Note

**[1]This is a simplification, but there is no real need to go into the details of the question of pronominal reference here, since the two languages are virtually identical in this respect.

In what follows I discuss some details of the use of nonreflexive pronouns, in those points where English and Portuguese differ, or where spoken Brazilian differs from standard written Portuguese.

38.2.1 Extensive use of the subject pronoun in Portuguese

We have already seen (section 35.5) that in Portuguese the subject pronoun is frequently omitted, so that the verb may appear without an overt subject in many cases where English requires a pronoun. On the other hand, there is a tendency in the spoken language to use the subject pronoun in most cases, even in contexts in which the written language usually avoids it. This happens, for instance, in sequences of coordinated sentences, e.g.,

> *Zé vendeu o carro, <u>ele</u> vendeu o lote, e <u>ele</u> queria vender até a mobília.*
> 'Zé sold the car, he sold the lot, and he tried to sell even the furniture.'

The same also happens with subordinate clauses:

> *Eu acho que <u>eu</u> vou desmaiar.*
> 'I think that I am going to faint.'

> *Carvalho contratou o rapaz que <u>ele</u> achava mais competente.*
> 'Carvalho hired the young man whom he found most competent.'

> *O lutador desistiu quando <u>ele</u> viu o tamanho do adversário.*
> 'The fighter gave up when he saw the size of the opponent.'

In presentative sentences (that is, those that introduce the existence of something and often begin with *eu tenho* 'I have . . . ,' or *tem . . .* 'there is . . .') including a relative construction, a subject pronoun often follows the relative pronoun, even when the latter is itself a subject:

Eu tenho uma amiga que <u>ela</u> só veste de branco.   **SpBr**
'I have a friend who (she) only dresses in white.'

In all these cases the pronoun in question is optional but very frequent.

38.2.2 Ambiguous pronouns

In some cases the presence of the pronoun causes ambiguity, so that ellipsis is preferred:

A mãe disse à filha que <u>ela</u> estava com febre.
'The mother told her daughter that she had a fever.'

Here there is no way of knowing who had the fever, the mother or the daughter. But if the pronoun is omitted, reference is unambiguously to the mother:

A mãe disse à filha que estava com febre.
'The mother told her daughter that she (the mother) had a fever.'

This happens when there are two noun phrases in the main clause that may be the antecedent of the pronoun (in the above sentences, *a mãe* 'the mother' and *a filha* 'the daughter'). Ellipsis causes the verb to refer to the **subject of the main clause,** while the pronoun can refer to either candidate.

38.2.3 Resumptive pronoun

The pronoun *o* can be used to represent the complement of a verb; this use is most frequent with complements of *ser* 'to be' and of anaphoric *fazer* 'to do':

Ele declarou ser solteiro, mas não <u>o</u> era.   **Wr**
'He stated that he was single, but he was not (it).'

O governo prometeu eliminar a corrupção, mas não <u>o</u> fez.   **Wr**
'The government promised to wipe out corruption, but didn't do it.'

This use is confined to the written language. In more informal language (both written and spoken) one may repeat the verb or simply omit it in the second member of the sentence:

Ele declarou ser solteiro, mas não era.
'He stated that he was single, but he was not.'

O governo prometeu eliminar a corrupção, mas não eliminou.
'The government promised to wipe out corruption, but didn't do it.'

38.3 Ellipsis in parallel structures

38.3.1 Missing verbs and qualificatives

When two coordinated sentences have the same verb, the second is frequently omitted, especially in the written language:

> *Meu irmão adora mamão, e minha tia melancia* [= . . . *adora melancia*].
> 'My brother likes papaya, and my aunt, watermelon.'

Since the same process occurs in English, no explanations are needed. It may be noted, though, that in the spoken language it is more usual *not* to omit the second verb, thus keeping to the general tendency of colloquial Portuguese toward more redundant ways of expression.

Também 'also, too' is used when the verb and at least one of its complements are repeated; in these cases it is possible just to add *também,* without omissions; or to omit the complement; or to omit the complement and the verb:

> *O vizinho planta rosas e eu planto rosas também.*
> 'The neighbor grows roses and I grow roses too.'

This sentence can be reduced in the following ways:

> *O vizinho planta rosas e eu planto também.*
> 'The neighbor grows roses and I grow (them) too.'
>
> *O vizinho planta rosas e eu também.*
> 'The neighbor grows roses and I (do) too.'

The two last sentences illustrate two points in which Portuguese differs from English.

Missing qualificatives are often represented in English by *so;* in Portuguese they are left unrepresented, e.g.,

> *—Seu pai está preocupado?*
> *—Muito.*
> "Is your father worried?"
> "Very much <u>so</u>."

The items *sim* 'yes' and *não* 'no' can also be used anaphorically in contexts in which English has *so* or a negative:

—*Seu pai está preocupado?*
—*Talvez <u>sim</u>. / Talvez <u>não</u>.*
"Is your father worried?"
"Perhaps (so)." / "Perhaps not."

38.3.2 Omission of the object

In the sentence just examined,

O vizinho planta rosas e eu planto também.
'The neighbor grows roses and I grow (them) too.'

the object of the second verb is omitted, whereas in English a pronoun is required: . . . *e eu planto também*' . . . and I grow *them* too.' This is typical of Portuguese, which allows omission of the object in many cases, for example,

Alaíde picou o pato e pôs Ø na panela.[1]
'Alaíde chopped up the duck and put (it) in the pan.'

Note

[1] I indicate the location of the ellipsis with 'Ø'.

—*Alguém me chamou?*
—*Eu não ouvi Ø.*
"Did someone call me?
"I didn't hear (anyone)."

Ele vive começando livros, mas nunca termina Ø.
'He is always starting books, but never finishes (them).'

38.3.3 *Fazer* as a pro-form

The sentence

O vizinho planta rosas e eu Ø também.
'The neighbor grows roses and I (do) too.'

shows that Portuguese lacks a general anaphoric verb like English *to do* and has resource to ellipsis in its stead.

There is an anaphoric verb, *fazer* 'to do,' but it is used only in very restricted environments. *Fazer* is used anaphorically only to refer to a whole verb phrase (that is, a verb plus its complements), as in

> *O governo prometeu combater o desemprego, mas não **o** fez.*   **Wr**
> 'The government promised to fight unemployment, but <u>didn't</u> do it.'

Here we may note that (a) *fazer* occurs with a pronominal object, *o* (in the spoken language, *isso* 'this'); (b) *o fez* refers to a whole verb phrase, namely, *combater o desemprego*.
Fazer corresponds also to *do so* in affirmative sentences, e.g.,

> *O governo prometeu combater o desemprego, e **o** fez.*   **Wr**
> 'The government promised to fight unemployment, and <u>did so</u>.'

Another example of the anaphoric use of *fazer* is

> *A professora prometeu anular a prova, e foi **o** que ela fez.*
> 'The teacher promised to annul the test, and that was what she did.'

The required object is present as *o que;* we might say as well

> *A professora prometeu anular a prova, e foi **isso** que ela fez.*
> 'id.'

38.3.4 Comparatives

In comparative structures English often repeats a verb whereas Portuguese prefers ellipsis, e.g.,

> *O Brasil é mais montanhoso do que o Canadá.*
> 'Brazil is more mountainous than Canada (is).'

In this construction the verb is never repeated in Portuguese; sentences like

> * *O Brasil é mais montanhoso do que o Canadá é.*

are found only in poor translations from English.

38.4 Lexical anaphora

Finally, Portuguese uses certain nonpronominal lexical items as anaphoric elements. Their English counterparts are such words as *thing, stuff, whatchamacallit, guy,* and the like. These items, unlike pronouns, are semantically restricted in various ways, so that they cannot be substituted for any noun phrase as pronouns like *they* can. The item *coisa* 'thing' is of course the most common and also the least specific of all lexical anaphorics. In the spoken language it gives rise to a verbal derivative, *coisar* 'to do something,' and is also used as a modifier:

> *Esse menino é meio coisa.*
> 'This boy is rather I-don't-know-what.'

Other items used anaphorically are the following:

negócio	'thing'	**SpBr**
troço, treco	'thing'	**SpBr**
trem	'thing'	**SpBr** (the use of *trem* is said to be a shibboleth denouncing speakers from Minas Gerais)
como-é-que-chama	'whatchamacallit'	**SpBr**
cara	'guy'	**SpBr**
dona	'woman'	**SpBr**
gata	'gal'	**SpBr**

and many others; as can be seen, this is a typical resource of the spoken language. These words pattern like normal nominals (they are preceded by articles, may be modified, etc.), but from a semantic point of view they are anaphoric.

VII The Discourse

39

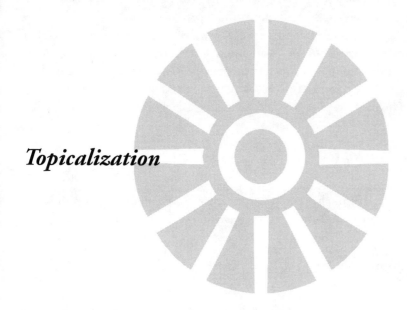

39.1 Topic and topic marking

The **topic** is an element that has the function of delimiting the main theme of an utterance. It may also have, concomitantly, a purely syntactic function (such as object, subject, etc.), but, as we will see, this is not a necessary feature. The topic has been described as "the peg on which the utterance is hung," which may be a little vague but gives us an idea to start with. In Portuguese, as in English, it is typically marked by being placed at the head of the utterance, e.g.,

> <u>*Essa cerveja*</u> *ninguém vai beber.*
> 'This beer nobody is going to drink.'

The object *essa cerveja* 'this beer' is carried to the head of the sentence, and the resulting effect is something like saying 'as for this beer . . . ' or 'concerning this beer . . . '—an instruction to the receptor to understand what follows as a comment on the beer in question. Compare the above sentence with the following:

> *Ninguém vai beber* <u>*essa cerveja*</u>.
> 'Nobody is going to drink this beer.'

Topicalization

The two versions mean the same in terms of information; what changes is the way the information is presented. In the first version, with *essa cerveja* at the head of the utterance, it is presented as a comment on a privileged element (the beer); in the second version, with *essa cerveja* at the end, it is presented neutrally, without privileging any of the terms. This is a very frequent phenomenon in English, and it is even more important in Portuguese, although most grammars give it little or no attention. One of the ways to mark the topic in Portuguese, seen in the examples above, is to prepose the topicalized element. But there are several other ways to do it, some of them common to speaking and writing, some specific to the spoken language.

39.2 Syntactic topics

The topic may be marked through syntactic constructions of the traditional kind, among which the most important are **left-dislocation, passive,** and the use of **cleft sentences.**

39.2.1 Left-dislocation

Left-dislocation is simply the placement of the topicalized element at the head of the sentence, as we saw in the examples given in the previous section. Portuguese is very liberal as to the major terms of the clause that may be preposed, and only the verbal elements (main verb, auxiliary, modals) and the predicative cannot be dislocated at all. Some examples follow:

O Guilherme nós pegamos no centro da cidade.   [**direct object**]
'Guilherme we picked up downtown.'

Para você eu faria qualquer coisa.   [**indirect object**]
'For you I'd do anything.'

Inteligente ele é, sem dúvida.   [**subjective complement**]
'Intelligent he is, without doubt.'

No Ceará a gente comprou umas rendas lindas.   [**adverbial adjunct**]
'In Ceará we bought some beautiful lacework.'

For most speakers, the predicative (see definition in chapter 28) cannot be dislocated; accordingly, the following sentence is usually rejected:

* *Um completo idiota Maria considera seu marido.*   [**predicative**]
'Maria considers her husband a complete fool.'

Even elements internal to noun phrases can be topicalized:

> *Dessa menina* <u>*eu conheci a mãe e o pai.*</u> [**modifier**]
> 'I met this girl's mother and father [literally, Of this girl I met the mother and the father].'

39.2.2 Passive

One of the functions of passive sentences is, as we saw in chapter 21, to omit the agent in certain cases. Another is to mark the patient as the topic:

> <u>*Dona Eulália*</u> *foi homenageada pelos membros do clube.*
> 'Dona Eulália was honored by the members of the club.'

Here one understands that the utterance is primarily motivated by the desire to say something about Dona Eulália—not, say, about the members of the club.

39.2.3 Cleft sentences

Cleft sentences are formed by means of a form of the verb *ser* 'to be' plus a relative pronoun. In Portuguese as in English, cleft sentences come in two varieties; in the first, *ser* and the relative bracket the topicalized element:

> **Foi** <u>*a professora*</u> **que** *mandou trancar a sala.*
> '(It) was <u>the teacher</u> who ordered the room to be locked.'

In the second variety (usually called **pseudo-cleft**), the relative comes first, and the sequence of *ser* plus the topicalized element occurs at the end of the sentence:

> **Quem** *mandou trancar a sala* **foi** <u>*a professora*</u>.
> 'Who ordered the room to be locked was <u>the teacher</u>.'

In pseudo-cleft sentences the relative has no antecedent, which explains why *quem* is used when referring to a person (see chapter 36 on the use of "free" relatives). Since these two constructions exist in a parallel form in English, they present no special learning problems to the English-speaking student.

The pseudo-cleft construction can be used to topicalize a verb phrase. For this, one uses the pro-form *fazer,* according to the following model:

O que *ele fez* **foi** <u>*limpar a cozinha*</u>.
'What he did was to clean the kitchen.'

As in English, the topicalized verb is in the infinitive.

39.3 Discursive topics

So far we have examined constructions with close correspondents in English. But spoken Portuguese also marks topics in very peculiar ways, unlike anything in standard English; such constructions are, moreover, extremely frequent in spontaneous speech, so that their acquisition is essential to enable the student to speak in a natural and idiomatic manner. And, since they practically never occur in writing, they are not included in traditional grammatical descriptions. Here is an example:[1]

> (**EP**) <u>*Essa bolsa aberta*</u>, *alguém podia te roubar a carteira.*   **SpBr**
> '[literally,   <u>That open purse</u>, someone might steal your wallet.]'

Note

[1]A few of the examples in this section were gathered by Eunice Pontes and published in her book on the topic in spoken Brazilian Portuguese (Pontes 1987); her examples, sometimes slightly adapted, are marked with (**EP**). In the examples I am separating the topic from the rest of the utterance with a comma; there is no established tradition on punctuation for these structures, since they are rare in the written language. The translations, given between brackets, are very literal, and may not sound like good English.

The utterance is composed of two main portions:

(a) the topic, announcing the main theme of the discourse; and
(b) a complete sentence.

Formally speaking, this is the typical structure of most topicalized utterances of the kind we are examining; other examples are

> <u>*Os meninos*</u>, *a gente vai telefonar para eles agora mesmo.*   **SpBr**
> '[literally, The boys, we'll call them right now.]'

No Ceará, lá a gente compra umas rendas lindas.　　　　**SpBr**
'[literally, In Ceará, there one buys some beautiful lacework.]'

<u>*A Beatriz*</u>, *ela viajou para a Europa.*　　　　**SpBr**[1]
'[literally, Beatriz, she traveled to Europe.]'

Note

**[1]This last example can also be analyzed as a case of topicalized subject, with an obligatory resumptive pronoun (*ela*). This kind of topicalization of a subject is very frequent in the spoken language.

In these examples the sentence contains a pronoun (*eles, ela*) which refers back to the topic. This is not always the case, though:

<u>*O shopping Del Rey*</u>, *você já foi na Casa Bahia?*　　　　**SpBr**
'[literally, (The) Del Rey Mall, have you already been to Casa Bahia?]'

Here the topic simply delimits an area, and it is understood that Casa Bahia is a store in that shopping mall. See also

(**EP**) <u>*Essa minha barriga*</u>, *só jejum.*　　　　**SpBr**
'[literally, This potbelly of mine, only fasting.]'

The semantic connection between the topic and the sentence can be very loose. Sometimes the topic serves as a way to ensure continuity within the dialogue. Suppose someone mentions the president in some context; then someone else may reply

<u>*Esse presidente*</u>, *o imposto está cada vez mais alto.*　　　　**SpBr**
'[literally, This president, taxes are getting higher and higher.]'

On the other hand, the topic often corresponds to an element that would be preceded by a preposition in a more "regular" sentence (but the preposition does not occur):

<u>*Illinois*</u>, *tornado é muito comum.*　　　　**SpBr**
'[literally, Illinois, tornadoes are very common.]'

<u>*Os meninos pequenos*</u>, *a mãe vai ter que vir buscar.*　　　　**SpBr**
'[literally, The small children, the mother will have to pick them up.]'

(**EP**) *O Márcio, pifou o freio de mão do carro.*   **SpBr**
'[literally, Márcio, the hand brake of the car broke down.]'

The function of the topic in all cases is to set up a context in which the rest of the utterance can be understood without difficulty. For instance, take the last utterance given: once established that we are speaking about Márcio, it would make no sense to start talking about someone else's car; therefore, the car mentioned in the sentence must be Márcio's car.

39.4 Comparing the two kinds of topics

Discursive topics, discussed in section 39.3, have no grammatical relationship with the verb: no agreement relation and no semantic restriction. And apparently any element may function as a topic, even the verb:

Dormir cedo, eu até mandei colocar cortina de blecaute.   **SpBr**
'[literally, Sleeping early, I even had blackout drapes installed.]'

In this they differ markedly from the syntactic topics covered in 39.2. For instance, in

O Guilherme, nós pegamos no centro da cidade.   [**direct object**]
'Guilherme we picked up downtown.'

there is a semantic relation between the verb and the (syntactic) topic, that is, the topic is understood as the patient of the action expressed by the verb. This conditions the meaning of the verb (*pegamos* 'we picked up'); if we substitute *essa gripe* 'this flu' as a topic,

Essa gripe, nós pegamos no centro da cidade.
'This flu we caught downtown.'

the verb automatically changes its meaning, as seen in the gloss.

Nothing of the sort occurs with discursive topics, which are semantically and syntactically independent. In most cases there is simply no way to insert them into the sentence at all; they are an external element, essential as to meaning, but structurally extraneous to the sentence. Accordingly, they have never been analyzed in traditional terms—which does not mean that they cannot, or should not, be analyzed, of course; we just need new categories in order to account for them.

40

Discourse and Dialogue Markers

40.1 Discourse markers

Discourse markers are elements used to connect syntactically independent sentences or other portions of a text, either by expressing logical relations or simply by giving continuity to the discourse. Coordinators such as *e* 'and,' *mas* 'but,' *porém* 'however,' and so on typically perform the first of these functions, as in

> *Os diplomatas tentaram evitar a guerra. <u>Mas</u> não tiveram sucesso.*
> 'The diplomats tried to avoid the war. <u>But</u> they had no success.'

In this particular English and Portuguese are alike, and no extended comments are necessary.

The second function of discourse markers, that is, giving continuity to the discourse, is carried out by items that have also the functions of certain types of adverbs (and are usually so classified in traditional grammars), of which the most important are given below. These items normally connect sentences separated by periods or equivalent punctuation marks and also may serve as a way to tie a sentence uttered by one speaker to previous sentences uttered by another speaker.

afinal / afinal de contas   'after all'

> *Não vou ligar para ele. <u>Afinal</u>, nós nem nos falamos.*
> '(I) am not going to call him. After all, we are not on speaking terms.'

aí   'then'
Aí is very frequently used to mark sentences referring to sequential events:

> *O Bruno ficou sem ter o que dizer. <u>Aí</u>, ela virou as costas e foi embora.*
> 'Bruno couldn't say anything at all. Then, she turned her back and went away.'

> —*Cecília saiu do emprego.*
> —*E <u>aí</u>?*
> "Cecília quit her job."
> "And then?"

E daí (*de* + *aí*) is used for 'so what?', e.g.,

> —*Meu pai ganha mais do que o seu.*
> —*E <u>daí</u>?*
> "My father earns more than yours."
> "So what?"

assim   'thus, therefore'

> *Ninguém se apresentou para limpar o pátio. <u>Assim</u>, tive que ir eu mesmo.*
> 'Nobody volunteered to clean the patio. Therefore, I had to do it myself.'

em suma   'in short'

> *Ele era desonesto, dissimulado, incompetente. <u>Em suma</u>, um patife.*
> 'He was dishonest, sly, incompetent. In short, a scoundrel.'

enfim   'after all'

> *Ele recebeu o dinheiro e foi embora. <u>Enfim</u>, era isso que ele queria.*
> 'He got the money and went away. After all, that was what he wanted.'

então   'then, consequently'
Então was formerly used to express time (as in *now and then*), but nowadays it is used only to introduce a consequence; as a temporal expression it is replaced by *naquele tempo, naquela época* 'at that time.'

As portas estavam trancadas. <u>Então</u> tivemos que pular a janela.
'The doors were locked. Consequently, we had to enter through the window.'

melhor dizendo / ou melhor   'or rather'

Elza saiu do emprego. <u>Ou melhor</u>, foi despedida.
'Elza quit her job. Rather, (she) was fired.'

quer dizer   'that is, in other words'

O rapaz resolveu casar. <u>Quer dizer</u>, arranjou noiva rica.
'The young man decided to marry. In other words, he found a rich bride.'

vamos dizer / vamos dizer assim / digamos   'let us put it this way'

Trata-se de um problema, <u>vamos dizer</u>, que exige uma abordagem diplomática.
'It is a problem, let us put it this way, requiring a diplomatic approach.'

40.2 Dialogue markers

These elements are used by speakers and hearers in order to keep a conversation going by checking whether the communication channel is working properly or by keeping the other person from taking a turn in the conversation. We may distinguish several kinds of such markers, according to their function in the dialogue; thus, they may signal that

    a. the speaker has not yet finished
    b. the hearer is following the speaker
    c. the hearer is not following the speaker
    d. the speaker asks the hearer whether he or she is following
    e. the hearer emphatically agrees with the speaker

For each of these functions there are specialized items, of which the most important are listed below.

The speaker has not yet finished
These items fill the time needed for thought, and they keep the other person from taking the floor:

   é . . .   that is, a long [ɛ::][1]

This element corresponds to English *er . . .* and marks a moment taken for organizing one's thoughts, or just a hesitation:

Ele disse que trabalhava para . . . é . . . para a CEMIG.
'He said he was working for . . . er . . . for CEMIG.'

In the same function one sometimes finds *ã* . . . [ɐ̃ːː].

Note

[1]The spelling of several of these elements is problematical, since they are used primarily in the spoken language. *É . . .*, for instance, may be found as *ééé . . .*

quer dizer [kɛˈdze]
assim
bom
tipo assim   **SpBr**
né   **SpBr**

These items are used (apart from their use as discourse markers) as semantically empty elements, with the function of filling time and signaling that the speaker has not yet finished:

Elas queriam, <u>assim</u>, sair da festa logo no início.
'They wanted to, say, leave the party right at the beginning.'

The hearer is following the speaker
Besides such items as *claro* 'sure,' *certo* 'right,' *é . . .*, and the like, one may also use
arrã [ɐ̃ˈhɐ̃]

—Aí eu achei que tinha que tomar uma decisão.
—Arrã.
"Then I thought that I had to make up my mind."
"Hm."

sei   '(I) know'

The hearer is not following the speaker
In this case one may use
quê?
como?
como é?
como assim?

como é que é?
hem?
all of which are interpreted as a request for repetition or explanation.

The speaker asks the hearer whether he or she is following
The most common items are
sabe?
viu?
está vendo?
entende?
sabe como é   often pronounced   [saku'mɛ]   **SpBr**
não é?
né?
The items ***não é?*** and ***né?*** are used to ask for a sign of agreement on the part of the hearer
and correspond to English tag questions:

> *Você anda meio nervoso, não é?*
> 'You've been a bit nervous, haven't you?'

The hearer emphatically agrees with the speaker
For this one may use
é isso aí!
isso!
isso mesmo!
claro!

> —*Eu vou é mandar tudo de volta para ela.*
> —*É isso aí!*
> "What I'm going to do is to return all the stuff to her."
> "Great!"

One of the participants wants to start speaking
The following items are used to call the attention of the hearer:
olha / olha só   'look'
escuta   'listen'
escuta aqui   'listen here'
gente   'folks'
ó   'hey'

> *Olha aqui, eu também tenho uma coisa para dizer.*
> 'Look here, I also have something to say.'

Gente, talvez seja melhor encerrar a discussão.
'Folks, perhaps it is better to close the discussion.'

40.3 Interjections

Some interjections may be considered discourse markers, as they often function in ways parallel to the items seen in the previous sections. For instance, *pô*, very frequent in the spoken language as an interjection, can be used discursively as in

A Catarina nunca mais telefonou. Pô, eu tenho que esquecer ela.   **SpBr**
'Catarina never phoned again. Damn, I have to forget her.'

Other interjections, like *ai!* 'ouch!' do not have this function. And, since we are at it, here is a list of the most usual interjections in the modern spoken language:

ah   'ah, oh'

—*Eu não apareci porque meu menino ficou doente.*
—*Ah!*
"I didn't show up because my child was sick."
"Ah!"

ai   'ouch'
alô   'hallo'   (used in answering the telephone)
bolas   'damn'   (a bit old-fashioned)
credo   denotes astonishment mixed with some fear

—*Lá no Chile tem terremoto todo ano.*
—*Credo!*
"In Chile there are earthquakes every year."
"Goodness!"

cruz credo   expresses fear

—*Dizem que aqui tem lobisomem.*
—*Cruz credo!*
"They say there are werewolves around here."
"Heavens!"

nossa / nó   expresses astonishment

>—*O Cláudio está ganhando mais de dez mil por mês.*
>—*Nossa!*
>"Cláudio is making more than ten thousand a month."
>"Wow!"

oba   'wow'

>*Oba! Papai comprou seis garrafas de uísque!*
>'Wow! Dad bought six bottles of whiskey!"

oh [ɔ:]   besides being a synonym of *ah, oh* also denotes disappointment

>—*Titia vem, mas os primos não.*
>—*Oh!*
>"Auntie is coming. But the cousins aren't."
>"Oh!"

oi   'hi'
ok   [oˈkej]   'OK'   this English loanword is very frequent in informal speech
opa   used to express mild disapproval

>—*Vou levar esse livro emprestado.*
>—*Opa!*
>"(I)'m borrowing this book."
>"Wait a minute!"

It can also be used as a translation for English *oops*.
ora / ora bolas   'bah'

>*Ele comentou que eu não ando de bicicleta. Ora bolas, eu nunca tentei.*
>'He pointed out that I can't ride a bicycle. Bah, I've never tried to.'

Pô / poxa   'damn, hey' (these interjections are rather mild and do not correspond to a really angry *damn*)

>*Pô, você vai deixar essa louça aí?*
>'Hey, are you going to leave these dishes over there?'

pronto   like *alô*, used in answering the telephone

psiu   used to ask for silence or to call someone without making too much noise; sometimes written (and pronounced) *pst*

puxa / puxa vida   synonyms of *credo, nossa,* and *nó*

quem dera / quem me dera   'I wish'   (followed by a subjunctive or an infinitive)

> *Quem me dera que vocês me entendessem!*
> 'I wish you could understand me!'

socorro   'help'

tá   'OK'

tchau   'bye-bye'

uai / ué   used to denote astonishment; use of *uai* is said to be a shibboleth for natives of Minas Gerais, the only Brazilians who use it

ui   'ouch'

Besides these, there are many other interjections of a more coarse or obscene character; I do not list them here, leaving to the reader the pleasure of learning them directly from native Brazilians.

VIII Word Formation

41

Derivation and Word Formation

41.1 Inflection vs. derivation

Noncompound words are formed according to two processes, **inflection** and **derivation.** The difference between them is their respective degree of systematicness: whereas inflection is highly systematic and contains mostly regularities, derivation is much less so, and much less regular in its formal appearance and in the semantic relations it expresses.

Take, for instance, verb conjugation, an instance of inflection. For all verbs, without exception, there is an infinitive (*vender*), a present tense (*vendo, vende, vendemos, vendem*), and a gerund (*vendendo*), etc. Furthermore, each of these forms is built in an essentially regular way: there is always a final -*r* in the infinitive and a final -*ndo* in the gerund; the present varies but follows the three basic models provided by the three conjugations. There are irregularities, but irregular verbs are only a small subset of all verbs.

On the other hand, derivation is much less well organized. Take, for instance, the word *amarrar* 'to tie.' If we add the prefix *des*- we get another word, *desamarrar,* which means 'to untie.' Yet, this is not a systematic process with all verbs; for instance, we cannot add *des*- to *pintar* to get * *despintar* * 'to unpaint,' although this new word would, potentially, make sense. Another example: from *pintar* 'to paint' we may derive, by means of a suffix, *pintura,* which means the action of painting. Most verbs, provided they express an event, have such derivatives; but the formal way they are built is not predictable, as the following list shows:

pintar	'to paint'	*pintura*	'painting'
estudar	'to study'	*estudo*	'study'
correr	'to run'	*corrida*	'race'
lavar	'to wash'	*lavagem*	'washing'
ligar	'to bind'	*ligação*	'binding'
cair	'to fall'	*queda*	'fall'
desmoronar	'to collapse'	*desmoronamento*	'collapse'
limpar	'to clean'	*limpeza*	'cleaning'
etc.			

Moreover, the same derivational element often occurs in different meanings with different bases. For instance, the prefix *re-* means 'repetition' in *refazer* 'to remake,' but it means an intensification of the action in *repuxar* 'to stretch energetically,' and does not mean anything in *rechear* 'to fill,' where it is just a required part of the verb. This is typical of many derivational suffixes and prefixes.

A consequence of this situation is that many words that are derived from each other, technically speaking, are best learned as independent items; learning them as cases of derivation would entail learning also, for each word, which suffix or prefix to use and what meaning that suffix or prefix has in that particular context. Accordingly, in this chapter I limit the exposition to cases tolerably amenable to generalization. I examine first cases of derivation by means of prefixes; then, I turn to derivation by suffixes.

41.2 Prefixes

The list includes only prefixes used productively, that is, those which can be added to a word to make up a novel sequence. For instance, it is possible to add *auto-* 'self-' to *cirurgia* 'surgery,' and the result, *auto-cirurgia* 'self-surgery,' will be understood without recourse to a dictionary as meaning 'surgery performed on oneself.' In other words, a student is hereby authorized to add *auto-* to whatever word, provided it makes sense.

This is not the case with, say, *a-*, which occurs in words like *abater* 'to bring down,' *acolher* 'to welcome,' *achatar* 'to flatten.' There is no way to assign this prefix a general meaning, and it appears only in ready-made words; speakers never *add* the prefix *a-* to some previously existing word in order to convey some novel idea with a new word. There is therefore little sense in calling the *a-* in *abater* a prefix, at least in terms of the current language; for our purposes, *abater* is not composed of *a+ bater* but is rather an unanalyzable word like *abrigar* 'to shelter,' which historically does not contain the prefix *a-*.

I do not include prefixes used primarily in technical and scientific terms, such as *hiper-* 'hyper-' and *hipo* 'hypo-,' since most formations in which they participate are transparent enough (for the specialist!); neither do I include some that are international in form and meaning, like *mega-, mini-,* and *pseudo-*. As for the use of the hyphen, see section 6.5.

For each prefix I give the corresponding English prefix, if any; otherwise, I give a translation:

anti-	'anti-'	*antidemocrático*	'antidemocratic'
auto-	'self-'	*auto-destruição*	'self-destruction'
contra-	'counter-'	*contra-ofensiva*	'counteroffensive'

des- expresses an opposite phenomenon or process

	desfazer	'to undo'
	desequilíbrio	'unbalance'

ex-	'ex-'	*ex-marido*	'ex-husband'

(pronounced [es])

extra- 'extra-' as in English, it is used to express an intensification or to express the idea of 'outside'

extra-oficial	'unofficial'
extrajudicial	'extrajudicial'
extraforte	'extra strong'

in- corresponds to English *un-* and *in-*, sometimes to *mis-*

incompleto	'incomplete'
incompreendido	'misunderstood'
ilegal	'illegal'
imerecido	'undeserved'
impensável	'unthinkable'

inter-	'inter-'	*interestadual*	'interstate'
multi-	'multi-'	*multimilionário*	'multimillionaire'
		multicor	'polychrome'

não- as expected, expresses a negation; corresponds to English *non-*

não-conformista	'nonconformist'
não-Freudiano	'non-Freudian'

pós-	'post-'	*pospor*	'to postpone'
		pós-operatório	'postoperative'
		pós-guerra	'postwar'
pré-	'pre-'	*pré-aquecer*	'to preheat'
		pré-história	'prehistory'
re-	're-'	*refazer*	'to remake'
		recalcular	'to recalculate'

This prefix is useful, and in its meaning of 'repetition' it is very widely used. But the student should not try to generalize this usage for all of its occurrences, as it appears very often with other meanings or without any separately discernible meaning: *reclamar* 'to complain,' *receber* 'to receive,' etc. Perhaps one should not analyze *reclamar, receber,* and the like as being composed of *re-* plus a verb, but rather as prefixless items; but of course the student cannot know this in advance.

recém-	refers to recent events		
		recém-falecido	'recently deceased'
		recém-eleito	'newly elected'
semi-	'*semi-*'	*semivogal*	'semivowel'
		semitom	'semitone'
sub-	'*sub-*', '*under-*'	*subterrâneo*	'underground'
		subgerente	'assistant manager'
		subdividir	'to subdivide'
super-	besides its traditional meaning corresponding to English *over-*, as in		
		superpopulação	'overpopulation'
		supernutrido	'overfed'

this prefix is frequently used as a quality intensifier (corresponding in meaning to a superlative):

		super-interessante	'very interesting'
		super-animado	'extremely motivated'
vice-	'*vice-*'	*vice-presidente*	'vice-president'

41.3 Suffixes

In what follows I list only the **productive** uses of each suffix. Many of them appear in other words, with other meanings, but not productively:

-ada
Used productively to express an action; it is added to the nominal designating the instrument of the action: *pincelada* 'brush stroke,' *machadada* 'hatchet blow,' *patada* 'kick,' *olhada* 'look':

> *Você podia dar uma <u>olhada</u> na minha tese?*
> 'Could you have a look at my thesis?'

-al ~ -ar

These suffixes are similar to English *-al* in *national,* that is, they form qualificatives out of referentials; the semantic effect is quite variable but may be described as including the ingredient 'appertaining to'-thus, *national* means 'appertaining to the nation,' and *central* means 'appertaining to the center.' The form *-ar* occurs when the original word contains **l,** otherwise *-al* is used: *nacional* 'national,' *racional* 'rational,' *central* 'central,' but *familiar* 'familiar,' *elementar* 'elementary,' *solar* 'solar.' *Global* is an exception: one would expect *-ar* because of the **l.**

-ão   SpBr

This suffix is used in the spoken language to denote someone who performs an action with particular frequency. It is added to a verbal root, e.g., *respondão* 'someone given to rude answers,' *trotão* 'trotter (said of a horse),' *babão* 'drooler.'[1]

Note

[1] For the use of *-ão* in augmentatives, see below.

-ção   SpBr

In the spoken language, *-ção* is added to a verbal root to name an excessively intensive or repeated action: *falação* 'excessive speaking,' *começão* 'excessive eating.'

-dor

This suffix corresponds to English *-er,* expressing an agent: *trabalhador* 'worker,' *pescador* 'fisher,' *desanimador* 'something that discourages people.' With some words, this suffix appears as *-tor*: *escritor* 'writer,' *construtor* 'builder.'

-ense

This suffix is used to form designations of national or regional origin: *canadense* 'Canadian,' *parisiense* 'Parisian,' *maranhense* 'native of the State of Maranhão.'

-ento   'full of,' as in *perebento* 'full of mange,' *ciumento* 'jealous,' *sedento* 'thirsty'

-ês

This is another suffix used for designations of national origin: *francês* 'French,' *inglês* 'English,' *português* 'Portuguese.'

-ismo   corresponds to English *-ism*: *formalismo* 'formalism,' *socialismo* 'socialism'

-ista   corresponds to English *-ist* and may express either a profession or an intellectual commitment: *pianista* 'pianist,' *marxista* 'Marxist'

-mente

This suffix forms adverbs out of nominals and corresponds to English *-ly,* as in *certamente* 'certainly,' *rapidamente* 'rapidly.'

-nte

Added to verbal roots, it conveys a qualificative meaning and corresponds to English *-ing:* *ardente* 'burning,' from *arder* 'to burn,' *comovente* 'touching,' from *comover* 'to touch,' *falante* 'speaking,' as in *ave falante* 'talking bird.'

-udo

Added to a nominal root, it denotes possession of something in particularly great quantity: *barbudo* 'heavily bearded,' *bochechudo* 'having fat cheeks,' *barrigudo* 'paunchy.'

-vel   corresponds to English *-ble,* with a similar meaning: *comível* 'edible,' *solúvel* 'soluble,' *descartável* 'disposable'

Suffixes denoting verbal action

As noted above, the derivation of action words from verbs is not regular, and there are so many idiosyncrasies that it is better to learn them as independent items. But there is one suffix that may be considered the **unmarked** action suffix, namely, *-mento*. It appears in many action words as the sole alternative, e.g.,

arrependimento	'repentance'	**from**	*arrepender(-se)*	'to repent'
casamento	'marriage'	**from**	*casar*	'to marry'
polimento	'polishing'	**from**	*polir*	'to polish'

Whenever a verb lacks an action word, speakers tend to use *-mento* productively; thus, the great writer Monteiro Lobato, when he needed an action word for *comer* 'to eat,' wrote *comimento*—a word nobody had ever seen before, but which is perfectly understandable.

Augmentatives

-ão, -zão   (feminine -ona, -zona)

These suffixes are augmentative, that is, they basically express big size. As a general rule, *-ão* is added to nominals ending in *-a, -o,* and *-e;* this final vowel is dropped and the suffix is added: *gato* 'cat,' *gatão* 'big cat,' *casa* 'house,' *casona* 'big house.' The form *-zão* is added to words ending in a consonant, a diphthong, or the vowels **u** and **i**: *tatu* 'armadillo,' *tatuzão* 'big armadillo,' *bazar* 'novelties store,' *bazarzão, canal* 'canal', *canalzão,* etc.

But there are exceptions, and in many cases either suffix can be used; furthermore, there are several other augmentative suffixes that are used with particular nominals, such as *bocarra* 'big mouth,' from *boca* 'mouth'; or the root may undergo some mutation, as in *rapagão* 'big boy,' from *rapaz* 'boy.' This means that learning augmentatives is largely a lexical question, only partially amenable to rules. On the other hand, in the spoken language *-ão* or *-zão* added to almost any nominal is acceptable, and one often hears forms like *rapazão, bocão,* and the like.[1]

Note

[1]Many words ending in *-ão* are incorrectly given in grammars as derived with the suffix *-ão,* which is not true in the modern language. For example, *portão* 'gate' is not an augmentative of *porta* 'door,' but denotes a different object, and so on.

Augmentatives, unlike diminutives, do not need to have the same gender as their original nominals; as a matter of fact, they tend to become masculine even sometimes when referring to women: *um mulherão* 'a great woman,' *um casão* 'a big house,' and so on. As for their meaning, see below, under **diminutives.**

Diminutives
-inho, -zinho

Diminutives, like augmentatives, are very much used in the spoken language. Their formation is not always regular. The suffixes *-inho* and *-zinho* are the most common and can be added in principle to any word. For words ending in *-a, -e,* and *-o* it is usual (but not mandatory in all cases) to prefer *-inho,* dropping the final vowel of the original word: *gatinho* 'little cat,' *cadeirinha* 'little chair' (in more informal style it is possible to say *gatozinho, cadeirazinha* as well). This rule does not work for words ending in a diphthong, which always make their diminutive with *-zinho: pão* 'bread,' *pãozinho; chapéu* 'hat,' *chapeuzinho; mãe* 'mother,' *mãezinha* (*mãinha* 'Mom' and *painho* 'Dad' are regional forms, current only in Bahia).

A word never switches its gender when becoming a diminutive, and the diminutive of, say, a feminine nominal is always feminine. But masculine words ending in *-a* keep their *-a* in the diminutive, while remaining masculine, if the suffix is *-inho: o problema* 'the problem,' *o probleminha* 'the little problem.' Now, with the suffix *-zinho* masculine words always end in *-o: o problemazinho* 'id.'

The diminutive of the word *pequeno* 'small' is *pequenininho* or, in the written language, *pequenino.*

Words ending in *-inho* take *-zinho: passarinhozinho* 'small bird,' *ninhozinho* 'small nest,' *galinhazinha* 'small hen.'

Both augmentatives and diminutives have several secondary meanings, apart from their main function of expressing size. The general tendency is for diminutives to express affection, as in *meu benzinho* 'my sweet love,' *vou buscar um sorvetinho para você* '(I)'m going to get a little ice cream for you.'

Use of diminutives and augmentatives with qualifying nominals

Another meaning frequently conveyed by the diminutive is an intensification of or emphasis on a quality, e.g.,

> *O cachorro estava <u>quietinho</u>.*
> 'The dog was very quiet.'

> *Meu pé ficou <u>geladinho</u>.*
> 'My foot became very cold.'

But with some nominals the diminutive expresses precisely the opposite, that is, attenuated quality:

> *O barco dele é <u>grandinho</u>.*
> 'His boat is a bit large.'

As for augmentatives, they may also express intensification of a quality:

> *Meu pé ficou <u>quentão</u>.*
> 'My foot became very hot.'

When added to a referential nominal, the augmentative may express appreciation of quality:

> *O Amaro é um <u>professorzão</u>.*
> 'Amaro is a great teacher.'

The above notes give only a slight idea of the complexity of the usages of which augmentatives and diminutives are capable. Unfortunately, this interesting problem has not been studied in depth, so that the most one can do is to mention the use of augmentatives and diminutives as one of the areas of Portuguese grammar deserving particular attention by the student.

Superlatives

We have finally the suffix *-íssimo,* which forms superlatives out of qualifying nominals: *forte* 'strong,' *fortíssimo* 'extremely strong.' Some nominals never take *-íssimo* for semantic reasons: *quarto,* 'fourth,' *posterior* 'posterior,' *gramatical* 'grammatical' never appear with *-íssimo* because their meaning does not admit of intensification.

The addition of *-íssimo* to a nominal may cause some adaptation of the last consonant in the root, of the same kind as we saw in 11.3.4 for the verbs; thus, for *largo* 'wide' we have *larguíssimo,* that is, **g** changes into **gu** in order to preserve its pronunciation [g] before **i**; see table in 11.3.4 for a complete list of such mutations.

Besides this, there are several irregularities in the formation of superlatives (the reason is that superlatives are not a native feature of Portuguese, but are Latin borrowings dating from the sixteenth century and follow the Latin rules). We begin with some rules:

nominals ending in *-vel* form the superlative in *-bilíssimo*:
terrível	'terrible'	*terribilíssimo*
amável	'kind'	*amabilíssimo*

nominals ending in *-z* change the *-z* into *-c*:
veloz	'rapid'	*velocíssimo*

nominals ending in a nasal sound form the superlative in *-níssimo*:
bom	'kind'	*boníssimo*
pagão	'heathen'	*paganíssimo*

Then there are the truly irregular ones; I give below a list of the most common. Those marked with '#' can also form superlatives in the regular way:

amigo	'friendly'	*amicíssimo*
antigo	'ancient'	*antiqüíssimo*
bom	'good'	*ótimo*[1]
célebre	'famous'	*celebérrimo*
cristão	'Christian'	*cristianíssimo*
difícil	'difficult'	*dificílimo*
doce	'sweet'	*dulcíssimo* #
fácil	'easy'	*facílimo*
grande	'big'	*enorme*
humilde	'humble'	*humílimo*
magro	'thin'	*magérrimo* #

(continued)		
mau	'bad'	*péssimo*
nobre	'noble'	*nobilíssimo*
pobre	'poor'	*paupérrimo #*
simples	'simple'	*simplíssimo/simplicíssimo*

Note

[1] *Bom* in its general meaning 'good' makes *ótimo;* when it means 'kind' (said of persons) its superlative is *boníssimo.*

An alternative to the use of superlatives is the use of intensifiers, such as *super:*

Eu hoje tou super cansada.   **SpBr**
'I am very tired today.'

Such usage is particularly frequent nowadays in the language of young people.

IX Final Notes

42

Trends of the Language

Throughout this grammar I have paid particular attention to features of the spoken language. I have done so because, first, the differences between the written and spoken language are numerous and sometimes deep; and, second, because the variety of Portuguese I call *spoken Brazilian* is the native language of all Brazilians, regardless of region, social status, and degree of schooling.

In this chapter I give a miscellaneous selection of such grammatical features. These important forms and rules are frequently found in the speech of Brazilians of all classes, regions, and degrees of schooling and should therefore be known to students. Nevertheless, they are generally ignored in the grammars, and speakers, led by linguistic prejudice, sometimes deny that they use them. Yet they are necessary to give the speech of the student that fluent, idiomatic quality that characterizes good spoken Portuguese. As for regional and social variation, as well as slang expressions, they must for the moment be treated in specific works, not in a general grammar like this one. I start with pronunciation features then turn to morphosyntactic and lexical points.

42.1 Pronunciation

42.1.1 Reduced forms

The most important pronunciation feature to be noted is the reduction of some extremely common words; these items almost always occur in reduced form, the full forms being limited to very careful speech, public addresses, reading aloud, etc. There follows a list of the most important of these items. Some of them have no traditional spelling and may be found in different form when written (in dialogues, in plays, etc.); and, since they are most likely to occur in spoken form, I give them also in phonetic transcription.

tá ['ta] (reduction of *está [bem]*) 'okay'
See below for the reduction of other forms of *estar*.
pra [pɾa] (reduction of *para*)
This is the normal pronunciation of the preposition *para*.
xô [ʃo] (reduction of *deixa eu*) 'let me'

> —*Ganhei um relógio, olha aqui.*
> —*Xô ver!*   **SpBr**
> "(I) got a watch, look."
> "Lemme see!"

cê [se] (reduction of *você*) 'you'
The personal pronoun *você* may be reduced to *ocê* [o'se] or, more frequently, to *cê*. The use of each of these forms depends on personal taste (some preferring the full forms in all cases) and also on the syntactic context. After prepositions the reduced form to be used is *ocê*, not *cê*, as in the contraction *procê* 'for you,' or in *sem ocê* 'without you.' With prepositions *cê* is used only after *com* 'with,' which makes *com cê* 'with you.'
pera / peraí ['pɛɾə] / [pɛɾə'i] (reductions of *espera* 'wait' and *espera aí* 'wait a moment,' respectively)
These expresssions are frequently used in informal speech; *pera* may be translated as 'wait,' while *peraí* conveys a sense of urgency and corresponds to English 'wait a minute!' spoken quickly.
pó ['pɔ] (reduction of *pode* 'may')[1]
This pronunciation of *pode* is used in proclitic situations, immediately before a main verb beginning with a consonant; it seems to be appropriate only at the beginning of an utterance:

> *Pode sair!*   ['pɔ sa'i]   **SpBr**
> '(You) may come out!'

Note

[1]The spelling *pó* is not official, of course, since this form is never written; I have kept the spelling *pode* in the example because *pó* there would probably not be understood by a native reader.

psia [psjə] (reduction of *precisa* 'it is necessary')
This reduction is used before a main verb:

> *Precisa levantar essa caixa.* [psjə levʌ̃'ta 'ɛsə 'kaʃə] **SpBr**
> 'It is necessary to lift this box.'

It is particularly frequent with a negative, meaning 'never mind,' 'there's no need':

> —*Você acha que tem que levantar a caixa?*
> —*Precisa não.* [psjə 'nʌ̃w] **SpBr**
> "Do you think we need to lift the box?"
> "No."

42.1.2 Deletion of the initial vowel

Initial **a** is very often omitted in informal, unguarded speech in a number of words, resulting in forms like the following:

té logo (from *até logo* 'bye-bye')
bissurdo [bi'suhdu] (from *absurdo* 'absurd,' often used in exclamations)

This process is particularly active with some very common verbs; the initial **a** is deleted so as to leave at least two syllables (that is, no two-syllable verbs lose their initial **a**). The most common cases are

cabar (from *acabar* 'to end')
garrar (from *agarrar* 'to grab')
güentar (from *agüentar* 'to stand, to bear')

> *Não güento mais esse emprego.* **SpBr**
> '(I) can't stand this job any more.'

panhar (from *apanhar* 'to catch')

> *Esse menino vai panhar* [pʌ̃'ɉa] *uma gripe.* **SpBr**
> 'This child is going to catch the flu.'

rancar (from *arrancar* 'to pull out')

> *Vou rancar* [hʌ̃'ka] *todas essas plantas do quintal.* **SpBr**
> '(I)'m going to pull out all those plants in the backyard.'

Curiously, *arrancar* in its other meaning 'to start (an engine)' does not reduce to *rancar*:

O carro arrancou com um barulho doido.
'The car started with a hell of a noise.'

rastar (from *arrastar* 'to drag')

O cavalo rastou ele uns dez metros. **SpBr**
'The horse dragged him for about ten meters.'

In some cases both forms have been accepted in the standard language:
baixar (and *abaixar* 'to lower')
sentar (and *assentar* 'to sit down')

A velhinha sempre assentava / sentava nesse tamborete.
'The old lady always sat down on this stool.'

Initial **o** is also often omitted in *obrigado* 'thank you,' pronounced [bɾiˈgadu].

42.1.3 *Des, tes* pronounced *ds, ts*

In the very common unstressed word endings *-tes, -des* (*limites* 'limits,' *verdades* 'truths')
the pronunciation, according to the rules given in chapter 2, is [dʒis], [tʃis], respectively.
Yet, even in relatively slow speech, these sequences usually reduce to [ds], [ts], so that *limites, verdades* are pronounced [liˈmits], [vehˈdads], respectively.[1]

Note

¹The sequence [ds] is voiceless throughout, but it does not merge with [ts] because in the former we have a **lenis consonant, in the latter a **fortis** one. This may sound too subtle, but Portuguese speakers have no difficulty whatsoever in making the distinction.

Word-initial *des-* / *dis-* also reduce to [ds] (before a voiceless consonant) or [dz] (before a vowel or a voiced consonant) in longer words, in which the stressed syllable is comparatively far ahead in the word. Thus, *desembargador* 'judge' normally is pronounced [dzĩbahgaˈdoh], while *dizer* 'to say' does not reduce. Other examples are *disponibilidade* 'availability' [dsponibiliˈdadʒi], *desbocado* 'foul-mouthed' [dzboˈkadu].

42.1.4 Other

Omission of final -r in verb forms

Final *r* is not pronounced when part of a verb form (see chapter 2). Thus, *cantar* is pronounced [kʌˈta] and *fizer* is pronounced [fiˈzɛ].

Reduction of the gerund morpheme

In Minas Gerais it is very common to omit the *-d-* in the gerund ending *-ndo;* thus, *fazendo* is pronounced *fazeno* [fa'zẽnu], *cantando* becomes *cantano,* etc. This reduction occurs only in the gerund ending; thus *Fernando* (a man's name), *vendo* '(I) sell,' and *quando* 'when' all keep their **d**'s.

ni *for* **em**

The preposition *em* is very frequently pronounced *ni* [ni] when it occurs before *mim:*

> *Ele queria bater ni mim* [ni mĩ].   **SpBr**   [**standard:** *em mim*]
> 'He wanted to hit me.'

Some speakers use *ni* with other items, but this is not very common:

> *Ele mexeu ni tudo.*   **SpBr [substandard]**
> 'He fussed with everything.'

Contraction of **pra** *with personal pronouns*

In rapid speech *para* (pronounced [pɾa]) combines with *ele* 'he' and *você* 'you,' giving rise to the following contractions:

para + ele =   **prele** [pɾeli] (and *prela, preles, prelas*)
para + você = procê

Para may even contract with *eu* 'I' when the latter is the subject of a following clause:

> *Ele fez tudo <u>preu</u>* (= *para eu*) *fracassar.*   **SpBr**
> 'He did everything so that I might fail.'

As we saw in chapter 5, contraction occurs before the demonstratives *esse* 'this' and *aquele* 'that' and with the articles *o* 'the' and *um* 'a':

> *Ela trabalha o dia todo <u>praquele</u>* (= *para aquele*) *vagabundo do marido.*   **SpBr**
> 'She works all day for that bum of a husband.'

42.2 Syntax

42.2.1 Imperative, first person plural

As we saw in chapter 11, the imperative has special forms in the spoken language. Besides those, there is also a form for the first person plural, which translates into English *let's* + **infinitive.** In the spoken language, the first person plural of the imperative is formed with *ir* as an auxiliary, e.g.,

Vamos sair depressa!
'Let us get out quick!'

The above form is acceptable in writing as well, besides more formal *saiamos*. In speech it is normal to reduce the *vamos* to *vamo* [ˈvãmu] or, more frequently, to *vam'* [vãm], with a final nasal consonant [m], not otherwise heard in Portuguese; this form may be further reduced to *vão* [vãw]. Thus, the above sentence is normally pronounced

Vam' sair depressa! [vãm saˈi dʒiˈprɛsə]　　**SpBr**

This is the usual way to say 'let's + infinitive' in colloquial Brazilian Portuguese.

The auxiliary *ir* is used with all verbs, *except* with *ir* itself; the imperative, first person singular of *ir* is simply *vamos* (*vamo, vam', vão*), without the infinitive.

42.2.2. *Lá, aqui* as a reinforcement of adverbials of place

The particles *lá* 'there' and *aqui* 'here' are commonly added to adverbials of place as a sort of reinforcement, so that instead of

Eu cheguei ontem da roça.
'I came yesterday from the country.'

it is more frequent to say

Eu cheguei ontem lá da roça.
'id.'

Other examples are

Em 87 ele veio morar aqui em Belo Horizonte.
'In '87 he came to live here in Belo Horizonte.'

Lá no Paraná é que faz frio de verdade.
'In Paraná it becomes real cold.'

42.2.3 Use of *tudo* for *todos*

There is a tendency to substitute *tudo* for *todos; tudo* in this usage always follows, never precedes, the nominal it quantifies. For example,

Todos os meninos estão doentes.
Os menino tudo tão doente.　　**SpBr**
'All the boys are sick.'

This construction is still regarded as substandard but seems to be gaining ground in informal speech. For the moment, it is to be avoided, but it is good to call the student's attention to it because it is certain to occur now and then.

42.2.4 Plural marking on the first element of the NP

We saw in chapter 34 that the plural morpheme *-s* tends to occur only on the first element of the noun phrase; thus, we have

> *Esses livros velhos*
> *Esses livro velho*   **SpBr**
> 'These old books'

In informal speech this tendency goes sometimes to the point of marking exclamatories and interrogatives (which are always phrase-initial), giving rise to noun phrases like

> <u>*Ques*</u> [kis] *porta suja!*   **SpBr**
> 'What dirty doors!'

> <u>*Ôs*</u> *menino capeta!*   **SpBr**
> 'What naughty children!'

This construction would probably sound odd if used by a nonnative and is avoided by many natives; but since it is frequent in the speech of some people, I mention it here.

42.2.5 *Mim* for *eu*

As we saw in chapter 8, the form of the first person singular pronoun after prepositions is *mim: para mim* 'for me,' etc. But the pronoun keeps its subjective form *eu* if it is the subject of a clause, even when the clause is preceded by a preposition:

> *Ela trouxe a manga para <u>eu</u> comer.*
> 'She brought the mango for me to eat [literally, for I to eat].'

The alleged reason is that the preposition governs not the pronoun, but rather the whole clause. Yet in the spoken language there is a strong tendency to use the oblique form *mim* even in these cases:

> *Ela trouxe a manga para <u>mim</u> comer.*   **SpBr**
> 'id.'

This construction, frowned upon by many people, is not in universal usage. But it does occur in the spontaneous speech of many educated persons, and it is useful to know about it.

42.3 Lexicon

estar / tar

The verb *estar* 'to be' is pronounced *tar* by most speakers; this reduction applies to all its forms: *estou* > *tou; esteve* > *teve; estando* > *tando; estivessem* > *tivessem*, etc. Yet *estar* is normally pronounced in full in the expression instanced by

> *Marlene está?*
> 'Is Marlene (at home)?'

como, feito, que nem

These forms are used as comparative particles. *Como* is the standard one:

> *Ele trabalha <u>como</u> um burro de carga.*
> 'He works like a beast of burden.'

Feito and *que nem* [ki'nẽj] are colloquial and occur rarely in the written language:

> *Ele trabalha <u>feito</u> um burro de carga.*   **SpBr**
> *Ele trabalha <u>que nem</u> um burro de carga.*   **SpBr**
> 'id.'

42.4 Changes in the written language

The written language is naturally more conservative than the spoken one, and changes are comparatively slow. But, as the distance between the two main varieties of the language increases, there is a growing tendency to adapt the written language to the realities of everyday speech; and this process has been particularly active in the past forty years or so. As of the mid–twentieth century, the written language of Brazil was very close to the European standard, but changes have been numerous since then. A text published in the 1950s looks archaic, sometimes even difficult to understand, to younger readers today.

This important phenomenon (which has not been researched as much as it deserves) is partially reflected, for instance, in the manuals of style published by the large Brazilian newspapers. In these documents one may confirm the imminent death of such constructions as mesoclitic pronouns (*tratar-se-ia*); the use of the hyphen between a verb and an oblique pronoun when the latter comes between two verbs (*tinha-se tratado*); the requirement that *assistir* 'to attend' and *visar* 'to intend' be followed by the preposition *a;* the use of *todo o mundo,* instead of *todo mundo,* to mean 'everybody.' But this is just a drop in an ocean; the whole language is changing, and much research is needed before we will have a coherent, realistic view of the current situation in written Brazilian Portuguese. For the moment, all we can do is to call the attention of the interested student, teacher, or researcher to the magnitude of the phenomenon.

Appendixes

Appendix 1: Regular Verbs

Regular verbs

	1<u>st</u> conjugation	2<u>nd</u> conjugation	3<u>rd</u> conjugation
Indicative			
Present	*ando*	*vendo*	*parto*
	andas Wr	*vendes* Wr	*partes* Wr
	anda	*vende*	*parte*
	andamos	*vendemos*	*partimos*
	andais Wr	*vendeis* Wr	*partis* Wr
	andam	*vendem*	*partem*
Imperfect	*andava*	*vendia*	*partia*

	andavas Wr	*vendias* Wr	*partias* Wr
	andava	*vendia*	*partia*
	andávamos	*vendíamos*	*partíamos*
	andáveis Wr	*vendíeis* Wr	*partíeis* Wr
	andavam	*vendiam*	*partiam*
Preterit	*andei*	*vendi*	*parti*
	andaste Wr	*vendeste* Wr	*partiste* Wr
	andou	*vendeu*	*partiu*
	andamos	*vendemos*	*partimos*
	andastes Wr	*vendestes* Wr	*partistes* Wr
	andaram	*venderam*	*partiram*
Pluperfect	*andara* Wr	*vendera* Wr	*partira* Wr
	andaras Wr	*venderas* Wr	*partiras* Wr
	andara Wr	*vendera* Wr	*partira* Wr
	andáramos Wr	*vendêramos* Wr	*partíramos* Wr
	andáreis Wr	*vendêreis* Wr	*partíreis* Wr
	andaram Wr	*venderam* Wr	*partiram* Wr
Future	*andarei* Wr	*venderei* Wr	*partirei* Wr
	andarás Wr	*venderás* Wr	*partirás* Wr
	andará Wr	*venderá* Wr	*partirá* Wr

Handwritten annotations: "Simple past" (next to Preterit); "había comido sp." and "Port. uses no auxiliary sp. does" (next to Pluperfect).

	andaremos Wr	venderemos Wr	partiremos Wr
	andareis Wr	vendereis Wr	partireis Wr
	andarão Wr	venderão Wr	partirão Wr

Conditional

	andaria	venderia	partiria
	andarias Wr	venderias Wr	partirias Wr
	andaria	venderia	partiria
	andaríamos	venderíamos	partiríamos
	andaríeis Wr	venderíeis Wr	partiríeis Wr
	andariam	venderiam	partiriam

Subjunctive

Present

eu	ande	venda	parta
tu	andes Wr	vendas Wr	partas Wr
vał,oł,ła	ande	venda	parta
	andemos	vendamos	partamos
	andeis Wr	vendais Wr	partais Wr
	andem	vendam	partam

Imperfect

	andasse	vendesse	partisse
	andasses Wr	vendesses Wr	partisses Wr
	andasse	vendesse	partisse
	andássemos	vendêssemos	partíssemos

	andásseis Wr	*vendêsseis* Wr	*partísseis* Wr
	andassem	*vendessem*	*partissem*
Future	*andar*	*vender*	*partir*
	andares Wr	*venderes* Wr	*partires* Wr
	andar	*vender*	*partir*
	andarmos	*vendermos*	*partirmos*
	andardes Wr	*venderdes* Wr	*partirdes* Wr
	andarem	*venderem*	*partirem*

Imperative (standard form)

(affirmative)	*anda (tu)* Wr	*vende (tu)* Wr	*parte (tu)* Wr
	ande (você) Wr	*venda (você)* Wr	*parta (você)* Wr
	andai (vós) Wr	*vendei (vós)* Wr	*parti (vós)* Wr
	andem (vocês) Wr	*vendam (vocês)* Wr	*partam (vocês)* Wr

(negative)	*não andes (tu)* Wr	*não vendas (tu)* Wr	*não partas (tu)* Wr
	não andem (vocês) Wr	*não vendam (vocês)* Wr	*não partam (vocês)* W
	não andeis (vós) Wr	*não vendais (vós)* Wr	*não partais (vós)* Wr
	não andem (vocês) Wr	*não vendam (vocês)* Wr	*não partam (vocês)* W

Imperative (colloquial form)

	anda (você) SpBr	*vende (você)* SpBr	*parte (você)* SpBr
	andem (vocês) SpBr	*vendam (vocês)* SpBr	*partam (vocês)* SpBr

Infinitive

Impersonal	*andar*	*vender*	*partir*
Personal	*andar*	*vender*	*partir*
	andares Wr	*venderes* Wr	*partires* Wr
	andar	*vender*	*partir*
	andarmos	*vendermos*	*partirmos*
	andardes Wr	*venderdes* Wr	*partirdes* Wr
	andarem	*venderem*	*partirem*
Gerund	*andando*	*vendendo*	*partindo*
(Past) Participle	*andado*	*vendido*	*partido*

Appendix 2: Irregular and Anomalous Verbs

Here I give the primitive forms of the most common irregular verbs. The following list includes all irregular verbs found among the fifteen hundred most frequent words of Portuguese, according to Duncan 1971. There are twenty-four verbs in all, but some are identical in their irregularity, so that there are only sixteen models. Anomalous verbs are given in complete paradigms, since deriving them from primitive forms is not economical.

Irregular verbs

I give all six primitive forms for each verb; the ones in boldface are irregular, the others are regular. Under certain verbs I add the other verbs in the list that conjugate identically. The following verbs can be readily conjugated by means of their primitive forms, plus the rules given in chapters 11–12 (plus a few notes, given below):

Infinitive	Present indicative 1st singular	Present indicative 3rd singular	Preterit 1st singular	Preterit 3rd singular	Past participle
produzir	*produzo*	**produz**	*produzi*	*produziu*	*produzido*
'to produce'					

similar verbs: *conduzir* 'to lead,'   *reduzir* 'to reduce,'   *reproduzir* 'to reproduce'

caber[1,2]	**caibo**	*cabe*	**coube**	**coube**	*cabido*
'to fit in'					

pedir	**peço**	*pede*	*pedi*	*pediu*	*pedido*
'to ask for'					

similar verb: *medir* 'to measure'

perder	**perco**	*perde*	*perdi*	*perdeu*	*perdido*
'to lose'					

ouvir	**ouço**	*ouve*	*ouvi*	*ouviu*	*ouvido*
'to hear'					

poder [2]	**posso**	*pode*	**pude**	**pôde**	*podido*
'to be able'					

saber [2,3]	**sei**	*sabe*	**soube**	**soube**	*sabido*
'to know'					

fazer [2,4]	**faço**	**faz**	**fiz**	**fez**	**feito**
'to make'					
similar verb: *satisfazer* 'to satisfy'					

dizer [2,4]	**digo**	**diz**	**disse**	**disse**	**dito**
'to say'					

trazer[2,4]	**trago**	**traz**	**trouxe**	**trouxe**[2]	*trazido*
'to bring'					

querer [2,3]	*quero*	**quer**	**quis**	**quis**	*querido*
'to want'					

valer	**valho**	*vale*	*vali*	*valeu*	*valido*
'to be worth'					

…*diar*	**odeio**	**odeia**	*odiei*	*odiou*	*odiado*

'to hate'

…imilar verbs: *ansiar* 'to long for,' *incendiar* 'to set on fire'

Notes

[1]The diphthong represented by *ou* in *trouxe, coube* is regularly pronounced [o]: *trouxe* ['trosi], *coubesse* [ko'bɛsi]; but one often hears [u] when it is unstressed: [tru'sɛsi], [ku'bɛsi]. The **x** in *trouxe, trouxesse, trouxer,* etc. is pronounced [s].

[2]For these verbs, all tenses derived from the preterit have an open [ɛ] whenever the ending begins with a stressed **e,** e.g., *coubesse* [ko'bɛsi], *dissermos* [dʒi'sɛhmus] (see section 12.2).

[3]The present subjunctive of *saber* is *saiba;* of *querer* is *queira.*

[4]The future and the conditional of *fazer, dizer,* and *trazer* are, respectively, *farei / faria, direi / diria,* and *trarei / traria.* These three verbs are the only ones that show any irregularity in these two tenses. Furthermore, their imperative, second person singular form is *faze, dize, traze,* thus making them different from the corresponding form of the present indicative (*faz, diz, traz*). It may be repeated that those imperative forms are practically never used in modern Brazilian Portuguese (even written).

The three verbs below have a very irregular present indicative, which correspondingly is given in full, along with the remaining primitive forms:

ler	Present indicative:	**leio**	**lês** Wr	**lê**	*lemos*	**ledes** Wr	**lêem**

'to read'

Other primitive forms:

Preterit 1st singular	Preterit 3rd singular	Past participle
li	*leu*	*lido*

identical verb: *crer* 'to believe'[1]

ver[2]   Present indicative: **vejo** **vês** Wr **vê** *vemos* **vedes** Wr **vêem**

'to see'

Other primitive forms:

	Preterit	Preterit	Past participle
	1st singular	3rd singular	
	vi	*viu*	*visto*

---

rir   Present indicative: **rio** *ris* Wr **ri** *rimos* **rides** Wr **riem**

'to laugh'

Other primitive forms:

	Preterit	Preterit	Past participle
	1st singular	3rd singular	
	ri	*riu*	*rido*

Notes

[1]Most forms of *crer* 'to believe' are little used, apart from the present tenses; it is normally replaced by its synonym *acreditar* (regular, first conjugation).

[2]The future subjunctive of *ver* 'to see' is *ver* in the spoken language, and increasingly in the written language as well. Grammars still insist on the traditional form *vir,* but this is normally avoided and sometimes is not even understood as a form of *ver* (Brazilians tend to interpret it as a form of *vir* 'to come').

Anomalous verbs

There are eight anomalous verbs; I give their complete conjugations below. For tenses showing irregularity in person formation, I give all six forms; for tenses regular as far as person is concerned, I give only the first person singular. Only one form of the infinitive is given, because the personal infinitive is always regularly formed by adding personal endings to the impersonal infinitive. All anomalous verbs are subjected to the opening of *e* mentioned in section 12.2, so that, for instance, *desse* is pronounced ['dɛsi] and *tiveram* [tʃi'vɛɾãw].

Dar 'to give'

Indicative

Present	*dou*	*dás* **Wr**	*dá*	*damos*	*dais* **Wr**	*dão*
Imperfect	*dava*					
Preterit	*dei*	*deste* **Wr**	*deu*	*demos*	*destes* **Wr**	*deram*
Pluperfect	*dera* **Wr**					
Future	*darei* **Wr**					
Conditional	*daria*					

Subjunctive

Present	*dê*	*dês* **Wr**	*dê*	*demos*	*deis* **Wr**	*dêem*
Imperfect	*desse*					
Future	*der*					

Imperative

(standard)	*dá* **Wr** *dai* **Wr**
(colloquial)	*dá*

Infinitive	*dar*
Gerund	*dando*
Past participle	*dado*

Estar   'to be'

Indicative

Present	*estou*	*estás*	**Wr**	*está*	*estamos*	*estais*	**Wr**	*estão*
Imperfect	*estava*							
Preterit	*estive*	*estiveste*	**Wr**	*esteve*	*estivemos*	*estivestes*	**Wr**	*estiveram*
Pluperfect	*estivera*	**Wr**						
Future	*estarei*	**Wr**						
Conditional	*estaria*							

Subjunctive

Present	*esteja*	*estejas*	**Wr**	*esteja*	*estejamos*	*estejais*	**Wr**	*estejam*
Imperfect	*estivesse*							
Future	*estiver*							

Imperative

(standard)	*está*	**Wr** *estai*	**Wr**
(colloquial)	*esteja*		

Infinitive	*estar*
Gerund	*estando*
Past participle	*estado*

Haver 'there to be' (all forms **Wr**)

Indicative

Present	*hei*	*hás*	*há*	*havemos*	*haveis*	*hão*
Imperfect	*havia*					
Preterit	*houve*	*houveste*	*houve*	*houvemos*	*houvestes*	*houveram*
Pluperfect	*houvera*					
Future	*haverei*					
Conditional	*haveria*					

Subjunctive

Present	*haja*	*hajas*	*haja*	*hajamos*	*hajais*	*hajam*
Imperfect	*houvesse*					
Future	*houver*					

Imperative

(standard)	[none]
(colloquial)	[none][1]

Infinitive	*haver*
Gerund	*havendo*
Past participle	*havido*

Note

[1]Grammars usually give an imperative for *haver* (*há, havei*); in half a century of speaking, hearing, writing, and reading Portuguese, I have never come across these forms, nor can I tell what they are supposed to mean.

Ir   'to go'

Indicative

Present	*vou*	*vais*	**Wr**	*vai*	*vamos*	*ides* **Wr**	*vão*
Imperfect	*ia*						
Preterit	*fui*	*foste* **Wr**		*foi*	*fomos*	*fostes* **Wr**	*foram*
Pluperfect	*fora* **Wr**						
Future	*irei* **Wr**						
Conditional	*iria*						

Subjunctive

Present	*vá*	*vás* **Wr**		*vá*	*vamos*	*vades* **Wr**	*vão*
Imperfect	*fosse*						
Future	*for*						

Imperative

(standard)	*vai* **Wr**		*ide* **Wr**	
(colloquial)	*vai*			

Infinitive   *ir*

| Gerund | *indo* |
| Past participle | *ido* |

Pôr   'to put'

Indicative

Present	*ponho*	*pões*	**Wr**	*põe*	*pomos*	*pondes*	**Wr**	*põem*
Imperfect	*punha*	*punhas*	**Wr**	*punha*	*púnhamos*	*púnheis*	**Wr**	*punham*
Preterit	*pus*	*puseste*	**Wr**	*pôs*	*pusemos*	*pusestes*	**Wr**	*puseram*
Pluperfect	*pusera*	**Wr**						
Future	*porei*	**Wr**						
Conditional	*poria*							

Subjunctive

Present	*ponha*	*ponhas*	**Wr**	*ponha*	*ponhamos*	*ponhais*	**Wr**	*ponham*
Imperfect	*pusesse*							
Future	*puser*							

Imperative

| (standard) | *põe* | **Wr** | | *ponde* | **Wr** |
| (colloquial) | *põe* | | | | |

Infinitive	*pôr*[1]
Gerund	*pondo*
Past participle	*posto*

Note

[1]The infinitive of *pôr* has an accent in order to distinguish it from the preposition *por;* the accent is dropped in derived verbs like *impor, compor, dispor,* etc.

Ser   'to be'

Indicative

Present	*sou*	*és* **Wr**	*é*	*somos*	*sois* **Wr**	*são*
Imperfect	*era*	*eras* **Wr**	*era*	*éramos*	*éreis* **Wr**	*eram*
Preterit	*fui*	*foste* **Wr**	*foi*	*fomos*	*fostes* **Wr**	*foram*
Pluperfect	*fora* **Wr**					
Future	*serei* **Wr**					
Conditional	*seria*					

Subjunctive

Present	*seja*	*sejas* **Wr**	*seja*	*sejamos*	*sejais* **Wr**	*sejam*
Imperfect	*fosse*					
Future	*for*					

Imperative

(standard)	*sê* **Wr** *sede* **Wr**
(colloquial)	*seja*

Infinitive	*ser*
Gerund	*sendo*
Past participle	*sido*

Ter   'to have'

Indicative

Present	*tenho*	*tens* **Wr**	*tem*	*temos*	*tendes* **Wr**	*têm*
Imperfect	*tinha*	*tinhas* **Wr**	*tinha*	*tínhamos*	*tínheis* **Wr**	*tinham*
Preterit	*tive*	*tiveste* **Wr**	*teve*	*tivemos*	*tivestes* **Wr**	*tiveram*
Pluperfect	*tivera* **Wr**					
Future	*terei* **Wr**					
Conditional	*teria*					

Subjunctive

Present	*tenha*	*tenhas* **Wr**	*tenha*	*tenhamos*	*tenhais* **Wr**	*tenham*
Imperfect	*tivesse*					
Future	*tiver*					

Imperative

(standard)	*tem* **Wr**	*tende* **Wr**
(colloquial)	*tem*	

Infinitive	*ter*
Gerund	*tendo*
Past participle	*tido*

Vir   'to come'

Indicative

Present	*venho*	*vens* **Wr**	*vem*	*viemos*[1]	*vindes* **Wr**	*vêm*
Imperfect	*vinha*	*vinhas* **Wr**	*vinha*	*vínhamos*	*vínheis* **Wr**	*vinham*

Preterit	*vim*	*vieste* **Wr**	*veio*	*viemos*	*viestes* **Wr**	*vieram*

Pluperfect	*viera* **Wr**

Future	*virei* **Wr**

Conditional	*viria*

Subjunctive

Present	*venha*	*venhas* **Wr**	*venha*	*venhamos*	*venhais* **Wr**	*venham*

Imperfect	*viesse*

Future	*vier*

Imperative

(standard)	*vem* **Wr**		*vinde* **Wr**
(colloquial)	*vem*		

Infinitive	*vir*

Gerund	*vindo*

Past participle	*vindo*

Note

[1]Grammars usually give *vimos* as the first person singular of the present indicative, but all speakers use *viemos* instead, even in writing. A sequence like *nós vimos* meaning 'we come' is never used and would not be understood (it would be taken to be a form of *ver,* meaning 'we saw').

Appendix 3: Contractions

The prepositions *a, de, em, para,* and *por* when appearing before some items beginning with a vowel contract with them, the sequence being pronounced and written as one word. In some cases contraction is optional (marked **opt**), but in most cases it is obligatory and must be learned. A list of all contractions found in the modern language follows:

Preposition <u>a</u>

+ articles

$$a + a = à$$
$$a + o = ao$$
$$a + as = às$$
$$a + os = aos$$

+ demonstrative *aquele*

    a + *aquele* = *àquele* (*àquela, àqueles, àquelas*)

As we saw in chapter 5, the pronunciation of **à** in these forms is identical to that of **a**, the difference being purely graphic.

Preposition <u>*em*</u>

+ articles

    em + o = *no* (*na, nos, nas*)
    em + *um* = *num* (*numa*, etc.) [**opt**]

Contraction of *em* plus forms of *um* is optional in writing and generally used in speaking.

+ demonstratives

    em + *esse* = *nesse* (*nessa*, etc.)
    em + *este* = *neste* (*nesta*, etc.)
    em + *aquele* = *naquele* (*naquela*, etc.)

+ personal pronouns

    em + *ele* = *nele* (*nela*, etc.)

Preposition <u>*de*</u>

+ articles

    de + o = *do* (*da, dos, das*)

de + *um* = *dum*   (*duma*, etc.) [**opt**]

Contraction of *de* plus forms of *um* is very rare in writing and common, but not obligatory, in speaking.

+ demonstratives

   de + *esse*   = *desse*   (*dessa*, etc.)
   de + *este*   = *deste*   (*desta*, etc.)
   de + *aquele* = *daquele* (*daquela*, etc.)

+ personal pronouns

   de + *ele* = *dele*   (*dela*, etc.)

+ adverbs of place

   de + *aqui* = *daqui*
   de + *ali*   = *dali*
   de + *aí*   = *daí*
   de + *onde* = *donde* [**opt**]

Preposition *para*

All contractions with *para* are exclusive of the spoken language. The preposition, when appearing alone, is always pronounced *pra* [pɾa] and contracts as shown below.

+ articles

   para + *o* = *pro*   (*pra*, etc.)   **SpBr**
   para + *um* = *prum* (*pruma*, etc.)   **SpBr** [**opt**]

+ demonstratives

   para + *esse*   = *presse*   **SpBr** [**opt**]
   para + *aquele* = *praquele*   **SpBr** [**opt**]

There is no contraction of *para* with *este,* because this demonstrative does not occur in the spoken language.

+ personal pronouns

> *para* + *ele* = *prele* (*prela,* etc.)   **SpBr [opt]**
> *para* + *você* = *procê*   **SpBr [opt]**

+ adverbs of place

> *para* + *aqui* = *praqui*   **SpBr**
> *para* + *aí*   = *praí*   **SpBr**

Preposition por

This preposition becomes *pel-* when contracting.

+ articles

> *por* + *o* = *pelo* (*pela,* etc.)

Appendix 4: Days of the Week, Times of the Day, Dates

Days of the week

domingo	'Sunday'
segunda-feira	'Monday'
terça-feira	'Tuesday'
quarta-feira	'Wednesday'
quinta-feira	'Thursday'
sexta-feira	'Friday'
sábado	'Saturday'

They are not capitalized, and, as in English, they may be used without a preposition:

> *Ela vai chegar sábado* **or** . . . *no sábado.*
> 'She is arriving (on) Saturday.'

Times of the day
A.M. and P.M.

There are two ways to distinguish 'A.M.' from 'P.M.':
  —By using the expressions

da manhã	for	'A.M.'
da tarde	for	'P.M.' until 6 P.M.
da noite	for	'P.M.' after 7 P.M.

For instance, *seis horas da tarde* 'six P.M.'; *quatro e meia da manhã* 'four-thirty A.M.' For the hours in the morning before 6 A.M. the expression *da madrugada* can also be used: *duas da madrugada* 'two A.M.' or *duas da manhã*. With *uma* 'one,' one uses the singular: *uma hora da tarde* 'one P.M.' 'Midnight' is *meia noite;* 'noon' is *meio dia*.
  —By numbering the hours from one to twenty-four:

vinte horas	'eight P.M.'
treze horas	'one P.M.'
vinte e três horas	'eleven P.M.'

'Midnight' is *zero hora*.
  This system is rarely used in speech, but it occurs in official documents and posted announcements:

> *O concerto se realizará pontualmente às vinte e uma horas.*
> 'The concert will take place punctually at nine P.M.'

Hours and minutes
  —From :01 until :39, add *e* 'and' plus the number of minutes:

duas horas e dez minutos	'2:10'
doze e trinta e três	'12:33'

—For :30, one may say regularly *trinta* 'thirty' or, more frequently, *meia:*

cinco e meia **or** *cinco e trinta*	'5:30'

—From :40 to :59, one may follow the general rule,

seis horas e cinquenta	'6:50'

But it is more common to *subtract* the minutes until the next hour in the following manner:

dez para as sete	'6:50'
quinze para as nove	'8:45'

Observe that the word *horas* may be omitted; this is most common when the expression includes hours and minutes. Thus, one generally says *duas horas* 2:00, but *duas e quinze* 2:15. The word *minutos* is omitted more often than not.

Dates
Months

janeiro	'January'
fevereiro	'February'
março	'March'
abril	'April'
maio	'May'
junho	'June'
julho	'July'

(continued)

agosto	'August'
setembro	'September'
outubro	'October'
novembro	'November'
dezembro	'December'

Like the days of the week, they are not capitalized.

How to say and write dates

For the days of the month, *primeiro* is used for the first day, and cardinals (*dois, três,* etc.) for the other days; and the day is joined to the month with *de:*

primeiro de maio	'May 1'
quatro de janeiro	'January 4'
vinte e nove de outubro	'October 29'

De is also used before the year:

seis de março de 1990	'March 6, 1990'

When abbreviated, dates in Portuguese follow the European ordering, that is, *day, month, year,* so that 2-5-96 (or, more commonly, 02-05-96) means May 2, 1996, and not February 5, 1996.

References

This being a work written with practical purposes in mind, I have kept scholarly references in the text to a minimum. Nevertheless, it is to be understood that many of the analyses here presented are traditional or have been proposed by researchers other than myself in the recent literature. I list below all works that I have consulted while writing this *Grammar* and that have been useful in some way or other, as well as some of my own works that I think can be useful to the interested researcher. In some cases I add a short commentary on the contents and merits of the work.

Alkimim, Mônica G. G., and Gomes, Cristina A. (1982). "Dois fenômenos de supressão em limite de palavra." *Ensaios de Lingüística 7*. Belo Horizonte: UFMG.

Allerton, D. J. (1982). *Valency and the English Verb*. London: Academic Press.

Álvarez, Jesús Fernández (1987). *El Subjuntivo*. Madrid: Edi-6 S.A.

Amaral, Emília et al. (1991). *Redação—Gramática—Literatura—Interpretação de Texto: Testes e Exercícios*. São Paulo: Nova Cultural.

> A work intended for students "cramming" for entrance examinations at the university; yet, exactly because it is used in emergencies, often more to the point than traditional grammars.

Andrade, Ernesto d' (1993). *Dicionário Inverso do Português*. Lisboa: Edições Cosmos.

> An inverse dictionary can be a very useful tool in phonology or morphology. Suppose you need to know whether there is a word in Portuguese ending in unstressed *-al*: an inverse dictionary gives a ready answer (there are a few: *jângal* 'jungle,' *Setúbal*, name of a town in Portugal).

Asher, R. E., and Simpson, J. M.Y. (eds.). *The Encyclopedia of Language and Linguistics*. Oxford, England: Pergamon Press.

Azevedo, Milton M. (1981). *A Contrastive Phonology of Portuguese and English*. Washington: Georgetown University Press.

Berruto, Gaetano (1987). *Sociolinguistica dell'Italiano Contemporaneo*. Roma: La Nuova Italia Scientifica.

Bosque, Ignacio, and Demonte, Violeta (1999). *Gramática Descriptiva de la Lengua Española*. Madrid: Espasa.

> This huge (5,351 pages) work is best viewed as a collection of often valuable articles on most

important points of the structure of Spanish; but it is not a unified grammar and it is very technical, so that many chapters are difficult reading for the nonspecialist.

Bull, W. E. (1965). *Spanish for Teachers, Applied Linguistics.* New York: Ronald Press.

Butt, John, and Benjamin, Carmen (1995). *A New Reference Grammar of Modern Spanish.* Lincolnwood, Ill.: NTC Publishing Group.

This excellent Spanish grammar is a source of good ideas, both about how to organize a grammar of a Romance language and about suggestions on how to treat particular points.

Castilho, Ataliba T. de, *et al.* [ed.] (1990–99). *Gramática do Português Falado.* Campinas, SP: Editora da UNICAMP.

This is the first serious attempt to present a comprehensive description of spoken Brazilian Portuguese (seven volumes have been published so far). A success, considering the tremendous difficulties of the task. The work is directed to professional linguists and is therefore somewhat difficult for the general reader.

Cunha, Celso, and Cintra, L. F. Lindley (1985). *Nova Gramática do Português Contemporâneo.* Rio de Janeiro: Nova Fronteira.

Cunha and Cintra's grammar is perhaps the best representative of the Luso-Brazilian grammatical tradition—both in its strengths and in its defects. If carefully used, this book may be a source of information. On the other hand, it is deficient in organization, somewhat inconsistent in theory, and not always accurate as to the facts of the modern standard language.

Dardano, Maurizio, and Trifone, Pietro (1985). *La Lingua Italiana.* Bologna: Zanichelli.

Duncan, John C. (1971). *A Frequency Dictionary of Portuguese Words.* (Stanford University Doctoral Dissertation). Ann Arbor, Mich.: University Microfilms.

Fernandes, Francisco (1957). *Dicionário de Verbos e Regimes.* Porto Alegre: Globo.

None of the valency dictionaries published in recent years is as complete and accurate as Fernandes's work. Its main drawback is that it focuses almost exclusively on traditional usage, but it is still a most useful work.

——— (1958). *Dicionário de Regimes de Substantivos e Adjetivos.* Porto Alegre: Globo.

Same comments as for Fernandes's verb valency dictionary (see above).

Ferris, Connor (1993). *The Meaning of Syntax: A Study in the Adjectives of English.* London: Longman.

Folha de S. Paulo (1987). *Manual Geral da Redação.* São Paulo: Folha de S. Paulo.

Fulgêncio, Lúcia, and Bastianetto, Patrizia (1993). *In Italiano—Manual de Gramática Contrastiva.* Perugia: Guerra Edizioni.

Gärtner, Eberhard (1998). *Grammatik der portugiesischen Sprache.* Tübingen: Max Niemeyer.

A comprehensive description of modern Portuguese, focusing on the European variety of the language.

Greenbaum, Sidney (1969). *Studies in English Adverbial Usage.* Coral Gables, Fla.: University of Miami Press.

HarperCollins (1997). *Harper Collins Portuguese Dictionary.* Glasgow: HarperCollins Publishers.

A small English-Portuguese, Portuguese-English dictionary, very good for its size. Includes a reasonably accurate phonetic transcription of the Brazilian pronunciation.

Hauy, Amini B. (1989). *Acentuação Gráfica em Vigor.* São Paulo: Ática.

A complete and accurate account of the conventions governing the use of graphic accents.

Houaiss, Antônio, and Avery, Catherine B., eds. (1967). *The New Barsa Dictionary of the English and Portuguese Languages.* New York: Appleton-Century-Crofts.

This is, to my knowledge, the best English-Portuguese and Portuguese-English dictionary. Very complete and accurate; includes pronunciation, using the International Phonetic Association (IPA) transcription system. Published in the United States as *The New Appleton Dictionary of the English and Portuguese Languages* (New York: Appleton-Century-Crofts, 1964), it has unfortunately been out of print for some years.

Huddleston, Rodney (1984). *Introduction to the Grammar of English.* Cambridge: Cambridge University Press.

Although Huddleston's book is concerned primarily with English grammar, it is useful also to readers interested in a lucid discussion of such general grammatical notions as sentences and clauses, clause types, inflection and derivation, parts of speech, topicalization systems, and many others.

Kury, Adriano da Gama (1972). *Gramática Fundamental da Língua Portuguesa.* São Paulo: LISA S.A.

Levy, Paulette (1983). *Las Completivas Objeto en Español.* México: Colegio de México.

A highly accurate, clear, and brilliantly argued study of the nominal clauses in Spanish. Although some of Levy's results do not apply to Portuguese, her text is very useful as a guide on what to look for when studying mood, complementation, and related matters.

Liberato, Yara G. (1978). "Alterações vocálicas em final de palavra e a regra de palatalização." *Ensaios de Lingüística 1.* Belo Horizonte: UFMG.

Michaelis (1985). *Novo Michaelis—Dicionário Ilustrado.* São Paulo: Melhoramentos.

A large English-Portuguese, Portuguese-English dictionary. Definitely not as good as Houaiss and Avery, but more easily available.

Nøjgaard, Morten (1995). *Les adverbes français—Essai de description fonctionnelle.* Copenhagen: Kongelike Danske Videnskabernes Selskab.

Novo Dicionário Aurélio da Língua Portuguesa (1986). Rio de Janeiro: Nova Fronteira.

Certainly the best existing monolingual dictionary of Portuguese. Very complete, including slang, archaisms, regional words, etc.

Pecoraro, Walter, and Pisacane, Chiara (1984). *L'avverbio.* Bologna: Zanichelli.

Pérez-Saldanya, Manuel (1988). *Els Sistemes Modals d'Indicatiu i de Subjuntiu.* Valencia: Abadia de Montserrat.

An excellent study of the indicative-subjunctive opposition in Catalan. Many of Pérez-Saldanya's findings are valid for Portuguese as well.

Perini, Mário A. (1995). *Gramática Descritiva do Português.* São Paulo: Ática.

——— (forthcoming). "A posição do adjetivo em português: preliminares a uma análise."

Perini, Mário A. *et al.* (1996). *O Sintagma Nominal em Português: Estrutura, Significado e Função.* Special number of *Revista de Estudos da Linguagem.* Belo Horizonte: UFMG.

Pontes, Eunice (1965). *Estrutura do Verbo no Português Coloquial.* Belo Horizonte.

> The standard work on the morphology of the verb in the modern Brazilian colloquial language.

—— (1973). *Verbos Auxiliares em Português.* Petrópolis: Vozes.

> Perhaps the best discussion to date on the analysis of the auxiliaries.

—— (1987). *O Tópico no Português do Brasil.* Campinas: Pontes.

> This book was the main source for the exposition in chapter 39.

Renzi, Lorenzo (ed.) (1988). *Grande Grammatica Italiana di Consultazione.* Bologna: Il Mulino.

Rodrigues, Daniele M. G. (1992). *Brazilian Portuguese—Your Questions Answered.* Campinas: Ed. da UNICAMP.

Saraiva, António J., and Lopes, Óscar (undated). *História da Literatura Portuguesa.* Porto: Porto Editora Lda.

> Besides being a history of Portuguese literature, this book includes a useful introductory chapter on the early history of the Portuguese language.

Thomas, Earl W. (1969). *The Syntax of Spoken Brazilian Portuguese.* Nashville: Vanderbilt University Press.

> An excellent overview of Brazilian Portuguese syntax, packed with interesting insights on the structure of the language; unfortunately it has been out of print for years.

Index of Grammatical Subjects

(References are made to section numbers)